Identity Technologies

Wisconsin Studies in Autobiography

WILLIAM L. ANDREWS
General Editor

Identity Technologies

Constructing the Self Online

Edited by

ANNA POLETTI *and* JULIE RAK

THE UNIVERSITY OF WISCONSIN PRESS

Publication of this volume has been made possible, in part, through support
from the Anonymous Fund of the College of Letters and Science at the
University of Wisconsin–Madison.

The University of Wisconsin Press
1930 Monroe Street, 3rd Floor
Madison, Wisconsin 53711-2059
uwpress.wisc.edu

3 Henrietta Street
London WC2E 8LU, England
eurospanbookstore.com

Library of Congress Cataloging-in-Publication Data

Identity technologies : constructing the self online / edited by Anna Poletti and Julie Rak.
pages   cm — (Wisconsin studies in autobiography)
Includes bibliographical references and index.
ISBN 978-0-299-29644-5 (pbk. : alk. paper) — ISBN 978-0-299-29643-8 (e-book)
1. Autobiography. 2. Online identities. 3. Identity (Psychology) and mass media.
4. Online social networks. 5. Internet—Social aspects. I. Poletti, Anna, editor.
II. Rak, Julie, 1966–, editor. III. Series: Wisconsin studies in autobiography.
CT25.I34   2014
302.3—dc23
2013011469

Contents

Acknowledgments   vii

Introduction: *Digital Dialogues*
ANNA POLETTI *and* JULIE RAK   3

FOUNDATIONS

Beyond Anonymity, or Future Directions for Internet Identity Research
HELEN KENNEDY   25

Cyberrace
LISA NAKAMURA   42

Becoming and Belonging: *Performativity, Subjectivity, and the*
Cultural Purposes of Social Networking
ROB COVER   55

Virtually Me: A *Toolbox about Online Self-Presentation*
SIDONIE SMITH *and* JULIA WATSON   70

IDENTITY AFFORDANCES

Adultery Technologies
MELISSA GREGG   99

Facebook and Coaxed Affordances
AIMÉE MORRISON   112

Archiving Disaster and National Identity in the Digital Realm:
The September 11 Digital Archive and the Hurricane Digital Memory Bank
COURTNEY RIVARD   132

Life Bytes: *Six-Word Memoir and the Exigencies of Auto/tweetographies*
  LAURIE McNEILL   144

MEDIATED COMMUNITIES

Negotiating Identities/Queering Desires: *Coming Out Online and the
Remediation of the Coming-Out Story*
  MARY L. GRAY   167

"Treat Us Right!": *Digital Publics, Emerging Biosocialities, and
the Female Complaint*
  OLIVIA BANNER   198

Cyber-Self: *In Search of a Lost Identity?*
  ALESSANDRA MICALIZZI   217

Homeless Nation: *Producing Legal Subjectivities through New Media*
  SUZANNE BOUCLIN   229

REFLECTIONS

Autobiography and New Communication Tools
  PHILIPPE LEJEUNE, *translated by* KATHERINE DURNIN   247

The Blog as Experimental Setting: *An Interview with Lauren Berlant*
  ANNA POLETTI *and* JULIE RAK   259

Contributors   273
Index   279

Acknowledgments

We absolutely must thank Bill Andrews, who invited us to begin this project, supported us through it, and encouraged us to think big. We also thank Raphael Kadushin, Matthew Cosby, and the rest of the team at the University of Wisconsin Press for their stewardship of the project over many years. Thanks to the editorial board of the press for their suggestions and support. We thank Katherine Durnin for her sensitive translation of Philippe Lejeune's work.

We also thank Lauren Berlant, who has been unfailingly supportive, provocative, generous, and hospitable to us as individuals and as a team. Thanks also to Nicole Matthews, an Australian ally for the interdisciplinary nature of the project. Thanks to Susan Brown, Linda Warley, and Aimée Morrison for their assistance early in the process. As always, we thank our colleagues in the International Association for Biography and Autobiography (IABA) for their enthusiasm. We thank Arpit Gutpa, Priit Kasesalu, and Jaan Tallinn, the original inventors of Skype, without whom this project would have been impossible.

Julie particularly wants to thank Danielle Fuller for her constant encouragement, wisdom, and love throughout this project, and Mr. T. for being supportive in the feline sense.

Anna would like to thank Johannes Klabbers for his technical troubleshooting, humor, and optimism. She also thanks Amanda Kerley, and Stripe.

Anna received financial assistance for participation in the project from the Faculty of Arts, Monash University, who provide excellent support for early career researchers. Julie received support from the Faculty of Arts at the University of Alberta.

We thank all our contributors for their work and their patience. Thanks particularly to our contributors who graciously gave permission to reprint essays in this collection.

"Beyond Anonymity, or Future Directions for Internet Identity Research," by Helen Kennedy, was first published in *New Media and Society*, Sage Publications, vol. 8, no. 6 (2006): 859–76. Reproduced with permission and copyedited for inclusion in this volume.

"Cyberrace," by Lisa Nakamura, was first published in *PMLA*, Publications of the Modern Languages Association of America, vol. 123, no. 5 (2008): 1673–2. Reproduced with permission.

"Negotiating Identities/Queering Desires: Coming Out Online and the Remediation of the Coming-Out Story," by Mary L. Gray, was first published in *Journal of Computer-Mediated Communication*, International Communication Association, vol. 14 (2009): 1162–89. Reproduced with permission.

Identity Technologies

Introduction

Digital Dialogues

ANNA POLETTI *and* JULIE RAK

This collection is an experiment in interdisciplinary dialogue. As scholars of autobiography, we are intensely interested in the rise of autobiographical discourse in contemporary culture. Nowhere is the power and diversity of the auto-biographical more visible than online, where it is the raison d'être for many of the activities and practices associated with Web 2.0, and where acquiring and maintaining online identities make up the core activities of many users. Research into how identity is presented online is occurring in a number of fields, such as auto/biography studies (a widely used term for the study of autobiography, biography, and life writing), communications and new media studies, cultural studies, education, game studies, psychology, and sociology. Each field draws upon its own methods and prominent theorists to gather data and analyze the diverse range of identity technologies that have become available. Each field, too, rests on a confidence in the methods and approaches it deploys to under-take this research, and how the key questions and issues raised by the spread of identity technologies are to be identified and defined.

As our individual research interests have led us further into the analysis and theorizing of online identity, we have become excited by the prospect of creat-ing a bridge between auto/biography studies and media studies, which could be mutually beneficial to researchers in both fields. The aim of this bridge is to productively challenge a founding assumption, or tendency, in each field, using the approaches and ways of thinking of the other in order to problematize "iden-tity" as a frame through which to examine online texts and practices. To do this, we have included a mix of new and established scholarship on the topic of online identity from the areas of media studies, sociology, cultural studies, and auto/ biography studies. This variety of approaches brings together a range of examples of how "identity" can be read in order to encourage researchers and students in the field to revisit the question of what it means to pay attention to identity online. As researchers adapt the methods of their discipline to the expanding field of identity technologies, we must question how preexisting ways of defining, identifying, and interpreting online texts shape not only what is visible as evidence of online identity but also the conclusions drawn about that evidence. We realize that it is not possible to trace the contours of each approach to online identity in their entirety, but we do think that it is possible to think about how the study of online media can benefit from the insights of auto/biography studies about identity construction. In turn, auto/biography studies could benefit from the long engagement scholars from media studies and other disciplines have had with specific aspects of online life. Beyond thinking about specific software packages or hardware designs, this book discusses what it actually means to *be* online and to have an online life, and the ways in which we can study this question in all its complexity. *Identity Technologies* represents one way to approach these issues.

WHY STUDY ONLINE IDENTITY?

It is now commonplace to assume that personal identity work is foundational to the production of social media and even of hardware interfaces. There are many possible reasons for this. One reason involves the connection of Web 2.0—with its insistence on digital forms of participation between individuals— to liberal ideas of subjectivity. Internet subjects can be many things: they can be citizens, consumers, participants, gamers, lurkers, or stalkers, but generally the conditions of Internet subjectivity remain indebted to classic liberalism. Internet users understand themselves to be individuals who are unique, have agency, and exhibit commonly understood forms of consciousness, as discussed by Helen Kennedy in her foundational article (this volume, 25–41). Arguably, the structure of the Internet works to support this understanding of identity, which originated in Europe, spread via various forms of print culture, and became part of Western ideas about what the self is. These assumptions about the subject have continued to travel worldwide, via the grammar of Internet interfaces. Moreover, if these conditions of selfhood are not present, then there are usually traces of active resistance to normative Internet culture present as well (Rak 2005). Therefore, the study of online activity needs to take into account ideas about what identity is, how it is formed, and how stories about identity are made.

We also believe that the understanding of affordances in new media studies should enter the vocabulary of humanist scholars who are interested in studying online practices. In the work of the psychologist J. J. Gibson (1979), an affordance is an expression of a relationship between an actor (animal or human) and its environment. In *The Psychology of Everyday Things*, Donald Norman adapted the concept for design purposes; for him, an affordance "refers to the perceived and actual properties of the thing, primarily those fundamental properties that determine just how the thing could possibly be used" (1988, 14). Designers of computer hardware and software use the idea of affordances to help them design interfaces that can be used efficiently (McGrenere and Ho 2000), but increasingly, Internet designers and media theorists understand affordances to be social (Wellman et al. 2006). Internet affordances help to determine how we will behave online, because they direct us to act in certain ways and even be a certain type of person. The constant directive to "share" personal information on social media sites such as Facebook or Linked In is an example of a media affordance, which asks for users to create a specific type of identity, one that can be shared. In the same way that the genres of life writing such as memoir or diary create the terms within which people create identities, Internet affordances can work (sometimes covertly) to create the terms for identification and the rules for social interaction. Affordances are therefore an important aspect of studying the ideological aspects of the production of online identities and communities.

These two examples of ways to understand online identity production are indicative lines of inquiry that are beginning to converge in the study of digital life, particularly in the areas of auto/biography studies and new media. We believe that it is time for these areas of research to join forces so that we can begin to answer questions about identity that move beyond specific examples of online and digital activity. The development of research into online identity has key studies within it, which already try to bring these areas together. We have included some of these studies here as reprints, and we also have commentaries by established scholars, which reflect on what a confluence between these areas might mean, and essays by emerging scholars who are working on these questions. In this introduction, we present our case for thinking through identity technologies in a way that pays attention to how identity has been theorized and remains open to the new directions that could occasion revisiting common assumptions about identity in an online environment.

In new media studies, future work on identity technologies could be enhanced by attention to the complex relationship between self and self-representation. The *production* of a self through representation is a more complex affair than a conscious performance as commonly argued in new media studies (see, e.g., Papacharissi 2011, 307). On the one hand we agree with, and respect, Nick Couldry's suggestion that in new media studies "understanding digital storytelling as a broad social phenomenon involves moving beyond such storytelling's status merely as texts or processes of production or distribution. Ever since Lazarsfeld and Merton (1969 [1948]) identified the first and most important question of 'media effects' as the 'effect' of the existence of media institutions as such, media scholars have developed answers to this classic question within a variety of methodological paradigms" (Couldry 2008, 374). There is no doubt that new media studies moved beyond "mere" textual analysis long ago. In the case of online practices where people are representing themselves *through* text—and often through multimedia texts—we must carefully consider the processes of mediation inherent in self-representation. We argue that when it comes to analyzing the effect of self-representational media our analysis must remain attentive to the self as an effect of representation—the affordances, strategies, techniques, and intended audiences—rather than one's identity being expressed through online practices. The extent to which identity is evidenced through online practices relies more on the implicit assumptions underpinning methodologies of reading and interpretation, which treat textual features as facts, than it does on the truth claims of the texts themselves.

We owe this insight to the area of auto/biography studies, which has rigorously critiqued the "givens" of autobiography (literally "self," "life," and "writing"). For example, the idea that the self or personality is expressed in writing has given way to the assumption that identity is in fact a product of the writing or composing process (Ashley et al. 1994; Smith 1998). In some cases, the form of identity expression works to give the writer access to certain kinds of power and knowledge formations, which were not available to him or her before. In other cases, the form of representation constructs the limits of what an identity can be. Collaborative autobiographies, letter writing, and personal zines are all examples of life-writing practices, which create the conditions for some kinds of identity-work but not others. In a similar way, the idea of "writing" as the only way to create documentation about our lives has been expanded to include all kinds of modes of representation. Some genres of writing, for example, are heavily gendered. Others are associated with specific subject positions in structures of power. What is composed, and how, and by whom has come to have intense significance in auto/biography studies itself. And finally, the idea that "life" is a given is also open to question. Who gets to "have" a life worthy of representation? Can one "make" a life from representation, and how does this process work? What are the ethics of representing another's life, and in a posthuman sense, is human life the only life that matters? These kinds of considerations could be brought into productive tension with online media studies work so that we could work through what affordances such as these have to do with identity construction.

When it comes to self-representation, online media studies approaches to online self-representational practices could do well to incorporate the kinds of insights into the relationship between self and text cultivated in auto/biography studies to tease out the relationship between "the self" and "the self online." So too, the methods for interpreting the interplay between the distribution, reception, embedding, and archiving of self-representation and larger trends in the formulation and recognition of political agency and cultural authority developed in auto/biography studies (e.g., see Smith and Schaffer 2004; and Whitlock 2007) could contribute to current debates in media studies regarding the characteristics and impact of digital storytelling (Couldry 2008). A number of essays in this collection use the insights of auto/biography studies in order to bring together the history of studying what identity is with the productions of identity in a digital environment.

Just as the insights of auto/biography studies about identity and narrative could prove to be very fruitful when we theorize Internet identities and how they are constructed through rapidly developing ideas about personhood, representations of experience, privacy, and data, so auto/biography studies could benefit from the work of media studies on non-narrative forms of identity work. Because the Internet is the site of a convergence of media technologies, it is now possible for users to have many different kinds of media available to them, such as music, video, print, and imaging technologies, and it is also now possible for users to make use of any or all of these technologies at the same time when something is constructed.

However, not all of these types of media depend on narrative to transmit meaning. In fact, some activities that constitute communicative identity-work, such as social media posting, search records, the use of SMS, apps for the handheld devices that locate where you are, or the posting of photographs, do not constitute the building of a narrative at all. And yet these activities and the technological affordances that make certain kinds of identity presentation possible (and others unthinkable) form much of the basis for the advent of auto/biographical discourse in digital media. In some cases, though, we are still using older analytical tools to try to understand this new situation. Self-representation online challenges the tendency to read for narrative, which has been a hallmark of auto/biography studies, and demands a consideration of how researching identity online causes us to rethink the basic assumption that has animated the field to date. One example of this tendency is the persistence of narrative as a frame for understanding how online identity is formed.

NARRATIVE AND IDENTITY:
RETHINKING THE ONLINE CONNECTION

In this section, we look at what some of these connections have been, with a view to rethinking that central connection between life and narrative, which has formed much of the basis for auto/biographical theory, in some alternate ways that fit better with what digital media and identity production are about.

In the area of auto/biography studies the connection between narratives as presentations of information in a sequence of events (Lacey 2000, 13) and the concept of "life" as both the represented and performative aspect of identity is long standing.[1] In a recent and explicit articulation of the link between these ideas that summarizes much of the work in the area, Sidonie Smith and Julia Watson use "life narrative" in their guide *Reading Autobiography* as a way to describe "autobiographical acts of any sort," which do not have to be written down but can be "written, performative, visual, filmic or digital" (Smith and Watson 2010, 4). "Life narrative" is seen by Smith and Watson as a more accommodating term than autobiography, because it can be about the representation of another person's life as well as one's own, and it also can describe nonwritten forms of self-representation, which are found in new media, including digital media. To this, Smith and Watson connect their sense of "identity" as a discursive construction of available models, which autobiographers (and others) use in their narratives. These models do not necessarily preexist the writing or composing subject but are historically specific, culturally marked, and often multiple and provisional (39–40). As they say, "the stuff of autobiographical storytelling, then, is drawn from multiple, disparate and discontinuous experiences and the multiple identities constructed from and constructing those experiences" (40).

In this formulation, identity and life occupy similar positions as both process and product: they exist socially and historically, and interact dynamically. But "narrative" does not. It is assumed here that all lives are to be understood as narrativized: autobiography as narrative is what results from the attempt to arrange the chaotic process of identity formation into a causal framework. Paul John Eakin in his later work has claimed that this process does not even occur at the level of writing but at the level of living, so that identity formation is the result of narrative-building (Eakin 2008, 2). In Eakin's work in particular, we can see evidence of John Locke's contention that identity is the expression of consciousness that is continuous over time, but that identity is also a product, one's own property, which is a legal entity (Rak 2004, 4–5; Poster 2006, 101–8). Identity as we understand it today is the process of knowing oneself by an interplay of difference and similarity; at the same time it is also about knowing one's social place due to a host of technologies outside of one's self, which authenticate and delimit one's existence, such as identity cards, dog tags, or PIN numbers. In a similar way, Mark Poster thinks about how the very possibility of identity theft denotes a shift in our understanding of identity itself. Poster maps the process by which systems of governmentality that document and authenticate identity are laid over Lockean and psychoanalytic conceptions of identity as a process of self-knowing. In other words, the possibility of identity theft underscores Locke's belief that identity is in fact personal property (because it can be stolen) *as* it challenges other ideas from Locke and later from psychoanalysis about identity as a process of self-incorporation. If identity can be stolen, then the process of identity formation is not unique to individuals. Therefore, "individual identity is being transformed," Poster argues, "by dint of information media, into something that both captures individuality and yet exists in forms of external traces" (Poster 2006, 111). But how can identity be this expression of inner self-processing *and* the result of identification of micropractices? Where does agency begin and end? As more and more people use electronic banking, engage in online commercial transactions, and communicate with each other online, the idea of identity as property as well as one's essence is put under increasing pressure. Identity theft has been called "the quintessential crime of the information age" (Kahn and Roberds 2008, 251) because it highlights the fact that the term "identity" now refers to *both* "an aspect of consciousness (an awareness of continuity in time and space) and a complex of media content contained in information machines that combine to define an individual" (Poster 2006, 114). If we are the sum total of our data, and if our data is not only indicative of a self but also symbolic of what we possess, then our existence becomes precarious, since data (unlike memories) can be relatively easily taken from us and used in ways we do not intend (LoPucki 2001–2). We agree with Mark Poster that this dual understanding of identity "has not been adequately recognized in cultural discourse, and its implications have not been fully explored" (Poster 2006, 114).

When we turn to the study of identity-production in digital media, this slippage between identity as a process and as a product is attenuated, particularly when we add "narrative" as an idea to the mix. But is "narrative" the best way to understand identity generation in contemporary digital media? Although auto/biography studies has contributed important work to the study of narratives by and about the self, here is where it is necessary to rethink the operation of narrative, and its relation to identity so that we can understand and study the

explosion of digital identity work in all its forms. A common use of narrative as
a term in literary studies (which is one of the areas from which auto/biography
studies developed) is to conflate the idea of narrative process and narrative as
product. As Ann Jurecic says in *Illness as Narrative*, literary critics could easily
dismiss the sociological work on life narratives by sociologists such as Ulrich
Beck and Anthony Giddens because "their work never addresses *actual* biogra-
phies or autobiographies" (Jurecic 2012, 20). Beck and Giddens's description of
narrative as social process runs directly into the idea that there are real narratives that are products. As products they should be read or interpreted in that
light. The tendency in much of literary studies and in some uses of auto/biog-
raphy studies to assume that a narrative is a product (the same thing as a text)
does not translate well to studies of other kinds of media productions. For one
thing, not all autobiographical media productions exist in narrative form, and
thinking of them as "stories" actually serves to close down elements in film or
new media that work outside of or threaten the idea of narrative as the primary
or only way to understand self-representation (Poletti 2012, 158). For another,
practices such as playing or designing an online game, texting a friend, posting
about a topic on a Facebook wall, or circulating a video may not be "narrative"
practices that build identity into a story but are instead expressions of identification, which might, through repetition, result in that internal sense of identity
as an effect (Butler 1990, 24–25). If we think of narrative as an act, as Smith and
Watson often do when they use the term "autobiographical acts" to describe
non-narrative or even just commonly circulating ways of self-representation,
we get at ways to think about how the disruptive features of identity-formation
and attempts to normalize these disruptions operate in digital media. We can
ask what the "products" of identity are and whether they are part of late capitalist circulations of goods, and we can find out who produces and who con-
sumes certain kinds of identities. As Smith and Watson point out, the study of
online productions involves many kinds of analysis, which must include what
a producer makes or codes, and what the affordances of the representation are.
For example, it is just as important to understand how advertisements work to
disrupt the idea of the Internet as a public or democratic space (this volume,
79–80). And as Philippe Lejeune also points out, "new communication tools are
not only changing autobiography—the expression of a life—but are also attacking life itself" in that they are changing the way we understand how fast someone should live, and they multiply how many media registers are available to
many of us to communicate things about our lives to others (this volume, 249).
The result, Lejeune says, may be a breakdown of what he calls narrative identity,

since the speed of technology means that the development of the idea of a life cannot depend on older ideas of what the past and the future for an individual might be (249–50). Whether technology succeeds in breaking down older ideas about the self, Lejeune's observation signals that the idea of narrative may not fit what identity formation looks like in digital media, and we may have to look to other ways to think about what is happening.

For example, the proliferation of self-representation in digital media has the effect of making anyone into a celebrity, a cultural construction where the representations of one's person becomes a commodity, which is traded legally or stolen. Celebrity in the United States necessitated the development of privacy law, which conflated the images of a person with that person so that she could exert "control" over what was produced. Privacy law was created because public identities within capitalism (through the medium of celebrity) were coded as threats (Barnett 1999, 555). The development of digital forms of identity production and circulation has followed a similar path. As Lynn LoPucki (2003) states, the existence of capitalist forms of identity production, such as the concept of the individual consumer, has eroded the idea of online public identities. In the process, this operation has created a micropolitics based on secrecy maintained by the use of passwords or the granting of access. Online identities then become closely guarded things (rather than processes), which can be stolen or misrepresented. The casting of identities as properties under constant threat necessitates the increase of security (and its inevitable failure as controls are "breached") and can even result in a neoliberal interpretation of citizenship as the assumption of individual responsibility for security (Milne 2003). But the anxieties about security are in fact caused by the existence of the idea of privacy itself (LoPucki 2003). The operations of online living within late capitalism are beginning to result in changes to the way ideas about security, citizenship, and identity itself are understood.

Taking Up the Questions

The chapters in this volume take up in various ways how we can think about identity and technology in digital media, and what auto/biographical representation looks like within some of these newer forms of representation and communication. This work is, by necessity, speculative, tentative, and concerned with specific cases in addition to their historical, geographical, social, and political contexts. But some patterns emerge in the study of online identity in different fields. We have organized these chapters to clearly show what we think is at stake in the study of online identity. We begin with Foundations, a collection of work by leaders in the areas of auto/biography theory and new media studies. Next, Identity Affordances contains essays about online and handheld interfaces that work to construct certain ideas about identity; Mediated Communities contains works that explore the idea of remediation and online community-building. In the final section, Reflections, an essay by Philippe Lejeune reflects on the development of online identity, and an interview with Lauren Berlant discusses the scene-setting possibilities of blogging. These chapters constitute separate meditations on possible futures for online life and writing. Some of the essays have been reprinted so that we can see where the methods and theories for the study of online identity began; others are newer investigations into specific instances of self-representation online, or they create theoretical paradigms to assist with the study of identity technologies.

In Foundations, Helen Kennedy's chapter from a 2006 issue of *New Media and Society* is reprinted here for its prescient analysis of the problems raised by (overuse of) "identity" as frame for analyzing and discussing activity online. Kennedy's argument, using empirical research with the ethnic minority women involved in Project Her@ in the UK in the 1990s as its foundation, asks productive questions about the history of identity as a concept and demonstrates the benefits that can come from an interdisciplinary approach, particularly in rethinking the divide between online and offline practices of identification. Lisa Nakamura's landmark essay "Cyberrace" is reprinted here; it provides a history of early Internet user-communities, and then critiques the assumption that people using them could "pass" as other races because the interfaces allowed them this freedom. This chapter shows that what she calls "identity tourism" in online environments (where people can "play" a person of any race, particularly in gaming environments) actually serves to obscure the fact that the same stereotypes about race, and practices involving racism, persist in online environments, just as they do in offline life. Rob Cover analyzes Facebook as a technology of identity performance. He suggests that Facebook is an excellent tool for the production and maintenance of a coherent identity—fundamental to social inclusion, as theorized by Judith Butler. This chapter is an excellent example of a cultural studies approach to identity technologies. Cover argues for the usefulness of Judith Butler's theory of performativity for thinking about the utility of social networking as means for individuals to satisfy the social and political demand for an intelligible and coherent subjectivity. In arguing that our analysis of social networking use must take into account both the conscious and the unconscious elements of identity performance, Cover's work is a timely reminder that approaches to identity technologies risk oversimplifying identity technologies when they focus on reporting intended uses as stated by users in empirical research.

The final entry in the Foundations section is from pioneering scholars of auto-biography Sidonie Smith and Julia Watson. Extending on their work in *Reading Autobiography* (2010), Smith and Watson take up the challenge of providing an overview of current approaches to thinking about identity online in both media studies and auto/biography studies, and suggest possible future lines of inquiry through the formulation of a variety of questions. This section will be of par-ticular interest and use to researchers and students who are conceptualizing research projects on identity technologies. Read in conjunction with the con-tributions from Lauren Berlant and Philippe Lejeune in the Reflections section, Smith and Watson provide many points of departure for future work, which can capitalize on the insights made possible by looking at the topic from mul-tiple perspectives.

One of the most important aspects of the study of online identity in the area of new media is the emphasis on affordances as examples of technologies, which create specific responses to an interface. We begin the Identity Affordances sec-tion with Melissa Gregg's chapter, which explores "spouse busting" apps: smart-phone applications aimed at couples who may wish to monitor their partner's behavior or protect against a partner who wants access to the digital traces of activity left in a smartphone. Gregg begins with the important work of putting these apps—and the anxieties they seek to exploit and allay—into both their historical and cultural context. By doing so, her work extends beyond a mere report on the rise of these apps, and examines how their development, release, and continued refinement intersects with the structural changes in white collar work and the changing nature of coupledom in the twentieth and twenty-first centuries. As a leading theorist of intimacy and work, Gregg's contribution to the collection is a fascinating case study, and an exemplar of theorizing the rela-tionship between identity technologies and the desires they evoke and formu-late. She demonstrates the need for attentive and flexible methods that can make visible the complex intermingling of online and offline practices.

Aimée Morrison's chapter presents a much-needed analysis of the evolution of the status update on Facebook as an identity technology by framing it as an affordance that coaxes autobiographical statements from users. Morrison blends approaches from auto/biography studies and new media studies to analyze and account for the complex interaction between software affordances and self-representation in the social networking context. From auto/biography studies, Morrison takes an interest in the historical development of form (in this case, the Facebook status update). This approach yields insights into how users have adapted to Facebook's changing interface, the kinds of identity performances the interface facilitates, and how the history of that interface is important to users' understanding and engagement with the platform. Morrison outlines the difficulties facing researchers interested in tracking the development of a site available only in its present iteration, and overcomes this limitation through her use of a variety of sources. Morrison's analysis of the changing iterations of the invitation to share an update—from an incomplete sentence that begins with the user's name to the current "what's on your mind?"—demonstrates an interdisciplinary approach to understanding how social networking occasions particular kinds of self-representation by bringing together the concepts of the affordance and the role of coaxers in the production of self-representation.

Courtney Rivard's chapter, "Archiving Disaster and National Identity in the Digital Realm," compares the affordances created by the attempt to archive responses to the 9/11 attacks in the United States and another, less successful, attempt to archive responses to the Hurricane Katrina disaster in 2005. Rivard argues that the structure of the archives was similar, but that differences in deeply entrenched beliefs in the United States about race, gender, class position, and public presentation meant that the affordances in the archives resulted in widely divergent responses to each project. Rivard concludes that online technologies of identity are not in fact democratic in themselves, as some commentators have assumed. Offline ideas about what identity *is* affect how affordances are taken up in digital environments. Laurie McNeill's chapter, "Life Bytes: Six-Word Memoir and the Exigencies of Auto/tweetographies," examines the website and online community Six-Word Memoir.com in order to look at how exigence, a term from the study of genre that explains how a form can emerge within a community and create among the community's members a sense that the form must be taken up immediately, helps explain the popularity of the Six-Word memoir form and its development into a reporting form, which resembles Twitter discourse in its immediacy and repeatability.

The study of online identity is not just the study of individual activity. It is also intimately involved with the idea of community in all its forms. But community in a digital sense is not merely an opaque concept. It is mediated and remediated through the technologies that are used to facilitate and express it. The Mediated Communities section begins with a reprint of an essay by Mary L. Gray titled "Negotiating Identities/Queering Desires: Coming Out Online and the Remediation of the Coming-Out Story." Gray explores how rural youth weave digital-media materials into their own formulations of identity, particularly as they navigate what Gray calls the master narrative of gay/lesbian/bisexual and transgendered identification: the coming-out story. This process can result in identifications that work against the established belief that media representations helps youth to "come out." Gray shows that online communities provide a way for rural youth to engage in what, after Judith/Jack Halberstam, she calls "queer realness," a generic effect of online media images, which help rural youth identify with a queer community through experiencing the repetition of the signs of queerness in various ways. Online representations have the effect of confirming the identity work some rural youth undergo as they work out what their identities as queer people could mean. Queer realness, then, is the result of rural teens' investigation of their immediate (small-town) situation, encounters with media, and discoveries of online community. Gray asks us to consider the web of these associations as the work of negotiating identity over time rather than simply assuming that exposure to mass media queer interpretations plays the central role in a coming-out process.

Olivia Banner's chapter examines a different type of community and its ideas about medical data with a theorization of Foucauldian biopower. In "'Treat Us Right!': Digital Publics, Emerging Biosocialities, and the Female Complaint," Banner looks at how "informatics," the state where a (often medical) subject is thought to be composed of unmediated data, informs the community-building of a group of women who suffer from chronic pain. The forum they use, PatientsLikeMe.com, represents a type of biomediated community, where users are encouraged to "life log," or upload their experiences with their illness in order to help researchers find a cure for these conditions. Banner shows that the expectation of the site's creators that users will give over their symptoms and even their lives to the cause of data-building is imperfectly realized, as users in the community sometimes choose to respond differently to the idea of medicalization than originally intended. Banner's discussion is also indicative of how the proliferation of identity technologies and practices unsettles some practices of knowledge production in the humanities, particularly what we can and cannot assume about the relationships between audiences and texts.

Alessandra Micalizzi examines a culturally specific and temporary online environment where Italian women who have experienced the loss of an unborn child come together in a community of grief. The question motivating Micalizzi's research involves understanding how the women use the identity technology of the online forum for identity reorganization after a traumatic event. Like Banner, Micalizzi examines a specific instance of online identity practices stemming from medical experience. Her chapter, "Cyber-Self: In Search of a Lost

Identity?" analyzes the recent development of community sites for perinatal death mourning in Italy. Based on an empirical study of the most successful sites for women who have experienced the loss of an infant, Micalizzi examines how the Internet can serve as a means of creating an identity that is under-recognized or taboo in a society. Drawing on narrative theories of identity, her analysis demonstrates that identity technologies can be temporary—taken up at a point of crisis, and set aside once the individual has adjusted to her "new" identity—and address very specific needs. Importantly, Micalizzi's contribution to the collection also reminds us that the processes of globalization have not completely eroded the potential for communities based on language, location, and culture to use the web for identity work.

Suzanne Bouclin's piece, "Homeless Nation: Producing Legal Subjectivities through New Media," tracks the development of a Web 2.0 site, which street people in Quebec and the rest of Canada can use in order to post images and videos, to report a missing person, and to build an online version of street community. Homeless Nation is an admittedly utopian use of social media by activists who want the site to help protect and enhance the lives of people on the street. But Bouclin says that the site embodies a version of what she calls "street law," a network of unwritten rules (sometimes about official law such as vagrancy legislation), which members of street communities use as part of surviving and thriving in precarious urban environments. Bouclin argues that Homeless Nation's goal is to provide a way to facilitate three kinds of identities that street people can use: the identity of mediator between street practices and urban laws about street people, a resistant identity that contests official law and opens up new practices on the street, and an identity that allows street people to communicate and interact with each other using online technologies. The special character of the Homeless Nation website (until its hiatus in 2009) was to move past its existence as an archive and become a way for its members to be part of what Bouclin calls a "legal community" that seeks to govern its own interactions and not just be governed by the state.

We intend for the Reflections section to be a meditation on the future of digital identity in light of early work in new media and auto/biography studies, and a way to move the study of online writing and other representation into new areas of theoretical enquiry. The Reflections section begins with a chapter by Philippe Lejeune titled, in English, "Autobiography and New Communication Tools." Originally a talk given in French at the University of Lyons, it appears here in print for the first time, in an English translation undertaken by Katherine Durnin for this volume. Philippe Lejeune is one of the most significant autobiography and diary theorists: more than four decades after he published the essay "The Autobiographical Pact," this way of understanding what autobiography is as a genre is still central to the discipline. But there is much more to Lejeune's work than his famous pact. In "Autobiography and New Communication Tools," Lejeune looks back at the historic development of autobiography and the diary as genres, concluding that without technological developments such as printing, these forms would not exist as we know them today. The Foucauldian idea of "the care of the self" is intimately connected to technological change. Therefore, new developments in digital and online communication need to be seen in the same way: they are not just changing the forms of self-expression, but they are in the process of changing our understanding of what life itself is going to mean. What Lejeune calls new communication tools have two features: fusion and speed. By fusion, he means that media convergence in newer technologies has combined an older practice, writing, with newer practices of representation, such as video. By speed, Lejeune means that new communication tools are breaking down older ideas about the divisions between time and space. The result may be not only new ways to tell stories about identity but also new ways to conceive of identity itself. It may be, Lejeune suggests, that the older ideas in the Western world of the desirability of a "good life" or of a life project that one undertakes will be changed by the advent of new technologies for representing life. It may be too, Lejeune thinks, that older forms of writing such as the diary persist within the newer environments, changing in light of different technological demands but never disappearing entirely. These forms may not even take the shape of life narrative as we have known it. But they are here, and they are evolving, and they deserve our full attention.

The Reflections section, and the volume itself, concludes with our interview with Lauren Berlant, whose work as a theorist of intimacy, women's culture, and American citizenship is widely recognized. In 2007 Berlant began a research blog, called *Supervalent Thought*, which is the topic of our conversation. Organized as a series of scenes, the interview opens the topic of identity technologies out to a consideration of blogging as practice, as an attempt to bring about other ways of being in the world; along the way Berlant shares with us, and extrapolates, some vital methodological insights for the study of online practices as scenes of aspiration and transformation. In the inaugural post on *Supervalent Thought* Berlant observes: "A supervalent thought produces an atmosphere in the world, makes an opening in the potential for apprehension, consciousness, and experience" (2007); and in conversation with us, Berlant considers the potential for online writing practice to be a means of bringing new genres of writing and identity into being that not only de-prioritize the narrative imperative but also make possible other forms of attachment to people and the world. Like all Berlant's work, the interview provokes us to scrutinize the relationship between our method and our subject, and provides new avenues for thinking about what "counts" as identity activity and how. How then can we study the operations of identity in digital media, and particularly in the case of online communication and production if we don't wish to just use the idea of narrative as a heuristic?

One way to think of this problem is through Lauren Berlant's discussion of scene and encounter in her interview. Berlant's injunction to think of scene as a place from which representations about an event originate counters a more established tendency to write about or conceptualize events as episodes, which is a way to temporalize them. Eakin understands such a tendency as connected to memory itself, where episodes from one's life constitute the building blocks of identity in daily life. When we read or write episodically, we are doing what we already know how to do naturally. If we do not live this way, we have a mental or physical illness (Eakin 2008, 12–15). However, as Cathy Caruth and many other theorists of trauma point out, life events can cause a narrative problem that prevents the construction of episodes either for oneself, or in the act of representing experience (Caruth 1996, 6–7; Laub 1992, 57–58). In many ways, trauma is about the inability to create narrative, whether it is because the impact of the event is too great for an individual to bear, or whether there is no one present to make a narrative from what is recalled. It is, we would say, about narrative's failure to be the language for the event, an event that is often interpreted as catastrophic. Marianne Hirsch's formulation of postmemory (2008) or Celia Lury's (1998) idea that photographs can act as a prosthetic memory are only two of many ways to understand how individuals make sense of memories that cannot be made into narrative. Both make use of the technologies of photography as the way to make connections that are not episodic, but that are nonetheless vital to the survivor's own process of identification with the past and the present. Technology provides a way to survive an event, or the loss of people one loves, which may be too much to bear without it.

The point here is that narrative constructions of identity should not be seen as normal, but as one way among many to understand events in terms of some kind of identification. Berlant's sense of what a scene is, taken from psychoanalysis, has a number of parallels to understanding trauma. She states, "In psychoanalysis, what is a scene? A scene exists where there is a perturbation in an atmosphere that overwhelms, that reveals and unravels structure, but it also induces a kind of stuckness in relation to the revelation of the event. That is, it produces a kind of slowness or a paralysis or incapacity" (this volume, 268). A scene contains the possibility that the subject is overwhelmed by an event, where narration is not possible because "your seeing of it is accompanied by an over-presence of affect that makes it impossible to narrate it away and to narrate your-self away from it" (269). What Berlant calls "genre" is a way of making sense of a scene that involves a gradual process of recognizing its terms. Eventually, Berlant says, a scene can become event. And that can take on a narrative shape, which can start to have resonances with other events in that genre.

If certain kinds of autobiography are thought about not as episodic and gen-erative but as a series of scenes, which can become episodic (but may not, or may for someone else who performs this act of recognition), then it becomes more possible to think about how autobiographical discourse surfaces within different types of media, including online media, in ways that may not be tem-poral and that may exceed the original terms set for them. An example of this could be the transgender activist and performance artist Micha Cárdenas's grad-uate work at the University College of San Diego, where Cárdenas created a proj-ect called "Becoming Dragon." With the help of video technology, which shut off her sense that there is an outside world so that her movements and experi-ences were contained entirely in-world, Cárdenas spent 365 consecutive hours in the online world Second Life as her avatar, a dragon named Azdel Slade. She chose this time period because one hour represents each day that a transgender person has to live in the offline world as their chosen gender in order to qualify for gender confirmation/sex reassignment surgery (365 days). Cárdenas's proj-ect raises the question whether it would be possible to live a Second Life for a virtual year, and then qualify for species-reassignment surgery, and also to see if living as another species creates the same sets of disjunctures that transgen-dered people experience when they have to live as the gender with which they were born, but with which they do not identify.[2] In this case, understanding Cár-denas's online experiences as a dragon or offline experiences as a transgendered person as scenes rather than as episodes, which "generate" a life, can call into question the conflation between the living of a life and the representation of life that is also part of auto/biography studies. What "life" is she living in Second Life during the project, for example? Is it more real or more of a "good life" than liv-ing in the so-called real world without experiencing one's gender as real, or with-out other people understanding what gender one might be? What kind of story might be told about this life? There is no narrative here, but rather a dialectical connection between the two states of being, online and offline, and a series of scenes in both where the avatar/artist learns literally to "walk around" (as Berant puts it [ooo]) in a genre and understand its parameters within a disturbance. Rather than assuming—as early theorists sometimes did—that the Internet is a utopic space, which promises to change the conditions of identity, here online life is a thought-experiment, which calls into question the homology between life and narrative, and where identity is staged as a problem of design in both registers.

These examples show that the production of identity in digital and online registers can be understood in other than narrative terms in a way that we hope opens up issues about what identity is, how it is related to technology, and what older identity forms such as citizenship might mean in light of proliferating forms of self-expression through various media. We are not suggesting that the identities that appear online are always radical, or that they always represent a departure from what is known. In fact, older genres such as documentary film, written diaries, or the discourses of written and spoken confession persist within digital media; they help create that language of genre, which allows these forms to continue and inform other uses of them. But we do think that the long-standing connection between identity and its technologies deserves new critical tools, which can help us to rethink the connection between identity, narrative, and the idea of life.

Here, we come full circle in our argument that the scholars of auto/biography studies and new media studies have much to say to each other. We agree with Lejeune that changes in technology have always meant changes to the idea of the self, and that identity work is both a work of mediation and remediation between technology and life. Like him, we are not sure where this latest mediation between identity and technology will lead. But we are committed to studying it, and to studying it in new ways. In this collection, we seek to bring together many approaches to the study of identity in digital environments, keeping in mind the important work we have seen about identity as a rhetorical effect, and the promise (as well as the problems) of technology itself. What we are, who we love, how we live and communicate with others, how we think of our life histories, even if we make our lives as stories at all, and even what being alive means: these are all states of being increasingly mediated through online digital environments. *Identity Technologies* is part of a move to try to understand what being online, and what online being, is about. We invite you to be part of this digital dialogue.

NOTES

1. The term "auto/biography" is often used by scholars in this area to denote the studies of published and discursive forms of autobiography and biography as well as to acknowledge that there is often a mixing of these forms in individual examples. Auto/biography also appears here as a term that includes what is often called life writing or life narrative in scholarly circles.

2. For details, see the short video feature "Becoming Dragon" at http://www.youtube .com/watch?v=pHEDym1aOZs. Thanks to Lauren Berlant for pointing us to this video. See also Cárdenas 2010.

REFERENCES

Ashley, Kathleen M., Leigh Gilmore, and Gerald P. Peters, eds. 1994. *Autobiography and Postmodernism*. Amherst: University of Massachusetts Press.

Barnett, Stephen. 1999. "'The Right to One's Own Image': Publicity and Privacy Rights in the United States and Spain." *American Journal of Comparative Law* 47 (Fall): 555.

Berlant, Lauren. 2007. "Supervalent Thought." *Supervalent Thought*. December 23. Accessed June 6, 2012. http://supervalentthought.com/2007/12/23/hello-world/.

——— 2008. "Thinking about Feeling Historical." *Emotion, Space and Society* 1, no. 1: 4–9.

Butler, Judith. 1990. *Gender Trouble: Feminism and the Subversion of Identity*. New York: Routledge.

Cárdenas, Micha. 2010. "Becoming Dragon: A Transversal Technology Study." *Code Drift: Essays in Critical Digital Studies* 9. http://www.ctheory.net/articles.aspx?id=639.

Caruth, Cathy. 1996. *Unclaimed Experience: Trauma, Narrative, History*. Baltimore: Johns Hopkins University Press.

Couldry, Nick. 2008. "Mediatization or Mediation? Alternative Understandings of the Emergent Space of Digital Storytelling." *New Media and Society* 10, no. 3: 373–91.

Eakin, Paul John. 2008. *Living Autobiographically: How We Create Identity in Narrative*. Ithaca, NY: Cornell University Press.

Foucault, Michel. 1998. *The Will To Knowledge: The History of Sexuality*. Part 1. London: Penguin Books.

Gibson, J. J. 1979. *The Ecological Approach to Visual Perception*. Boston: Houghton Mifflin.

Hirsch, Marianne. 2008. "The Generation of Postmemory." *Poetics Today* 29, no. 1: 103–28.

Jurecic, Ann. 2012. *Illness and Narrative*. Pittsburgh: University of Pittsburgh Press.

Kahn, Charles M., and William Roberds. 2008. "Credit and Identity Theft." *Journal of Monetary Economics* 55, no. 2: 251–64.

Lacey, Nick. 2000. *Narrative and Genre: Key Concepts in Media Studies*. New York: St. Martin's Press.

Laub, Dori. 1992. "Bearing Witness, or the Vicissitudes of Listening." In *Testimony: Crises of Witnessing in Literature, Psychoanalysis and History*, edited by Shoshana Felman and Dori Laub, 57–74. New York: Routledge.

Lejeune, Philippe. 1989. "The Autobiographical Pact." Translated by Kathleen Leary. In *On Autobiography*, edited by Paul Jean Eakin, 3–30. Minneapolis: University of Minnesota Press.

LoPucki, Lynn. 2001–2. "Human Identification Theory and Identity Theft." *Texas Law Review* 80:89–135.

————. 2003. "Did Privacy Cause Identity Theft?" *Hastings Law Journal* 54, no. 4. Accessed June 15, 2012. http://dx.doi.org/10.2139/ssrn.386881

Lury, Celia. 1998. *Prosthetic Culture: Photography, Memory and Identity*. London: Routledge.

McGrenere, Joanne, and Wayne Ho. 2000. "Affordances: Clarifying and Evolving a Concept." *Proceedings of Graphics Interface 2000*. 179–86. http://teaching.polishedsolid .com/spring2006/iti/read/affordances.pdf.

Milne, George R. 2003. "How Well Do Consumers Protect Themselves from Identity Theft?" *Journal of Consumer Affairs* 37, no. 2: 388–402.

Norman, Donald A. 1988. *The Psychology of Everyday Things*. New York: Basic Books.

Papacharissi, Zizi. 2011. "A Networked Self." In *A Networked Self: Identity, Community and Culture on Social Network Sites*, edited by Zizi Papacharissi, 304–18. New York: Routledge.

Poletti, Anna. 2012. "Reading for Excess: Relational Autobiography, Affect and Popular Culture in *Tarnation*." *Life Writing* 9, no. 2: 157–72.

Poster, Mark. 2006. "Identity Theft and Media." In *Information Please? Culture and Politics in the Age of Digital Machines*, 88–115. Durham, NC: Duke University Press.

Rak, Julie. 2004. *Negotiated Memory: Doukhobor Autobiographical Discourse*. Waterloo, ON: Wilfrid Laurier University Press.

————. 2005. "The Digital Queer: Weblogs and Internet Identity." *Biography: An Interdisciplinary Quarterly* 28, no. 1 (Winter): 166–82.

Smith, Sidonie. 1998. "Performativity, Autobiographical Practice, Resistance." In *Women, Autobiography, Theory: A Reader*, edited by Sidonie Smith and Julia Watson, 108–15. Madison: University of Wisconsin Press.

Smith, Sidonie, and Kay Schaffer. 2004. "Conjunctions: Life Narratives in the Field of Human Rights." *Biography: An Interdisciplinary Quarterly* 27, no. 1: 1–24.

Smith, Sidonie, and Julia Watson. 2010. *Reading Autobiography: A Guide for Interpreting Life Narratives*. 2nd ed. Minneapolis: University of Minnesota Press.

Wellman, B., A. Quan-Haase, J. Boase, W. Chen, K. Hampton, I. Díaz, and K. Miyata. 2006. "The Social Affordances of the Internet for Networked Individualism." *Journal of Computer-Mediated Communication* 8, no. 3. doi:10.1111/j.1083-6101.2003b00216.

Whitlock, Gillian. 2007. *Soft Weapons: Autobiography in Transit*. Chicago: University of Chicago Press.

FOUNDATIONS

Beyond Anonymity, or Future Directions for Internet Identity Research

HELEN KENNEDY

THE INTERNET, IDENTITY, AND ANONYMITY

In his overview of the short history of the field that he defines as cyberculture studies (which has many overlaps with new media studies), David Silver (2000) suggests that the area has moved through three key phases. The first phase he defines as "popular cyberculture," consisting of descriptive journalism, often in the columns of magazines. The second phase builds on this and is defined as "cyberculture studies": while more academic and less journalistic, it was marked by equally celebratory literature such as Rheingold's *The Virtual Community* (1993) and Turkle's *Life on the Screen* (1995). These texts also reflect the focus on virtual communities and online identities that marked this historical phase. Silver claims that we are now in a phase of "critical cybercultural studies," characterized by a concern with contextualizing cyber-experiences and by the emergence of a broader range of empirical studies of cyber-worlds. Consequently, cyberculture studies are now more theoretically nuanced and more empirically based than they have been in the past.

Although the neat chronology of events implied in Silver's account is somewhat oversimplified, he makes a number of important claims: today, cyberculture studies is increasingly populated by empirical research and focused on a broader range of concerns than identity and community, resulting in more diverse and richer theorizations than existed fifteen years ago. Nevertheless, a number of writers continue to argue that there has been too much focus on identity in cultural studies of the Internet. For example, Christine Hine (2001) proposes that conceiving of web pages as performances of identity fails to acknowledge the social and cultural meaning of web page production; Tara McPherson (2000) argues that instead of focusing on identity play online, we should consider politics and participation, in order to understand cyber-worlds. Furthermore, within some sectors of cultural studies, there has been ongoing debate about the usefulness of the very concept of identity—from Stuart Hall's essay "Who Needs Identity" (1996), which criticizes the essentialist model of human subjectivity embodied in this concept, to more recent literature influenced by the work of Gilles Deleuze, which proposes alternatives to identity such as affect, as more effective starting points for carrying out sociocultural research (e.g., Parisi and Terranova 2001).

Despite these critical interventions, the tropes of identity and community endure. This chapter addresses the debates about whether identity remains a useful focus for studies of the Internet and other new media.[1] Its aim is to map the field of Internet identity research, to point to some of its limitations, and to suggest some future directions. I question the specific claim in Internet identity research that virtual identities are anonymous (Turkle 1995); some of them might be, but there are problems with this generalized, enduring claim. I argue that online identities are often continuous with offline selves, not reconfigured versions of subjectivities IRL; for this reason it is necessary to go *beyond* Internet identities, to look at offline contexts of online selves, in order to fully comprehend virtual life. More importantly, the concept of anonymity is problematic because it fixes the relationship between being and feeling in a way that limits the exploration of the significant differences between these two conditions—concepts other than anonymity might therefore be more helpful in conceptualizing Internet identities. If Internet identity research is to reposition itself conceptually, then it needs to engage with and learn from ongoing debates within cultural studies, which call into question the usefulness of the concept of identity. To date, such an engagement has been surprisingly absent from considerations of identity within new media studies, despite the close relationship between these two fields. This engagement may lead Internet identity researchers to start with a different set of conceptual tools than those mobilized to date, which, in turn, might lead to some new conceptual developments within the broader field of new media studies, within which Internet identity research is located.

This chapter draws on empirical research into Internet use by a group of ethnic minority women in the UK on Project Her@, which took place in the late 1990s.[2] Project Her@ was an experiment in computer-mediated distance learning that aimed to enhance access to university education for women from disadvantaged backgrounds. Fourteen mature (i.e., over twenty-one years old), ethnic minority, working-class women took part in the project, whose purpose was to respond to a range of inequalities in a region of the UK that is characterized by economic disadvantage, limited engagement in university education, and subsequent high unemployment. The extent of the digital divide at the time meant that many inhabitants of the region were unlikely to have access to digital networks. It is within this social and economic context that Project Her@ was developed.[3]

Project Her@ developed a foundation course, delivered partly by computer-mediated distance learning, that offered women who had been out of education for some time the opportunity to improve study and communication skills, and that guaranteed its students places on degree courses upon successful completion. Both the foundation course and the degree courses to which successful students could progress aimed to develop students' technical skills in media, multimedia or IT, as well as their critical understanding of the range of complex relationships between technologies and societies. By providing a flexible learning environment in which communication could take place asynchronously, these distance and e-learning approaches might attract a group of women otherwise unable to commit to full-time study. The project funded the purchase of PCs that were loaned to students and installed in their own homes for the duration of the course. It subsidized students' online time for several hours a week in addition to their phone calls to their tutors, each other, and the project's technical support team.

A condition of acceptance onto Project Her@ was that students consented to our use of their distance-learning assessed work as research data and to participating in interviews with us—the students chose their own pseudonyms for research purposes. The assessed work included written reflections about students' techno-experiences and individual home pages, the latter of which became the central focus of this chapter. Individual interviews were carried out in students' own homes about halfway through the course. Later, when the majority of the students had entered the first year of their degree programs, a second round of interviews was completed, this time in small groups on the university campus. Less than three years later, I attempted to contact those students who had produced individual home pages while on the Her@ course, asking them if they would be willing to answer more research questions. Given the passage of time, it was not surprising that I received only four responses to my request. One of my arguments is that it is necessary to look at the offline contexts in which Internet identities are produced; it is inevitable, then, that I draw on the students' written narratives and on interview material, as well as their home pages. I discuss this empirical material and its implications for Internet identity research after an overview of the literature within the field.

IDENTITY IN THE AGE OF THE INTERNET:
MAPPING THE FIELD

A history of Internet identity research has no better starting point than Turkle's *Life on the Screen* (1995). A classic study of the relationship between identity construction and networked technologies, Turkle argues that, online, identity changes, becoming fluid and fragmented (1995). Most of what Turkle claims about the relationship between the Internet and fragmented identity is based on the experiences of her research subjects, largely college students, in MUDs (Multi-User Dungeons).[4] The comment of one MUD participant, who said that "part of me, a very important part of me, only exists inside PernMUD" (12), is symptomatic of her respondents' experiences, which suggest that in such anonymous environments, identity can be broken into fragments, deconstructed, and reconstructed. Turkle also argues that home pages reflect fragmented identities, as "home pages on the Web are one recent and dramatic illustration of new notions of identity as multiple yet coherent" (259). Turkle indicates that despite her attraction to the postmodern notion of decentered identity and the experiences of fragmentation that her research subjects reported, she ultimately had difficulty with these concepts. Other writers have demonstrated a greater commitment to the notion of digitally fragmented identity, such as Plant (1997) and Haraway (1998). Haraway argues that it is politically important to split identity because acknowl-edging identity as always partial, never complete, allows the subject to join with and understand other partial beings, therefore facilitating political alliances and coalitions across difference: "the split and contradictory self is the one who can interrogate positionings and be accountable; the one who can construct and join rational conversations and fantastic imaginings that change history" (Haraway 1998, 195).

In contrast, Turkle demonstrates a commitment to the centered and unified self, stating, "Virtual environments are valuable as places where we can acknowledge our inner diversity. But we still want an authentic experience of self. One's fear is, of course, that in the culture of simulation, a word like authenticity can no longer apply" (Turkle 1995, 254). Despite this conclusion, Turkle's work is not known for its ultimate loyalty to authentic, coherent identity but for its celebration of fragmented and multiple identity experimentation. Indeed, this latter reading of Turkle informs much writing on digital, virtual identity (e.g., Shields 1996; Poster 1999; and Cheung 2000). More recently, as detailed empirical, ethnographic, and biographical studies are being carried out, different conceptualizations of Internet identity begin to populate the theoretical landscape. As a result of her ethnographic study of the online forum BlueSky, Lori Kendall concludes that, despite prevailing claims about multiple and fluid identities in such environments, BlueSky participants "continually work to reincorporate their experiences of themselves and of others' selves into integrated, consistent wholes" (Kendall 1999, 62). In other words, in some cases, virtual identity is not fragmented but stable; in some forums, relatively unified cyber-identities are presented.

Furthermore, it is now necessary to differentiate between the types of identity presented in distinct Internet environments. Tetzlaff, for instance, makes a distinction between digital identities in home pages and other, more text-based forums, arguing that in the latter, identity may be fluid; in the former, it is more fixed because of the types of "data" located there—photographs, contact details, and so on (Tetzlaff 2000; see also Miller and Mather 1998). Clearly, new digital forms may result in new digital identities and, as Nina Wakeford argues, it is necessary to specify which aspects of new media are under examination in order to avoid the kind of "conceptual leakage" (Wakeford 1997, 54) that occurs when ideas about identity in one virtual context are then applied to others. At the same time, it may not be helpful to polarize virtual identity types as Tetzlaff does.

Perhaps the most enduring concern about Internet identity to emerge from Turkle's work addresses the relationship between virtuality and anonymity. Turkle argued that in anonymous MOOs and MUDs (both object-oriented, text-based, online vr systems), people can disguise certain aspects of identity that might lead to discrimination, such as race or gender, and so can perform a range of identity positions, hiding marginal identities and becoming part of the mainstream. Implicit in Turkle's claim is the assumption that anonymity in cyberspace is potentially empowering: because we cannot see each other, we cannot judge each other; consequently, virtual worlds are equalizing. What's more, anonymous online settings are empowering because they facilitate identity exploration, or they can occupy identity positions, which may be difficult to fill in real life (see Shaw 1997 for an example of this argument). Not surprisingly, a number of scholars have pointed out that online anonymity is more problematic than this. For example, discussing the increased incivility in the electronic exchanges he witnessed in the site of his research, Santa Monica's Public Electronic Network, Joseph Schmitz (1997) disputes the claim that such environments are necessarily democratic because of the absence of visual clues to identity. Instead, he argues that although some "markers of difference" are difficult to detect in online communication, others are easy to identify, so that judgment and discrimination still exist. He wrote that "although physical appearance, dress, and other status cues recede, educational competencies and linguistic skills increase in importance. Computer-communication media are not neutral with regard to culture, education, and socio-economic class. And electronic persons are not more 'equal' than proximate individuals, we just use different criteria to rate them" (85). Other more recent studies also indicate that not all online communities are created for anonymous identity performance and not all participants engage in virtual environments anonymously. As a result of their research, Roberts and Parks (2001) conclude that the performance of alternative genders is practiced by a small minority and viewed by many as dishonest. Similarly, Kendall (1999) argues that anonymity is not a factor in the MUD she studied and that many MUDders would object to the trivializing of all MUDs as forums for playing identity games. Baym summed up the issues at stake in 1998 when she wrote, "Judging from the scholarly attention paid to anonymous CMC interaction and its uses in identity play, one would think most on-line interaction is anonymous and few people ever interact as themselves. The reality seems to be that many, probably most, social users of CMC create on-line selves consistent with their off-line identities" (Baym 1998, 55). Of course, the fluidity and fragmentation that Turkle claims for Internet identities can also be found in a broader range of literature concerned with postmodern identity more generally—digital, virtual environments are commonly seen as arenas in which fragmented, fluid postmodern identities can be realized. Debates about Internet identities within new media studies, therefore, need to be located in the context of wider debates about identity. Despite the origins of much new media studies in the more established discipline of cultural studies, few discussions of Internet identities locate themselves within the rich debate about identity than can be found within cultural studies (see Bell 2001 for one exception to this). This absence is problematic, because it means that studies of Internet identities in particular, and new media studies more generally, fail to engage with debates that might help to develop new media theory. What is needed is an identification of and engagement with important debates about identity that can inform future new media studies.

In his seminal essay "Who Needs Identity?" (1996), Stuart Hall traces a move in cultural studies toward an understanding of identity as decentered and multiple, along similar lines to those outlined by Turkle. Despite increasing acknowledgement of identity as hybrid, Hall claims that the term "identity" itself is too bound up with essentialist approaches to human subjectivity, which leads him to reject this concept in favor of his preferred notion of identification. He favors identification because "it accepts that identities are never unified and, in late modern times, increasingly fragmented and fractured; never singular but multiply constructed across different, often intersecting and antagonistic, discourses, practices and positions. They are subject to a radical historicization, and are constantly in the process of change and transformation" (Hall 1996, 4). For Hall, identification means "points of temporary attachment to the subject positions which discursive practices construct for us" (19); it is less fixed than identity, more fluid and contingent. Like Hall, Braidotti seeks a more useful term than "identity" with which to theorize contemporary subjectivity; she settles upon the concept of "nomadic subjects" (Braidotti 1994). For Braidotti, this term also captures the positionality that characterizes postmodern identity. The nomad is thoroughly postmodern for Braidotti, because he "has relinquished all idea, desire, or nostalgia for fixity" (22). Identity is a matter of constant becomings, which Braidotti refers to as the practice of "as-if": "the affirmation of fluid boundaries, a practice of the intervals, of the interfaces, and the interstices" (7).

Braidotti takes her concept of becoming from Deleuze (1973), who has influenced a number of contemporary cultural theorists to reject the concept of identity and to start the project of cultural theorization with a different set of conceptual tools. For Deleuze, like for Hall, the problem with identity is that it implies stability and stasis, whereas what really offers creative and theoretical potential is difference—not being (as implied in the term "identity"), but becoming. Building on the work of Deleuze and others, a number of alternatives to identity are proposed—for example, some writers argue that the concept of affect is a useful starting point for cultural theory (such as Parisi and Terranova 2001). Affects in cultural objects result in affections, or emotional and bodily reactions, in experiencing subjects, but affects themselves are free from "the particular observers or bodies who experience them" (Colebrook 2002, 22) so that the concept of affect moves beyond identity or that of the experiencing subject. The concept of affect also shifts the focus of analysis away from what cultural objects *mean*, which has been the central concern in cultural studies to date, by encouraging consideration of what such objects *are* and *do*, how they *feel*, and their bodily impacts, intensities, and intimacies.

When I first analyzed the home pages of Project Her@ students (Kennedy 1999), I wanted to explore the extent to which some of the generalized claims that took hold as a result of Turkle's study, particularly regarding online anonymity, could be applied to the home page form. The conclusions I drew as a result of my analysis changed over time, as I moved from a focus on the home page text to consider the contexts of their production and the meanings of the texts for their producers. This process led me to rethink my original conclusions about the apparent absence of anonymity in the home pages. It led me to identify the limitations of not only focusing on the home page texts but also of common uses of the concept of anonymity in Internet identity research, which assume a fixed, continuous relationship between *being* and *feeling*. In contrast, my empirical material pointed to a distinction between being and feeling, between being anonymous and feeling anonymous in the Internet identities of the research subjects. Recognizing the limits of anonymity for making sense of Internet identities and the subsequent need to seek a different set of conceptual tools, I suggest that there is much to be learned from the cultural studies debates about identity, in which the problems associated with markedly fixed concepts is addressed and alternative theoretical tools are sought.

Anonymity in Her@ Students' Home Pages

The Her@ students' personal home pages were produced at the end of their year-long studies, after they had carried out a range of preparatory activities, including thinking about the uses, advantages, disadvantages, and potential risks of having a home page. They also participated in the production of a collective, group home page in order to learn about the process of web page production. The students did not receive any guidance about the specific content that they should include in their home pages. Instead, the criteria for assessing their efforts focused on the extent to which they had considered technical and design issues like quantity of text, size of images, download time, balance, and use of hyperlinks. Clearly, Her@ students' familiarity with the home page genre, the themes of the course they were undertaking, and the fact that they were submitting their home pages for assessment influenced, to some extent, their production of this "research data." Reflecting on the research data that interviews generate, Day Sclater has written that "the interview is an intersubjective process, and the narrative account is jointly produced" (Day Sclater 1998, 90), a claim that applies to all research data. The general educational context and specific assessment conditions set by the Her@ research team contributed to the joint production of the students' home pages, but other research data is also produced in conditions controlled by the researcher, like interviews. The Her@ students' home pages can, therefore, be read as expressions of their identity in conditions that were not of their making.

In my initial analysis of the Her@ students' home pages (Kennedy 1999), I questioned the claim that people, online, hide aspects of their identity, which might otherwise lead to discrimination (such as race or gender) and that this hiding is empowering, for a number of reasons. First, home pages generate different types of online identities and experiences than textual forums like MUDs; in addition, Turkle's findings in relation to these text-based spaces (Turkle 1995) did not apply to the more visual and multimedia form of the World Wide Web home pages of the Her@ students. More importantly, I found that the students showed no signs of wanting to hide their gender and ethnicity and so "benefit" from the possibility of anonymity that cyberspace offers them. Rather, they made explicit and implicit references to their gender and ethnicity in their home pages. Many of the Her@ students made their ethnicity central to their home pages, just as it is central to their identity, through the inclusion of images such as an image of an African mother and child on Askari's site; a painting of a group of black graduates on Teti's; Sasha's link to Flavortown, a black entertainment site; and Tessa's inclusion of a flag of Trinidad.

In addition to images, another way in which identity is constructed in home pages is through links—as Miller (1995) claims, "Show me what your links are, and I'll tell you what kind of person you are." In this case, the sites to which Her@ students linked are also statements of their ethnicity. Lorraine linked to a black cultural bookshop, Sasha to BlackNetUK, Roni to a site about beauty products for black women, with the words "Black women need cosmetics that are specific to *our* skin types" (emphasis added). In one version of her site, Teti included a link to "World of Black Studies," and Noori linked to a site by and about Asian women. Once students were familiar with surfing the web, it became clear that, as Askari put it, "being part of the Black Internet community" was important to many students. Furthermore, their identities and experiences as ethnic minority *women* led them to make their gender, like their ethnicity, central to their home pages, particularly through references to their roles as mothers. Askari's image of an African mother and child could be read as a representation of her own motherhood; Teti and Lorraine stated that the most important role in their lives was being a mother; Sha and Tessa mentioned that they were mothers; Roni chose to share her site with her daughter; Lorraine's links to educational sites could be read as evidence of her motherly concerns; and Noori and Chimwe wrote about their difficulties combining their responsibilities as mothers with their studies. Noori's home page reflected on the difficulties she experienced fulfilling the conventional expectations of a Muslim wife and mother. At one point she wrote on her page, "During Ramadan I used to wake up to cook at 3 or 4 a.m. and not go back to sleep again because I would not be able to wake up to take the children to school or go to class. I used the time wisely, though I managed to get the revision done for the exam, sometimes I would almost miss the Fajar (dawn) prayer because I was on the computer."

Like links, guestbooks could be conceived as spaces in which the identity of the self is constructed through identifications with and recognition from others. The people who signed Sasha's guestbook constitute the community of which she was a part, and the language that they used, like Sasha's, identified them as young and black. For example, "Mr. Lover" made the following entry in Sasha's guestbook:

> Say Wha happen Miss Sasha how come mi never did see you from time and you kyant call Mr Lover But still mi have nuff love fi you, Anyway mi come fi say BIG up your Sexy and Fine self and mi go talk to you soon coz mi have someting fi say to you (I bet you worried now don't be) seen.
> one love Girl!!
> The one and only MR LOVER XXXX.[5]

While Mr. Lover's message needs to be paraphrased in a note so that it can be understood by the geographically dispersed and ethnically diverse readership, it would be more easily recognized and understood by young African Caribbeans in the UK as locating both Mr. Lover and Sasha as part of a young, black, Internet community. Indeed, throughout her site, Sasha's identity as a young woman was communicated through the language she used—she made extensive use of exclamation marks, abbreviations (like "coz," "ya" and "yall") and slang (such as the phrase "Big Up," or praise). The type of music she liked, ragga and rap, underlined her young age as well as her ethnicity; this is also the case for Roni, who wrote extensively about the music (and physical appearance) of black Gangsta Rappers.

Consideration of the students' comments in their written reflections about their home pages suggests that although their Internet identities could not be defined as anonymous, neither are they "fixed," as Tetzlaff (2000) and Miller and Mather (1998) argue. Consequently, these polarized understandings of Internet identities—fragmented and anonymous or fixed and archived—are not helpful. After all, a web page is a media form, which is never entirely finished, just as identity composition is a continuous process—both are constantly "under construction." Sasha's home page, which has changed several times since she first built it, suggests that she wanted the representation of herself on the web to change, not to be fixed. The numerous versions of her website that Teti produced indicate that she constructed slightly altered representations of her identity in each new version, none of which was more or less her. The final version was chosen not because it was a "better" or "truer" representation of herself, but rather because time was up and the latest version had to do. Askari wrote of her website, "I felt it was difficult to incorporate the 'right' image of myself, an image I wanted the rest of the world to see and like." Her use of quotation marks around the word "right" problematizes this concept, and her words suggest that she struggled to capture an "accurate" representation of herself and toyed with more than one construction of herself as she developed her website. She is one Her@ student who happily left her site explicitly "under construction."

Nevertheless, despite my initial conclusion that Her@ students showed no signs of anonymous identity experimentation in their home pages, the intimate, confessional style of some of their content suggested that, in fact, they appeared to *feel* anonymous online. A number of students demonstrated a tendency to be "extraordinarily frank and revealing," to use Daniel Chandler's description of the authors of the home pages he studied (Chandler 1998). Noori, for example, wrote at length about the lack of support offered to her by her husband, who insisted that she continue her domestic duties while studying full time, even though he was out of work at the time. In the first draft of her home page, she was very critical of her husband, writing that "it hasn't been easy with a husband who won't lift a finger or offer any kind of support. Sometimes I am in the middle of typing an assignment and he will ask for a cup of tea, if I don't get it for him right away he will start complaining." After some discussion with her tutors about home pages as public documents, she decided to remove these comments from her final draft. Although some students demonstrated caution over the inclusion of personal information on their home pages (only one student, Sasha, included photographs of herself; only one other, Roni, included her e-mail address), and some, like Oyen and Lorraine, reflected on the need to be careful about the inclusion of personal data in home pages, there is still a lot of personal detail on the Her@ students' home pages. For example, all of them include their first names, and the majority of them include their surnames.

As a result of these apparently contradictory tendencies, on the one hand confessional and intimate (*feeling* anonymous) and on the other, including detailed personal data (not *being* anonymous), three years after the home pages had been produced, I returned to interview some of the former Her@ students to ask about the issue of anonymity in Internet identities. I asked those students whether anonymity had been an issue for them—had they wanted to preserve their anonymity, or remove it by stating openly who they were? Their responses questioned my earlier reading of the home pages (which had depended heavily on a textual analysis of the students' online selves), in which I felt that their references to their gender and race, as well as their inclusion of names and surnames, meant that their virtual identities were, indeed, not anonymous. As I discovered during these interviews, the concept of anonymity is more complex than this.

One student, Tessa, questioned my reading of her inclusion on her home page of an image of a Trinidadian flag and her reference to Caribbean foods such as plantain and avocado as an indication of her black identity. She suggested that this aspect of her identity was less visible than I thought; she pointed out that there are white Trinidadians and that white people like Caribbean food, so her ethnicity was more hidden than my reading suggested. Noori, the student who wrote critically about her husband, said that she still felt a degree of anonymity in her home page, despite including her name and surname—she might identify herself as Noori Begum, but which Noori Begum? These interview responses suggested that for some home page producers, there is a distinction between *being* anonymous and *feeling* anonymous, which arguably derives from the dual role of the World Wide Web as both public (publishing thoughts, feelings, and identities to a potentially large audience) and private (located in the home, a medium used to construct thoughts, feelings, and identities) (Chandler 1998). Some Her@ students may have given their names and surnames, but they still appeared to feel a degree of anonymity in their home pages. Anonymity, therefore, was not as absent from the Her@ students' home pages as I first thought.

My findings indicate the need for Internet identity research to move beyond a simple acceptance of the claim that whereas people experiment with anonymous identities in virtual contexts like MUDs, the inclusion of photographs and other autobiographical detail in home pages reveals the "true" identities of their authors and so erases the possibility of anonymity (Tetzlaff 2000). Such understandings need to take account of the importance of going beyond online lives and selves to consider the offline context of their production and consumption. This means not just acknowledging who the producers of online selves are offline but also considering how they feel about their online selves. To use Hine's phrase, it is necessary to think about the ways in which online selves are socially meaningful to their offline counterparts: "In order to understand the form of WWW pages it is crucial to understand their significance for their authors" (Hine 2001, 183). Studying online texts in offline contexts makes this possible, and such an approach enhances understanding of the context of production of the online text, as well as the text itself. That many of the Her@ students identify as black women in their home pages and, arguably, empower themselves and other black women in this process, indicates the importance of who the Her@ students are offline in shaping who they are online, and demonstrates that online lives are lived and produced in the context of life offline—as Kendall points out, "nobody lives only in cyberspace" (Kendall 1999, 70).

From an initial conclusion that the Her@ students did not engage in the presentation of anonymous identities to an acknowledgement that there were traces of anonymity in their online representations of selves indicates that there are degrees of anonymity in Internet identities, which are varied and situated, and so problematizes the very concept of anonymity. It also suggests that more complex categories than "anonymity" are needed to conceptualize Internet identities and comprehend them more fully. Magnus Åkesson discovered comparable complexity in his study of the Swedish gay men's portal Sylvester, in which one of his respondents included photographs of himself and other personal details on his home page on the portal but did not want Åkesson to use his (the respondent's) real name in his final study. Consequently, the author suggests that "half-anonymity" is a more useful concept than "anonymity" for analyzing his data.

In contrast to refining the concept of anonymity, it may be more productive to turn to some new conceptual tools. The problem with the concept of anonymity is that it is too fixed and stable to allow for recognition of the differences between being anonymous and feeling anonymous—Internet identities either are or are not anonymous. Consequently, the being/feeling relationship is fixed: being and feeling are locked together in a way that limits exploration of the significant differences between them and what these differences might reveal about the simultaneously public/private character of the Internet. It is here that Internet identity research could learn from cultural studies debates about identities. The parallels between the problem with identity, which has been identified in cultural studies, and the problem with anonymity is that both are too fixed to recognize the fragmentation, temporality, and contingency of the experiencing subject. This suggests that Internet identity research could benefit from considering whether there are other conceptual tools, which could be more effectively mobilized and which acknowledge the distinction between being and feeling in Internet identities, concepts like identification, affect, as-if, and becoming. I do not argue that Internet identity researchers should abandon all existing conceptual tools but rather that a more rudimentary step needs to be taken, and that might be to engage with such cultural studies debates about identity. This is the next conceptual step for Internet identity research in particular and new media studies in general.

FUTURE DIRECTIONS FOR INTERNET IDENTITY RESEARCH

Identity has been a significant theme in studies of the overlapping terrains of the Internet, cyberculture, and new media because of the opportunities for identity experimentation that virtual networked environments initially seemed to open up, and because of the centrality of identity in political life. Early celebrations of the possibilities of online identity play have more recently been grounded by empirical research, which has proposed a more complex range of relationships between online and offline identity. This research has questioned some of the key terms of Internet identity research and pointed to the need to understand virtuality in relation to and as part of reality. The empirical research from Project Her@ does these two things. I have demonstrated how moving beyond the Project Her@ student home pages to discuss their meanings for their producers with the producers themselves led me to a richer reading of the online texts. A result of this process is that the concept of anonymity is more complex than it seems at first glance—there is a distinction between feeling and being anonymous, and there are indeed varied and situated degrees of anonymity. Like others, I, too, have found the terms of Internet identity research limited and problematic.

While some academics before me have identified that terms like anonymity are too simplistic for understanding Internet identities (e.g., Baym 1998; Åkesson 2001) and others have stressed the importance of looking at contexts (e.g., Kendall 1999; Hine 2001), very few Internet identity researchers have engaged with contemporary cultural studies debates about identity itself. Even fewer have brought all three together, and this is what is now needed—for future research to move beyond anonymity, to look at contexts, and to engage with and learn from the theoretical work taking place within cultural studies. In particular, researchers of virtual identities need to consider whether those concepts that are taking ground in cultural studies (affect, identification, nomadic practice, as-if, and becoming), might open up new insights and allow for new conceptual developments, within Internet identity research in particular and new media research in general. For empirical researchers, this means two things. The first is to reflect on how research is conceived and whether identity remains a useful and illuminating starting point for new media research. The second is to reflect on the way empirical material is analyzed and to consider whether the alternative notions identified here provide new methodological and analytical tools as well as conceptual ones.

The argument here raises the question of whether identity still matters, in theory, in Internet and new media research, and in practice, "as a contested fact of contemporary political life" (Gilroy 1997, 301). Theoretically, it is time for Internet identity research to reposition itself conceptually and that reflection is needed on the appropriateness of the concepts mobilized in this field for future research, concepts like anonymity, or, if we are to follow cultural studies' lead, identity itself. Although academics may have a duty to contemplate whether identity retains validity conceptually and theoretically, those involved in identity politics on the ground—those experiencing hostility because of their "different" identities, for example—may not feel that they share this duty (or indeed luxury). Therefore, what is important is to take these conceptual steps without losing sight of identity as embodied experience, of the real struggles of real people whose identities are fiercely contested or defended—in other words, without losing sight of identity-as-practice. This is the real challenge for Internet identity research.

NOTES

1. Although there is no simple definition of identity suitable for my purposes, some brief introductory comments are useful in framing the discussion. Even a dictionary gives useful pointers to some of the characteristics of identity. *The Collins English Dictionary*, for example, defines identity simultaneously as "the state of having unique identifying characteristics held by no other person or thing," "the individual characteristics by which a person or thing is identifiable," and "the state of being the same in nature, quality etc." (1979, 728). In these definitions, identity is characterized by uniqueness and sameness. Woodward argues that the construction of identity, the process of actively taking up identity positions and presenting the resulting constructions to others, is what distinguishes identity from other, similar terms such as subjectivity (Woodward 1997). The concept of subjectivity also embodies some of the tensions, contradictions, and characteristics of identity. Subjectivity, the state of being a subject, implies agency, yet to be a subject can also mean to be subjected, as well as to be the grammatical subject of a sentence, constructed through language, ideology, and processes of representation. However, while subjectivity is necessarily subjective, identity works to connect the subjective, or the internal, with the external; identity construction makes connections between who we are, how we imagine ourselves, and how we want others to see us.

2. Project Her@ is a pseudonym, taken from the Greek goddess Hera, worshipped by women at every stage of their lives. It was funded by a British Telecommunications PLC University Development Award and was staffed by Linda Leung, Nod Miller, and me.

3. For further discussion of the context of Project Her@, see Miller, Kennedy, and Leung 2000.

4. PernMUD is one of the text-based, online spaces in which Turkle's research subjects participated.

5. To paraphrase, Mr. Lover asks why he has not seen Sasha around, and tells her that he likes her and wants to meet up with her because he has something to say to her.

REFERENCES

Åkesson, Magnus. 2001. "Gay Identities On-line and Off-line." Master's thesis, University of Amsterdam.

Baym, Nancy K. 1998. "The Emergence of On-line Community." In *Cybersociety 2.0: Revisiting Computer-mediated Communication and Community*, edited by Steve Jones, 35–68. Thousand Oaks, CA: Sage.

Bell, David. 2001. *An Introduction to Cybercultures*. London: Routledge.

Braidotti, Rosi. 1994. *Nomadic Subjects: Embodiment and Sexual Difference in Contemporary Feminist Theory*. New York: Columbia University Press.

Chandler, Daniel. 1998. "Personal Home Pages and the Construction of Identities on the Web." Accessed November 1, 2001. http://www.aber.ac.uk/media/Documents/short/webident.html.

Cheung, Charles. 2000. "A Home on the Web: Presentations of Self in Personal Home Pages." In *Web.Studies: Rewiring Media Studies for the Digital Age*, edited by David Gauntlett, 43–51. London: Arnold.

Colebrook, Claire. 2002. *Gilles Deleuze*. London: Routledge.

Collins Dictionary of the English Language. 1979. London: Collins.

Day Sclater, Shelley.1998. "Creating the Self: Stories as Transitional Phenomena." *Auto/biography* 6, no. 1–2: 85–92.

Deleuze, Gilles. 1973. *Proust and Signs*. Translated by Richard Howard. London: Allen Lane/Penguin.

Gilroy, Paul. 1997. "Diaspora and the Detours of Identity." In *Identity and Difference*, edited by Kathryn Woodward, 299–346. London: Sage/Open University Press.

Hall, Stuart. 1996. "Who Needs Identity." In *Questions of Cultural Identity*, edited by Stuart Hall and Paul du Gay, 1–17. London: Sage.

Haraway, Donna. 1998. "The Persistence of Vision." In *The Visual Culture Reader*, edited by Nicholas Mirzoeff, 191–98. London: Routledge.

Hine, Christine. 2001. "Web Pages, Authors and Audiences: The Meaning of a Mouse Click." *Information, Communication, and Society* 4, no. 2: 182–98.

Kendall, Lori. 1999. "Recontextualising 'Cyberspace': Methodological Considerations for Online Research." In *Doing Internet Research: Critical Issues and Methods for Examining the Net*, edited by Steve Jones, 57–74. London: Sage.

Kennedy, Helen. 1999. "Identity Construction in a Virtual World: The Home Page as Auto/biographical Practice." *Auto/biography* 7, nos. 1–2: 91–98.

McPherson, Tara. 2000. "I'll Take My Stand in Dixie-Net: White Guys, the South, and Cyberspace." In *Race in Cyberspace*, edited by Beth E. Kolko, Lisa Nakamura, and Gilbert B. Rodman, 117–32. New York: Routledge.

Miller, Hugh. 1995. "The Presentation of Self in Electronic Life: Goffman on the Internet." Paper presented at "Embodied Knowledge and Virtual Space" conference, Goldsmiths' College, University of London, June.

Miller, Hugh, and Russell Mather. 1998. "The Presentation of Self in WWW Home Pages." Accessed October 25, 2001. http://www.intute.ac.uk/socialsciences/archive/iriss/papers/paper21tm.

Miller, Nod, Helen Kennedy, and Linda Leung. 2000. "Tending the Tamagotchi: Rhetoric and Reality in the Use of New Technologies for Distance Learning." In *Technology and In/equality: Questioning the Information Society*, edited by Sally Wyatt, Flis Henwood, Nod Miller, and Peter Senker, 129–46. London: Routledge.

Parisi, Luciana, and Tiziana Terranova. 2001. "A Matter of Affect: Digital Images and the Cybernetic Re-wiring of Vision." *Parallax* 7, no. 4: 122–27.

Plant, Sadie. 1997. *Zeros + Ones: Digital Women and the New Technoculture*. London: 4th Estate.

Poster, Mark. 1999. "Underdetermination." *New Media and Society* 1, no. 1: 12–17.

Rheingold, Howard. 1993. *The Virtual Community: Homesteading on the Electronic Frontier*. Reading, MA: Addison-Wesley.

Roberts, Lynne D., and Malcolm R. Parks. 2001. "The Social Geography of Gender-Switching in Virtual Environments on the Internet." In *Virtual Gender: Technology, Consumption, and Identity*, edited by Eileen Green and Alison Adam, 265–85. London: Routledge.

Schmitz, Joseph. 1997. "Structural Relations, Electronic Media, and Social Change: The Public Electronic Network and the Homeless." In *Virtual Culture: Identity and Communication in Cyberspace*, edited by Steven G. Jones, 80–101. London: Sage.

Shaw, David F. 1997. "Gay Men and Computer Communication: A Discourse of Sex and Identity in Cyberspace." In *Virtual Culture: Identity and Communication in Cyberspace*, edited by Steven G. Jones, 133–45. London: Sage.

Shields, Robert M. 1996. "Introduction: Virtual Spaces, Real Histories and Living Bodies." In *Cultures of Internet: Virtual Spaces, Real Histories, Living Bodies*, edited by Robert M. Shields, 1–10. London: Sage.

Silver, David. 2000. "Looking Backwards, Looking Forwards: Cyberculture Studies 1990–2000." In *Web.Studies: Rewiring Media Studies for the Digital Age*, edited by David Gauntlett, 19–30. London: Arnold.

Tetzlaff, David. 2000. "Yo-Ho-Ho and a Server of Warez: Internet Software Piracy and the New Global Information Economy." In *The World Wide Web and Contemporary Cultural Theory*, edited by Andrew Herman and Thomas Swiss, 99–126. London: Routledge.

Turkle, Sherry. 1995. *Life on the Screen: Identity in the Age of the Internet*. New York: Simon and Schuster.

Wakeford, Nina. 1997. "Networking Women and Grrrls with Information/Communication Technology." In *Processed Lives: Gender and Technology in Everyday Life*, edited by Jennifer Terry and Melodie Calvert, 51–66. London: Routledge.

Woodward, Kathryn. 1997. "Introduction." In *Identity and Difference*, edited by Kathryn Woodward, 1–6. London: Sage/Open University Press.

———. 2000. *Questioning Identity*. London: Routledge/Open University Press.

Cyberrace

LISA NAKAMURA

Remember *cyber*? Surely one of the most irritating and ubiquitous prefixes of the 1990s, the word "cyber" quickly became attached to all kinds of products (the Sony Cybershot camera), labor styles (cybercommuting), and communicative practices (cyberspace), which have now become so normalized as already digital that the prefix has dropped out of the language. Photography, work, and social discourse no longer need be flagged as cyber since we can more or less assume that in postindustrial, informationalized societies they usually are. Cyber migrated widely during the nineties, but the legal scholar Jerry Kang's (2000) article "Cyber-race" was the first to attach this prefix to race. Kang answers the question "can cyberspace change the very way that race structures our daily lives?" (1133) with an affirmative: "race and racism are already in cyberspace" (1135). He then proposes three potential "design strategies" for lawmakers to deal with the problem of race and racism in cyberspace: the abolitionist approach, in which users take advantage of the Internet's anonymity as a means of preventing racism by hiding race; the integrationist approach, in which race is made visible in online social discourse; and the most radical one, the transmutation approach (1135). Strategies for transmuting race in cyberspace reprise some of the discourse about identity and performance that was often associated with Judith Butler—"it seeks racial pseudonymity, or cyber-passing, in order to disrupt the very notion of racial categories. By adopting multiple racialized identities in cyberspace, identities may slowly dissolve the one-to-one relationship between identity and the physical body" (1206).

The notion that racial passing is good for you—and, what's more, good for everyone else since it works to break down the rigidly essentialist notion of the body as the source and locus of racial identity—legitimated a widespread practice in the pre-graphic Internet period. In the days before widely supported graphic images generated on the fly using web browsers became a common aspect of Internet use, the Internet was effectively a text-only space and a conversation by new media as defined by Lev Manovich and others. As Manovich puts it, "new media technology acts as the perfect realization of the utopia of an ideal society composed of unique individuals" (Manovich 2001, 42) because the variability of a new media object guarantees that every user will generate and receive her or his own version of it. New media appeals to us so powerfully partly because it satisfies our needs in postindustrial society to "construct [our] own custom lifestyle from a large (but not infinite) number of choices" (42). Manovich questions this rosy picture of new media as infinite choice by calling attention to the bound quality of choice in digital interactive environments, and Jennifer Gonzalez extends this notion by questioning the nature of the objects themselves. If identity construction and performance in digital space is a process of selection and recombination much like shopping (another privileged activity of the nineties), what types of objects are offered, what price is paid, who pays, who labors, and who profits? Gonzalez calls out neoliberal digital utopians by characterizing bodies as an infinitely modifiable assemblage defined by "consumption, not opposition" (Gonzalez 2000, 48). The illusion of diversity through digitally enabled racial passing and recombination produces a false feeling of diversity and tolerance born of entitlement: "What this creation of this appended subject presupposes is the possibility of a new cosmopolitanism constituting all the necessary requirements for a global citizen who speaks multiple languages, inhabits multiple cultures, wears whatever skin color or body part desired, elaborates a language of romantic union with technology or nature, and moves easily between positions of identification with movie stars, action heroes, and other ethnicities of races" (Gonzalez 2000, 48). If cyberrace is distinguished from "real" race by its anonymity, composability, variability, and modularity, the task of debunking it as inherently liberatory is linked to e-mail, chat, bulletin board, or MUD (Multi-User Dungeon), then the most popular way to communicate. Users' racial identities could not be seen as they interacted with others, yet as Kang rightly predicted, technological innovations and user desire would change that, and "it [would] become increasingly difficult to delay the disclosure of race" (Kang 2000, 1203). Improvements in interfaces, video devices, and bandwidth have made us more visual social actors; Kang claims that "as we move from communications that are text-only to text-plus, avatars will become more popular," and indeed they have (1151). The wide range of imaging practices available to users, such as profile photographs on social network sites like Facebook and graphic avatars created by using the extremely popular

Simpsons avatar-building engine, guarantee that racial identity is now often visually signified as part of users' self-presentational practices. Yet while it lasted, the pre-graphic Internet overlapped with the rise of digital utopianism, the beginnings of a Clinton-led neoliberal political dynasty in the United States, and a concomitant strategy of addressing racial problems by refusing to see race—Kang's abolitionist strategy writ large, which Patricia Williams identifies as the "colorblind" approach (Williams 1997). At the same time, in the academy, theories of social constructionism strongly challenged and indeed displaced essentialist understandings of race by asserting that race is an effect of social performance, thus empowering the individual agent to "jam" race through playful acts of recombining, confounding, and cutting and pasting existing identity markers. This is a form of pastiche characteristic of "participatory media" such as mashups, animutations, and other contemporary forms of web-user production, practices that fall under the umbrella term "Web 2.0."

Indeed, the notion of identity as variable, modular, and granular, resembling most closely a program in perpetual beta release rather than a stable object, recalls the logic of critiquing new media utopianism generally. It was necessary for new media to be discussed in a more critical way, in the light of structural constraint, industrial imperatives, and global inequality, for race to be viewed as a salient category in what was then known as cyberspace. This was an uphill battle in the nineties, however, because the fetish of interactivity had yet to be exposed either as a marketing strategy or as a racial ideology.

The fetish of interactivity is alive and well—my students frequently claim that "the world is at their fingertips" when they use the Internet, a formulation that recalls television's vast claims to "give us ten minutes, and we'll give you the world"—but it was even more alive and well ten years ago. The ability to manipulate the "look and feel" of race by online role-playing, digital gaming, and other forms of digital media use encouraged and fed the desire for control over self-construction and self-representation. This was quite an empowering ideology, and scholars such as Sherry Turkle (1995) claimed that the cyberspace was postmodern because it permitted unprecedented fluidity and composable identities. Edward Castronova (2005) makes similar claims for MMORPGs (massively multiplayer online role-playing games) as a radically level playing field and thus as radically democratic. Turkle's psychoanalytic approach took identity play extremely seriously, as identity work: this first wave of theoretical writing confirming the formative and subversive influence of online subjectivity, which included Julian Dibbell's important "A Rape in Cyberspace" (Dibbell 1994), attempted to persuade us that virtual life and gender were real, not a difficult feat since many of us were already convinced. Yet this brought up a vexing question: If life online is real, are race and racism online real too? My article (Nakamura 1995) discusses cross-racial role-playing and passing in MUDs as a form of identity tourism. Drawing on Edward Said's (1979) work on tourism, racial passing, and travel in the imperial context, I discuss in *Cybertypes* (Nakamura 2002) how MUD users who created orientalist avatars such as samurai and geisha were able to temporarily "appropriate an Asian racial identity without any of the risks associated with being a racial minority in real life," and how online communities often punished users who wished to discuss race and racism (40). Identity tourism resembled offline tourism because it gave users a false notion of cultural and racial understanding based on an episodic, highly mediated experience of travel, an experience rhetorically linked with digital technology use as the "information superhighway" and the "cyberfrontier," as well as with the burgeoning travel industry.[1] Community hostility toward discussions of race and racism in LambdaMOO reflected the color-blind attitude held about race that characterized neoliberalism in the nineties, when neither asking nor telling was encouraged. Race in virtual space was "on you" in more than one sense: when users "wore" race in the form of a racialized avatar or performed it as racialized speech or conveyed it by sharing their "performance of tastes (favorite music, books, film, etc)," or "taste fabric," this form of display was viewed as a personal decision, an exercise of individual choice. It was also "on you" because users were considered to be solely responsible for any negative consequences, such as racism.[2]

Identity tourism let users "wear" racially stereotyped avatars without feeling racist, yet it also blamed users who revealed their real races and thus became victims of racism online. The logic of identity tourism figured race as modular, ideally mobile, recreational, and interactive in ways that were good for you—part of the transmutation strategy with the supposed potential to "break" race as a concept and rupture its hold on our imaginations and bodies. The narrow range of racialized performance visibly enacted in many online social spaces—gangstas, samurai, geisha, Latin lovers, and hot Latin mamas—attested to the problem with seeing digital interactivity as infinite rather than bounded. Zabet Patterson (2004) writes that "the illusory nature of choice in many interactive situations" contributed toward the conviction that the Internet was a postracial space because it was possible to "choose" a race as an identity tourist, as well as to withhold, or "cover," racial identity; however, these choices were preconstituted by existing media texts (117). Cultural images of race—our database of bodies, discourses, behaviors, and images—resemble all database-driven new media objects in that they are experienced by users as much more profuse and open than they really are. Patterson writes that "we often find this compensatory rhetoric and narrative of free choice, a cornerstone of American cultural ideology, inhabiting precisely those situations that, on a basic structural level, admit of little or no choice at all" (116). The limited interactivity available to identity tourists online promoted a comforting amnesia in regard to the lack of choice racial minorities faced in everyday life.

In 2000 Tiziana Terranova advocated a turn toward the political economy of digital culture and away from reveries of idealized Internet digital identities (Terranova 2000). Even though race is not discussed overtly in her analysis, this turn is useful to new media scholars because it enables a grounded discussion of race, power, and labor in digital culture. If postracial cosmopolitans refused to acknowledge the ways that unequal access, limited forms of representation in digital culture, and images of race under globalization were shaping cyberrace, it could not be denied that labor in postindustrial societies is racialized and gendered. She urged us to examine how the "'outernet'—the network of social, cultural and economic relationships which crisscrosses and exceeds the Internet—surrounds and connects the latter to larger flows of labour, culture and power. It is fundamental to move beyond the notion that cyberspace is about escaping reality in order to understand how the reality of the Internet is deeply connected to the development of late postindustrial societies as a whole" (Terranova 2007, 75).

Seeing the Internet as a virtual space that was like real life while being separate from it—a second life—figured it as a place to escape from reality, especially racial realities. Several new media scholars studying race and gender before 2002 challenged this state of exemption. In 1996 Cameron Bailey wrote, "Faced with the delirious prospect of leaving their bodies behind for the cool swoon of digital communication, many leading theorists of cyberspace have addressed the philosophical implications of a new technology by retreating to old ground. In a landscape of contemporary cultural criticism where the discourses of race, gender, class, and sexuality have often led to great leaps in understanding— where, in fact, they have been so thoroughly used as to become a mantra— these interpretive tools have come curiously late to the debate around cyberspace" (Bailey 2001, 334). In the 1990s and after, the Internet was pitched as a curative to racism, which was always framed as a problem of too much visibility by the telecommunications and computing industries and scholars alike, since the Internet permitted users to hide their race or pass as a different one. The term "Cyberrace" was thus deemed an oxymoron at that time, a useful strategy for a computer industry and for a political regime struggling to get users to invest in, purchase, and believe in the technology. Updating the Internet's image as a clubhouse for hobbyists and geeks involved representing it as a solution to especially knotty social problems like racism. Alondra Nelson wrote, "Public discourse about race and technology, led by advertisers (and aided and abetted by cybertheorists), was preoccupied with the imagined new social arrangements that might be made possible by technological advance. Advertisers relied on a shared message about race and ethnicity—the disappearance of the DuBoisian 'color line'—to promote their products" (Nelson 2002, 5). As Nelson notes, this digital racial-abolitionist strategy was waged on two fronts—the commercial and the academic. Much of the important critical scholarship on race and new media noted this alliance and traced its trajectory through close readings of technology industry texts such as advertisements.

Advertisements, films, novels, and the Internet itself produced a rich stream of content during this period that depicted racialized bodies in exotic locales juxtaposed with digital technologies. This advertising blitz was a result of the "thriving and competitive market for high-speed nationwide computer networking services" that quickly developed in the early nineties (Abbate 1999, 197). In 1995 the Internet's backbone became a series of networks run by private companies (Shah and Kesan 2007). Cisco, IBM, MCI, Worldcom, and others produced almost only this type of image, but it became a staple as well in cyberpunk science fiction film, television, and literature. Wendy Chun's (2005), Tom Foster's (2005), and Alondra Nelson's (2002) critiques of postracial utopianism analyze digital networking advertisements and cyberpunk films and fiction, and explain why race and cultural difference are continually invoked in them. Chun's adept unpacking of digital racialization in telecommunications company commercials from the nineties such as MCI's "anthem" identifies how a "[r]ewriting of the Internet as emancipatory, as 'freeing' oneself from one's body, also naturalizes racism. The logic framing MCI's commercial reduces to what they can't see, can't hurt you. Since race, gender, age, and infirmities are only skin-deep (or so this logic goes), moving to a text-based medium makes them—and thus the discrimination that stems from them—disappear" (Chun 2005, 132). The racial-abolitionist rhetoric advocated technologically enabled disembodiment as a solution to social problems; Foster's (2005) cogent critique of this strategy discusses this discourse's roots in cyberpunk science fiction such as William Gibson's *Neuromancer*. Simply put, race and racism don't disappear when bodies become virtual or electronically mediated. In Foster's discussion of the Deathlok comic book series, he writes that "neither becoming a cyborg nor accessing cyberspace is conceptualized as escaping the body, but rather in terms of a more complex relationship that is both productive and problematic" (156).

Critical race theory and political-economic approaches caught up to the Internet around the turn of the century, at a time when it was particularly ready to be caught—shortly after the stock market crash of 2001 and right around the time when the term "cyber" started to vanish. It was only after the digital bloom was off the dot-com rose that it became possible to discuss cyberspace as anything other than a site of exception from identity, especially racial identity. Several collections (Kolko, Nakamura, and Rodman 2000; Nelson, Tu, and Hines 2001; Lee and Wong 2003; and Everett 2007) have been published since 2000. Just as important, general new media and cyberculture anthologies include chapters on race (Trend 2001; Bell and Kennedy 2007; Raessens and Goldstein 2005; Chun and Thomas Keenan 2006), as did popular culture anthologies (Guins and Cruz 2005 and Mirzoeff 2002). Digital media, an area of study that an entire generation of undergraduate students experienced as the last couple of weeks of their courses on writing, media literacy, television and film, and literature, not only came to the fore as a discipline that merited its own courses but also began to integrate discussions of racial identity in digital media and online social space.[3] The publication of several monographs signaled the growth of the field (Nakamura 2002; Chun 2005; Foster 2005; Adam Banks 2006; Christopher McGahan 2007; and Nakamura 2007).

Terranova writes that the "larger flows of labour, culture and power" that surround and shape digital media travel along unevenly distributed racial, gendered, and class channels (2007, 75). And Caren Kaplan states, "Questions about divisions of labor cannot be left out of an inquiry into representational practices in information and communication technologies. . . . [T]here is no discussion of the people who make the devices that are used to achieve the dream of subjectivity" (Kaplan 2002, 40).

Coco Fusco (2001), Donna Haraway (1991), Toby Miller (2006), and Kaplan (2002) all urge us toward a concern with labor and embodiment, which tells us less about fleeing, refashioning, and augmenting bodies with technology and more about viewing bodies within technophilic, informationalized societies—and noting the costs paid by racialized bodies. In contrast with the Internet's early claims to transform and eliminate both race and labor, digital communication technologies today racialize labor, employing "virtual migrants" who perform tasks such as help-line staffing, online gamers who sell their virtual gold and leveled-up avatars to busy Americans and Europeans to use in MMORPGs, and a class of truly miserable workers who "pick away without protection at

discarded First World computers full of leaded glass to find precious metals"
(Miller 2006, 9). Significantly, these workers are primarily Asian, a phenomenon that has led to robust anti-Asian racism in MMORPGs such as World of
Warcraft (WoW), where "gold farmers" are despised and abused as their services are used promiscuously among its ten million players. Most players con-
demn gold selling as the rankest form of cheating yet purchase virtual gold in
such quantity that they have turned the secondary market in virtual property
into a massively profitable industry, one that is predicted to outstrip the primary digital games market in the years to come.[4] The anti-Chinese gold-farmer
media produced by WoW players and distributed through Warcraftmovies.com
and YouTube is especially salient in the US context because it echoes anti-
immigration discourse. The racialization of this type of digital labor as Asian,
abject, and despised bears comparison with the ways the other forms of racialized labor are controlled and managed.

In 2005 the Internet entered a new industrial, historical, and cultural period:
Web 2.0.[5] The software publisher Tim O'Reilly (2005) first circulated this term
in his article, which claims that the web as we use it today is a much more participatory and potentially profitable medium than it was before 2005, and indeed
there has been a renewed interest and faith in the web as a renascent source of
capital, as well as a new utopianism regarding user interactivity. In semantic
terms, today's 2.0 is tomorrow's cyber, but it is worth unpacking it to see what
kind of ideological baggage it has. Web 1.0, or "cyber" space, conceptualized the
Internet as an alternative reality, a different place in which one could exercise
agency and live out fantasies of control. This control extended to all aspects of
personal identity, including (and especially) race. Web 2.0 comes with a different
imaginary. While it neither posits a postracial utopia based on racial abolition-
ism online nor envisions racialized others and primitives as signs of cosmopol-
itan technofetishism, it does make claims to harness collective intelligence by
allowing everyone to participate in a more or less equal fashion. These claims
are implicitly postracial, and many contemporary advertisements for telecommunications hardware and software visually address the stubborn problem of
digital inequality by showing "global kids" broadcasting video of themselves on
the Internet in the most meaningful way possible—to be famous.

Cisco's "Human Network" ad campaign, running since 2007, figures racialized performance and publicity through digital video broadcasting as both the
ends and the means to a radical Web 2.0-inflected democracy. Its thirty-second
video spot "Fame" depicts children of color in the United States and "global" children broadcasting digital video of themselves to ubiquitous digital screens viewed

by their parents, red-robed monks in Tibet, other children around the world, and an idealized global public. In a reprise of famous viral performance videos such as the Chinese boys who lip-synched to the Backstreet Boys' "I Want It That Way," the "Human Network" website depicts an African American boy popping and locking for his father's cell phone camera, a Latina girl flamenco dancing, a Russian man performing a "Russian" dance while his PC's camera captures the performance, buskers in Europe playing violins, and an Asian woman in a kimono dancing with a fan, with the subtitle "one dance moves and grooves the world."[6] Uncannily, one of these video ads is titled "Anthem," harking back to the MCI ad from the nineties and conveying a similar message of digital-cultural triumphalism with a 2.0 twist: it reads "welcome to the network where anyone can be famous—welcome to the human network." Yet while, as Chun notes, the original MCI-anthem ad touted cyberspace's ability to hide users' bodies and races, Cisco's "Anthem" 2.0 works differently, by selling the network as a site of racialized performance and visibility (Chun 2005). The site's users are also invited to contribute content in the form of stories, which are incorporated into the site in the true spirit of user-generated content. The work of racialization, or making race through digital means, is passed on and eagerly accepted by the children in these ads, just as the logic of Web 2.0 passes on and accepts all kinds of software and content-development work. The performance of stylized images of race and ethnicity is industriously undertaken by children of color in the Cisco "Human Network" campaign and is accepted as an inevitable and natural part of the compulsory immaterial labor of becoming "famous" and of being seen on the multiple mediated screens embedded in everyday life—on cell phones, PDAs, PCs, televisions, and, in the case of Cisco's "Myles" commercial, on the megascreens on tall buildings in Times Square. This is a privilege figured as an entitlement of digital citizens and as a justification for our continuing faith in the web—so long as those citizens are able to labor properly, performing race in ways that will appeal to other users.

As Terranova notes in her pre–Web 2.0 article, "The Internet does not automatically turn every user into an active producer, and every worker into a creative subject" (Terranova 2000, 34). The question of what constitutes a creative subject in our current digital culture is racialized in terms of Web 2.0 entrepreneurship, the grueling immaterial labor of "making yourself." Tila Tequila, the Vietnamese American star of the 2007 VH1 reality television program *A Shot at Love with Tila Tequila*, is most likely the first Internet star, for the "signal reason for [her] breakout success may also be the basis for Ms. Tequila's unconventional fame, her boast that she has 1,771,920 MySpace friends" (Trebay 2007).

Tequila's immense popularity on a widely used social network site (she had 2,940,387 friends as of March 19, 2008 on MySpace—a number that grew after Trebay wrote his article, partly because of the new audience generated by *A Shot at Love*) was leveraged on "the classic show-business redemption narrative" but, more important, also on constant claims of possessive individualism and rehabilitation through digital racial self-fashioning. Tequila's profile, like any Web 2.0 object, is in perpetual beta release. It is a valuable new media object because it employs the labor of her "friends," using the posts both as a sounding board for Tequila and as unique content; it also capitalizes on her own racial and sexual ambiguity. The profile captures the sense of liveness characteristic of digital media that has migrated across so many other genres and platforms; it maps the development of Tequila's "deeply disoriented" identity growing up in a Houston housing project after emigrating from Singapore (Trebay 2007). In an interview with *Car Tuner Magazine*, she explains, "I was really confused then, because at first I thought I was black, then I thought I was Hispanic and joined a cholo gang" (2007).

Although Tequila's story has been read as a symptom of a radical change in the nature of media celebrity—as Trebay puts it, "a shift from top-down manufactured celebrity to a kind of lateral, hyper-democratic celebrity" (2007)—Tequila emphasizes her own digital labor in the manufacture of her celebrity on MySpace, a celebrity that is racialized as diasporic and polysexual. Tequila depicts herself as a bisexual Asian woman fleeing religious repression, poverty, and urban violence—a modern day Horatio Alger in a G-string—and her constant references to her "fans" on MySpace as the source of her visibility and fame highlight the ways in which she needs to construct herself as "user-generated" as well as self-made. Clearly Tequila's MySpace profile exemplifies what Celine Parreñas Shimizu (2007) terms the "hypersexuality of race"—it describes an Asian woman who will "friend" anyone and everyone, and who is endlessly responsive, invoking Asian American porn megastars such as Annabel Chong. Like other Asian female stars such as Anna May Wong, Nancy Kwan, and Lucy Liu before her, whose "hypersexuality is essentialized to their race and gender ontology and is constructed in direct relation to the innocence and moral superiority of white women" (62), Tequila is unfavorably compared to Paris Hilton by Trebay. Tequila's purported lack of talent is articulated to her racialized hypersexuality, digital promiscuity, and racio-sexual ambivalence.

Tequila's Web 2.0 narrative repeats the message of the Cisco "Human Network" campaign—digital fame accrues to racialized performance. Instead of "routing around" race, Web 2.0 creates Race 2.0 (Silver 2000, 138). Tequila and Cisco's human network demonstrate that while Race 1.0 was understood as socially constructed, a process that at least acknowledges that race and gender are historical formations, Race 2.0 is user-generated. Once again race is "on us," as Web 2.0 rhetoric positions us all as entrepreneurial content creators. The Internet's resurgence and rebranding as Web 2.0 incessantly recruits its users to generate content in the form of profiles, avatars, favorites, comments, pictures, wiki postings, and blog entries. Cyberrace has gone the way of the Cybershot, cybercommuting, and cyberspace, and for much the same reason: racialization has become a digital process, just as visual imaging practices, labor, and social discourse have. The process of racialization continues on both the Internet and its outernet, as the "dirty work" of virtual labor continues to get distributed along racial lines.

NOTES

1. In her analysis of cyberspace's advertising discourse, Megan Boler describes this false sense of cultural understanding as "'drive-by difference' [that] presents difference and the other as something that can be 'safely' met or experienced—at a distance" (Boler 2007, 146).

2. In their study of friend connections in social network sites, Liu, Maes, and Davenport formulated the term "taste fabric" to describe users' creation of alternative networks for community formation (qtd. in Ellison and Boyd 2007).

3. See Boler (2007) and Galloway (2007) for two excellent examples of new media critique that incorporate critical race theory.

4. "The International Game Exchange states that the '2005 marketplace for virtual assets in MMOG's is approaching 900 million,' and that 'some experts believe that the market for virtual assets will overcome the primary market—projected to reach 7 billion by 2009—within the next few years'" (Consalvo 182).

5. Geert Lovink writes that "by 2005, the Internet had recovered from the dot-com crash and, in line with the global economic figures, reincarnated as Web 2.0" (Lovink 2007, ix).

6. The "Chinese Backstreet Boys" had been viewed over six million times on YouTube as of March 26, 2008. When a user typed in "Backstreet Boys" as a search query on this site, the Chinese video for "That Way" came in as number seven, ahead of some of the "official" Backstreet Boys content.

REFERENCES

Abbate, Janet. 1999. *Inventing the Internet*. Cambridge, MA: MIT Press.
Aneesh, A. 2006. *Virtual Migration: The Programming of Globalization*. Durham, NC: Duke University Press.
Bailey, Cameron. 2001. "Virtual Skin: Articulating Race in Cyberspace." In *Reading Digital Culture*, edited by David Trend, 334–46. London: Blackwell.
Banks, Adam J. 2006. *Race, Rhetoric, and Technology: Searching for Higher Ground*. NCTE-LEA Research Series in Literacy and Composition. Mahwah: Erlbaum; Urbana, IL: National Council of Teachers of English.

Bell, David, and Barbara M. Kennedy, eds. 2007. *The Cybercultures Reader*. 2nd ed. London: Routledge.

Boler, Megan. 2007. "Hypes, Hopes, and Actualities: New Digital Cartesianism and Bodies in Cyberspace." *New Media and Society* 9, no. 1: 139–68.

Castronova, Edward. 2005. *Synthetic Worlds: The Business of Culture and of Online Games*. Chicago: University of Chicago Press.

Chun, Wendy. 2005. *Control and Freedom: Power and Paranoia in the Age of Fiber Optics*. Cambridge, MA: MIT Press.

Chun, Wendy Hui Kyong, and Thomas Keenan. 2006. *New Media, Old Media: A History and Theory Reader*. New York: Routledge.

Cisco Systems, Inc. 2007. "The Human Network." Cisco. Accessed May 21, 2008. http://www.cisco.com/web/about/humannetwork/.

Consalvo, Mia. 2007. *Cheating: Gaining Advantage in Video Games*. Cambridge, MA: MIT Press.

Dibbell, Julian. 1993. "A Rape in Cyberspace." *Scribble, Scribble, Scribble: Selected Texts, Published and Unpublished*. December 23, 1993. Accessed June 11, 2008. http://www.juliandibbell.com/texts/bungle_vv.html.

Ellison, Nicole, and danah boyd. 2007. "Social Network Sites: Definition, History, and Scholarship." *Journal of Computer Mediated Communication* 13, no. 1. Accessed June 11, 2008. http://jcmc.indiana.edu/vol13/issue1.

Everett, Anna. 2007. *Learning Race and Ethnicity: Youth and Digital Media*. John D. and Catherine T. Macarthur Foundation Series on Digital Media and Learning. Cambridge, MA: MIT Press.

Foster, Tom. 2005. *The Souls of Cyberfolk: Posthumanism as Vernacular Theory*. Minneapolis: University of Minnesota Press.

Fusco, Coco. 2001. *The Bodies That Were Not Ours and Other Writings*. London: Routledge, in collaboration with inIVA, Institute of International Visual Arts.

Galloway, Alexander. 2007. "StarCraft, or, Balance." *Grey Room* 28:86–107.

Gonzalez, Jennifer. 2000. "The Appended Subject: Race and Identity as Digital Assemblage." In *Race in Cyberspace*, edited by Beth E. Kolko, Lisa Nakamura, and Gilbert B. Rodman, 27–50. New York: Routledge.

Guins, Raiford, and Omayra Zaragoza Cruz. 2005. *Popular Culture: A Reader*. London: Sage.

Haraway, Donna. 1991. *Simians, Cyborgs, and Women: The Reinvention of Nature*. London: Routledge.

Kang, Jerry. 2000. "Cyber-race." *Harvard Law Review* 113:1130–1208.

Kaplan, Caren. 2002. "Transporting the Subject: Technologies of Mobility and Location in an Era of Globalization." *PMLA* 117:32–42.

Kolko, Beth E., Lisa Nakamura, and Gilbert B. Rodman. 2000. *Race in Cyberspace*. New York: Routledge.

Lee, Rachel C., and Sau-ling Cynthia Wong. 2003. *Asian America.Net: Ethnicity, Nationalism, and Cyberspace*. New York: Routledge.

Lovink, Geert. 2007. *Zero Comments: Blogging and Critical Internet Culture*. New York: Routledge.

Manovich, Lev. 2001. *The Language of New Media*. Cambridge, MA: MIT Press.

McGahan, Christopher. 2007. *Racing Cybercultures: Minoritarian Art and Cultural Politics on the Internet*. Routledge Studies in New Media and Cyberculture. New York: Routledge.

Miller, Toby. 2006. "Gaming for Beginners." *Games and Culture* 1, no. 1: 5–12.

Mirzoeff, Nicholas, ed. 2002. *The Visual Culture Reader*. 2nd ed. London: Routledge.

Nakamura, Lisa. 1995. "Race in/for Cyberspace: Identity Tourism and Racial Passing on the Internet." *Works and Days* 13, no. 1–2: 181–93.

———. 2002. *Cybertypes: Race, Ethnicity, and Identity on the Internet*. New York: Routledge.

———. 2007. *Digitizing Race: Visual Cultures of the Internet*. Minneapolis: University of Minnesota Press.

Nelson, Alondra. 2002. "Introduction: Future Texts." *Social Text* 20, no. 2: 1–15.

Nelson, Alondra, and Tuy Tu, with Alicia Hines. 2001. *Technicolor: Race, Technology, and Everyday Life*. New York: New York University Press.

O'Reilly, Tim. 2005. "What Is Web 2.0: Design Patterns and Business Models for the Next Generation of Software." *O'Reilly*, September 30, 2005. Accessed May 1, 2008. http://oreillynet .com/pub/a/oreilly/tim/news/2005/09/30/what-is-web-20tml.

Patterson, Zabet. 2004. "Going On-line: Consuming Pornography in the Digital Era." In *Porn Studies*, edited by Linda Williams, 105–23. Durham, NC: Duke University Press.

Raessens, Joost, and Jeffrey H. Goldstein. 2005. *Handbook of Computer Game Studies*. Cambridge, MA: MIT Press.

Said, Edward. 1979. *Orientalism*. New York: Vintage Books.

Shah, Rajiv C., and Jay P. Kesan. 2007. "The Privatization of the Internet's Backbone Network." *Journal of Broadcasting and Electronic Media* 51, no. 1: 93–109.

Shimizu, Celine Parreñas. 2007. *The Hypersexuality of Race: Performing Asian/American Women on Screen and Scene*. Durham, NC: Duke University Press.

Silver, David. 2000. "Margins in the Wires: Looking for Race, Gender, and Sexuality in the Blacksburg Electronic Village." In *Race in Cyberspace*, edited by Beth E. Kolko, Lisa Nakamura, and Gilbert B. Rodman, 133–50. New York: Routledge.

Terranova, Tiziana. 2000. "Free Labor: Producing Culture for the Digital Economy." *Social Text* 18, no. 2: 33–58.

———. 2007. *Network Culture: Politics for the Information Age*. London: Pluto.

Trebay, Guy. 2007. "She's Famous (and So Can You)." *New York Times*, October 28. http://www.nytimes.com/2007/10/28/fashion/28fame.html.

Trend, David, ed. 2001. *Reading Digital Culture*. London: Blackwell.

Turkle, Sherry. 1995. *Life on the Screen: Identity in the Age of the Internet*. New York: Simon and Schuster.

Williams, Patricia. 1997. *Seeing a Colorblind Future: The Paradox of Race*. New York: Noonday.

Becoming and Belonging

Performativity, Subjectivity, and the Cultural Purposes of Social Networking

~~~~~

ROB COVER

WHAT IS FACEBOOK FOR?

A problem with the ways that social networking sites have been investigated and discussed by researchers, journalists, and public commentators is that much of the time, just one out of a broad range of purposes, uses, tools, functions, or gratifications of social networking is articulated as the primary purpose of sites such as Facebook, MySpace, Friendster, Twitter, and YouTube. These include seeing social networking as a site for a number of different, categorizable purposes: personal experiences among friends, whether known or strangers (Ellison et al. 2007, 1143); articulation of identity-based interests through the construction of taste statements (Liu 2008, 253); relationship maintenance and new introductions (friending) (Hoadley et al. 2010, 52; Tong et al. 2008, 531); representation of preexisting and salient aspects of users' identities for others to view, interpret, and engage with (boyd 2007, 11; Buffardi and Campbell 2008); and youth engagement and communication outside of geographic constraints and parental surveillance (boyd 2007, 18). These are all ostensible reasons for the use of social networking—conscious, self-aware purposes articulated by different users in different combinations. When it comes to the relationship between the multiplicity of uses and identity, there is a common tendency in both scholarship and popular discourse to assume that the identities of users are fixed, static, and merely represented or expressed through online activities. An alternative view is to consider the ways in which social networking sites operate as a space for the continued, ongoing construction of subjectivity—neither a site for identity play nor for static representation of the self, but as an ongoing reflexive performance and articulation of selfhood that utilizes the full range of tools made available through common social networking sites such as MySpace and Facebook.

Judith Butler's theories of identity performativity have enormous capacity to further our understanding of how people use the profile functions of social networking and *why* so many people invest such a great deal of time, energy, effort, and emotional investment in social networking maintenance, contact, and communication. Working from a poststructuralist antifoundationalist perspective that draws on Foucault, Lacan, and Derrida, Butler's theory of performativity is based on the idea that identity and subjectivity is an ongoing process of becoming, rather than an ontological state of being, whereby becoming is a sequence of acts that retroactively constitute identity (Salih 2002, 46; Butler 1990). That is, the performance of a facet of identity in accord with discursively given knowledge establishes the necessary fiction of an actor behind the act, a doer behind the deed: the self or "I" is made up of a matrix of identity categories, experiences, and labels (Butler 1990, 40) that through repetition lend the illusion of an inner identity core (Butler 1993, 12). Where Butler's theories provide an important perspective for the study of social networking and identity construction is in extending the very idea of performance from the bodily, the experiential, the affective into the field of online acts. In other words, online social networking behavior is as performative as "real life" acts, and just as equally implies a stabilized core inner self behind the profile. Importantly, this shifts our understanding of social networking from one in which identity is understood through ideas of representation of the "real" in the realm of the "digital." Instead, it opens the possibility of thinking about social networking and identity in the context of being a matrix of acts of profile building, maintenance, friending, updating, tagging, album adding, and other networked communication, contiguous with the many everyday nonvoluntarist and nonconscious performances of selfhood.

This is, in part, to respond to Helen Kennedy's call for Internet identity research to move away from claims of online anonymous, multiple, and fragmented selves but also to look at the continuities between online and offline identity by engaging with cultural studies debates that call into question the self-evidence of subjectivity and the usefulness of concepts of identity (Kennedy 2006, 859–61; see also this volume, 25–41). Indeed, as we have shifted from the text-based online world of Web 1.0 to a more interactive matrix of online behaviors in Web 2.0, characterized by social networking, audio-visual representation, and everyday tools for creative expression, we can see that online applications are taken up for anything but anonymity. Instead they are part of a complex response to an older, ongoing cultural demand that we process our selves and our actions into coherence, intelligibility, and recognizability, and thus disavow the instability of identity. I argue here that social networking sites are popular because they are the most effective means to achieve this cultural demand and respond to contemporary anxieties around subject intelligibility and recognizability. Important in this examination is that the refinement of theories of identity performativity into methodologies of investigation to account for the mass popularity of social networking profiles is, as Deleuze and Foucault in conversation suggested, not about the development of a totalizing formula by which to make a unilateral set of claims but a multiplication of possible narratives that work to "show up" the condition of subjectivity as contingent and historical (Foucault 1977, 208).

I explore the ways in which social networking sites have been taken up and become popular as an efficient, effective yet also problematic site for the performance of coherent, intelligible, and recognizable identities and subjectivities. I begin with an overview of the ways in which Butler's (1990, 1991, 1993, 1997) theories of identity performativity can be utilized within a media and digital media context, and how these highlight subjecthood as a never-ending process of "always becoming," which is a response to the cultural demand for identity coherence necessary for social participation and belonging (Bell 1999). This approach allows us to investigate the selection of social networking profile "identity categories" and tastes as part of the performance of selfhood that requires time, effort, energy, and investment in order to work toward identity coherence. I deal here only with profile establishment and maintenance as an act of performativity that constitutes, stabilizes, reiterates, and alters the subjectivity of the user. Friending, and the complex relationship between friends, plays an important part in the identification with others and the representation and performance of the self, but that aspect is an investigation for another time. Finally, I consider how concerns about changes to Facebook's interface demonstrate the deep investment users have in these sites as spaces of identity performance, arguing that social networking's relationship with identity performance is not determined by the technological elements and tools of the interface, but that it fulfills a deep-seated cultural demand for ways to "play out" subjecthood coherently and intelligibly for ourselves and others.

PROCESS AND PURPOSE:
SOCIAL NETWORKING AND IDENTITY COHERENCE

Judith Butler's early 1990s work on gender performativity presented an influential approach to understanding subjectivity from a poststructuralist perspective. The notion of the performativity of identity and selfhood puts both "essentialist" and "constructionist" notions of subjectivity in question in favor of a radically antifoundationalist view. This is an important consideration for furthering the study of identity and social networking, as it allows us to move beyond two common positions that limit our understanding of the relationship between social networking and identity. The first of these positions is a popular conception of social network users as simply representing or *expressing* their identities online through profiles and interaction (boyd 2007, 2, 12–13) and—in risk discourses— saying too much about a real self and real behaviors that are seen to stem from an essential "real life." We find this position particularly in the popular press coverage of the frequent panics about younger persons' use of online communication applications, and the celebrationist account of the uses of learning about the self through profile construction and online social interaction (Livingstone 2008). The second position is the view that there is a real, essential self and a consciously and voluntarily constructed fluid self that one can create online, as a number of writers such as Sherry Turkle (1995) saw particularly in the pre–Web 2.0 text-based chat room. This has proved to be a reductive and oversimplified attempt to map together a real/digital binary with essentialist/ constructivist identities and body/mind dichotomies (Cover 2004a).

In both these positions, there is a tendency, as Lelia Green has argued, to think about the relationship between online activities and selfhood as one where users have preexisting identities "brought to computers from the culture at large" (Green 2008, 11), as if the very process of identity construction, constitution, and formation ceases the moment one sits down at the computer. Following Butler, and viewing identity and selfhood as nonvoluntarist, those unconscious performances that cite and repeat discursively given identity categories or stereotypes allows us to explore how online behavior is more than an expression of different ways of doing identity and, instead, as a set of acts and behaviors that constitute those very identities.

Although Butler's work is complex and wide-ranging, there are four nodes of her theory of performative identity that are significant in the study of identity and digital media in an online, interactive, Web 2.0 framework. First, following Nietzsche and Foucault, Butler (1993) argues that the "self" is an *effect* of a performance constituted in and through language, discourse, and culture. In the case of social networking, this includes the discursive frameworks of online rituals within the context of broader everyday acts. Second, the self is performed reiteratively as a process in accord with a discursively given set of norms, stabilizing over time to produce the fiction of a fixed, inner, essential selfhood, which retroactively produces the illusion that there is a core doer behind the deed (12). In social networking sites, we see this in the simultaneous citation and articulation of user profile categories ranging from gender and relationship status to choices around favorite films and other taste categories. Third, Butler (1991) recognizes that while selves are constituted in discourse, they can be reconstituted or reconfigured differently in encounters with different, new, imaginative discursive arrangements (18), which can include new categories or alternative names and norms of identity encountered online. For example, the decision to add or "like" a fan page on, say, animal rights might reconstitute a coordinate of that user's identity as vegetarian. Finally, Butler (1997) emphasizes that the motivation to be articulated as a coherent, intelligible self stems from a cultural imperative for coherence in order for the individual to participate in being and society (27). Moreover, the demand for coherence requires that the individual forge a sense of self and belonging across an array of identity categories, or what I refer to as "identity coordinates" (Cover 2004b). These include common axes of discrimination such as gender, ethnicity, ability, and age but might also be comprised of spurious experiences, which are less easily categorizable and less well demarcated in an identity/difference dichotomy. Coherence is performed through an ongoing process of "shoring up" or "answering" any anomalies between those coordinates to present a coherent, recognizable, and intelligible self. Performativity, then, is subjecthood as the nonvoluntary citation of culturally given identity categories or norms in a reiterative process.

Social networking sites such as Facebook and MySpace are the tools par excellence for performing identity coherence over time. As Helen Kennedy has pointed out about web pages generally, they are a media form, which is never entirely finished, just as identity composition is a continuous process—both are constantly "under construction" (Kennedy 2006, 869). Using Facebook or MySpace for performing identity in a never-ending process toward coherence and intelligibility is, effectively, not dissimilar from the identity work of having a conversation whereby a subject relates narratives of selfhood, desire, experiences, recent actions, and tastes. Within a disciplinary society of surveillance (Foucault 1977), we police each other's subjecthood for coherence in such scenes: one subject's taste for classical music and punk clothing requires an explanation for consistency in order that one's identity be intelligible and allow one to belong and maintain participation in the social. Conflicting or unrecognizable selves narrated outside the restrictive norm or stereotype demand explanation. Two conflicting views must be smoothed over: the statement "But you said earlier . . ." demands the *work* of bringing the performance, articulations, and expressions back into coherence and stabilizing once again the project of identity. On Facebook, the tools for performative coherence are supplied, even though one does not necessarily need to utilize them all. The profile basics: gender, birthdate, gender of sexual/romantic interest, relationship status (and who), a biographical statement, political views, religious views, a short written biography, a profile photograph or image, a favorite quotation, education and work, likes and interests. For Sonia Livingstone, such choices are an act of autobiography in which users "select a more or less complex representation of themselves" (Livingstone 2008, 403). However, to view this in a framework of performativity, the establishment and maintenance of a profile is not a conscious self-representation but a series of performative acts that constitute the self and stabilize it over time as the effect of those choices. Written, selected, and revised, this is a performance that requires carefully chosen responses, which present an intelligible self through integrity across those coordinates. To fail the demand for coherence requires an explanation from those who surveil the profile through being networked to the users profile. For example, an inconsistency (conservative political views that rub awkwardly against the act of "liking" an antiwar fan page) can be made intelligible and consistent through dialogue on the user's page. A straight man's status of being in a relationship with another man can be indicated or recognized as an act of irony, leaving the identity of heterosexuality intact (depending on the reader's digital-cultural literacy or knowledge of the person). The important element here in understanding social networking as a site for an intelligible identity performance is that different users will exploit these tools in different ways and to varying degrees. At no stage is this necessarily a conscious, voluntary moment of identity construction but just as reiterative, hidden, and disavowed as a masculine way of walking performs, stabilizes, and is consistent with a male identity, or that choices around household furnishing performs and coheres with, say, a middle-class income bracket, affiliation, or identification. These are never complete but always and forever a process—persistent maintenance of the self and constant maintenance of the profile.

But why this ongoing process of refining, sorting, and organizing the self toward coherence and smoothing out of anomalies? As Butler argues, the "'I' emerges upon the condition that it deny its formation in dependency, the conditions of its own possibility" (Butler 1997, 9–10). Here she identifies the necessity of ongoing reiteration of the self, stating that "a subject only remains a subject through a reiteration or rearticulating of itself as a subject" (1997, 99). While it is necessary for a constant reiterative performance of that subjectivity, and while the very fact of reiteration may well constitute a subject's incoherence or incompleteness (1997, 99), there remains the point that this reiteration may not necessarily need to occur in what is ostensibly understood as the present-future, as ongoing in a bodily performance of the categorical and normalized codes of intelligibility, but it can just as easily be relegated to the continued resignification of memory, a sort of disembodying of the subject such that the reiterative play is "always having had been." The necessity of social categorization for existence indicates the double promise of categorization of subordination (to the category) and the continuation of existence. Subjection, Butler suggests, "exploits the desire for existence" (1997, 20–21). The desire for existence is the desire for categorization and coherence, the desire "to be" ("this" or "that" in an intelligible and socially recognizable way). What occurs in contemporary late-capitalist society is a push-and-pull of multiple demands: the Enlightenment demand that one articulate oneself as a rational, reasonable, coherent, and intelligible subject (Woodward 2002, 89), and a decentered and fragmented subjectivity, which fulfills the demand that we express identity in fleeting ways through forms of consumption that emerge at the nexus of late capitalism and postmodernism (Jameson 1985). Social networking sites are effective in answering the contemporary cultural anxiety between these competing demands. As the work of self-coherence becomes ever more difficult, the time spent in profile maintenance (which may be as complex as widespread profile revision or as simple as making a status update and adding an image caption) pays off as the (never quite) coherent and intelligible profile remains over time, and as the café conversation that established a moment of coherence does not.

A reason social networking profiles are so effective for the self-governance and performative articulation of subjective coherence relates to the fact that a subject's performance is only stable, intelligible, and recognizable if it is repeated. Performativity, as Butler (1993) points out, "must be understood not as a singular or deliberate 'act,' but, rather, as the reiterative and citational practice by which discourse produces the effects that it names" (2). If either a social networking profile or a set of conversations with a friend will serve adequately as a mode of identificatory behavior that reiteratively performs a stable identity, then it is by virtue of linear performativity that coherence over time is best established. Anxieties around (frequently younger) Facebook and MySpace users' privacy, sexual behavior, attitudes to friendship, sharing of images, and so on, risks focusing on an exaggerated view of what is new and distinctive about what such sites provide, ignoring what is continuous with existing, historically constituted cultural needs and desires, as Meaghan Morris points out (2009). A space for the better performative articulation of identity coherence and subject intelligibility is a product of Enlightenment rationality: Facebook and MySpace can thus be seen as the latest development fulfilling this demand within the contemporary slippages of postmodern fragmentation.

Ironically, this point can be illustrated by reversing the common metaphors of technological distinction between the analog and the digital: the digital world of a social networking profile is analog and the café conversations are digital in terms of the linear repetition of identity performativity. The analog performance cites the culturally given codes of intelligible sexuality; it corresponds and re-presents (as the Greek root *analogia* indicates—analogy) the discursively given and intelligible codes of subjectivity; and much like the analog sound wave or the analog photograph, it is a smooth wave, ongoing and uninterrupted, gaps filled out and unseen over time. The ephemeral conversations that smooth over anomalies to produce a coherent self are, on the other hand, digital. Like a digital recording or a digital photograph, they are a series of "offs" and "ons," close enough to appear as a coherent image or sound but, upon very close examination (like the photograph in newsprint), not continuous or coherent at all. In other words, where the "real life" performances are founded on the idea of multiple moments of performance in succession, the profile that is tweaked over time erasing past anomalies and appearing to represent forward into the future is, in and of itself, repetitious. It does not require performances, which are culturally perceived as repetitive acts and thus betray the possibility that such acts may not be repeated, but instead presents the performativity of subjecthood as intelligible and ongoing, disguising the possibility of a fragmentary "gap" in its repetition. Interestingly, this distinction is the focus of much risk discourse around the use of social networking sites: where a spoken conversation is understood as ephemeral, but a profile update or a compromising party photo is a risk because it remains persistent, searchable, and cross-indexable (Tufekci 2008, 20–21). We might argue that the reason these alleged risks are taken is because the privacy concerns are, unconsciously at least, far less important to selves than fulfilling the demands for selfhood.

COORDINATES AND CONSTRAINTS:
SOCIAL NETWORKING CATEGORIES AND IDENTIFICATIONS

I expand this theorization of performativity in the context of social networking by exploring how profile maintenance, status updates, photograph uploads and captioning, wall posts, fan page additions, and comments on friends' posts are in themselves performative acts, which not only operate as a space of coherence but also constitute the subjectivity of the user. For Butler (1993), where there is a self "who utters or speaks and thereby produces an effect in discourse, there is first a discourse which precedes and enables that 'I' and forms in language the constraining trajectory of its will" (225). There is no presocial integrity, as Butler tells us (1990, 29). Subjectivity, in poststructuralist terms, does not emanate from a "naturally given" essential self but as a discursively given code. Likewise, the array of identity positions or coordinates that make up the self are given discursively and do not emanate from an essentialist, pregiven body and self. While much application of Butler's theory of performativity has considered—often in "political" terms—the cultural constitution of the identity categories of gender, race, and sexuality (Disch 1999), they are well equipped to analyze the ways in which the individual subject of being, the "I," is constituted and performed more broadly. For Butler, the "I" is performed through a materializing body, a psyche, a Foucauldian "soul," which imprisons and makes the body docile in coherence and the citation of categories that are given in a discursive framework. Some categories, of course, operate to a totalized identity performance more so than others. For example, sexual orientation may be the identity coordinate that for a particular subject may direct all other coordinates and categories of identity from career to musical tastes. This is in part a result of what Diana Fuss (1989) identifies as the "synecdochical tendency to see only one part of a subject's identity (usually the most visible part) and to make that part stand for the whole" (116).

If identities are the citation of a set of culturally shared attributes that in their performance and repetition constitute the self, then the act of selecting profile categories, choosing tastes, updating statuses, "friending" others, and "liking" fan pages is an encounter with a discursive and technological framework, one that for some users may stabilize elements of identity and for others may invoke wholly new concepts of identity categories, names, and norms. There is always the possibility of an initial "encounter" with the discourse that posits the possibility of an identity. It is not that the performative and reiterative play of the "self" initiates a subject position; there must also be an interpellative act of *naming*, which performs this function prior to the reiterative play and which is the subjectivity-in-process. This naming may be, as Butler (1997) has suggested, the use of a proper name but equally can be an act of categorization (95–96). This is not to suggest that the subject comes into being at the moment one articulates the name or the category: performativity is never merely a set of serialized acts (1993, 12); there can never be a first or a founding act. Rather than a subject coming into being when it is "named," a subject performs his or her subjectivity in accord with a discourse in which the name or categorization occurs.

For boyd (2007), the act of building an intricate profile is an initiate rite
through which a digital selfhood is written into being (13). This is not a representation of a preexisting self but just another, effective node of performance
that constitutes the self. Writing from a Deleuzian perspective, Ian Buchanan
has recently made the point that the body has been replaced by our online profiles, which include our credit ratings, the aggregated data in government agency
databases, among other elements of our online life (Buchanan 2007). But such
profiling constitutes and constrains the embodied self, just as Foucault's "soul"
produces the docile and productive body in *Discipline and Punish* (1977). The
management of the profile, then, is an act of self-governance, which produces
embodied selves and subjects through an interpellation that "hails" one to choose
the coordinates of identityhood within the framework provided by Facebook
or MySpace. In other words, subjectivity as an effect within an interactive digital environment occurs not through an external act of "naming" but in choosing the name *as if* it were an interpellation, giving the sense, however, *as if* it
were simply a choice for a convenient representation.

What takes place, then, is that a user, in an attempt to fulfill the demand for
coherent identity, is called upon to choose from a resource (a drop-down menu
of common identity coordinates), and by simultaneously citing and choosing,
one constitutes oneself in a manner that disavows the lack of foundation and
appears to be recognizing oneself in *that* discursive list given and in *that* choice
made. The act of choosing is a recognition of a beginning, a trajectory, undertaken to negate the performative effect of discourse and present a coherent,
essential self. The subject is thus required to recognize the self—in a retrospect,
which is disavowed—by denying the nonfoundation of subjectivity. In that sense,
one selects, builds, updates, and maintains a social networking profile by recognizing oneself in the "provided" identity categories of the drop-down menus,
the linguistics of social networking, and the rituals of its use. But this recognition is always also a *re*-cognition of one's selfhood (Düttmann 1996, 31). At the
moment when one "names" by choosing a profile identity coordinate, such as
sexual orientation or a particular taste category, this is an act of citation of the
coordinate, made available by the social networking site that masquerades as
a recognition but is an inauguration, adjustment, stabilization, or new performance of a coordinate of the user's subjectivity. I recognize my relationship status by choosing from the drop-down menu. But simultaneously I *re*-cognize
that status, *re*-think the self, *re*-constitute my status and its related identity facets
in the act of making that apparent choice. Of course, persistent reconstitution
of the self comes with the performative acts of every status update, every wall

post, every new image upload, caption, tag—but this is always hidden within the broader performance of the profile as a whole and the fiction of the whole self it serves.

The online performance of subjectivity is, then, articulated in three ways. First, by modifying one's own profile (boyd 2007, 3), which includes developing the profile through choosing particular categories of common identity coordinates, providing and deciding on particular information, which in the act of deciding is itself a performance of identity, such as age, gender, relationship status, indicators of sexual orientation, and making biographical statements; as well as ongoing activities such as status updates, uploading and captioning photos, sending messages, rewriting biographical statements and other forms of updating, refining, and manipulating one's profile. Second, it involves identifying with various friends and networks through invitations to be added to another user's network—and, of course, updating, changing, and making new additions or deletions to the friends list. Third, there is identification with particular taste groups on social networking sites through adding, becoming a fan of, or "liking" particular pages. However, none of these forms of performativity online is without constraint but is, in fact, discursively given. Social networking sites are not a free space for the performance of coherent and intelligible subjectivities; they provide, however, discursively given categories or "coordinates" of identity, which operate within a framework of limits and restrictions. Relationship status on MySpace, for example, is forced—Liu points out that only 0.3 percent of users analyzed in his research avoided responding to it by using software hacks (Liu 2008, 272). Furthermore, the sorts of choices one can make are also limited: the gender drop-down category has until recently offered just two options (male/female), which foreclosed on the performance of intersexed or transgender identities, gender fluidity, and non-Western androgynies. As Ian Buchanan put it in discussing the cultural, linguistic, and discursive options available to us around gender identity, "you can choose to be man, woman, or transgendered, but you cannot choose to be nongendered" (Buchanan 2007). In the categories available in making profile choices in social networking, the sites provide the same limitations—if not stricter ones—as the discourses available to us offline. In Butler's (1990) terms, these are "constitutive categories that seek to keep gender in its place by posturing as the foundational illusions of identity" (33–34). Although not wholly constrictive given the range of counteroptions for performing otherwise (e.g., the biography text-box or ongoing status updates), the profile-provided categories on social networking sites offer a notion of freedom to "choose," which is endemic to neoliberalist thinking and digital technology's either/or framework (Lazzarato 2004, 2009). Yet they risk for some users the violence of a normative truth-regime, which excludes alternative, postmodern, poststructuralist ways of reconfiguring or complexifying identity or doing subjectivity otherwise (Butler 1993, 53). Thus, the social networking tools of subject performance provide limited scope for playing out an identity in accord with anything but the most simplistic and simplified discourses articulating only the most limited normative choices—at least around gender, age, and relationship status as three areas of demarcated and heavily politicized identity coordinates.

ANGER AND ANXIETIES: SOCIAL NETWORKING'S CULTURAL PURPOSES AND IDENTITY PERFORMANCE

According to Facebook's own statistics (Facebook 2011), there are currently more than 750 million Facebook users with 50 percent of those logging on daily and with the average user creating seventy pieces of content per month. Facebook members analyzed in research by Ellison et al. (2007, 1153) reported spending between ten and thirty minutes on average using Facebook each day. So from the perspective of the performativity of identity, subjective becoming, and social belonging, why are social networking sites so popular? One acknowledges, of course, that all media and technological practices have a range of levels of participation and purpose (Burgess and Green 2009, 82). Taking the approach I have discussed, the popularity of social networking is not about fads, digital communication, and networking, keeping in touch with friends, or having a space to archive photographs, nor is it even about "hooking up" with others sexually or romantically, although all of these can be the "conscious" ostensible reasons for the popularity of such sites and their related activities both online and offline. Rather, we might argue that Facebook's popularity is in itself an effect of the contemporary anxieties over subjectivity and its performance: the push-and-pull struggle between the demands for intelligibility and the late-capitalist postmodern "slippage" of identity categories into the ephemeral, temporal, fragmented, and consumption-driven expressions. To say this is to return to early cultural studies approaches to the introduction of new media technologies and to avoid the popular media panics about the impact of social networking that are so firmly grounded in a technological determinism, which focuses on social ills and places the blame on the sites' introduction itself. Rather, we can turn to the cultural studies forefather Raymond Williams and adapt his analysis of the social history of television as a technology to remind ourselves that social networking, like other media technologies, is no accident of invention nor are its effects a symptom of other social qualities. Instead it should be viewed as a product of cultural desires, demands, and needs that responds to specific social purposes and practices (Williams 1990, 13). That is, social networking sites, applications, frameworks, and establishments can be said to serve the specific, historical purpose of aiding our contemporary cultural anxieties over subjectivity and intelligibility. This is not, as Livingstone points out in her rejection of technologically determinist accounts, to ignore the mutual shaping of technology and social practices (Livingstone 2008, 396).

To test this point, we might look at the near-hysteria that emerged globally when Facebook made a number of relatively minor changes to its profile layout and format between May and September 2008. No information or activities were altered; mini-applications were preserved. The change was predominantly to the layout, which included some simplification and reorganization of the profiles with tabs for various sections (info, wall photos, etc.) and various adjustments to the ways in which information is shared—making it easier for others (friends) to see information about the user without deeper searching, causing some concerns about privacy and user capacity to control information (Tufekci 2008, 21). While the privacy issues are understandable, the remainder of the changes were predominantly cosmetic; Facebook users were said to be "fuming" (*Courier Mail* 2008) with allegedly tens of millions angry and upset about the change. As Meaghan Morris (2009) put it, this reaction was "anger endemic to living passionately in an environment that the owner can alter at will (a condition a bit like being in love and a lot like being a tenant)." One possibility here is to see the reaction to the profile format and layout changes as a "disruption" to the expression of identity coherence; altering the familiar space in which identities are played out in a performative theoretical framework can be seen to be as significant, perhaps, to users as waking up to find one's body has changed ethnicity or gender overnight. Social networking sites allow us, then, the most effective opportunity to "shore up" and simultaneously "adjust" our subjectivity. Where conversations with others, self-reflection, and other activities (not all of them necessarily conscious and voluntary) once gave us the opportunity to forge recognizable identities as part of the ongoing process of becoming in order to belong, social networking sites allow us to do so by bringing various elements of ourselves together as an expression of identity coherence. Changes, alterations, and manipulations of this cultural technology impact not on convenience or familiarity but on the very subjectivities and identities that are constituted in its use.

REFERENCES

Bell, Vikki. 1999. "Performativity and Belonging." *Theory, Culture and Society* 16:1–10.
boyd, danah. 2007. "Why Youth (Heart) Social Network Sites: The Role of Networked Publics in Teenage Social Life." In *MacArthur Foundation Series on Digital Learning—Youth, Identity, and Digital Media Volume*, edited by David Buckingham, 1–18. Cambridge, MA: MIT Press.
Buchanan, Ian. 2007. "Deleuze and the Internet." *Australian Humanities Review* 43. Accessed February 12, 2008. http://www.australianhumanitiesreview.org/archive/.
Buffardi, Laura E., and Keith W. Campbell. 2008. "Narcissism and Social Networking Web Sites." *Personality and Social Psychology Bulletin* 34:1303–14.
Burgess, Jean, and Joshua Green. 2009. *YouTube: Online Video and Participatory Culture*. Cambridge: Polity.
Butler, Judith. 1990. *Gender Trouble: Feminism and the Subversion of Identity*. London: Routledge.
———. 1991. "Imitation and Gender Insubordination." In *Inside/Out: Lesbian Theories, Gay Theories*, edited by Diana Fuss, 13–31. London: Routledge.
———. 1993. *Bodies That Matter: On The Discursive Limits of "Sex."* London: Routledge.
———. 1997. *The Psychic Life of Power: Theories in Subjection*. Stanford, CA: Stanford University Press.
Courier Mail. 2008. "Facebook Makeover Leaves Some Subscribers Fuming." *Courier Mail*, September 11.
Cover, Rob. 2004a. "Digital Addiction: The Cultural Production of Online and Video Game Junkies." *Media International Australia* 113:110–23.
———. 2004b. "From Butler To Buffy: Notes Towards a Strategy for Identity Analysis in Contemporary Television Narrative." *Reconstruction: Studies in Contemporary Culture* 4. Accessed May 31, 2009. http://reconstruction.eserver.org/042/cover.htm.
Disch, Lisa. 1999. "Judith Butler and the Politics of the Performative." *Political Theory* 27:545–59.
Düttmann, Alexander García. 1996. *At Odds With AIDS: Thinking and Talking About a Virus*. Translated by Peter Gilgen and Conrad Scott-Curtis. Stanford, CA: Stanford University Press.
Ellison, Nicole B., Charles Steinfeld, and Cliff Lampe. 2007. "The Benefits of Facebook 'Friends': Social Capital and College Students' Use of Online Social Network Sites." *Journal of Computer-Mediated Communication* 12:1143–68.
Facebook. 2011. "Statistics." Accessed June 5, 2011. http://www.facebook.com/press/info.php?statistics.
Foucault, Michel. 1977. *Discipline and Punish: The Birth of the Prison*. Translated by Alan Sheridan. London: Penguin.
Fuss, Diana. 1989. *Essentially Speaking: Feminism, Nature and Difference*. New York: Routledge.
Green, Lelia. 2008. "Is it Meaningless to Talk about 'the Internet'?" *Australian Journal of Communication* 35:1–14.
Hoadley, Christopher M.; Heng Xu, Joey J. Lee, and Mary Beth Rosson. 2010. "Privacy as Information Access and Illusory Control: The Case of the Facebook News Feed Privacy Outcry." *Electronic Commerce Research and Applications* 9, no. 1: 50–60.

Jameson, Fredric. 1985. "Postmodernism and Consumer Society." In *Postmodern Culture*, edited by Hal Foster, 111–25. London: Pluto Press.

Kennedy, Helen. 2006. "Beyond Anonymity, or Future Directions for Internet Identity Research." *New Media and Society* 8:859–76.

Lazzarato, Maurizio. 2004. "From Capital-Labour to Capital-Life." Translated by Valerie Fournier, Akseli Virtanen, and Jussi Vahamaki. *Ephemera: Theory and Politics in Organization* 4:187–208.

———. 2009. "Neoliberalism in Action: Inequality, Insecurity and the Reconstitution of the Social." *Theory, Culture and Society* 26:109–33.

Liu, Hugo. 2008. "Social Network Profiles as Taste Performances." *Journal of Computer-Mediated Communication* 13:252–75.

Livingstone, Sonia. 2008. "Taking Risk Opportunities in Youthful Content Creation: Teenagers' Use of Social Networking Sites for Intimacy, Privacy and Self-Expression." *New Media and Society* 10:393–411.

Morris, Meaghan. 2009. "Grizzling about Facebook." *Australian Humanities Review* 47. Accessed May 18, 2010. http://www.australianhumanitiesreview.org/archive/Issue-November/.

Salih, Sara. 2002. *Judith Butler*. London: Routledge.

Tong, Stephanie Tom, Brandon Van Der Heide, Lindsey Langwell, and Joseph B. Walther. 2008. "Too Much of a Good Thing? The Relationship Between Number of Friends and Interpersonal Impressions on Facebook." *Journal of Computer-Mediated Communication* 13, no. 3: 531–49.

Tufekci, Zeynep. 2008. "Can You See Me Now? Audience and Disclosure Regulation in Online Social Network Sites." *Bulletin of Science, Technology, and Society* 28:20–36.

Turkle, Sherry. 1995. *Life on the Screen: Identity in the Age of the Internet*. New York: Simon and Schuster.

Williams, Raymond. 1990. "The Technology and the Society." In *Popular Fiction: Technology, Ideology, Production, Reading*, edited by Tony Bennett, 9–22. London: Routledge.

Woodward, Kath. 2002. *Understanding Identity*. London: Arnold.

Virtually Me

A Toolbox about Online Self-Presentation

SIDONIE SMITH *and* JULIA WATSON

Opportunities for composing, assembling, and networking lives have expanded exponentially since the advent of Web 2.0. The sites and software of digital media provide occasions for young people to narrate moments in coming of age; for families to track and narrate their genealogical histories; for people seeking friends and lovers or those with similar hobbies to make connections; for political activists to organize around movements and causes. These everyday sites of self-presentation appear to be categorically different from what is understood as traditional life writing, be it published autobiography, memoir, or confession. And yet, as Nancy Baym (2006) observes, "online spaces are constructed and the activities that people do online are intimately interwoven with the construction of the offline world and the activities and structures in which we participate, whether we are using the Internet or not" (86, qtd in Gray 2009, 1168). Thus, online lives exist in complicated relationship to offline lives and to what has been termed the "outernet" (Nakamura 2008, 1676). And "electronic persons" have multiple connections to "proximate individuals," as J. Schmitz (1997) has observed (qtd in Kennedy 2006, 4). For these reasons, the analytical frames and theoretical positions of scholarship on life writing can provide helpful concepts and categories for thinking about the proliferation of online lives in varied media and across a wide range of sites.

Our contribution to understanding subjectivity and identities online, as well as the modes and media mobilized to present and perform lives, is this toolkit, organized alphabetically through rubrics derived from the framework we developed in *Reading Autobiography* (Smith and Watson 2010).[1] Studying the presentation of online lives makes clear that both the self and its presentation are only apparently autonomous, as many life narrative theorists, as well as media theorists, argue. In fact, online lives are fundamentally relational or refracted through engagement with the lives of their significant others: the lives presented are often interactive; they are co-constructed; they are linked to others—family, friends, employers, causes, and affiliations. Many online lives profess attachments not to flesh-and-blood others but to media personages, consumer products, and works of art or music linked to online resources such as YouTube videos. As N. Katherine Hayles asserts for electronic literature, so for online relationships and subjectivities: they are re-described and re-presented "in terms of a networked environment in which individual selves blend into a collectivity, human boundaries blur as people merge with technological apparatus, and cultural formations are reconfigured to reflect and embody a cyborgian reality" (Hayles 2003).

Here we offer two preliminary comments. The first clarifies the key terms "self," "subject," and "subject position" as used in this toolkit. Throughout, we use the term "self" as a pronominal marker of reflexivity, the shorthand term for acts of self-reference. This sense of the term should not, however, be conflated with the liberal humanist concept of the self as a rational, autonomous, self-knowing, and coherent actor, which is a legacy of the Enlightenment. Indeed, this liberal humanist self, understood as essential, free, and agentic, has been a focus of critique for four decades. When constructing personal web pages or the like, users themselves often imagine that they are revealing their "real" or "true" essence, a person or "me" who is unique, singular, and outside social constructions and constraints.[2] Theorists of media and autobiography, however, approach the constructed self not as an essence but as a subject, a moving target, which provisionally conjoins memory, identity, experience, relationality, embodiment, affect, and limited agency.

In online self-presentation as in offline life narration, then, the "I" of reference is constructed and situated, and not identical with its flesh-and-blood maker.[3] Moreover, that "I" is constituted through discursive formations, which are heterogeneous, conflictual, and intersectional, and which allocate subject positions to those who are interpellated through their ideological frames, tropes, and language. Those subject positions in turn attach to salient cultural and historical identities. Both offline and online, the autobiographical subject can be approached as an ensemble or assemblage of subject positions through which self-understanding and self-positioning are negotiated.

Our second comment clarifies what the term "online lives" encompasses in this chapter.[4] Many media theorists invoke the term "digital storytelling" to refer to the transmission of personal stories in digital forms. Nick Couldry, for example, refers to "the whole range of personal stories now being told in potentially public form using digital media resources" (Couldry 2008, 347). We follow Couldry's lead in limiting online lives to "online personal narrative formats . . . [now] prevalent: . . . multimedia formats such as MySpace and Facebook, textual forms such as webblogs (blogs), the various story forms prevalent on more specialist digital storytelling sites or the many sites where images and videos, including material captured on personal mobile devices, can be collected for wider circulation (such as YouTube)" (381–82). We oscillate between the forms attached to particular sites, and the acts and practices of self-representation and self-performance employed by users on a range of standardized forms and templates.

Further, we do not take up oral storytelling such as co-produced stories told in offline workshops and then mounted online. Others have focused on the contrast of online narrative forms to practices of oral storytelling and projects involving listening to others' stories, as does Joe Lambert (2012) and scholars and writers affiliated with the Center for Digital Storytelling in Berkeley, California. Nor do we consider the collective websites that make available collaboratively produced life stories of ordinary people, such as StoryCorps, Lifebio.com, or My Life Is True. While many kinds of online life stories use autobiographical templates for narration, not all are produced by the single subject/user telling, performing, and/or imaging a life, the focus of this chapter.

In our toolkit of fifteen concepts presented in alphabetical order, each brief discussion is followed by questions to enable scholars and students to productively engage with the vast variety of sites presenting lives online. You might pose these questions as you produce or interact with online "life" presentations of many sorts: an opinion blog, a profile of a desirable self on a dating site, a webcam "reality" video, a Facebook profile or LiveJournal entry. The questions offer points of entry for analyzing online self-presentations and points of departure for constructing, and critiquing, your own online life and those of others.

Archive and Database

Online sites gather, authorize, and conserve the version of self a user is assembling. Various kinds of documents become evidence capturing varied aspects of the presenter's life, habits, desires, and the like. That is, a site incorporates and organizes documents about a self as a personal archive, and that personal archive may become incorporated into other archives, official or unofficial, designed or accidental. Moreover, the algorithmic data generated by the site directs information about the self into online databases. The prodigious capacities of online archives have therefore shifted how we understand the relationship of archives to databases. Tara McPherson (2011) argues that today's database has supplanted the archive, and distinguishes the archive—which has an archivist of some kind, a principle of collection, and a design for storage and structure for categorization—from the database, which is an instrument of a governmentality that bureaucratizes and commodifies bits and pieces of information.

Neither the archive nor the database has a fail-safe delete button for past tidbits of the self. Code may break down, and the new service industry of reputation management may eventually delete substantial data archives. Nonetheless, online users are implicated in contributing user-generated content, which can return in digital afterlives, as online archives and databases become ever more searchable. Thus, the archival possibilities of the web include deliberate efforts by users to store a profile that becomes an online version of the self; the random bits that are dispersed across the Internet that could be pulled in to construct, alter, or contest a user profile; accidental archives assembled by others such as Wikileaks, which disseminate personal data that has been kept out of public circulation; reassemblages of the data of the self circulated by others with varied motivations; and the "digital character" (Noguchi 2011) that data aggregators assemble from user's buying habits, GPS locations, phone connections, and the like.

In examining an online site of self-presentation, consider the following questions related to archiving and producing data. What comprises a database through which "digital character" is constructed? Who benefits from the accumulation of data about users? What comprises an archive of self and how is it built? Are official documents scanned in, such as birth, marriage, or death certificates, or citizenship records? How are the documents authenticated, and is that certification persuasive? What kind of authority does the user seek to establish in assembling documentation to curate a life? Is a motive or purpose given for this documentation? Are the testimonies of others included or links made to them? Is there a link to evidence asserting the history and legitimacy of a larger group?

Over time, online presentation of embodiment creates an archive of the body. What kind of archive of embodiment can be observed on various sites? Does it make visible segments of the life cycle, or particular bodily forms, or particular conditions of the body? Which aspects of the body archive are drawn from history, and which are projected as fantasies of a future moment in the life cycle?

For what occasions, to what extent, and for whom is an archive or database being assembled? Which media of archiving have been employed and to what effects? Is the purpose of self-archiving to build a legacy, to mislead or deceive by creating a false identity, and/or to register a history of successfully overcoming a past identity? Has the user's life story been inserted into someone else's archive, for example in the collection of stories amassed by the StoryCorps project on National Public Radio, in sports histories, or in opposition research for political campaigns? What larger story does the archive produce? Does the site construct a history that aims to counteract or undermine other information available online about the user?

Digital archives are unlike print archives in several ways: the categories and hierarchies of information storage are leveled; the incidental and the characteristic seem of the same magnitude and significance. Careless users can lie and conflate people sharing a characteristic such as name or birthdate. What is involved in searching an archive for some part of one's story or history? How do the archives of such institutions as the Church of the Latter-day Saints or websites such as ancestry.com contribute to a user's story and how might their protocols co-construct that story?

AUDIENCES

Online venues assume, invite, and depend on audiences, sometimes intimate, sometimes not. How a site appeals to an audience and the kind of response it solicits deserve attention. It may seek to enhance its authority with endorsements from, or links to, celebrities, experts, or an index of commercial success. It may invite a voyeuristic response by offering access to intimate details about the subject of the site or others. It may feed an appetite for the melancholic, sensational, morbid, or violent. Visitors also need to follow the money, evaluating who has funded and who is asked to contribute to the site. It may espouse a social need or cause, but users may want to determine who paid to mount the site or who ultimately profits from it.

What kind of audience does the site call for? Whom does the site explicitly address as its imagined audience? What verbal or visual rhetorics does the site deploy to engage visitors? How does the site attempt to bracket out potentially hostile users from its audience? What is the reach of the assumed or desired audience—local, national, transnational? Are issues of language or cultural difference foregrounded and are ways of translating those differences provided on the site?

What action does the site invite its audience to undertake or support? What affect does the site seek to produce in readers—for instance, shame, pity, anger, or melancholy? And how might actual users respond in ways aligned or unaligned with an affect? How is audience interaction incorporated into the self-presentation? Over a longer period of time, how much change or continuity can be observed in the self presented?

In terms of actual users, who are the frequent users, and what are their demographics or characteristics as a group? What other audiences might use or interact with the site? Are there potentially hostile users, or user groups, that the site tries to bracket out? Has the demographic of the audience changed over time, and if so, in what ways? Is the audience a potential market, and what kind of a market?

Authenticity

Users find online environments potent sites for constructing and trying out versions of self. The availability of multiple and heterogeneous sites for self-presentation promises seemingly endless opportunities for conveying some "truth" about an "authentic" self for those with access to web technologies. The selves produced through various sites can convey to visitors and users a sense of intimacy—the intimacy of the quotidian details of daily life, the intimacy of shared confession and self-revelation, the intimacy of a unique voice or persona or virtual sensibility, contributory to the intimate public sphere theorized by Lauren Berlant (1997) and Anna Poletti (2011).

Yet cultural commentators question the extent to which presenters can be "authentic" in virtual environments. If by authenticity one means the unmediated access to some "essence" or "truth" of a subject, virtual environments only make clearer the critique made by poststructural theorists that all self-presentation is performative, that authenticity is an effect, not an essence. Jeff Pooley (2011), for instance, observes that "authenticity today is more accurately described as 'calculated authenticity'—. . . stage management. The best way to sell yourself is to not appear to be selling yourself." David Graxian even more strongly emphasizes that authenticity is "manufactured." Graxian is exploring the ways in which authenticity is "manufactured" within the context of the Chicago blues club, but his observations on this offline environment are productive for thinking about digital authenticity: "Broadly speaking," he writes, "the notion of authenticity suggests two separate but related attributes. First, it can refer to the ability of a place or event to conform to an idealized representation of reality: that is, to a set of expectations regarding how such a thing ought to look, sound, and feel. At the same time, authenticity can refer to the credibility or sincerity of a performance and its ability to come off as natural and effortless" (Graxian 2003, 10–11; cited in Gray 2009, 1164).

If authenticity can be "manufactured," if it is an effect of features of self-performance, then credibility, veracity, and sincerity acquire a slipperiness that can prompt suspicious readings (see Smith and Watson 2012). And indeed, users themselves often read sites with a skeptical eye, assessing the presenter's degree of sincerity or speculating about whether he or she is posing as a false identity. Alternatively, authenticity can be rethought through the concept of "realness" proposed by Judith/Jack Halberstam. Halberstam shifts attention from questions of authenticity to the unpredictability of effects in the world. She defines "realness" as "not exactly performance, not exactly an imitation; it is the way that people, minorities, excluded from the domain of the real, appropriate the real and its effects" (Halberstam 2005, 51; cited in Gray 2009, 1163). Appropriations of realness in online environments may reinforce social norms and they may open a space for recognition of the constructedness of those norms.

In interacting with online performances of self, the following questions arise with regard to authenticity and realness. Is this a site where the authenticity of self-presentation matters and if so, for whom and for what reasons? What strategies for creating a situated, historical subject does the user or site mobilize? Does an aura of authenticity attach to a particular identity category on particular kinds of sites; for example, sites acknowledging victimization or transgression such as coming-out sites, weight sites, illness sites, or grief sites?

What strategies for winning belief are deployed? What are identified as guarantors of authenticity on a site? How convincing are those guarantors? Are there different kinds of guarantors for different kinds of sites? For example, webcam sites seem to guarantee the moment-to-moment authenticity of the subject of their surveillance, and yet "surveillance realism" can be manufactured, as in reality television. The web-based video series that began in June 2006 named LonelyGirl15, for instance, was unmasked in September 2006 as inauthentic, a bid to gain celebrity status for an aspiring nineteen-year-old American actor (Jessica Lee Rose as Bree Avery). The narration of personal histories on video sites such as YouTube appears to be a slice of life, but the production of a video is a collective project involving a camera person, a sound person, and sometimes a director other than the performing "I." How, then, is the aura of authenticity attached to an online performance constructed by a crew, which could include a camera person, sound person, director, and script-writer? Do you find this self-presentation to be sincere or to be calculated authenticity, a pose or "manufactured" pseudo-individuality?

How is "authenticity" surveilled online? How does the site try to convince visitors of its creator's "truthfulness"? What degree of fabrication or exaggeration do visitors tolerate and correct for in an online environment? For instance, on dating sites users may expect idealized representations of others as younger, thinner, and more attractive, and adjust for a vanity-driven profile. How does an aura of authenticity get attached to "anonymity" in sites where the user is not identified? Can a fabricated online identity contribute to a different kind of "truth" aimed at correcting a social harm or inequity? That is, to what extent does it matter that an online identity is inauthentic if the blogger or journal writer claims to speak on behalf of victims who cannot dare to risk speaking out publicly? What are the larger politics of authenticity in the global traffic in narratives of suffering? What is the relationship of authenticity to the ideological formations of global capitalism, to transnational activism, to online marketing, to reputation management?

Automediality

Scholars in media studies and autobiography studies invoke a set of related terms to illuminate the relationship of technologies and subjectivity: medium, mediation, mediatization, automediality, autobiomediality, and transmediality. Jay David Bolter and Richard Grusin (2000), for instance, describe the relation of medium and mediation in this way: "A medium is that which remediates. It is that which appropriates the techniques, forms, and social significance of other media and attempts to rival or refashion them in the name of the real" (65). British cultural studies theorists are concerned to distinguish mediatization generally from mediation. "Mediation," observes Nick Couldry, "emphasize[s] the heterogeneity of the transformations to which media give rise across a complex and divided social space" (Couldry 2008, 375). Mediatization, in contrast, "describes the transformation of many disparate social and cultural processes into forms or formats suitable for media representation" (377). His argument is that media cannot simply be conceptualized as "tools" for presenting a preexisting, essential self. Rather, the materiality of the medium constitutes and textures the subjectivity presented. Media technologies, that is, do not just transparently present the self. They constitute and expand it, and imagine new kinds of virtual sociality, which do not depend on direct or corporeal encounter. (See Smith and Watson 2010, 168.)

The concept of automediality (or autobiomediality) directs the concept of mediation to the terrain of the autobiographical and the self-presentation of online sites. It provides a theoretical framework for conceptualizing the way subjectivity is constructed online across visual and verbal forms in new media. Brian Rotman (2009) places the concept of autobiomediality in the long history of encounters between modes of self-enunciation and locates the present moment in "a radically altered regime of space-time" in which there is "an emerging copresence of mobile, networked selves with identities . . . 'in perpetual formation and reformation at the moment of use'" (121). Scholars in Germany and France, among them Joerg Dünne and Christian Moser (2008), have focused on the concept of automediality as well. Ruth E. Page (2008) refers to transmediality and multimodality as forms of electronic literature that are gaining attention in narrative studies. Automediality implies an aesthetics of collage, mosaic, pastiche. Subjectivity cannot be regarded as an entity or essence; it is a bricolage or set of disparate fragments, rather than a coherent, inborn unit of self. Automedial practices of digital life writing impact the prosthetic extension of self in networks, the reorientation of bodies in virtual space, the perspectival positioning of subjects, and alternative embodiments.

How does the choice of a medium or media contribute to the construction of subjectivity on a particular site? If you observe multiple media of self-presentation, where do you see them merging or conflicting in a self-presentation?

AVATARS

Embodiment is a translation in various media of the experienced and sensed materiality of the self. While the body is always dematerialized in virtual representation, embodiment in many forms and media is a prominent feature of online self-presentation. The possibility of configuring oneself as an avatar with nonhuman features and capacities on sites such as Second Life or World of Warcraft offer new dimensions to the performance of the self. Bodily extensions and fantasies (e.g., of animals, cartoon heroes, or machines; enhanced, streamlined, or transformed human capacities) are enabled. And yet, while avatars are assumed to function as the erasure of identity markers such as race or ethnicity, gender, sexuality, and age, the choice of an avatar can be a form of what Lisa Nakamura (2008) labels "identity tourism." This troubling practice, according to Nakamura, "let users 'wear' racially stereotyped avatars without feeling racist, yet it also blamed users who reveal their real races and were victims of racism online" (1675). She argues that the Internet is not "a postracial space" where users can "'choose' a race as an identity tourist" or withhold a racial identity (1676), and therefore that the avatar is not necessarily a medium for escaping identity.

What possibilities of avatar identity are generated by site templates and protocols? How is the avatar stylized—through, for instance, adornment of the contemporary or a historical period, body markings, prostheses, or amputation? What does the choice of an avatar suggest about the relationship among bodily systems and organs, visible bodily surfaces, and bodily histories and meaning? How might the codes or rules of a community affect the choice of an avatar?

What social boundaries are crossed or transgressed through self-presentation as an avatar? Are scenarios of desire or violence or mystical transformation enacted and to what end? Are fantasies of embodiment engaged through dreams, rituals, myths, or other projections? How is the avatar of the user related to other bodies? What are the effects of capturing the body in other ways than photos and video? If identity markers are referenced, is there evidence on the site for determining whether they are markers of race, ethnicity, gender, nationality, age? What contextualization in the form of chatting or blogging surrounds the avatar?

BRANDING

Online environments are fully corporatized, with sites ripe for data mining by aggregators and marketers. So, we can't be surprised that the discourse of corporate management has promoted "Brand Me" as the mode of online self-presentation. Or as William Deresiewicz (2011) observed, "The self today is an entrepreneurial self, a self that's packaged to be sold" (7). That is, the self is regarded as a commodity to be packaged for brokering in a variety of media sites, including YouTube, the personal websites of entrepreneurs, and product-related sites.

Online venues are preferred vehicles for composing, circulating, monitoring, and managing one's brand. Individual users adopt the methods of corporate marketers, simplifying and honing their self-images and presentational behaviors to project a desirable brand "Me"—digitally hip, successful, fully sociable, intriguing. Some identify what sets them apart in their quirky individuality; some emphasize achievements. Some turn themselves into a kind of "logo," which will consistently deliver a product and up-to-date status reports. As self-curators, users utilize the web to create a multimedia CV that marks "you" as a brand. The brand is consolidated and marketed through narratives and images, especially those on social networking sites. Thus, telling personal stories or performing one's sense of one's personality is critical to the conveyance of the brand "you." Narrative, profiles, images all link aspects of your experience and your character into a coherent presentation.

With the imperative of branding, however, comes the necessity of managing the brand by managing online reputation. To do this, users can contract with any one of the many reputation managers advertising their services, such as reputationmanagementconsultants.com and ironreputation.com. The message here is that the impulse to online self-disclosure can be reckless and can undermine the self-image or brand a creator wants to project.

Is the creator branding herself or himself on the site? How is the brand linked to autobiographical stories, about experiences, character features, achievements? And how convincing is the assertion of brand coherence? How consistently and coherently is branding employed on various sites where the user appears?

CONFESSION ONLINE

Many consider confession a prime motivation for self-presentation in online environments. The sense of intimacy within anonymity that a virtual community of sharers experience in online sites provide may encourage users to disclose secrets but at potential risk to their privacy. Many online sites invite confessional disclosure and set out protocols for the degree and kinds of intimacy they invite. PostSecret, one of the most widespread and intriguing of these, combines the discourse of confession with the material traces of personal forms such as handwriting, photos and drawings, and small objects to secure the promise of authenticity for the secrets disclosed on the handmade postcards mailed or uploaded (which are in turn adjudicated by the site's manager Frank Warren). As Anna Poletti (2011) observes, the "confessional meta-narrative" of Post-Secret protects anonymity through the postal system while connecting the secret to both the body of the creator and to the intimate public who comes to possess it. "The secrets," she emphasizes, "*remain secrets*" (32). The technologies that mark the confession as such may be multiplied and focused in online environments to emphasize its special status for creators and to call site-users to an ethical response to it, though the boundaries of the genre seem more blurred than in its written form as practiced by, say, Augustine, Rousseau, or Joan Didion, Annie Ernaux, and Maya Angelou.

How does the site invite confession of secrets, self-doubts, or fantasies? What guarantees of protection does it offer users, and are those reliable? Does the site link confession to anonymity? What form does the confession take? Is it framed as a "sin" by a religious template? Told as a psychological disclosure? Acknowledged as a political transgression? To what extent does the confession seem "sincere," and why or why not? (Consider both internal evidence within the narrative and its reference to external data.) Is the confession a reference to an incident in the teller's past or to an ongoing habit pattern? In what ways is, or isn't, the narrating "I" distinct from the narrated actor who did the deed or had the thought? Are others implicated as victims or as beneficiaries? Has some form of retribution been made, and if so, how? In your view, was it sufficient to redress the harm? Is the confessor overly scrupulous about her or his actions or motivations? Who benefits from this act of confession? What politics does the confession seem to serve? What communities?

What risks and rewards of the online confession are observable? What role did or do site visitors play in pardoning the confessor? Do they remain a multiple, impersonal audience or are they personalized? Does the confession generate similar acts by visitors, and if so, to what effect?

ETHICS

The web seems to be a fluid environment in which "anything goes"; but increasingly, users, corporations, and managers are confronting difficult ethical issues related to online behaviors, borrowing, copyright, repurposing of gathered materials (such as video clips and images), surveillance, and data-mining. Ethical questions about appropriate online behavior, for instance, relate to the site and its management and to users.

Site management can be a form of self-care or a form of surveillance. Does the site articulate an ethics as a protocol for its use, and does it observe that ethics? How do the site and its management assert or delimit zones of privacy? How does the site address issues related to disclosure of intimate details? Does the site protect anonymity? Does the site propose a code of use relating to borrowing from other sites? Is some form of remedy available to users with respect to these ethical issues? What implicit dangers or risks to self-disclosure exist on this site? Does the site address the implications for vulnerable users such as children?

Users engaged in acts and practices of online self-presentation also confront pressing ethical issues. Does the user assert or imply an ethical code or practice on his or her site? What is the ethics of going public with intimate material about family and friends in the context of online self-presentation? What is the ethics of appropriating materials from other people's lives or sites? How can users manage their personal sites to care for their privacy and vulnerability while pursuing self-exploration or trying out versions of selves? How does a personal ethics of online self-performance intersect with a corporatized system for developing and managing one's public image? What is at stake in the conjunction of excessive attention to performing one's self and the increasing scope of surveillance enabled by the technology and by site monitors?

GLOBAL CIRCUITS

The instantaneity and reach of Internet technologies join people together as what is considered a global community of users. But access to online technologies remains unevenly distributed across the globe. Moreover, the asymmetrical distribution of access and benefits; the differential treatment of the labor forces producing hardware, software, and cloudware; the differential degrees of technical literacy; the incommensurability of culturally specific idioms of self-presentation; and the persistence of larger formations of imperialism and neocolonialism all impact the lived realities of the digital divide and the digital future. At the same time, though, the increasing digital literacy and access to some kind of technology such as cell phones, the proliferation of translation sites, and the availability of nonlinguistic modes of communication mean that the possibilities for linking one's story and self-presentation across geographic, languages, and political borders have expanded.

To what extent does online self-presentation map onto transnational social identities, political movements, activist causes, or transnational formations such as global youth cultures, human rights movements, and transnational community-building among indigenous peoples across the globe? On sites that assemble an archive of life stories, such as those witnessing to histories of violence, how do paratexts around them, testimonials embedded in them, and their placement online affect the subject position of the witness, the form of story told, and the projected audience? What kinds of responses are invited from visitors to the site, for instance, a donation of money or a pledge of advocacy? To what extent is an online self-presentation implicated in programs and policies of a neoliberal nation-state or in efforts to subvert or challenge a neoliberal ideology? How might online acts and practices of self-presentation reassemble the textual legacies of one or diverse cultural traditions that extend back over centuries?

What means of self-translation are available to users addressing a global audience? How are photos and videos mobilized to translate a self across differences of language and culture? What kinds of online lives gain salience and why and how?

IDENTITY ONLINE

While identity is often regarded as a set of components of personhood, such as markers of gender, race, nationality, class, sexuality, generation, family genealogy, political belief, and religious affiliation, theorists have come to view identities as multiple, provisional, contextual, intersectional, and historically specific. That is, people are situated and situate themselves discursively in relation to context-specific social norms, which determine and constitute identities as subject positions. In the expanding array of virtual environments, identities become increasingly manipulable. Indeed, for some commentators online identity, as virtual, seems unbounded, purely a matter of choice and invention among avatars, roles, and subject positions. Paul Longley Arthur (2009), for instance, observes that "online identities are easily manipulated at any time by the individual subject or by others" and this "ability to 'manage' online content at will is changing the way we see ourselves and each other" (76).

The malleability and interchangeability of identities online, however, is qualified offline in several ways by both the complexity of identity performance and the *Realpolitik* of situated subjects. Considering the performance of identity, the sociolinguist Ruth E. Page (2011) distinguishes between those aspects that are "transportable identities," traveling across several kinds of discursive situations, and those aspects that are "discourse- and situated-specific, . . . locally occasioned roles adopted in relation to a particular speech situation" (18). In Real-Life (RL) social settings as well, Page observes that not all aspects of identity are intrinsic to a person's performed characteristics; some may be provisionally adopted for a particular occasion or context. While the origins and correlatives of virtual identities are not embodied as are those presented in RL social settings, distinguishing between transportable and role-based or assumed aspects of identity may enable more nuanced theorizing.

Furthermore, not all valences of identity are equalized and sharable online. New media scholars such as Lisa Nakamura, Helen Kennedy, and Mary L. Gray caution that the utopian vision of an Internet where the free play of identity is unbounded obscures the persistent asymmetries of power and access that attach to marginalized and normative identity positions on and offline, and to the labor of producing, circulating, and consuming lives in Web 2.0. Nakamura (2008, 1678), for instance, asserts that "the 'larger flows of labor, culture and power' that surround and shape digital media travel along unevenly distributed racial, gendered, and class channels" (see also this volume, 42–54).

In this environment, at once fluid yet inflected by asymmetrical power relations, some artists have created meta-identity projects that reformulate identity as contingent and arbitrarily networked. The Australian painter Jennifer Mills (2009–11), for example, developed *What's in a Name?* Googling her own name, she found more than 325 women from across the globe, especially the English-speaking world—the United States, Australia, Canada, New Zealand—who shared it. She then used their websites or Facebook pages to make candid watercolor images of her avatars as intimate "secret sharers." Exhibited at the Queensland Art Gallery, *What's in a Name?* illustrates how self-representation through online avatars is an increasingly important aspect of contemporary self-identity, yet it fractures social identity. One of Mills's "Googlegängers," Australian *writer*

Jennifer Mills, notes the compelling but dislocated intimacy of the Internet: "The idea that in the mass of difference and differentiation you might have something in common with a stranger has a kind of dizziness about it. . . . These Jennifers have traveled through the hyperreality of the network, and come back home."

What components of identity are presented in an online site, and which ones are assumed? How do site protocols and templates manage identity? Do discourses of a "true" self or an imaginary self inform the site? To what extent are distinctions of social identities blurred and dispersed in the online environment of self-presentation? To what extent are an individual's multiple or conflicting identities homogenized? Do you observe ways in which normative identities—as effects of racialization, heteronormativity, or ableism, and the like—are invoked, sidetracked, queered, reformulated, rematerialized?

Some self-presenters consider themselves as primarily embedded within online collectivities; that is, they are part of a group of actors speaking as a homogenous "we." How would you describe the community or collective? How large is it? How connected in time and space? Is the community multigenerational? Does it make links across sexes, ages, national, ethnic, or linguistic boundaries? What shared characteristics make this "I" part of a larger "we," and which are inherited, which consciously chosen? Is there a set of beliefs or an ideology at the core of the group's formation? Does the site assume that visitors are members of a particular community or provide a way for them to claim or participate in an identity through membership and/or IRL (In Real Life) meetings, activities, and rituals?

MEMORY

Processes of individual and collective memory are both changed and enabled by the Internet. The encoding of memory is also technologically vulnerable in that data may be lost or corrupted. But, as scholars of life narrative have argued, memory was always more than the storage of impressions of past events. There are many processes of memory: retrieval, association over time, flashback and flashbulb, dreams, traumatic memory, postmemory, and prosthetic memory, to name some kinds (see Smith and Watson 2010, ch. 2). It is important to distinguish between the "stored" memory of an online archive or database and what is available as historical and collective memory through other sites and non-online sources.

The Internet also provides technologies for creating what might be called "future memory," which is prospectively retrospective. Consider an ongoing project by the multimedia artist Christian Boltanski. Titled "Storage Memory," it is a project he hopes to continue for the rest of his life. Each month he will film ten one-minute movies, which can be watched separately but, as a set, will be a "jigsaw puzzle" as a "self-portrait depicting his emotions and sensations . . . a record as time goes by, of the transformations in his life."[5] Boltanski has solicited online subscribers (for an annual fee) to reach beyond his fans to individuals around the world. He describes the project as "a work in progress of unknown duration which only death will put an end to." Here, future memory is enabled by technologies for recording, storing, and sharing what an artist becomes, on a regular basis throughout his life, merging past and future with the reflexivity of an ever-moving present.

What does memory become on online sites where entries can be made episodically, and where both the site and the web itself serve as a kind of memory bank? In engaging a site, consider how it incorporates memory or practices of memory such as association, emplacements, or substitution. Are prompts to memory retrieval used, such as lists of "firsts" and genealogical trees? How is the emotional content or freight of a memory conveyed online? In authoring a self is there attention to forgetting or an effort to engage others in a search for lost memory? What sources of personal memory are mobilized online, such as genealogy, family albums, photos, and objects, and are they personal artifacts or public documents, events, or rituals?

How is individual memory linked to larger contexts, such as collective memory, historical record, and transnational processes of migration, exile, and diaspora? Does the user/creator highlight traumatic or belated memory as a self-authoring practice for telling about suffering or events that seem unrepresentable to him or her? Does the self-author use the site therapeutically for engaging, overcoming, and healing from painful memories?

PARATEXTS AND PARASITES

Paratext is the name given to material of several sorts, which supplements and mediates a written text, among them tables of contents, chapter headings, and endnotes; letters, documents, and endorsements; book covers, illustrations, and advertisements. Paratexts have various effects: they solicit specific audiences; they produce a certain "look" that brands a narrative for consumption; and they seek to influence reading publics (see Smith and Watson 2010, 99–102). In online environments, in addition to the kinds of paratexts associated with written texts, the screen content may include the visible features of the formal template, blog commentaries, hyperlinks, pop-up ads, associated inventories in sidebar suggestions, "I-like-this" options, and other algorithmically generated matter that mediates acts of self-presentation to contextualize an individual's self-presentation differently with rapid shifts in the environment.[6] Constantly changing frames, driven by behind-the-scenes algorithms, contextualize self-presentation relationally and in ever-changing juxtapositions, affecting how site visitors and reading publics view, read, understand, and respond to the self presented. For instance, the paratextual box registering the constantly changing number of site visitors on a particular site informs viewers about its popularity and can even create celebrity. The sources, purposes, and effects of paratextual apparatuses are thus radically altered in virtual media. Most critically, online paratexts are not only part of author- and/or publisher-generated content; they are also effects of online environments, including site architectures and algorithms, and the economic transactions and business models based on Big Data.

There are also new and striking parasitical aspects of online paratexts. In online environments, as noted above, paratexts may have no intrinsic relationship to the autobiographical project of the user/author, in terms of values, beliefs, and intentions. Indeed, as uninvited occupiers of the screen, paratexts can establish symbiotic relationships with sites: the sites provide advertising space and Big Data for businesses while the paratexts net resources to support site owners. An effect of this symbiotic relationship is that paratexts also project readings of the life and self of site-users by imputing habits, values, and identifications to them. They make linkages unanticipated and unintended by site-authors, and these can inflect, in dramatic and subtle ways, how the presenter is interpreted. They produce "digital character" and project imagined desires, interests, and affiliations. As parasitic, online paratexts mobilize the transport of identities to unanticipated locations and stimulate surprising cohabitations.

Because paratexts can be modified over time, online authors can find their self-presentations framed differently whenever they return to their sites. For example, thinspirational songs and photos of stick-thin models might change the interpretation of disclosures on a site where users monitor their eating habits. Self-presentations surrounded by pornographic or political-advocacy paratexts might influence how visitors interpret the self-presenter's motives and beliefs. Then, too, because fragments of self-presentations can be, and often are, copied without user-authorization, online lives can be resituated on another site, such as Tumblr, and reinterpreted through new paratextual juxtapositions. The circulation and recombination of paratexts open any online life to multiple framings, some of which are chosen by the author, some of which are algorithmic and impersonal, and some of which are effects of ceaselessly shifting placement and juxtaposition.

Consider what kinds of paratexts accompany and situate an online self-presentation. In what larger narrative does a particular paratext situate this self-presentation? For example, on sites that gather oral histories into an archive, individual stories are often organized within an interpretive apparatus dedicated to projecting a collective overview and a counterhistory. Are there contradictory, dissonant, or competing narratives set in motion by different paratextual frames? How might paratextual frames call into question the reliability or accuracy that a self-presenter claims?

Consider, as well, how the inevitability of parasitic paratextual frames commodifies a self-presentation as a demonstration of products, buying habits, and projected desires, making a "life" into a practice of self-branding. Can you distinguish between paratextual frames that impose branding and those that are intentional self-branding? And are there paratexts that are not oriented to commodifying the subject but rather to the projection of values or the exploration of ethical issues, such as a commitment to social justice or human rights activism?

SELF: COMPUTATIONAL OR QUANTIFIED

The shift from an alphabetical to a computational self has opened the way for individuals to become their own quantification engines. A case in point is the "loosely organized group known as the Quantified Self," centered in Boston. The Quantified Self is constituted of people who digitally self-monitor their bodily processes, intake, outgo, and activities. Gary Wolf (2010) has called this new dispensation of the computational self "the data-driven life." And he asks: "Does measuring what we eat and how much we sleep or how often we do the dishes change how we think about ourselves?" (38). In answering his own question, he observes that "almost imperceptibly, numbers are infiltrating the last redoubts of the personal" (40).

One might think of the self in this context as a site of time-stamped data. But what is interesting about the Quantified Self is the capacity of people to become contributors to Big Data; they can increasingly contribute their personal data to large databases, which will become a source of research in the biomedical sciences—through applications such as Foursquare and various weight-tracking programs and sites such as fitday.com or thedailyplate.com, as well as the online journals myfooddiary.com and weightwatchersonline.com. Emily Singer (2011) observes that "the most interesting consequences of the self-tracking movement will come when its adherents merge their findings into databases. The Zeo, for example, gives its users the option of making anonymized data available for research; the result is a database orders of magnitude larger than any other repository of information on sleep stages" (41). She also notes that "[p]atient groups formed around specific diseases have been among the first to recognize the benefits to be derived from aggregating such information and sharing it" (43). The quantified self, then, is more than a practice of self-monitoring; it suggests a shift to sharing such information for collectivized profiles of groups that serve as authorities on themselves.

Wolf recognizes that the Quantified Self, as an assemblage of data driven by the body and by habits, will reorient us to ourselves, even if the impetus to quantify remains attached to a logic of self-development, which is part of the cultural imaginary. "When we quantify ourselves," he observes, "there isn't the imperative to see through our daily existence into a truth buried at a deeper level. Instead, the self of our most trivial thoughts and actions, the self that, without technical help, we might barely notice or recall, is understood as the self we ought to get to know" (Wolf 2010, 44). Paradoxically, the Quantified Self is at once located as a singularity and made anonymous in numeric code.

Efforts to quantify the self, however, occur not just for the purpose of monitoring bodily functions. The Bangladeshi American media artist Hasan Elahi, for example, has created an ongoing project called Tracking Transience—The Orwell Project, which records his movements in multiple, specific ways on his website.[7] He began in response to being detained by the FBI on September 12, 2001. Elahi, an American citizen with a Muslim name who does not speak Arabic, was repeatedly questioned, nine times over six months, and given lie-detector tests concerning his whereabouts during the terrorist attacks (Mihm 2007). Despite his protestations, he remains a "person of interest" to the FBI (which has never charged him); but because of his status he cannot be issued an official letter of clearance and therefore remains vulnerable to rearrest.

As a response to his situation, Elahi has chosen to wear a GPS-positioning device and uses GoogleEarth to track his movements to and from airports and hotels, as well as his meals in restaurants and even use of public toilets. He regularly posts his movements, using a red arrow to show his location. As Siegel (2012) observes, the anonymous "eye" of the satellite camera acts as a kind of all-seeing, superhuman surveillance mechanism (94). In 2011 Elahi wrote in an essay for the *New York Times Magazine*, "You want to watch me? Fine. But I can watch myself better than you can, and I can get a level of detail that you will never have." Elahi's website, which is open so that *all* can track his movements, contained more than 46,000 images in early 2012 and is regularly updated. He points out that continuous self-surveillance, exposing everyday details about oneself, can be a response to the misapplication and uncritical use of identity management technologies. Elahi's strategy is to show his location every day but never any part of his body. Elahi's self-tracking project, which uses uploaded photos to quantify locational aspects of himself, suggests that the Quantified Self concerns not simply measurement but may be employed in self-representations with aesthetic and political implications. His response to government surveillance in "quantifying" himself, yet not revealing his own body, reverses the logic of public disclosure as a means of "establishing the paradoxical condition of public privacy" and suggests an innovative means of intervention in the imperative of Big Data (Siegel 2012, 92).[8]

Are aspects of the quantified self observable on a personal website—data about the body, habits, or measurable achievements of the site creator? To what extent does quantified data dominate the self-portrayal? Is there much personal narrative or self-reflection? How does this quantification shape the kinds of interactions the site invites or permits? For example, on a weight-monitoring site, what informs your response?

User-Authored and/or Protocol-Driven Sites

It is helpful to distinguish between two kinds of online sites. *Protocol-driven sites* have elaborate formats, driven by algorithms that dictate how users organize what they tell or present themselves. The protocols of Facebook, for example, require that users enumerate themselves in established formats, which may suppress some aspects of individual difference. Users can, however, modify or disrupt some site formats, which seem constricting or incomplete, in order to create more nuanced and complex self-presentations. They might add photographs or mention distinctive features of tastes to customize a self-presentation, or they might add a link to another site of self that complicates or expands the limits of the protocol template.

While *user-authored sites* observe some protocols, they are looser and may be minimal. For example, personal websites, such as LiveJournal and collaborative diary sites, permit blogging of unspecified length without a narrowly scripted protocol and extensive commentary by site visitors. Blogs permit users to modify their entries in successive posts and invite interactive comments from others.

What are the norms and rules of the site? What does it allow users to include or require that they exclude? What kind of "life" does the site's format solicit? If it employs the ready-made templates of protocol-driven sites, how does the template shape the user's projection of identity and communal affiliation? How do more constricting formats normalize or typicalize or deindividualize a certain kind of subject as a general social type? What is excluded, obscured, or deformed in a life ready-made through a template? What kind of subject is rendered abnormal through a site format? Are there ways that users can intervene in or innovate upon the protocols?

TEMPORALITY

Self-presentation in online environments, unlike in analog life writing, does not have narrative beginnings and ends distinguishable by birth or death. Its structuring is primarily episodic rather than emplotted. In this way, online presentation is located in time and ever-changing. This mobility of selves in online environments complicates our notions of temporality: it is both an eternal present of moments of self-accretion and extensible across time through the archive. Online, the chronicle is one temporal mode of self-presentation. On sites such as Facebook and blogs, time is successive and accreted, a form of chronology ever changing through modification. Temporality can also be organized by associative memory, by dispersed status updates, or by larger frameworks of historical periods, such as the framework of music history implied in changing attachments to certain kinds of music. Moreover, users can "go backward" in time to delete or amend content. For example, bloggers time travel when they edit earlier posts, which have been criticized as slanderous or offensive.

What time or times, whether a specific moment or a more general time, does the site set up? Does it situate itself in an ongoing series of moments, as in a blog or online journal or webcam site? Are temporal moments signaled through dates or other chronological distinctions? If the site is interactive, how do other users temporally mark their engagements in time? To what extent is the site changed or added to over successive moments? Is there a pattern of self-modification? How are the temporalities of different archives of the self mounted at different sites interarticulated? To what other temporalities is the site linked? Is the self-presentation conscious of the subject's location in generational time, or national time, or a religious moment, or a collective time? Can there be said to be a temporal "end" to a site and the creator's self-presentation? How many temporal dimensions are observable on a site?

CONCLUSION

We regard this toolkit as functional. The questions are intended to supply concepts and prompt analysis. They attend to new ways of presenting a self online, and new formations of subjectivity generated by combinations of media enabled by the Internet. We hope this assemblage of questions contributes to a better understanding of the transformations of subjectivities and lives that the revolutionary shift to digital environments has enabled.

Online self-presentation raises provocative questions for scholars of life narrative and cyber-environments alike. We might ask whether the formulas, protocols, and ready-made environments of online sites call the singularity and uniqueness of the authored self into question. Is this a new critical formation distinct from a postmodern view of subjectivity, such as Derrida's, that written selves are always already citational assemblages? Will the potential of online forms provoke new innovations in self-authoring to convey explorations of self-experience digitally in ways similar to the powerful innovations of Augustine and Rousseau in their *Confessions* and Montaigne in his *Essays*? Or will radically distinct models of prosthetic personhood emerge, as posthumanist theorists suggest?

Online environments can incorporate multiple media and juxtapose them in ways that produce new possibilities for self-representation. A site can configure the self of the user as, for example, a map, a puzzle, a portrait, an assemblage of tastes and habits, a genealogical chronology, a type representative of a group, an aficionado of particular celebrities, heroes, or sports figures. Users may choose to encode themselves through fantasies of being someone or something else, as avatars or alternative identities. The notion of "bricolage," assembling a profile from disparate parts and allowing other users to recombine it differently, is also a feature of some online sites.

Reflection on online self-presentation leads us to wonder what is added, what lost by the ease of assembling multiple versions of a self in disparate media, with different limits and emphases. And it provokes some concluding provocative questions:

- What consequences might the explosion of virtual self-authorship have for the de- or re-formation of subjectivities?
- How does the flattening of online lives into a successive chronicle of moments or an ongoing, updateable present alter expectations that the self in visual and written forms is a construct of depth, interiority, and reflexivity?
- Does the archival capacity for searchability among earlier entries on, or versions of, self-presentation foreclose or expand the prospect for complex self-representation?
- Do self-presentations and extensions through assemblages, links, and avatars signal the emergence of a new posthuman subjectivity? Or is the virtualization of the subject only a neoliberal manifestation of the mind-body split as a legacy of Enlightenment humanism?

- Do the archives and architecture of the web transform the self into a "switching point" or "transit" or "node"? That is, should acts of self-composition that are nonverbal and in constant flux be conceptualized as the extension of a self into multiple relations, or its evacuation?
- What becomes of the concept of agency ascribed to the self constructed through autobiographical performances in writing or other media? Where does agency reside in the narrating and performing subject; as a co-construction in networked interactivity? in the ideological orientation of templates and protocols? or in their intersections? Or is agency delusory? Because of interactivity and transpersonal fluidity, are "virtual me's" post-agentic?
- To what extent are the risks of public disclosure balanced by the new possibilities of self-exploration and self-expression for generations of users who were formerly inhibited about constructing versions of themselves and making enduring multimedia portraits?
- How might the social work of life narrative—for instance, memorialization of family or nation, political activism, group identification—be modified by the archiving, storage, and communicative networks and rhetorics of online environments?
- How might disciplinary norms and practices of online environments for self-presentation contribute to increased commodification and surveillance of selves and life stories? And how might the protocols, politics, and frames of online sites prescribe and enforce ideological norms of identity, belonging, and communicative practice?

We do not have answers to these questions, but we regard online self-presentation as neither Huxley's "brave new world" nor REM's "the end of the world as we know it." The prospect of being simultaneously self-presenters, self-curators, consumers of others' lives, and bricoleurs of individual and collective subjectivities heralds a new age in which the old certainties no longer apply, but spaces of experimental combination are likely to provoke new formations of self, relation, and community. As we confront these transformations, we might recall Sherry Turkle's (2012) trenchant observation: "We have to love our technology enough to describe it accurately. And we have to love ourselves enough to confront technology's true effects on us" (243).

NOTES

We are grateful to Tony Smith-Grieco, James Hixon, Andrew Mayer, and Kate Black for consulting on online concepts and environments. In the United States, David Herman was a helpful resource on work on narrative aspects of online storytelling. In Berlin,

Steffen Siegel helpfully enhanced our knowledge of the work of Hasan Elahi; and Christian Moser and Regina Straetling organized the "Ludic Self-Fashioning" Conference at the Free University in October 2012, which was a helpful forum for presenting and getting feedback on a condensed version of this chapter. Julie Rak and Anna Poletti provided us insightful editorial suggestions.

1. For a fuller toolkit of aspects of autobiographical subjectivity, such as memory, experience, identity, spatial location, embodiment, and agency, see *Reading Autobiography*, ch. 2 (2nd ed.).

2. We have not found the term "user" sufficient and distinctive for online self-representation but also have not been able to come up with an alternative. Sometimes we will use person, people, author, or individual.

3. In *Reading Autobiography*, we theorized the "I"s of autobiographical acts, distinguishing the flesh-and-blood historical "I" of the outernet, to whom others have no direct access, from the speaker or narrator or composer of the textual "I"; we also noted that that textual "I" is always composed of multiple narrated and narrating "I"s. (See Smith and Watson 2010, chs. 2–3).

4. We have not, by and large, pursued the burgeoning corpus of electronic autobiographical literature as such, narratives composed as literary creations conceived for the Internet. Dr. Ruth Page, who focuses on electronic "semi-autobiographical" narratives in innovative multimodal forms by the novelists Shelley Jackson and Tim Wright, trenchantly discusses some of the new possibilities that consciously literary electronic self-presentation can achieve and the effect they may have: "By defamiliarizing the linear reading process through hypertextual fragmentation, electronic literature reminds us that self-representation is inevitably partial, and storytelling an illusory creation of coherence. In a parallel move, readers might then reconsider their own attempts to build mental profiles of narrative participants as similarly partial and open to reconfiguration" (Page 2008).

5. See www.christian-boltanski.com and http://www.mariangoodman.com/artists/christian-boltanski/.

6. For a discussion of paratexts in online gaming, see Paul (2010).

7. See http://trackingtransience.net/.

8. Since this essay went to press, issues of state surveillance have become a focus of international debate, especially with the disclosure by Edward Snowden of data captured by the American National Security Agency. In a *New York Times* editorial, Malte Spitz noted that Germans, sensitized by the surveillance states of both Nazi Fascism and East German socialism, no longer trust President Obama. For six months Spitz published 35,830 pieces of metadata on himself that he downloaded from T-Mobile. The information, published online in *Die Zeit*, demonstrated how every aspect of his life and travels was visible with "just metadata" (*New York Times*, "Sunday Review," June 30, 2013, 4).

REFERENCES

Arthur, Paul Longley. 2009. "Digital Biography: Capturing Lives Online." *a/b: Auto/Biography Studies* 24, no. 1 (Summer): 74–92.

Baym, Nancy K. 2006. "Finding the Quality in Qualitative Research." In *Critical Cyberculture Studies*, edited by D. Silvery and A. Massanari, 79–87. New York: New York University Press.

Berlant, Lauren. 1997. "Introduction: The Intimate Public Sphere." In *The Queen of America Goes to Washington: Essays on Sex and Citizenship*, 1–24. Durham, NC: Duke University Press.

Boltanski, Christian. 2013. "Storage Memory." http://www.christian-boltanski.com/eng/2/presentatio-oeurvre and http://www.facebook.com/pages/Christian-Boltanski-Storage-Memory/258575834210811?sk=info. Accessed January 20, 2013.

Bolter, Jay David, and Richard Grusin. 2000. *Remediation: Understanding New Media.* Cambridge, MA: MIT Press.

Couldry. Nick. 2008. "Nediatization or Mediation? Alternative Understandings of the Emergent Space of Digital Storytelling." *New Media and Society* 10:373–91.

Deresiewicz, William. 2011. "Generation Sell." *New York Times Magazine*, November 12. http://www.nytimes.com/2011/11/13/opinion/sunday/the-entrepreneurial-generation.html?pagewanted=all&_r=0. Accessed January 20, 2013.

Dünne, Jorg, and Christian Moser. 2008. "Allgemeine Einleitung. Automedialität." In *Automedialität: Subjektkonstitution in Schrift, Bild und neuen Medien*, 7–18. Munich: W. Fink.

Elahi, Hasan. 2011. http://trackingtransience.net/. Accessed March 21, 2012.

Graxian, David. 2003. *Blue Chicago: The Search for Authenticity in Urban Blues Clubs.* Chicago: University of Chicago Press.

Gray, Mary. 2009. "Negotiating Identities/Queering Desires: Coming Out Online and the Remediation of the Coming-Out Story." *Journal of Computer-Mediated Communication* 14:1162–89.

Halberstam, Judith/Jack. 2005. *In a Queer Time and Place: Transgender Bodies, Subcultural Lives.* New York: New York University Press.

Hayles, N. Katherine. 2003. "Deeper into the Machine: The Future of Electronic Literature." *Culture Machine* 5. http://www.culturemachine.net/index.php/cm/article/viewArticle/245/241. Accessed June 15, 2012.

Jackson, Shelley. 1997. *My Body, A Wunderkammer.* Available at http://www.altx.com/thebody/, accessed by Ruth E. Page, November 20, 2007.

Kennedy, Helen. 2006. "Beyond Anonymity, or Future Directions for Internet Identity Research." *New Media and Society* 8, no. 6: 859–76.

Lambert, Joe. 2012. *Digital Storytelling: Capturing Lives, Creating Community.* 4th ed. New York: Routledge.

McPherson, Tara. 2011. "After the Archive: Scholarship in the Digital Era." Paper presented at the Institute for the Humanities, University of Michigan, November 29.

Nakamura, Lisa. 2008. "Cyberrace." *PMLA* 123, no. 5 (Winter): 1673–82.

Mihm, Stephen. 2007. "The 24/7 Alibi." *New York Times Magazine*, December 9. http://www.nytimes.com/2007/12/09/magazine/09247alibi.html?_r=0. Accessed January 20, 2013.

Mills, Jennifer. 2009–11. *What's in a Name?* Water color with pencil on paper. Queensland Art Gallery. http://www.qagoma.qld.gov.au/collection/contemporary_australian_art/jennifer_mills. Accessed January 20, 2013.

Noguchi, Yuki. 2011. "Following Digital Breadcrumbs to 'Big Data' Gold." National Public Radio, *Morning Edition*, November 29.

Page, Ruth E. 2008. "Stories of the Self on and off the Screen." In *Electronic Literature: New Horizons for the Literary*, edited by N. Katherine Hayles. http://newhorizons.eliterature.org/index.php. Accessed February 21, 2012.

————. 2011. *Stories and Social Media: Identities and Interaction.* London: Routledge.

Paul, Christopher A. 2010. "Process, Paratexts, and Texts: Rhetorical Analysis and Virtual Worlds." *Journal of Virtual Worlds Research* 3, no. 1 (November): 4–17. http://seattleu .academia.edu/ChristopherAPaul/Papers/1236770/Process_Paratexts_and_Texts_ Rhetorical_Analysis_and_Virtual_Worlds. Accessed June 15, 2012.

Poletti, Anna. 2011. "Intimate Economies: PostSecret and the Affect of Confession." *Biography* 34, no. 1 (Winter): 25–36.

Pooley, Jeff. 2011. "Authentic? Get Real." Quoted in the *New York Times*, Sunday Style Section, September 11, 1–2.

Rotman, Brian. 2009. "Gesture and the I Fold." *Parallax* 15, no. 4: 68–82.

Schmitz, J. 1997. "Structural Relations, Electronic Media, and Social Change: The Public Electronic Network and the Homeless." In *Virtual Culture: Technology, Consumption and Identity*, edited by S. G. Jones, 80–101. London: Routledge.

Siegel, Steffen. 2012. "Sich selbst im Auge behalten: Selbstüberwachung und die Bilderpolitik des Indiskreten." ("Keeping an Eye on Oneself: Self-surveillance and the Cultural Politics of Indiscretion.") *KulturPoetik* 12, no. 1: 92–108.

Singer, Emily. 2011. "The Measured Life." *Technology Review*, July/August, 38–45.

Smith, Sidonie, and Julia Watson. 2010. *Reading Autobiography.* 2nd ed. Minneapolis: University of Minnesota Press.

————. 2012. "Witness or False Witness? Metrics of Authenticity, Collective 'I'-Formations, and the Ethic of Verification in First-Person Testimony." *Biography* (Fall): 590–626.

Turkle, Sherry. 2012. *Alone Together: Why We Expect More from Technology and Less from Each Other.* New York: Basic Books.

Wolf, Gary. 2010. "The Data-Driven Life." *New York Times Magazine*, May 10, 38–45.

Wright, Tom. 2004. *In Search of Oldton.* http://www.oldton.com/my_oldton.html. Accessed November 20, 2007.

IDENTITY AFFORDANCES

Adultery Technologies

MELISSA GREGG

For some of us—perhaps the fortunate, or at least,
the affluent—monogamy is the only serious philosophical question.

—ADAM PHILLIPS, *Monogamy*

Life is short. Have an affair.

ashleymadison.com

In August 2011 the Japanese company Manuscript was forced to amend the settings of its new software application, *Karelog* (Boyfriend Log), in response to consumer complaints. Drawing on GPS technology, the service allowed users to log in from a computer to track another person's phone. In the program's first release, these surveillance capacities also stretched to include accessing the mobile's call history and remaining battery life. Promotional material for the product targeted anxious girlfriends wanting to know the whereabouts of partners. But within days of the public launch, the antivirus software giant McAfee labeled the app a "Potentially Unwanted Program," because users had no way of knowing the technology had been installed or what information was being logged and sent. The problem was not so much the capacity of the application—GPS tracking is already used for other caring purposes, such as parents staying in touch with children. The crime was that women were encouraged to install the app without their partners' permission. The language of Internet security literalized the threat that the program posed as an example of everyday spyware.

Facing the media, Yoshinori Miura, the president of the fledgling software firm, admitted the product's publicity involved some cynicism: "We were still a largely unknown company, so I thought that we could grab attention by focusing on anti-cheating programs, but we went too far. I didn't think we [would] get so much criticism" (MSN 2011). The official apology also addressed the gender discrimination inherent to the application design. Press reports acknowledged that there was nothing about the technology that stopped it from being used by both genders; nonetheless the aesthetics of design showed clear allegiance to the established traits of Japanese *kawaii*, or "cute" (Hjorth 2009; McLelland 2009).[1]

While Boyfriend Log made headlines in Japanese- and English-language media, gendered assumptions have also affected the release of similar surveillance programs in the United States. For example, iTrust is an iPhone app that reveals whether a significant other has been tampering with one's text. In contrast to the Boyfriend Log, iTrust turns the tables to allow phone owners to maintain privacy. A fake home screen locks the mobile in the user's absence at the same time as it records the traces of interfering fingers. In the demo video for the program, a female voice-over describes a failed attempt to read her boyfriend's messages in a moment of boredom. Like the men offended by Karelog's marketing, this casting decision did not escape the notice of commenters responding to the story on industry stalwart news website Mashable.[2]

Karelog and iTrust are only the tip of the iceberg when it comes to the booming market for online intimacy surveillance. The most heavily promoted spouse surveillance packages deploy familiar tropes, including "007 Spy," "stealth software" and "spy agent" alongside a host of popular detective imagery (hats and overcoats, magnifying glasses, zoom lenses) to reinforce the secrecy and strength of the service. High-ranking search results point to such websites as Catch Cheaters, E-Spy, Spouse Spy, and Spy Tech, all of which portray glamorous conniving couples with telltale signs of suspicious activity. These signs and symbols reinforce the software's capacity to encode the identity of "cheater" and "cheated" with great efficiency. Vague statistics on the prevalence of affairs promote the basis for these identities and the broader industry of infidelity.[3]

In these depictions, marital disloyalty often appears as a subcategory or niche demographic for a product also marketed to employers to ensure workers' appropriate behavior. Here the shop-floor discipline of the factory finds its equivalence in the domestic surveillance adultery technologies evoke and police (Kipnis 2003). Dubious promotional testimonies highlight the ease with which monitoring equipment can be deployed. These YouTube-style confessionals collected from ostensibly aggrieved and at times hostile and aggressive partners draw on authenticating "user-generated" aesthetics to reinforce product credentials. The willingness of these alleged customers to reveal themselves as users, with or without providing "real" names, raises important questions of legality, literacy, and class in contemporary friendship networks.

The very need for adultery technologies is symptomatic of a moment in which some individuals see limited options for intimate support—few visions or practices of community—other than the fulfillment to be gained from a dependent partner. As Laura Kipnis (2003) argues, the modern relationship is one in which lovers "must know everything there is to know about one another" (162). This accords with broader transformations in intimacy, which encourage openness and communication between self-directed individuals (Giddens 1992; Illouz 2007). The practice of "withholding information or having secrets is a definite warning sign of relationship distress," since "in principle nothing should be off limits (even if on occasion, 'making sure' may be required)" (Kipnis 2003, 162–63). Spouse-monitoring software provides the means for "making sure." It demonstrates a major tenet of contemporary intimacy in so far as it presumes there is no need for privacy "if there's nothing to hide" (163).

This same commitment to transparency is regularly expressed when the social media entrepreneur Mark Zuckerberg defends the privacy policies of Facebook (Lind 2010; Dash 2010). These mutually affirming logics regard surveillance and trust as equivalent, as if no other model of witnessing could provide a preferable form of security. Additional examples of adultery technologies along with practices, which while not explicitly sexual may produce adulterous effects, questions the symmetry of surveillance and security in its more paranoid registers (Sedgwick 2003). This chapter offers a reading of social media use to highlight the forms of communal witnessing taking place online and the networks of concern that are emerging in information rich work/lifestyles.

Busted: Criminal Conversations and the Crime of Secrecy

Spousebusting technologies use a range of measures, from keystroke logs to hidden voice recorders, to produce the certainty of adultery. The applications and their professional agents respond to long-standing anxieties about love, commitment, and faith that are not unique to the present, although their emergence is a useful reflection of the intensity and claustrophobia of modern monogamous coupledom (Kauffman 2009). On one level, intimacy surveillance of this kind might be read in terms of the wider shift, in Deleuzian terms, to a control society: the dimensions of power and knowledge that emerge when relationships are less a matter of intersubjectivity and more about negotiating packets of data that project an identity as meaningful (Deleuze 1992). In a related vein, Dominic Pettman (2006) argues that love is itself a technology following socially agreed scripts and protocols. Surveillance software heightens sensitivity to the "structural unknowability of one's beloved": "One's partner is no longer the immediate flesh-and-blood creature that one seeks to 'hold onto' but the nocturnal source of unfathomable, intangible, keyboard-based professions of love to someone known only as BayArea_Betty. Someone's 'personality' is—to use Heidegger's formula—unlocked, transformed, stored, distributed, and switched from home and hearth to the cold global mediascape which lurks on the other side of a modem" (176).

Data bits and code are thus the latest in a long history of discursive representation, which have been used to evince and police middle-class heterosexual etiquette, given the patriarchal exchanges traditionally dependent on marriage. David Turner (2002) reminds us that monitoring and surveillance strategies were key to proving cases of adultery in seventeenth-century England. In the shift from religious to civil discourse, both the charge of adultery and the insults attached to actors, had to convey appropriate condemnation at a time when the practice was thought to be quite widespread. Initial appeals to traits of "generosity" relied on a male code of honor of fellow feeling and belief in benevolent sociability. Adultery "was not just morally wrong but beyond the pale of polite society" (64). To engage in intimate relations with another was therefore to partake in a "criminal conversation" (47). Opportunities for men and women to engage in "wicked," "illegal," or "libidinous" conversations increased with wider social changes in the use of public and private space, whether it was the drapes dividing and secluding domestic interiors and chambers, or the parks and parties providing the social spaces of metropolitan culture. By the 1700s, the transgression of adultery carried specific consequences. For men this entailed a failure of responsibility and an abuse of domestic authority if the affair was with a servant. For women, adultery generated "revulsion" among society members who read the actions as upsetting convention in an act of "domestic rebellion."

Turner's study is a useful background for understanding the different geographical and social terrain of online platforms and mobile digital devices today. He isolates how legal cases of adultery came to be associated with location, namely "private and suspicious" places (2002, 157). It is here that adultery takes some of its modern meaning as being almost synonymous with secrecy. Court testimony from neighbors, servants, and others illustrates that the refusal to open a door, or having a locked as opposed to a "latched" door, were each taken to indicate "a crime of secrecy" between conspiring couples (158; see also Robertson 2012). Turner uses reporting from cuckoldry and adultery trials along with analysis of publishing avenues such as plays and novels to show how intimate encounters came to broader public attention. As Turner concludes, this focus on the affairs of the elite class "did much to further the opinion that the *beau monde* lived by a code of sexual manners significantly removed from the rest of society" (2002, 193). In an important addition, he notes that "for upper-class women who formed the majority of defendants in adultery suits, there are signs that physical intimacies, a desire for attention and attempts to escape boredom may have been important elements of love affairs alongside sexual attraction" (197).

Spousebusting websites list a host of incriminating activities performed by partners, from staying late at the office to extended phone calls with mysterious others. These "private and suspicious" practices are exacerbated by virtual and mobile platforms, which render physical space malleable. Cell phones that fit neatly in pockets, only to vibrate discreetly against the body without public intrusion, are design innovations that assist "libidinous conversations." Over the course of a decade, SMS (short message service) text has only consolidated its reputation for pithy flirtation (Shahin 2002).[4] The growing crop of adultery websites, alongside more generic channels like Skype and Facebook, provide further "publishing avenues" for private conversation in addition to the circulation of gossip. On the home page of Ashley Madison, Australia's leading dating service for the married, media testimonials prove the newsworthiness of adultery and its currency as an everyday preoccupation. The growing market for these services confirms the appetite for illicit conversations among a digitally literate and apparently promiscuous demographic, just as the quasi-publics of social networking sites stage witnessing opportunities for suspicious partners and heartbroken exes alike (Gershon 2010).

What counts as adultery in virtual space is subject to contention.[5] The case of Anthony Weiner (D-NY), the congressman forced to resign in the wake of a Twitter photo scandal in 2010, shows the loopholes that continue to exist in the United States as to what "having sexual relations" with a woman might mean (Berlant and Duggan 2001). Caught tweeting a picture of his underpants to a girl he'd met on his work website, the unfortunately named Weiner had little chance of surviving the uproar, given his initial panicked claim that his account had been hacked. That the *New York Times* could devote an entire "Room for Debate" opinion forum to "sexting" following the event remains a marker of the vast industry of commentary and opinion devoted to intimacy etiquette. In the history of adultery, it is never just the act of intercourse that is at issue, when it is even proven. Rather, it is the character of actors whose betrayal of the marriage institution is an affront to "every strained metaphor that it sustains" as a model of loyalty, consent, and trust (Kipnis 2003, 188).

ADULTERY AND BOREDOM

That adultery anxiety continues to focus on the elite class is certainly evident in the routine tactics of electoral politics whether of the Right or the Left. But

Turner's suggestion that women's extramarital activity is often the result of broader influences requires further consideration. The association between adultery and boredom takes on interesting inflections in a contemporary context when—in contrast to previous centuries—the professional and working class is just as likely to be female. Suzanne Leonard's (2007) account of boredom and adultery in Hollywood narratives sees feminist potential in films that "give voice to the condition of female boredom" and "do so in a way that is attentive to the sorts of economic arrangements" to which women are often condemned (112). Leonard outlines the dialectical balance between the feminist-positive legacy of paid work and the mythology of heterosexual marriage "as both the greatest achievement and the producer of the greatest happiness" for women (102). She reads "the female adultery trope" as a challenge to both the "celebratory rhetorics of the female worker and to the rampant overvaluation of the marital imperative" in postfeminist media culture (107). Acknowledging the repetitive drudgery of service industry work, an employment experience that only echoes the experience of women's unpaid labor in the home, the adultery narrative "persuasively connects an exploration of marital boredom" to working conditions that are far from liberating. These ideas accord with Kipnis's (2003) observation that "[i]nsofar as adultery represents discontent, insofar as it acts on that discontent—even in unformed, inchoate, often temporary ways 'it implies' a nascent demand for 'something else'" and "has the potential to model uprisings in other social spheres" (198). Leonard (2007) concurs that "the adultery narrative, already well able to debunk marital mythology, thus presents itself as a likely vehicle through which to *also* energize a workplace critique" (114).[6]

Leonard's project responds to the mainstream experience whereby women are increasingly encouraged to view the workplace as a complement, if not wholly an alternative, to the relationships available in the domestic sphere (McRobbie 2007). In this sense, Leonard's reading has pertinence beyond the low-wage sector that is, importantly, her focus. I began thinking about adultery seriously when researching the work and home lives of a range of employees in information jobs in cultural organizations and the media (Gregg 2011). In interviews and diary reflections, it became clear that work-related thoughts were an accommodating contrast to the concerns of domesticity, especially for those whose long-term relationships might require much more complicated attention. To take just one example, here is an excerpt from a diary entry made by Jenny, a project officer for a library, who was asked to record when she performs paid work at home:

Have noticed my partner does get annoyed when I log on at night to check my
email. I try to limit it but I sometimes find myself quickly checking my email
  - before he gets home
  - when he goes to the shop
  - when he is downstairs gardening etc.
I check my email constantly because I think to try and stay organized, "on top of
things." I do not want any surprises.

The final sentence indicates how Jenny's e-mail monitoring behavior is a somewhat conditioned response to her unpredictable workload and the coercive e-mail
preferences maintained by her colleagues. But her relationship to the technology also comes across as a series of opportunities to be seized in moments free
from surveillance. Indeed, Jenny's e-mail habit reads somewhat like a clandes-
tine affair that needs to be hidden from her partner. Contact with work here
manifests as a kind of adultery.

Jenny's attachment to work clearly competes with the other relationships in
her life, and others in the study, women and men alike, showed similar patterns.
This is what I call "presence bleed": where the expectation of professional availability presents new dilemmas about the appropriate spaces and drivers for intimacy. In Jenny's case, her regular contact with work and routine access to this
side of her identity offset some of the banalities of domestic space. She admitted
catching up on e-mail and other administrative labor at times when her partner's
preferences (watching football or a movie) took precedence. Jenny's satisfaction
in staying on top of her work makes us speculate whether professional women
may feel valued pursuing job-related tasks beyond necessary requirements when
their options for fulfillment are limited in the home, much like the adulterous
affairs of wealthy ladies in previous centuries. In this curious scenario, paid
work takes on the characteristics of consolation and distraction that we associate
with infatuation—adulterous or otherwise (Armstrong 2003). As professionals
acknowledge the "guilty pleasures" they gain from creative and rewarding work,
this prompts us to ask, along with adultery more generally, whether it poses a
complement or threat to the primacy of the couple.

LONG HOURS, HIGH BANDWIDTH

Another way of drawing connections between adultery and work is to observe
how long-hours cultures produce their own forms of intimacy, and not only
does this mean affiliations between coworkers who share a physical location in
an office or workspace. It is hardly incidental that the secretary/boss is an iconic

image of adultery; the genre of work-based romance is resilient enough to be a regularly actualized cliché. But more broadly, the online networks that have proven a major feature of the past decade encompass the chat windows of colleagues and micronetworking of "buddies," "followers," and "fans." Couples with jobs dependent on computer use took advantage of online platforms to communicate with each other during the long workday. Mood changes, events, and random trivia could be broadcast from distant locations, and the reach of these messages extended not only to partners but also to workmates, friends, and family. Patrick, a breakfast-radio producer, and Adam, a freelance writer, were particularly adept at keeping profiles up to date since their work schedules rarely saw them at home together. These online exchanges even took on the function of domestic intimacy in the sense that shared space, lived and inhabited together for a prolonged period, played host to the couple's relationship.

New media technologies' effects on long-term coupledom occur on at least two levels. First, partners reckon with the possibility of having unprecedented knowledge about their mate's daily travails beyond proximate observation. Time spent at work isn't neatly separate from intimate others, as social media relieve the loneliness and separation of home and market spheres. Meanwhile, returning home from the office, selected networks following online updates have the chance to witness the rhythms, realities, and even shortcomings of friends' domestic relationships. Ongoing commentary about home-based activities joins an accumulation of regular posted items as individuals log in more or less often at different times of the week. Friends can even provide a comforting role for each other when their partners are busy at work. The benefits of online intimacy here include the possibility of expanding the always limited caring capacities of the couple. Virtual friends assist and alleviate the pressure on partners when work and other commitments prevent them from acting as the sole source of intimacy.

Of course, the popularity of Facebook and other ambient media platforms is also due to their role in offsetting boredom, in similar ways to those outlined earlier, and this adds to their adulterous potential. The solitude of the lunch break or the suburban commute is softened as friends literally appear in the palm of one's hand, offering respite from the isolation of "alienated" labor. These online companions reconfigure the spatial organization of the Fordist work world, which relied on distinct realms of home and office, and an accompanying gender bias for each. Following friends across the course of the day is the unique experience of communal witnessing that mobile technologies facilitate. Their one-to-many address is not so much infinite as a "public" in Warner's (2002) sense: an audience that exists "at the moment of attention" (2002). As a model for community, it is preferable to the paranoid outlook of spousebusting sites, since it acknowledges the productive modes of interest, concern, and affection that dwell beyond the insularism of the couple. Such platforms provide a release valve for the normative and overbearing expectations of monogamy—the intense pressure that is placed on the couple when society offers few other possibilities for ethical conduct and recognition (Shumway 2003).

Beyond Adultery Anxiety

Mobile devices and their accompanying services hold the capacity to deliver all kinds of discreet communication, some of which may be compromising, amusing, and sexual. Take the example of TigerText, an application that allows users to "cover their tracks" by deleting SMS messages within predetermined time periods. Named after the animal notoriously difficult to trace, and emerging before Tiger Woods lay claim to the title of world's most notorious cheater, Tiger-Text is just one of the technical innovations enabling "criminal conversations" well into the present. In true *Get Smart* fashion, messages can now self-destruct. These design breakthroughs circumvent the obsession with knowingness and transparency that pervades contemporary understandings of intimacy, and this may be their great benefit. A politics of erasure is an alternative framework for care that a control society makes possible. By contrast, spousebusting epistemologies only continue the detective work inaugurated by "the love plot": where knowing *something* about what a person feels about us is *everything* (Berlant 2001; italics mine). But the wider question of what infidelity tells us is worth much greater discussion. According to Adam Phillips (1996): "Infidelity is as much about the drama of truth-telling as it is about the drama of sexuality. It is only because of sexuality that we think about truth at all; that we find honesty and kindness at odds with each other" (4). If a technological fix like TigerText can facilitate an overthrow of adultery's obsession with exposure, we may even be witnessing a shift away from the wider structural pressures that emphasize sex as the truth of oneself (Foucault 1978).

With the marriage institution under severe renovation as a result of feminist and queer political activism, adultery anxieties remain an important index of radicalism. But they are also a useful means to gain insights into the organization of knowledge in the present. To the extent that adultery remains an obsession, it reflects the paucity of intimate relationships that Western notions of love and romance actively harness (Rosa 1994). In an era of data flow and control, even "virtual" sex still resembles the ultimate transgression, requiring professional skills to navigate the broadening expanse of the "digital enclosure"

(Andrejevic 2007). Such epistemologies of entrapment need to be rethought in a context where the stakes involved in domesticity, property, and alimony are no longer so fraught. In a postfeminist culture, we must wonder whose interests are served by holding adultery as a technical and moral offense when women's material wealth is increasingly independently amassed.

For the middle classes to whom this argument applies, history has always shown them to be innovators in love (Bourdieu 1984). If the written word and print publishing were crucial to circulating knowledge of citizens' affairs in the past, what we are seeing today is a split in the forms of intimacy and discretion available to different social groups. In today's reconfiguration of middle-class subjectivity, online and mobile media provide a new discursive space to experiment and improvise in the realm of sexual politesse and manners. These elements of society and association available to professionals stand in contrast to the surveillance solutions adopted by isolated others. Spousebusting services are an inkling of what happens to those outside the sphere of digital literacy, those without access to elite networks of opportunity that provide salvation from love's material benefits. In this sense, the mundane pedagogy of intimate surveillance reveals less about our capacity to be desirable and more about the changing nature of social belonging.

Yet even for the middle class, in an era of "liquid love" (Bauman 2003), a decline in occupational security means the workplace and the domestic unit are equally challenged to provide reliable displays of recognition, identity, and support. Ashley Madison's claim, "life is short, have an affair," plays on the temporality of redundancy in software design and job security as much as it invokes the figure of the philanderer who trades in longevity for a new model. Such appeals gain traction in a culture enamored with the upgrade. However, outsourcing our concerns about ontological and economic precarity to the surveillance of strangers is not a necessary outcome. Anxieties about adultery are always anxieties about security, about understanding who can be counted upon to deliver something that may never remain the same but is expected to be in the absence of more sustaining relationships. To move beyond the "hermeneutics of suspicion" (Sedgwick 2003) that adultery technologies exacerbate, we must demand and promote a wider ecology of care that allows long-term relationships of all kinds to flourish. In this venture, "how we love and how we work can hardly be separate questions" (Kipnis 2003, 24). This chapter provides the opening for an argument suggesting that it is capitalism's insecure workplaces, more so than the sex lives of fallible partners, that hold the key to a wider drama. It is the amorality of this economic model, and its knock-on effects for our relationships, that continues to require our most vocal condemnation.

NOTES

1. Steve Levenstein at *Inventor Spot* wrote: "[I]t takes no knowledge of Japanese to know the pink and lacy graphics at the Karelog website are designed to attract a female demographic. If that's not enough, check out the image of a big-eyed black kitty (with pink hairbow à la Hello Kitty) gazing longfully at her Android-phone-clutching, pants-wearing tomcat. With that said, there's no reason why anyone of any gender can['t] use Karelog to spy on anyone of any gender. Let the paranoia-fest begin!" (Levenstein 2011).

2. One viewer, Pascal-Emmanuel Gobry, commented: "This video is really, really offensive. After all, everyone knows girls are dishonest and go through your stuff, and totally clueless about technology so unable to hit the 'home' button on an iPhone. Maybe this app is for men who have girlfriends but I'm pretty sure the guys who made the app don't have, and never will have one" (http://mashable.com/2010/01/18/itrust/, accessed March 7, 2012).

3. See http://catch-cheaters.net/, http://www.e-spy-software.com/signs_of_cheating_spouse.htm, http://www.spousespy.com.au, and http://www.spytech-web.com/spouse-monitoring.shtml, as well as www.spousebusters.com.au, a major inspiration for this chapter given its prominent advertising in suburban Australian pubs at the time of writing. The legalities of these monitoring programs are complex given that many developed and advertised on U.S. websites are distributed worldwide.

4. Shahin's article on use of SMS in India is notable not only for its historical interest but also its recognition of the significant consequences for women engaged in extra-marital relationships in religious and caste-controlled cultures. See also Vasudev (2002). In Iran, "temporary marriages" have emerged as a stopgap solution to avoid the serious consequences of adultery for women (Sciolino 2000), which include flogging, fines, and even death—the latter also being the case in parts of India (Blakely 2010).

5. Recalling the memorable debates in Internet studies precipitated by Julian Dibbell's "A Rape in Cyberspace," originally published in the *Village Voice* in 1993.

6. Kipnis's work reinvigorates for a popular audience a tradition of anti-monogamy thinking within women's liberation movements through the 1970s and 1980s (as recounted by Jackson and Scott 2004) and even the early 1990s (see Rosa 1994) prior to the more wholesale ascension of queer theory in the academy.

REFERENCES

Andrejevic, Mark. 2007. "Ubiquitous Computing and the Digital Enclosure Movement." *Media International Australia* 125:106–17.

Armstrong, John. 2002. "The Romantic Vision." In *Conditions of Love: The Philosophy of Intimacy*, 1–7. New York: W. W. Norton and Co.

Bauman, Zygmunt. 2003. "Falling In and Out of Love." In *Liquid Love: On the Fragility of Human Bonds*, 1–37. Cambridge: Polity Press.

Berlant, Lauren. 2001. "Love, a Queer Feeling." In *Homosexuality and Psychoanalysis*, edited by Tim Dean and Christopher Lane, 432–51. Chicago: University of Chicago Press.

Berlant, Lauren, and Lisa Duggan, eds. 2001. *Our Monica, Ourselves: The Clinton Affair and the National Interest*. New York: New York University Press.

Blakely, Rhys. 2010. "Mobiles Ban 'to Save Arranged Marriages.'" *Australian*, November 26. http://www.theaustralian.com.au/news/world/mobiles-ban-to-save-arranged -marriages/story-e6frg6so-1225961109005. Accessed November 26, 2010.

Bourdieu, Pierre. 1984. *Distinction: A Social Critique of the Judgment of Taste*. Translated by Richard Nice. Cambridge, MA: Harvard University Press.

Dash, Anil. 2010. "The Facebook Reckoning." *Anil Dash*. September 13, 2010. http:// dashes.com/anil/2010/09/the-facebook-reckoning-1.html. Accessed March 7, 2012.

Deleuze, Gilles. 1992. "Postscript on the Societies of Control." *October* 59:3–7.

Dibbell, Julian. 1993. "A Rape in Cyberspace: How an Evil Clown, a Haitian Trickster Spirit, Two Wizards, and a Cast of Dozens Turned a Database Into a Society." *Village Voice*, December 23. http://www.juliandibbell.com/texts/bungle_vv.html. Accessed August 1, 2012.

Foucault, Michel. 1978. *The History of Sexuality*. Vol. 1. New York: Pantheon.

Gershon, Illana. 2010. *The Breakup 2.0: Disconnecting Over New Media*. Ithaca, NY: Cornell University Press.

Giddens, Anthony. 1992. *The Transformation of Intimacy: Sexuality, Love, and Eroticism in Modern Societies*. Stanford, CA: Stanford University Press.

Gregg, Melissa. 2011. *Work's Intimacy*. London: Polity Press.

Hjorth, Larissa. 2009. *Mobile Media in the Asia-Pacific: Gender and the Art of Being Mobile*. London: Routledge.

Huffington Post. 2011. "Anthony Weiner Resigns: Congressman Announces Resignation at Press Conference." June 16. http://www.huffingtonpost.com/2011/06/16/ Anthony-weiner-resigns_n_878229tml. Accessed March 7, 2012.

Illouz, Eva. 2007. *Cold Intimacies: The Making of Emotional Capitalism*. London: Polity Press.

Jackson, Stevi, and Sue Scott. 2004. "The Personal is Still Political: Heterosexuality, Feminism, and Monogamy." *Feminism and Psychology* 14, no. 1: 151–57.

Kaufmann, Jean-Claude. 2009. *Gripes: The Little Quarrels of Couples*. Translated by Helen Morrison. Cambridge, MA: Polity Press.

Kipnis, Laura. 2003. *Against Love: A Polemic*. New York: Pantheon Books.

Leonard, Suzanne. 2007. "'I Hate My Job, I Hate Everybody Here': Adultery, Boredom, and the 'Working Girl' in Twenty-First-Century American Cinema." In *Interrogating Postfeminism: Gender and the Politics of Popular Culture*, edited by Diane Negra and Yvonne Tasker, 100–131. Durham, NC: Duke University Press.

Levenstein, Steve. 2011. "Android App Allows Jealous Girls to Remotely Follow Their Boyfriends." *Investor Spot*. http://inventorspot.com/articles/android_app_allows_jeal ous_girls_remotely_follow_their_boyfriend. Accessed March 7, 2012.

Lind, Dara. 2010. "Mark Zuckerberg's Silver-Spoon Vanguardism." *Think Progress*. Last modified May 28. http://yglesias.thinkprogress.org/2010/05/mark-zuckerbergs-sil ver-spoon-vanguardism/. Accessed March 7, 2012.

McLelland, Mark, ed. 2009. "Japanese Transnational Fandoms and Female Consumers." *Intersections: Gender and Sexuality in Asia and the Pacific* 20. http://intersections.anu .edu.au/issue20_contents.htm.

McRobbie, Angela. 2007. "Top Girls? Young Women and the Postfeminist Sexual Contract." *Cultural Studies* 21, no. 4–5: 718–37.

MSN. 2011. "'Anti-cheating Boyfriend' App Forced to Change." *NineMSN*, October 17. http://news.ninemsn.com.au/article.aspx?id=8361319. Accessed March 7, 2012.

Pettman, Dominic. 2006. *Love and Other Technologies: Retrofitting Eros for the Information Age.* New York: Fordham University Press.

Phillips, Adam. 1996. *Monogamy.* New York: Random House.

Robertson, Stephen. 2012. "Private Detectives and Privacy." Paper presented at the "Surveillance and/in Everyday Life Conference," University of Sydney, February 20.

Rosa, Becky. 1994. "Anti-Monogamy: A Radical Challenge to Compulsory Heterosexuality?" In *Stirring it: Challenges for Feminism*, edited by Gabriele Griffin, Marianne Hester, Shirin Rai, and Sasha Roseneil, 107–20. London: Taylor and Francis.

Sciolino, Elaine. 2000. "Love Finds a Way in Iran: 'Temporary Marriage.'" *New York Times*, October 4. Archived at http://www.library.cornell.edu/colldev/mideast/tmpmrig .htm. Accessed March 7, 2012.

Sedgwick, Eve Kosofsky. 2003. "Paranoid Reading and Reparative Reading, or, You're So Paranoid, You Probably Think This Essay Is About You." In *Touching Feeling: Affect, Pedagogy, Performativity*, 123–52. Durham, NC: Duke University Press.

Shahin, Sultan. 2002. "India's Love Affair with Hi-Tech Flirting." *Asia Times Online*, November 8. http://www.atimes.com/atimes/South_Asia/DK08Df02tml. Accessed March 7, 2012.

Shumway, David. 2003. *Modern Love: Romance, Intimacy, and the Marriage Crisis.* New York: New York University Press.

Turner, David M. 2002. *Fashioning Adultery: Gender, Sex, and Civility in England, 1660–1740.* Cambridge: Cambridge University Press.

Vargas, Jose Antonio. 2010. "The Face of Facebook." *New Yorker*, September 20. http://www.newyorker.com/reporting/2010/09/20/100920fa_fact_vargas?currentPage=all. Accessed March 7, 2012.

Vasudev, Shefalee. 2002. "Love in the Time of SMS." *India Today*, October 14. http://www.india-today.com/itoday/20021014/cover.shtml. Accessed March 7, 2012.

Warner, Michael. 2002. *Publics and Counterpublics.* Cambridge, MA: MIT Press.

Facebook and Coaxed Affordances

AIMÉE MORRISON

In a 2007 *PMLA* article addressing "the changing profession," Nancy K. Miller (2007) suggests that "[a]utobiography may emerge as a master form in the twenty-first century" (545). Recognizing both the expansion and explosion of popular forms of published autobiography, and the strength and durability of what Sidonie Smith and Julia Watson have called "the memoir boom" (Smith and Watson 2010, 127), Miller points to the rich variety of texts and contexts animating autobiographical production and consumption, as well as to the necessity of promoting a similar richness in scholarly approach. She happily concludes that, in the face of such variety and plenitude, "[a]cademics have risen to the occasion with refreshing inventiveness" (Miller 2007, 546). Since that publication, popular Internet life writing forms—among them blogs, vlogs, and social network sites—have begun to demand a similar inventiveness.

Such invention proceeds in fits and starts, but the challenges presented by digital life writing are arguably more sweeping and various than those uncovered by the graphic memoirs and print "autobiofictionalography" Miller considers in her survey. Digital life writing maps a realm with no gatekeepers, editors, or canons, producing texts to excess on a scale of production and publication that completely overwhelms the boutique reading practices of literary scholarship. Digital life writing develops normative writing and reading practices that shift with each software upgrade or each new cultural meme. Digital life writing troubles the hard-won notion of the artfulness of auto/biographical texts as the basis for their appropriateness as objects of scholarly attention. Digital life writing, in fact, poses a kind of limit case of autobiographical theory and criticism, at once terrifying and compelling in its sheer scale and its wide-open popular production.

How can we understand the Facebook status update? This is a deceptively modest question, one that will generate further pointed inquiries into digital life writing practices in all their variety. Facebook offers both fertile ground and a terrible problem to auto/biography scholars. That the service cries out for auto-biographical analysis seems beyond doubt. That more than 1 billion people are enrolled in the network, with more than half of them accessing Facebook daily, renders that analysis as urgent as it is important (Facebook 2012). But fundamental questions confront the analyst, questions that are complicated to formulate, let alone answer: What are the ethics of the interpolation of the stories and voices of others into a user's digital life narrative? What to make of the use of photographs? What social pressures are at play in determining what is written on the site and who can see it? These are serious questions, but insofar as they pertain to the relationality of identity, the ethics of life storytelling, or the role of visual material in autographic narratives, auto/biography studies is well enough equipped already to handle them.

But what if, as Gillian Whitlock and Anna Poletti suggest, social network sites present "auto-assemblages" rather than authored texts as such (Whitlock and Poletti 2008, xiv)? Whitlock and Poletti describe these auto-assemblages as "the result of ongoing selection and appropriation of content across several modes brought together into a constellation for the purpose of self-representation or life narrative" (xv).[1] To account for the "auto" of this "assemblage" would be to acknowledge the necessity of dealing with the technological characteristics of digital media. And so the fact of Facebook poses us yet more questions, perhaps even thornier for auto/biography scholars to address and for which less groundwork has been laid. We must begin to consider the style sheets that organize display of user-generated materials; the input prompts that coax and restrict user action by turns; the ever-shifting privacy settings that dramatically and continually reset the boundaries between personal narrative and public dissemination; and the automated, algorithm-driven recitation of users' actions across their social graphs. Each shapes the resulting digital life writing "text" as much as do the more traditional authorial practices of a typing subject deliberately arranging her life into a story. Whitlock and Poletti (2008) assert that scholars must consider "how the functionality of the software, in conjunction with the cultures of usage . . . , shape the production of specific autographic performances" (xvi). One way to proceed, they note, is by "asking precise questions about software" (xvi). To do just this, the path forward must be mapped by both auto/biography and new media studies. A conjunction of the methods and insights of these fields offers real explanatory power, a means by which to engage substantively with online texts as instances and genres of digital life writing produced in and through both social practices and technological artifacts.

By opening the status update function of Facebook to analysis here, I delineate a generalizable interpretive methodology that balances key ideas from two scholarly discourse communities: from autobiography studies, the notion of "coaxing" imbricates with the theory of "affordances," drawn from the social studies of science and technology. Taken together, coaxing and affordances offer a theory and a method by which to read how and why Facebook and its users are mutually implicated in the construction of digital life writing texts on that site.

Is "Facebook" a Coercive Technology?

The question of what Facebook *is* seems to be a vexed one. How we understand the service and its relationship to its users necessarily colors our interpretations of the life-writing texts solicited, produced, and consumed through that platform. In February 2004, "Thefacebook" was a hobby project devised by some Harvard students to employ technical wizardry for intramural social purposes. There were no ads; it was a closed network; strong privacy was the default (Kirkpatrick 2010, 29). By February 2012, Facebook had become an enormous media company preparing for an initial public stock offering at a market valuation of $100 billion (Raice 2011). Advertising is its main source of revenue; the network is global and expanding exponentially; "radical transparency" is its new privacy mantra (Kirkpatrick 2010, 200). Depending on your own position relative to this ever-shifting platform, Facebook "is" an advertising medium, a public square, a place to play games, a place to nurture and maintain friendships, a digital photo album, a broadcast medium, and a place to document your daily doings.

From the average, everyday user's perspective, Facebook today works like this: to join the service, users provide (in addition to an e-mail address to which the account is anchored) a proper name, as well as information about their age, gender, relationship status, work and education networks, and tastes in movies, books, and music to create a "profile." While constructing this profile constitutes a user's first engagement with the site, the bulk of Facebook inheres in a dynamic user home page. This home page consists of a constantly updated stream of information created by the user herself (like photographs added or tagged, status updates, "Likes" on pages on the broader web, or "Likes" or comments left on the updates, and media created and shared by friends) and by anyone or anything she has become a "Fan" of (such as a product, an organization, a celebrity, or a politician) or identified as a "Friend." Facebook frequently and without warning makes both minor and major alterations to the content, features, and display of this page. For example, the earliest incarnation of the site, "Thefacebook," did not have a status update feature. The site consisted simply of browsable, largely static profiles. In other words, what is today simply the gateway exercise by which we are granted membership to the site was the sum total of possible activity it offered at its launch. Features have accreted over time; the point of the site has shifted.[2]

As the service grew and matured, Facebook and its users developed a sometimes-conflictual relationship. Facebook has suffered some well-publicized public outrages—from the introduction of the original News Feed in 2006 to the short-lived Beacon advertising program the following year to the perpetual rewriting of privacy permissions that is currently drawing the attention of legislators and watchdogs around the world (see boyd 2008a; Story and Stone 2007; Zuckerberg 2006). In the face of some of these outrages, Facebook has held steady (e.g., News Feed) and waited for users to accustom themselves to the new interface, and in others it has relented (e.g., Beacon) and cancelled the change outright. This tension is ultimately irremediable: the users of Facebook are not its customers but rather its product. Facebook's current revenue model is built on targeted marketing, where advertising is sold at a premium based on the depth of information the service harvests from its users.

Nevertheless, without engaged (i.e., happy) users, the service cannot survive. A kind of symbiosis necessarily develops, even if the lines of force and power are asymmetrical. The status update enacts both this tension and this symbiosis. A steady stream of status updates is important to Facebook. It provides value to the company in the form of greater consumer profile reporting by which to sell targeted advertising, and also the promise of longer time spent on the site both by the authoring user creating the updates and by that user's friends who become engaged in reading them. Of course, ever-growing user numbers and the increasing amount of time these users spend on the site indicate that these same features are as valuable to users as to Facebook's financial interests. A recent Nielsen report found, tellingly, that Americans spent a collective 53.5 billion minutes on Facebook in May 2011—this was more minutes than the four next-most popular sites (Yahoo, Google, AOL, and MSN) combined (Nielsen 2011).

Both Facebook's financial interest in coaxing these status updates and the evident pleasure that users take in authoring and in reading them must be taken equally into account. Auto/biography studies has been overly concerned with the former, too dismissive of the latter. In their introduction to the edited collection *Getting a Life: Everyday Uses of Autobiography*, Smith and Watson (1996) proclaim the urgency of attending to an explosion of everyday autobiographical practices in contemporary America. At the same time, however, they decry the resulting texts as somehow fundamentally inauthentic, either coerced by ideological state apparatuses like the church, government agencies, or the medical or education systems, or otherwise indelibly tainted by a commercial coaxing, as in daytime confessional talk shows, or celebrity ghostwritten memoirs. They conclude that "collecting autobiographical data is, perversely, a central instrument in the othering machinery of modern technological cultures" (9).

Smith and Watson (1996) seem to hold a special terror of digital media: "[O]ur personal histories are: dismembered into zeroes and ones; passed through electrons; stored on microchips . . . there for the taking by a host of unknown entities, including computers and their hackers" (8). In this reflexive fear of computing technologies, Smith and Watson echo a broader concern around the erosion of privacy, increased surveillance, or generally dehumanizing potential of life in the database society. The privacy researcher Helen Nissenbaum (2010) summarizes this fear: "The transformations facilitated by technology over the past two decades have affected the state and the practice of electronic engagement with personal information, which, in turn, are experienced as threats to privacy" (44–45). But in the Facebook era, it is important to remember, we gleefully database ourselves.

Facebook, it bears repeating, is an attractive service. It constantly attracts new users, of which a stunning proportion are vigorously engaged in its use. The pleasures, meanings, and consequences of this use remain to be accounted for.[3] But Smith and Watson (2010) are pessimistic about the value of Facebook and other social media, writing that social networks' "question protocols and limited formats restrict the possibilities of self-narration" (187). They decide that in the age of rampant digital life writing, "autobiographical performance may increasingly mean getting a prefabricated life" (187). It may well be that the vast majority of life writing online is undertaken under the aegis of commercial enterprise; it may well be that to engage in the practice of updating one's status on Facebook is to commodify one's life story.[4] It does not follow, however, that such narratives are in some fatal way inauthentic, or that they are coerced with such force or duplicity as to deny their ostensible authoring subjects of agency in their composition. It certainly does not follow that such texts are not worth analyzing: if nothing else, we might ask how such a compelling alignment between a commercial imperative toward ever greater data collection and the popular desire to self-narrate has come about.

AUTOBIOGRAPHICAL COAXING AND THE THEORY OF AFFORDANCES AND CONSTRAINTS

In asking every user "What's on your mind?" Facebook elicits personal disclosure. But how, exactly? The ways that compliant subjects answer the question demonstrate the way their practices are shaped by the coaxing technologies, both discursive and material, afforded by the moment of interaction between status update interface and human user. In constructing our life stories—or assembling the disclosures, facts, and documents that offer the basis for the inference of life story—we are guided not only by the often-implicit discursive precedent of the genre in which we write or speak but also by the material affordances and constraints of the objects through which we structure these stories of ourselves.

"Affordance" is a concept first articulated in ecological psychology, then moving through industrial design, and into human-computer interaction, usability, and user-experience design for digital environments. James Gibson (1986) devised the neologism "affordance" to describe the set of possibilities for action an environment presents to its users. Gibson's theory aims to explain the visual processing of the broader physical world by subjects moving through it: elements of the environment as thus perceived, relative to the perceiving subject, as "climb-on-able or fall-off-able or get-underneath-able or bump-into-able" (128). He describes this notion of the action-potentiating affordances of environments and objects as "a radical hypothesis, for it implies that the 'values' and 'meanings' of things in the environment can be directly perceived" (127). Later work by Donald Norman (2002) brought the concept of affordance into the realm of industrial design, famously tackling the problems of baffling car stereos and door handles that required instruction to be operated. Norman's work builds on Gibson's insights into the affordances of man-made objects by proposing ways that a designed object's potential-for-action could be more effectively and easily conveyed to a consumer.

Affordances in the world of manufactured objects should, Norman suggests, guide and structure our uses of these objects in ways that reduce the amount of cognitive friction involved in moving through the world: for example, a chef knife's size and weight indicates to us that we should hold it firmly in one hand, and the shape of the handgrip lets us know that the blade edge should point downward, for example. "Constraints," on the other hand, are features that restrict user action: they are often just as important as affordances. The child's plastic figurine has a head of larger diameter than that of the infant windpipe; the car cannot be shifted out of park unless the brake is depressed; the food processor's blades will not spin until all the components—bowl, lid, blade—are locked into position. Constraints in the object world are often devised to protect us from ourselves: from choking on a toy, from crashing into the garage, from slicing our fingers off or spraying the kitchen in hot soup. So beyond offering a set of potential actions to a perceiving user, designed objects discipline these actions by making some potential actions more obvious than others and even making other actions impossible. Manipulating affordances and constraints, a well-designed object teaches us how to use it without us ever consciously puzzling the matter out: it places "knowledge in the world," in Norman's phrase (Norman 2002, 74). A well-designed object leads us toward an appropriate use (sitting on a chair), and away from an inappropriate use (lying down on a chair) but not entirely away from all nonstandard uses (standing on a chair).

Digital environments require even greater care in their design. In digital environments, "the range of possible actions are limited to typing on a keyboard, pointing with a mouse, and clicking on mouse and keyboard switches. . . . All of these actions are abstract and arbitrary compared to the real, physical manipulation of objects" (Norman 1999, 41). With Jakob Nielsen, Norman further pushed idea of designed-affordance into the virtual landscape of potential action offered by what appears on a computer screen. The fields concerned are those of usability and human-computer interaction (Nielsen 2012). What's essential to a well-designed, functional web application is that the user can figure out what purpose the application is meant to serve, suss out the range of potential actions relating to that purpose, and easily accomplish a goal. Nielsen and Norman's work demonstrates that as the purely virtual perceptual field of the computer screen is necessarily filled with abstractions, designers must better disburse perceived affordances and constraints consistently and obviously to structure user action.[5]

Norman has further clarified that much of the effect of good design is achieved by calling upon conventional knowledge. He offers an example: "In today's screen design sometimes the cursor shape changes to indicate the desired action (e.g., the change from arrow to hand shape in a browser), but this is a convention, not an affordance" (Norman 1999, 40). There is nothing inherently "click-able" in the hand shape, but conventional use of this symbol to indicate a clicking affordance achieves the effect of one. Ian Hutchby (2011) makes a similar point: "[O]bjects and their values can also be tied in with complex sets of concepts and conventional rules governing their use, so there is an important sense in which we can, and indeed must, *learn* about some of the affordances that certain things offer" (448–49). That is, particular ways of doing things that are culturally learned and not directly perceivable in a way that, say, a fist-sized rock would be, in Gibsonian terms, "pick-up-able" and "throwable." Here, analytical methods derived from auto/biography—the reading for context as well as generic practice—can offer explanation where simple concerns of visual or interactional design might fail to predict or understand user practice.

Auto/biographical statements can be described as discursively coaxed in many situations, some of which veer toward the coercive, or at least the overdetermined, and are vehemently socially conditioned (Smith and Watson 2010, 64–69). A job interview, for example, requires the narration of a certain kind of life story, and this is different than the life stories elicited by a medical appointment. But many such coaxed or coerced life narratives are also disciplined at the material level, in the affordances that physically shape the solicitation and its answers. There is a forceful kind of coaxing at work in the layouts of bureaucratic forms, for example. The job application requires us to list our three most recent jobs, and it seems coded into the very document that to have had only one prior job is to mark oneself as unqualified. The online grant application demands we select an institutional affiliation from a pre-set list and will not let us proceed to the next screen until we do so.

This material disciplining of personal disclosures occurs in more voluntary forms of life writing as well. Photo albums are often shaped into particular length, organization, and subject matter by the same kinds of generic precedent and awareness of audience that mold narrative structure in memoirs: there are more pictures of smiling children than wailing ones in most family albums, for example. However, authoring practices are also determined by the material affordances and constraints of the physical album: the number of pages, whether the cover or other designed paratextual feature dictates a theme or appropriate subject matter (an album titled "Our Wedding" or "School Days," a page labeled "baby's first smile") or whether the page's geography is made up of plastic pockets with room only for landscape-orientation photos, or, by contrast, made of paper with no directed layout. Similarly, the "diary," in addition to a genre of personal life writing, is also a particular kind of print book with a set number of pages for each day or week of a year and sometimes categories within that: weather, mood, appointments, to-do, ideas.

The Coaxing Affordances of the Status Update Interface

Facebook's status update feature makes use of designed affordances and constraints, as well as emerging cultural convention, in order to coax life narratives from its users. Since the introduction of the feature in 2006, the interface by which a user engages as both an author and consumer of these brief texts has changed in subtle but consequential ways. By examining the status update's shifting composition and display interface, the shaping role of affordances becomes clear as do the kinds of coaxing the feature supports. Of course, some of the problems that bedevil scholarly analysis become apparent as well. To begin with, the primary text is highly individualized and unstable: my Facebook doesn't look like yours, and each might look and act differently tomorrow, in any case. Similarly, there is no archive of Facebook. The site exists in the perpetual present, with all traces of its prior incarnations, interfaces, functions, and displays obliterated at the moment the service is updated, rendering historical work nearly impossible. The simple question of versioning is thus complicated by Facebook's near constant, usually incremental updates: one day, a small shift to how photos are displayed in News Feed; another day, auto-tagging is introduced; all of a sudden, all the privacy options have been reset and reordered; then Timeline is announced, and while it is introduced over the course of a year, the change is massive and the prior forms irrecoverable. These characteristics make well-referenced scholarship based on close reading very difficult to produce.

Accessing the primary texts in question, then, requires the development of workarounds. The most voluminous research material can be found on the broader Internet, in the form of targeted Google image searches. These image files are often of poor resolution (making it difficult to read the text), may be impossible to date accurately, and may have been altered by their creator (as in the addition of captions, or cropping). Furthermore, while image files show what parts of Facebook looked like, the service is best understood as a series of micro-interactions between users and software, and these interactions are hard to assess through static images. Another possible source of reputable, dateable information lies within the pages of popular how-to texts, such as *Facebook for Dummies* (Abram and Pearlman 2010) or *Facebook: The Missing Manual* (Vander Veer 2010). These texts, again, can link particular iterations of the interface to approximate dates tied to their own publication; they are replete with screen shots and step-by-step descriptions of interactions and processes. Web-only tech journals, like *Mashable* or *Inside Facebook*, are very useful: major changes to Facebook are tracked, and often illustrated and reviewed, by these sites. As a new media scholar and necessarily early adopter of many social technologies, I rely as well on my own memory of (and notes from) using services like Facebook over many years. All these texts are useful, but insufficient to do a detailed close reading of how the service itself works: they are still secondhand reports.

The secondary works about Facebook do not entirely satisfy the needs of literary critics, either. Most scholarly work is based in the social sciences and communications studies, concerned more with motivations and effects of interpersonal communication on the site, and less with the life writing texts that result, and how these are produced (e.g., Zhao, Grasmuck and Martin 2008; Fovet

2009; Nosko, Wood, and Molema 2010; Tufekci 2008; Seder 2009; Skågeby 2009; Young 2009; Wang 2010; Debatin et al. 2009; Westlake 2008). A few popular press books have been published on Facebook, but these have focused on the history of the company while also tracking major changes in the software or user base (Kirkpatrick 2010; and to a lesser extent Mezrich 2009): these are the most authoritative sources available on Facebook and its history. With these caveats in mind, endemic perhaps to territory yet little explored, we can proceed to trace the general outlines and specific instances of the status update.

The early status update interface comprised a text-input field of a specified length in characters, preceded by a label reading: "[Firstname Lastname] is." The most obvious affordance of the text box is, in Gibsonian language, that it is "click-in-able" and subsequently "type-in-able." This perceived affordance is conventional to text-input boxes provided for in HTML forms, regardless of where they appear on the web, and so would be a familiar element of the digital environment to Facebook's early, college-student users. The HTML specifications allow for the length, size, and capacity of the input field to be customized. For example, it is possible to create a text box that appears to cover twenty characters on screen but which allows an infinite number of characters to be input; it is possible, too, to create an input field that covers multiple lines of screen space. The Facebook status update text box covers one line of text, at a visible length of not more than forty to sixty characters. The conventional affordance (click-in-able, type-in-able) of the text-input field leads the user to know that he is meant to type. The small size of the visible typing area indicates that brevity is expected. These characteristics afford a short, textual declaration: these are potential actions, directly perceivable, showing what *can* be done. The text-field label, however, further indicates what kind of short, textual declaration is appropriate, and the label thus performs a more explicitly social or discursive coaxing of the user.

The text-field label constitutes half a statement; the user is meant to complete it. This requires some deciphering to produce the desired speech in a socially competent way. While grammatically correct, "*Aimée Morrison is* an associate professor of English at the University of Waterloo" or "*Aimée Morrison is* married, and the mother of a seven-year-old girl" are not likely normative status updates, because they convey information already solicited by and visible in the profile. Additionally, these statements convey facts that don't really change and so do not seem to qualify as a status that might need frequent or repeated "updating" in the way this little box, soliciting the user at every login, seems to imply. Further implications might be derived from user experiences of other, similar software: in this case, users might discern a link to the generic precedent of the AIM (AOL Instant Messenger) "away message." These away messages are short statements a user could craft to appear online to indicate the user was away from his computer and thus not available to instant-message. Therefore, a statement like "*Jessica Louise Barber is* on campus, at the library" seems appropriate based on this generic precedent, and its conventional use. A more creative user could bend the norm without quite breaking it and write: "*Jessica Louise Barber is* hoping that the deadline gets extended." The designed affordance, that is, pushes users toward a particular kind of "correct" practice, while allowing for a certain degree of unanticipated, creative deployment of the feature.

As a solicitation of speech, the text-field's label is both subtle and economical; it coaxes the desired speech more implicitly and more briefly than a command to, for example, "Write something about yourself here."[6] In addition to suggesting, with the provided half-statement, what kind of disclosure is sought, the label also acts as a prompt that authorizes a subject to disclose at all. Such authorization is especially important when a user might be insecure about the social norms surrounding a given practice—self-narration on the site might be seen as unreasonably boastful, as it is in real life, for example. John Killoran (2003) notes the cultural constraints against disclosure that digital life writers may face. "In their autobiographical trespass into the public domain," he writes, "the work of these authors . . . must skirt the disrepute typically attending the public airing of the lower class to fashion a legitimate subject position for the ordinary human subject in the canon of public discourse" (70). Coaxing in this sense offers the necessary social precondition for near-continual self-disclosure. In the case of personal home pages, Killoran describes the emergent convention of the FAQ page, in which users ask themselves questions that they subsequently answer. In this way, "rather than delivering unsolicited monologues about themselves, [digital life writers] play off genres that furnish a second voice and thereby a dialogue, a dialogue that 'naturalizes' the presentation of self through conversational replies" (77). The format of the status update, placing the user herself as the subject of a sentence only half-completed, offers a similar injunction/justification for self-speech.

Conventional usage is reinforced by the way Facebook published the updates as flowing text constituting usually one sentence, mashing together the text-field label with the user-generated text. "*Marion Watier is* eating a sandwich" narrates an activity currently being undertaken. "*Aline Meakin is* blonde" describes a physical characteristic of the speaking subject but carries an additional potential connotative meaning of "Aline Meakin has done something dumb" in the tradition of the punchline of jokes whose protagonists are fair-haired. *"Ernest Barber is* unhappy" articulates an emotional state. The resulting status updates, no matter which user creates them, are uniformly crafted in the third person and, when assembled into the News Feed by which each user surveys her social universe, present a unified register and point of view, making the whole look more deliberate and more immediately comprehensible than similar sentiments expressed outside of the template might appear.

As much as the interface affords certain actions and coaxes or shapes particular kinds of disclosures, it also constrains other actions and disclosures. These constraints are inherent in the enforced "is" statement and in the shortness of the text-input box, as well as in the format in which the statements are published. This particular iteration of the status update does not admit of direct address, for example. The question "Can you tell me why everyone forgets how to drive when it snows?" would instead need to be phrased like this: *"George Cole is* wondering why everyone forgets how to drive when it snows." It's impossible, also, to craft an update in the first person: to express the statement "I love Justin Bieber," a user's passion needed the indirect devices of third-person narration and passive construction, as in *"Hope Desormeau is* in love with Justin Bieber." Thus the mode by which the published statements are displayed, in addition to the affordance of the text-input box and the coaxing function of the label text, constrain user practice, thus making some kinds of statements impossible.[7]

A more recent iteration of the status update removed the verb from the text-box label prompt, resulting in a terser opening to each update, thus: "[*First-name Lastname*] [blank field for user generated text]." This reconfiguration of input and display removed some of the constraints against variety of sentence construction and point of view, but did not alter the way the resulting text was displayed. A user could interpret the label as an indicator of the character who is speaking, like in a screenplay, where the appearance of the proper name set on its own, followed by some sort of first-person speech by the named character. A possible status update in this view could read: *"Hugh Donn* I want to eat ice cream for breakfast." The formatting of the published status update as flowing text does not seem to support this usage, but it was very common nevertheless. It is more orthodox, however, to interpret the removal of the verb "is" as an indication that another verb is meant to replace it; such a practice was supported by the display interface. In this view, the status update must take the same third-person narrator, but with a wider range of sensible statements. One might then see: *"Hugh Donn* wants ice cream for breakfast" or, again, *"George Cole* wonders why everyone forgets how to drive when it snows."

In this iteration of the feature, as in the first one discussed, what appears to be produced more often takes the form of self-biography rather than autobiography; that is, the subject of the (short) life story must be described in the third-person rather than the first. This particular constraint may be motivated by the exigence of display: one main way that status updates are read is in the context of another user's News Feed, where information drawn from all that user's friends is collated into a single stream.[8] This stream, which includes not only status updates but also auto-reported activity like changing a profile picture or joining a group, gains in legibility by this uniformity. The algorithmically generated news items are grammatically parallel to the user-authored ones, creating a news feed text that combines disparate information and actions into a unified narrative, grammatically at least. Thus, the status update "*Thomas Ouya* wishes he were sleeping," authored by that user, meshes neatly with the Facebook-generated "*Thomas Ouya* joined the group 'Insomniacs of Waterloo'" in my News Feed, for example.

The next innovation made first-person status updates possible, by simply shifting the way the text is displayed once "published"—in this case, moving the name of the user onto a separate line, distinct from the user-generated text:

Aimée Morrison
    My parents are five minutes away. They had to phone for directions, and also to ask me to have the cocktails ready.

The user's proper name now acts as a simple heading, like the title of a blog post or the byline of a (very short) newspaper article. Radical shifts in narration become possible, although, intriguingly, among longtime users of the site it is still not uncommon to see the prior forms of speech survive—third-person narration, with each statement taking the user's name as the opening of a sentence. This points both to the momentum a practice acquires as people become accustomed to it, as well as users' sometimes unwillingness to acquiesce to the new norms a shift in interface demands. As Norman (1999) notes, "Conventions are not arbitrary: they evolve, they require a community of practice. They are slow to be adopted and, once adopted, slow to go away"—this is a reality that literary and cultural scholars are quite familiar with. In any case, the News Feed where this information is published becomes more cacophonous, a series of short free-form monologues headed by a proper name. Statuses thus became longer and more various.

As the status update became conventionalized, with users both comfortably accustomed to providing these updates, and seeking out or being offered ever more opportunities to share information of all kinds, the features underwent a fundamental shift, rendering analysis yet more complicated. A 2009 version of the status update brings full multimedia capacity (and automation, too!) to bear on self-expression. Indeed, at this point, the status update interface is renamed "Publisher" to indicate the greater variety of user actions it can support (Eldon 2009). The text-input box is now much larger: it easily affords multiline text and even paragraphs. The prompt has shifted location: the text-input field is pre-filled with grayed-out text reading "What's on your mind?" Making use of new web-programming features, this prompt disappears once the user begins to type into the field, seamlessly making way for the user's own text. Rather than a direct question that labels the text-input field, the grayed-out text of the question seems rather to imply than to ask.

Additionally, the input interface is now tabbed, multiplying the user's possibilities of action. Beyond the textual status update feature, Publisher now affords several other interactions. A user can now use the feature to "share" a link, a video, a poll, or a photo. Currently, a user can "tag" other users in a post, or generate linked location data associated with where a post was composed and on what kind of device. In fact, the act of frequent real-time sharing inaugurated by the status update has become even more diffuse than the tabbed options indicate. Many user actions within and without the Facebook environment now result in an update being automatically generated and published—for example, if a user has checked into a location automatically, or posted to a blog, or "liked" something somewhere on the web, or completed an online yoga class, or earned a badge in a social game. This innovation raises the difficult question of how and if these "updates" are an act of authorship on the part of a life writer, and how we are to understand them as part of the digital life writing practices on Facebook.

Facebook's Evolving Users, Users Evolving Facebook

Digital life writing in the status update feature is coaxed, but it is not determined, even as users do not assert unmitigated free will in their authorship. Every user's Facebook page offers an environment for both authoring and reading, and thus their practices are conditioned by social norms among the Friends whose updates they read and the potential actions afforded by the software. Users are coached by what they read in the display interface at the same time that they are coaxed by Facebook's design of the composition interface. These relationships are tangled, but important. As Poletti (2011) notes, "[f]or considerations of new media practice and the paradigm shift to user-generated content, the concept of coaxing furthers our thinking beyond the professional/amateur,

producer/consumer binaries," which are no longer adequate categories by which
to structure our scholarly inquiries (79). She suggests that the notion of coaxing "provides a much needed way of positioning new media practices in relation
to existing social, bureaucratic, and cultural sites where life narrative serves a
range of purposes" (79). However, the current analysis, by further recourse to
affordance theory, demonstrates that these new media practices also relate meaningfully to the designed environment of the software platforms through which
digital life writers construct and author their texts. Indeed, much of the coaxing
is encoded in the visible, analyzable interfaces that mediate between life writers
and their texts, and between these texts and their audiences. For Hutchby (2001),
using the theory of affordances means that "technologies can be understood as
artifacts which may be both shaped by and shaping of the practices humans use
in interaction with, around and through them" (444). This relationship, while
asymmetrical, is co-determining, and teasing out its multidirectional influences is work that is only just beginning.

The online world increasingly presents "the extraordinary elasticity of autobiographical experimentation" (Miller 2007, 546) that Miller recognized in the
print world and that requires once more that we innovate in our methods and
our theories.[9] This elasticity risks stretching our interpretative faculties to the
snapping point. Paul Longley Arthur (2009) notes the disorientation that can
result when life writing now emanates so voluminously "from spheres of activity
that are so alien to the traditional study of biography that their rapid infiltration
of the field is being experienced as something of an ambush" (74). Ever-greater
sections of the population engage in digital life writing online, populating dating profiles, personal blogs, or social network sites with their life stories, or otherwise leaving numberless small traces of their ideas and experiences in their
daily digital travels: a comment on a news site, a contest form filled out, a shopping basket and personalized recommendations at Amazon, a collection of book-
marks and interests maintained in the cloud. Digital life writing runs the full
length of the field between the exacting, bureaucratic, computerized coercions
of life in the database society to an independent, creative, and liberatory "autobiography in real time" (Morrison 2010). Some categories of digital life writing
are easier to interpret in proportion to their adherence to the forms, purposes,
and content of established print modes. Others, in their deep imbrication of com-
putation and authorship, are much more difficult to fit to our established theories and practices. Blogs, for example, with their long-format, single-authored
texts arranged in reverse chronological order—even if they feature hyperlinks
and user comments and photographs—are much easier to relate to diary or

memoir or auto/biography than are the multivocal, multimediated, social network texts like Facebook that seem as much algorithmically produced as they do
authored.

There is no question—particularly since the introduction of the Timeline
interface—that Facebook and its users are producing life narratives. The company purports that Timeline will do nothing less than "tell the story of your life
with a new kind of profile" (Facebook 2011). The Timeline reconfigures how
materials already in its databases are displayed on a user's home page: it reor-
ganizes a user's entire social media history (increasingly conflated with that user's
entire life) chronologically, attaching all interactions with the site, other users,
and the broader web ecosystem to, well, a timeline. Each user's Facebook suddenly attains the classical structure of the biographical text, almost inadvertently.[10] For the first time, users are actively encouraged to go back in time to
fill out those parts of their lives that were not logged in real time over the service. Of course, users have for years uploaded unflattering photos of their friends
from high-school times—but the new interface allows these photos to be dated
according to when they were *taken*, rather than *uploaded*, creating Facebook
life stories that aim to account for the past as easily and comprehensively as the
present. The impact of this change remains to be examined. If not auto/biography
scholars, then who will interpret these texts with a view to all those concerns
that seem as evident in them as in Augustine, Augusten Burroughs, Alison Bechdel, "Alice B. Toklas"? This paper has dealt with only one aspect of the Facebook
platform, and its conclusions are tentative, marred by incomplete or unauthor-
itative primary textual data. But it begins the work of devising means by which
literary scholars trained in close textual reading and broad cultural contextualization can bring these methods to bear on digital life writing texts, by finding
points of overlap between auto/biography and new media studies.

NOTES

1. Whitlock and Poletti modify the neologism "autographics" to "online autographics" when describing digital life writing, hinting at the scale of critical creativity that will
be needed to meaningfully interpret these texts, even among scholars whose work already
pushes the boundaries of auto/biography criticism.

2. The profile has gradually become de-emphasized in favor of the ethic of constant
updating that currently structures use of the site. This shift in emphasis can be attributed to several factors. First, the original site was modeled on the print genre of the
freshman "facebook," a sort of college yearbook featuring the photos, names, and programs of new students (Kirkpatrick 2010, 23, 28). As Marshall McLuhan (1994) famously
claimed, the content of any new medium is the form of the medium it seeks to super-
sede; as Facebook matures, it comes to develop its own characteristic forms and content.
Second, as a tactic by which to draw users to the site again and again, and to encourage

them to stay online longer, dynamic content is far more compelling than static content: If nothing changes, why keep looking? This shift from primarily static content to more dynamic content is a hallmark of what has come to be called "Web 2.0," developing contemporaneously with Facebook (O'Reilly 2007). Third, from a dorm room pet project to a global company with a market valuation of $100 billion, Facebook grew in its ambition as much as in its reach. Furthermore, the technology itself—programming languages, algorithms for real-time processing of information from huge databases, a hardware and network infrastructure for instantly serving content globally (through "the cloud")—advanced over the period from Facebook's inception to the current moment, making possible the more advanced features of the current site.

3. Some of this work is proceeding in the social sciences if not in auto/biography studies. danah boyd's (2008b) work is exemplary and voluminous in this regard.

4. Along these lines, see Nicole S. Cohen and Leslie Regan Shade's (2008) article on commodified practices among young women on Facebook, which they link to the commodification of female subjectivity in commercial culture more generally.

5. An accessible and engaging introduction to this work can be found at Jakob Nielsen's website, in particular the weekly "Alertbox" columns on specific design issues in virtual environments.

6. The technology blogs track what kinds of prompts each social network service uses and infer major shifts in corporate strategy or user practice from alterations to these short phrases. One recent Twitter prompt change—from "What are you doing?" to "What's happening?"—was even commented upon by a linguist. See Cutler (2009), Stone (2009), and Tate (2009), for example.

7. The next major change in the status update was not in the input format but rather in the output: News Feed. The introduction of the news feed offers ample material for an analysis of the role of audience in digital life writing; this feature immediately made status updates much more visible to all of a user's friends, and prompted much hue and cry about privacy, even though the only thing altered was that already-public updates were much easier for Friends to read (see Kirkpatrick 2010, 180–82).

8. This mode of display made less sense in the "Mini Feed," which brought a dynamic element to a user's profile page by creating a news feed of that one user's interactions. Everyone looked like a narcissist with a whole stream of updates, each headed by "Aimée Morrison is" or "Aimée Morrison [verb]" (see Sanghvi 2006).

9. The special issue of Biography addressing "Online Lives," edited by John Zuern (2003), remains exemplary in this regard: the collected pieces demonstrate a depth of focus and attention to the technology unmatched in most scholarship since. This issue represents the most sustained and thorough engagement with digital life writing I've been able to find in auto/biography studies. See also articles by Julie Rak (2005) and by Margaretta Jolly (2004) in Biography; by Paul Longley Arthur (2009) in a/b: Auto/Biography Studies; and by me (Morrison 2011, "Suffused"), by Kate O'Riordan (2011), and by Nima Naghibi (2011) in a special issue on "Intimate Publics" in Biography, drawn from papers presented in IABA 2010.

10. Anecdotal reports of cognitive dissonance among users following this change are beginning to trickle out. One newspaper reporter was so discomfited by the "biography" his reconfigured Timeline told of him that he deleted his entire account and started fresh, with the Timeline's display structure in mind (Ladurantye 2011).

REFERENCES

Abram, Carolyn, and Leah Pearlman. 2010. *Facebook for Dummies*. 3rd ed. Hoboken, NJ: Wiley.

Arthur, Paul Longley. 2009. "Digital Biography: Capturing Lives Online." *a/b: Auto/Biography Studies* 24, no.1: 74–92.

boyd, danah. 2008a. "Facebook's Privacy Trainwreck: Exposure, Invasion, and Social Convergence." *Convergence* 14, no. 1 (2008): 13–20.

———. 2008b. "Why Youth (Heart) Social Network Sites: The Role of Networked Publics in Teenage Social Life." In *Youth, Identity, and Digital Media*, edited by David Buckingham, 119–42. Cambridge, MA: MIT Press.

boyd, danah, and Nicole B. Ellison. 2007. "Social Network Sites: Definition, History, and Scholarship." *Journal of Computer-Mediated Communication* 13, no. 1. http://jcmc.indiana.edu/vol13/issue1/boyd.ellison.html. Accessed April 8, 2012.

Cohen, Nicole S., and Leslie Regan Shade. 2008. "Gendering Facebook: Privacy and Commodification." *Feminist Media Studies* 8, no. 2: 210–14.

Cutler, Kim-Mai. 2009. "Twitter Retools Prompt, Asks 'What's Happening?'" *VentureBeat*, November 19. http://venturebeat.com/2009/11/19/twitter-retools-prompt-asks-whats-happening/.

Debatin, Bernhard, Jeanette P. Lovejoy, Ann-Kathrin Horn, and Brittany N. Hughes. 2009. "Facebook and Online Privacy: Attitudes, Behaviors, and Unintended Consequences." *Journal of Computer-Mediated Communication* 15, no. 1: 83–108.

Eldon, Eric. 2009. "Spoon Feeding: Facebook Redesign Brings Feeds (and Ads) to the Masses." *VentureBeat*, March 12. http://venturebeat.com/2009/03/12/spoon-feeding-facebook-redesign-brings-feeds-and-ads-to-the-masses/. Accessed March 29, 2012.

Facebook. 2011. "Introducing Timeline." http://www.facebook.com/about/timeline. Accessed March 29, 2012.

———. 2012. "Key Facts" *Facebook Newsroom*. http://newsroom.fb.com/content/default.aspx?NewsAreaId=22. Accessed March 27, 2012.

Fovet, Frédéric. 2009. "Impact of the Use of Facebook Amongst Students of High School Age with Social, Emotional and Behavioral Difficulties." Paper presented at the 39th IEEE Frontiers in Education Conference, October 18–21, San Antonio. http://fie-conference.org/fie2009/papers/1081df. Accessed April 18, 2010.

Gibson, James J. 1986. *The Ecological Approach to Visual Perception*. Hillsdale, NJ: Lawrence Erlbaum Associates.

Hutchby, Ian. 2001. "Technologies, Texts and Affordances." *Sociology* 35, no. 2: 441–56.

Inside Facebook. 2012. WebMediaBrands. http://www.insidefacebook.com/. Accessed March 27, 2012.

Jolly, Margaretta. 2004. "E-mail in a Global Age: The Ethical Story of 'Women on the Net.'" *Biography* 28, no.1: 152–65.

Killoran, John B. 2003. "The Gnome in the Front Yard and Other Public Figurations: Genres of Self-Presentation on Personal Home Pages." *Biography* 26, no.1: 66–83.

Kirkpatrick, David. 2010. *The Facebook Effect: The Inside Story of the Company That Is Connecting the World*. New York: Simon and Schuster.

Ladurantaye, Steve. 2011. "Facebook: Deactivated, and Back Again." December 24. http://www.steveladurantaye.ca/facebook-deactivated/. Accessed March 29, 2012.

Mashable.com. 2012. http://mashable.com/. Accessed March 27, 2012.

McLuhan, Marshall. 1994. *Understanding Media: The Extensions of Man*. Cambridge, MA: MIT Press.

Mezrich, Ben. 2009. *The Accidental Billionaires: The Founding of Facebook: A Tale of Sex, Money, Genius, and Betrayal*. New York: Anchor Books.

Miller, Nancy K. 2007. "The Entangled Self: Genre Bondage in the Age of the Memoir." *PMLA* 122, no. 2: 537–48.

Morrison, Aimée. 2010. "Autobiography in Real Time: A Genre Analysis of Personal Mommy Blogging." *Cyberpsychology: Journal of Psychosocial Research on Cyberspace* 4, no. 2. http://www.cyberpsychology.eu/view.php?cisloclanku=2010120801&article=5.

———. 2011. "'Suffused by Feeling and Affect': The Intimate Public of Personal Mommy Blogging." *Biography* 34, no. 1: 37–55.

Naghibi, Nima. 2011. "Diasporic Disclosures: Social Networking, Neda, and the 2009 Iranian Presidential Elections." *Biography* 34, no.1: 56–69.

Nielsen. 2011. *State of the Media: The Social Media Report*. http://blog.nielsen.com/nielsenwire/social/. Accessed March 27, 2012.

Nielsen, Jakob. 2012. *UseIt.com*. http://www.useit.com/. Accessed March 27, 2012.

Nielsen Norman Group. 2012. "About Nielsen Norman Group." http://www.nngroup.com/about/. Accessed March 27, 2012.

Nissenbaum, Helen Fay. 2010. *Privacy in Context: Technology, Policy, and the Integrity of Social Life*. Stanford, CA: Stanford University Press.

Norman, Donald A. 1999. "Affordances, Conventions, and Design." *Interactions* (June): 38–42.

———. 2002. *The Design of Everyday Things*. New York: Basic Books.

Nosko, Amanda, Eileen Wood, and Seija Molema. 2010. "All about Me: Disclosure in Online Social Networking Profiles: The Case of Facebook." *Computers in Human Behavior* 26, no. 3: 406–18.

O'Reilly, Tim. 2007. "What Is Web 2.0: Design Patterns and Business Models for the Next Generation of Software." *Communications and Strategies* 65:17–37.

O'Riordan, Kate. 2011. "Writing Biodigital Life: Personal Genomes and Digital Media." *Biography* 34, no. 1: 119–31.

Poletti, Anna. 2011. "Coaxing an Intimate Public: Life Narrative in Digital Storytelling." *Continuum: Journal of Media and Cultural Studies* 25, no. 1: 73–83.

Raice, Shayndi. 2011. "Facebook Targets Huge IPO." *Wall Street Journal*, November 29.

Rak, Julie. 2005. "The Digital Queer: Weblogs and Internet Identity." *Biography* 28:1 66–82.

Sanghvi, Ruchi. 2006. "Facebook Gets a Facelift." The Facebook Blog. Last modified September 5, 2006. http://blog.facebook.com/blog.php?post=2207967130. Accessed March 29, 2012.

Seder, J. Patrick. 2009. "Ethnic/Racial Homogeneity in College Students' Facebook Friendship Networks and Subjective Well-being." *Journal of Research in Personality* 43, no. 3: 438–43.

Skågeby, Jörgen. 2009. "Exploring Qualitative Sharing Practices of Social Metadata: Expanding the Attention Economy." *Information Society* 25, no. 1: 60–72.

Smith, Sidonie, and Julia Watson. 1996. "Introduction." In *Getting a Life: Everyday Uses of Autobiography*, edited by Sidonie Smith and Julia Watson, 1–24. Minneapolis: University of Minnesota Press.

————. 2010. *Reading Autobiography: A Guide for Interpreting Life Narratives.* 2nd ed. Minneapolis: University of Minnesota Press.

Stone, Biz. 2009. "What's Happening?" Twitter Blog, November 19. http://blog.twitter .com/2009/11/whats-happening.html. Accessed March 29, 2012.

Story, Louise, and Brad Stone. 2007. "Facebook Retreats on Online Tracking." *New York Times,* November 30.

Tate, Ryan. 2009. "Twitter's New Prompt: A Linguist Weighs In." *Gawker,* November 19. http://gawker.com/5408768/. Accessed March 29, 2012.

Tufekci, Zeynep. 2008. "Can You See Me Now? Audience and Disclosure Regulation in Online Social Network Sites." *Bulletin of Science, Technology and Society* 28, no 1: 20.

Vander Veer, E. A. 2010. *Facebook: The Missing Manual.* 2nd ed. Sebastopol, CA: O'Reilly Media.

Wang, Shaojung Sharon. 2010. "Face Off: Implications of Visual Cues on Initiating Friendship on Facebook." *Computers in Human Behavior* 26, no. 2: 226–34.

Westlake, E. J. 2008. "Friend Me If You Facebook: Generation Y and Performative Surveillance." *TDR/Drama Review* 52, no. 4: 21–40.

Whitlock, Gillian, and Anna Poletti. 2008. "Self-Regarding Art." *Biography* 31, no. 1: v–xxiii.

Young, Debo Dutta. 2009. "Extrapolating Psychological Insights from Facebook Profiles: A Study of Religion and Relationship Status." *CyberPsychology and Behavior* 12, no. 3: 347–50.

Zhao, Shanyang, Sherri Grasmuck, and Jason Martin. 2008."Identity Construction on Facebook: Digital Empowerment in Anchored Relationships." *Computers in Human Behavior* 24, no. 5: 1816–36.

Zuckerberg, Mark. 2006. "An Open Letter from Mark Zuckerberg." The Facebook Blog. Accessed March 29, 2012.

Zuern, John, ed. 2003. "Online Lives." Special issue, *Biography* 26, no. 1.

Archiving Disaster and National Identity in the Digital Realm

The September 11 Digital Archive and the Hurricane Digital Memory Bank

COURTNEY RIVARD

ARCHIVES OF THE FUTURE

"Archives of the future" capable of collecting "instant history"—this was the promising label given to both the September 11 Digital Archive (hereafter Digital Archive) and the Hurricane Digital Memory Bank (HDMB), launched in January 2002 and November 2005, respectively (Brennan and Kelly n.d.). While these comments heralding a new future in archiving may be a bit overblown, these two Internet archives mark a significant shift in the way that material is collected, stored, and organized for the purpose of future preservation. This chapter investigates these new digital methods in relation to how they both affect and reflect U.S. national identity. Interestingly, nearly identical methods yielded two drastically different outcomes; whereas the Digital Archive was deemed a resounding success with the collection of more than 150,000 digital objects, the HDMB was viewed as a disappointing failure with only 25,000 digital objects despite the advances in web-based social networking during the interim. This stark difference may be the result of the resurfacing of deeply entrenched cultural memories concerning race, gender, and class, which are usually ignored or even denied in the current multicultural policies in the United States. Moreover, the following analysis overturns any pretense that the Internet is exclusively used to create democratic and inclusive identities that transcend national borders.

In order to analyze the impact of these two digital archives, I conduct an ethnography of the archive, where one does not merely extract materials from an archive but instead analyzes the very production of the archive—the logics of its construction, the categorization and organization of its contents, and the conditions that made its existence possible.[1] Moreover, I use a cultural memory lens in order to further flesh out this method of analysis. This theory of cultural memory, informed by cultural theory scholars such as Marita Sturken (1997) and Macarena Gomez-Barris (2009), understands memory as inherently culturally framed, where culture is understood as a process of contestation and negotiation. Additionally, this conception of cultural memory sees the past as nonlinear and circular, so that the past informs the present and directs the future. Consequently, cultural memory is central to the formation and negotiation of identity. Therefore, by conducting an ethnography of the archive, where the archive is seen as an important technology of cultural memory, one is able to better understand the impact of the production of the archive as a reflection of current power structures, particularly as they relate to the issues of national belonging, and simultaneously as framing what can and cannot be known in the future about these two watershed events.

In order to accomplish this ethnography, this study brings together archival research into the production of the archives, detailed analysis of the two sites, and extensive interviews with the creators of the two archives in Washington, DC, New York City, and New Orleans. The chapter encompasses (1) a discussion of the power of archives, (2) a history of the creation of the two digital archives, (3) an explanation of the effect of the new methods employed by the digital archives, and (4) a discussion of the causes and consequences of the different outcomes yielded by the two archives.

The Power of Archives

Traditionally, archives have been thought as emerging in Western Europe in the eighteenth century in order to serve as neutral and objective storehouses of vital materials and records, which are dutifully preserved for future generations in their original format without any intervention. Consequently, the well-known historian David Lowenthal (2006) explains, "[A]rchival records came to be valued as reliable repositories of truth, seedbeds of unabridged and veracious history. Open to inspection by all and preserved for all time, archives promised an authentic, untampered-with past" (193). On the other hand, a more critical understanding of the power and role of archives emerged in the 1960s, fueled by the work of Michel Foucault (1976), Howard Zinn, and Jacques Derrida (1995). This camp of thought saw archives as creating knowledge and memories of the past through their very construction and maintenance, thereby rendering an "objective" stance impossible. Consequently, archives are hardly neutral but rather "produce knowledge, legitimize political systems, and construct identities" (Blouin and Rosenberg 2006, vii). This more critical understanding of archives is particularly important because it helps explain the relationship between archives and national identity. An analysis of the production and content of the September 11 Digital Archive and the HDMB demonstrates that these digital archives are not just storehouses of objective knowledge but rather affect and reflect U.S. national identity.

BUILDING DIGITAL ARCHIVES

Both the Digital Archive and the HMDB were exclusively funded by the Alfred P. Sloan Foundation. The Sloan Foundation became interested in funding a digital collection of historical events in the mid-1990s, and it gave significant funding to the Roy Rosenzweig Center for History and New Media (CHNM) at George Mason University to conduct a number of projects with increasing success.[2] Shortly after the attacks on September 11, 2001, the Sloan Foundation again contacted CHNM about the prospect of creating another project that would focus on "the public response to 9/11 and its aftermath captured in e-mails, digital images, online diaries, and other electronic media" (PRNewswire 2002). As a result, CHNM partnered with the American Social History Project/Center for Media and Learning at City University of New York's Graduate Center to create the Digital Archive. Daniel Cohen and Roy Rosenzweig, two key figures in the project, explain that their aim was "to collect—directly from their owners—those digital materials not available on the public Web: artifacts like e-mail, digital photographs, word processing documents, and personal narratives" (Cohen and Rosenzweig 2005). Two other key designers of the archive explained in a personal interview that they considered the Digital Archive to be "the archive of last resort," so they must collect material that was not being collected by larger databases (September 11 Digital Archive n.d., unpublished data).[3]

The Digital Archive has been deemed a resounding success, largely due to the number of items in the archive: "150,000 digital objects, including more than 40,000 personal stories and 15,000 digital images" (Brennan and Kelly n.d.). Because of the widespread success and popularity of this digital archive, when the full extent of Hurricane Katrina's devastation became understood, the CHNM (again with funding from the Sloan Foundation) wanted to use the same collection methods to create a digital archive focusing on the event. Therefore, they partnered with the University of New Orleans to create the HDMB. Sheila Brennan and T. Mills Kelly, two CHNM staff members, explain:

> Soon after Hurricane Katrina roared ashore on August 29, 2005, the staff at CHNM
> quickly realized that we were witnessing a very significant moment in American

history. Television and newspaper coverage of hurricane victims stranded on rooftops, houses blasted from their foundations along the Mississippi coast, the displacement of tens of thousands of Gulf Coast residents, and the subsequent failures of all levels of government convinced us that we needed to act quickly to begin collecting the history of this terrible disaster. Hurricane Rita's arrival a few weeks later merely reinforced that we had a job to do. (Brennan and Kelly n.d.)

The goals set forth by the HDMB are quite similar to the Digital Archive. HDMB's "about us" page explains, "The Hurricane Digital Memory Bank uses electronic media to collect, preserve, and present the stories and digital record of Hurricanes Katrina and Rita. . . . We hope to foster some positive legacies by allowing the people affected by these storms to tell their stories in their own words, which as part of the historical record will remain accessible to a wide audience for generations to come" (HDMB 2005). The similarity in goals and even wording can be seen with the Digital Archive: "Our goal is to create a permanent record of the events of September 11, 2001. In the process, we hope to foster some positive legacies of those terrible events by allowing people to tell their stories, making those stories available to a wide audience, providing historical context for understanding those events and their consequences, and helping historians and archivists improve their practices based on the lessons we learn from this project" (September 11 Digital Archive n.d.). Therefore, both projects sought contributions from those who directly experienced the disaster and those who witnessed it through another medium, such as television and the Internet.

Challenging Tradition: Digital Collection

In addition to the similarity in goals, the two digital archives employed similar collection methods. Interestingly, the collection methods employed by both sites actually turn a number of key tenets in the archival field on their head, including timing, scope, and verifiability. The traditional approach and often the popular understanding of archives is, according to Terry Cook (2006), that "Archivists remember *the past*, not the future; they deal with *history, not current or future events*. They do not construct social memory. . . . Archivists are guardians of the past, not its interpreters" (169–70; italics mine). In a similar vein, the well-known archivist Kenneth Foote directly cautions against collecting material too quickly, especially in regards to highly emotional events. He argues that "the key to understanding these sites [of violence] lies in the question what counts as 'significant,' a question whose answer can be determined only retrospectively.

Time must pass before the protagonist, participants, historians, and general public look back and assess the significance of events and struggle with their meaning" (Cox 2003, 22). Therefore, archivists have traditionally believed that their role is to collect material that is distant to them both in terms of time and personal experience so that their personal opinions do not cloud their judgment.

The current widespread use of the Internet to communicate and share feelings, combined with the highly ephemeral nature of digital communication, challenges the conception that archivists should collect only distant pasts. Sheila Brennan and Mills Kelly, members of the CHNM staff, describe this type of Internet communication as "instant history"—"history that was being created and published by thousands of average people in their personal blogs, on photosharing websites, and YouTube . . . many of which disappear almost as quickly as they are created" (Brennan and Kelly n.d.). Therefore, this "instant history" is a vulnerable history indeed. Peter Stearns, provost of George Mason University, explains that more than 100 million Americans sent e-mails in the few days after September 11, 2001; however, there "is a tremendous risk that a substantial amount of this information will be lost. A portion has certainly already disappeared as email messages and other digital records are purged from computer hard disks. The historical record of September 11 is in danger of being obscured as time softens our memories" (PRNewswire 2002). Thus, despite the established norms within the field, the staff of the two digital archives believed that the nature of each respective event actually required sweeping changes to the established tenets.

In addition to the uniqueness of the two events, the very nature of this "instant history" required drastically different collection methods. Unlike traditional archives, where archivists selectively piece together material from a distant past that may be culled from private collections, family heirlooms, or government records, the Digital Archive and the HDMB are based on the premise that in order to create an accurate historical record, they must collect all material submitted to the website with the only exception being overly offensive comments or SPAM. This shift in the scope of collected materials marks a dramatic change from the 1 to 2 percent of materials usually preserved by traditional archives. The managing director of the CHNM explains that the Digital Archive collected everything but would not post online "extreme racist, anti-Semitic, or lewd" contributions, even though these contributions were stored for future research purposes. They saw this policy as essential "for the public record, and so they were not going to judge what was and was not important."[4] This same policy was implemented for the HDMB. The HDMB's project manager explains that the staff wanted to make all contributions viewable, so they made "no judg-ments about opinions."[5] However, CHNM's managing director stressed that the staff did collect the Internet Protocol (IP) addresses of all contributions, so that they had documentation of where the contribution came from; therefore, as he explained, "theoretically [one] could verify the information, but that is the job of historians." This key principle of inclusiveness led to the implementation of a number of different ways in which users could submit materials, which were used in both digital archives. Contributors could (1) upload e-mails they had written or received regarding the respective event; (2) type their story, reflec-tion, or general feelings into a template; or (3) upload personal images or video relating to the respective event. Additionally, both sites are organized according to these different submission formats. In other words, there are separate virtual wings for each submission type.

Many scholars have seen this method of collecting everything as a new democratizing force within the field of archival preservation. Ekaterina Hask-ins (2007) explains, "The Internet levels the traditional hierarchy of author-text-audience. . . . Unlike traditional exhibitions, where the curator often exercises full control over the selection of materials, the September 11 Digital Archive epitomizes inclusiveness" (406–10). Cohen and Rosenzweig (2005) argue that "online accessibility means, moreover, that the documentary record of the past is open to people who rarely had entered before" (n.p.). Despite this democratic potential, other scholars view these changes as bringing about the demise of the legitimacy of archives as online collections cannot be verified because of mul-tiple and often anonymous authors. Gertrude Himmelfarb argues that "the Inter-net does not distinguish between the true and the false, the important and the trivial, the enduring and the ephemeral. . . . Every source appearing on the screen has the same weight and credibility as every other; no authority is 'priv-ileged' over any other" (Cohen and Rosenzweig 2005, n.p.). Similarly, Louise Craven explains:

Paper records have a set of "signs" which we absorb automatically . . . the outward form of paper records tells us about the significance and authority of the contents within. A book bound in red leather says "I'm important!" the way documents are folded in a bundle, the format of a pipe roll, the use of treasury tags, ties, and legal pink tape: these are all ways of telling us about the documents before we look at them. Secondly, the archivist's intervention here—putting the documents in order, describing them and producing finding aids—simply reinforces this notion of im-portance, and gives the user an indication of what to look at and where to start.

Signs of conservation are similarly significant: "ohh, this has been repaired: it must be valuable!" Electronic records have no such signs, no way of saying "I'm important!" Moreover, in the digital context . . . rearrangement and description by an archivist is unlikely. (Craven 2008, 22)

Barbara Abrash (2005) also comments on issues of scholarly rigor involved in digital collection: "[E]vidence that is fragmented, often unattributed, and recombinant raise questions of credibility and historical truth, as well as profoundly challenging conventions of linear narrative" (99). Of course, this lack of imposed authority is exactly what the proponents of digital archiving see as its greatest asset as the immense power usually afforded to archivists and curators, though rarely discussed, is greatly diminished, as theoretically anyone can contribute to the archive.

Understanding Different Outcomes: Race and National Identity

Given the similar methods employed by the two digital archives, one would expect similar results. In fact, the Sloan Foundation and CHNM actually expected even greater success for the HDMB because in 2005, social networking capabilities were being widely used, whereas they were just coming on the scene in 2001. Brennan and Kelly explain, "Our experiences with the September 11 Digital Archive had taught us a lot about collecting history online and so we expected that like the very successful earlier project, the HDMB would take off quickly and would rapidly become a central digital archive of original sources." However, they continue, "To our surprise, all the national media coverage and our efforts . . . did not result in anything like the flood of contributions that we expected" (Brennan and Kelly n.d., n.p.). The HDMB yielded 25,000 digital objects, including 1,300 personal reflections and more than 13,700 digital images, which is only a fraction of 150,000 digital objects in the Digital Archive. Brennan and Kelly explain this disappointing outcome as a result of lack of time, staff, and funds (Sloan gave HDMB $250,000, whereas they gave the Digital Archive $750,000).

Others might argue that the difference was the result of the sheer magnitude of devastation that was inflicted on an entire region by Hurricane Katrina and the massive flooding, where many people were understandably more concerned with surviving than writing their stories on the Internet, given that the chances of having access to a computer let alone electricity were slim. However, a comparison of the types of submissions from the two digital archives actually reveals more about the intersections of race, class, and gender in U.S. national identity than some logistical flaw in the administration of the HDMB. The goals concerning what to collect and the ways in which users could submit contributions were virtually identical for the two digital archives. Despite these similarities, both archives ultimately contained two very different types of contributions, which demonstrate the varying ways in which national identity was configured in the two events.

Two notable scholars at the American Social History Project/Center for Media and Learning at City University of New York's Graduate Center (CUNY), who were key members of the Digital Archive team, describe a significant shift in the types of contributions that occurred quite early on in digital archive's existence. They explain that "for the first year that the 9/11 digital archive was running we didn't get a whole a lot of contributions," which they assume was a function of how they collected the material.[6] For the first year they relied on their own social networks of leftist academics and artists, so the contributions reflect these liberal and leftist ideas; however, around the first anniversary of the 9/11 attacks, there is "a hard shift to [the] Right." They attribute this significant change in the content of the submissions to the increased publicity the Digital Archive received from major news outlets, most notably CNN. They note the shift in ideology behind the submissions is directly related to the types of experiences discussed in the submissions. The Digital Archive "started out as evidence of direct experience, people near the towers, those who saw the towers fall, but as time went on it became extended experience—the experience of people outside of New York City." Therefore, they conclude, "in some sense the early archive was about experience and later archive was about perception and ideology, or it was an archive of New York for the first six months and national archive after that." Additionally, they note that the flood of submissions only came after this turn. Therefore, the vast majority of submissions on the site are from indirect witnesses outside New York City, who saw the events unfold on television.

The majority of these submissions by indirect witnesses "recall their authors' first emotional reactions—disbelief, terror, and sympathy for victims and their families . . . some also go on to reflect on the meaning of the tragedy and its aftermath" (Haskins 2007, 411–12). Additionally, there are hundreds of instances of what has become known as "digital folk art," which consisted of either altered photographs, where contributors took existing photos, such as those of the Twin Towers, and Photoshopped pictures of themselves next to them, or short animations. The short animations, some of which were also video games, almost

exclusively depict horrifically violent images of white male Americans killing male
"Arab-appearing" terrorists, where the terrorist is racialized with Orientalist
tropes and often sexualized and feminized.[7] This virtual wing of digital folk art
most clearly demonstrates the hard shift to the Right as stated by the two
CUNY staff members. What is interesting, however, is that no such flood of
submissions from indirect witnesses occurred with the HDMB. Four and a half
years after its creation, the site remains almost exclusively a repository of first-
hand experiences of those who suffered through Hurricane Katrina, both from
those who attempted to weather out the storms in their homes and those who
were displaced throughout the country. Moreover, there are no cases of digital
folk art—still or animated images.

Why is there this profound difference? Why are there almost no submissions
that express complete shock of the sheer devastation, nostalgia for the way New
Orleans used to be, condolences for those affected by the storms, offers to help,
praise for the heroes, calls for determination and rebuilding, or blame for supposed culprits—all common themes in the Digital Archive? The answers to
these questions lie most probably with the fact that there was a strong lack of
identification with those affected by the storm, which is the result of two inter-
locking factors: (1) the way in which the supposed "natural" disaster revealed
existing and institutionalized cleavages and inequalities of race, gender, and class;
and (2) the media's framing of those affected by the storms as "refugees" rather
than national heroes, which certainly results from the very same historical inequalities and racialization of the poor.

In the days following the landfall of Hurricane Katrina and the levee breaks,
the media provided round-the-clock coverage of the desperate and horrific conditions that those who were unable to leave New Orleans and the surrounding
region were experiencing. As had been the case with September 11, millions of
people watched the tragedy unfold from the comfort of their homes. Many have
noted, though, that the media coverage of Hurricane Katrina was strikingly different, not in the use of graphic images or abhorring sensationalized accounts but
in the interpretations and the racialization of those images and accounts. Bettina
Aptheker (2005) explains, "In the flood waters of Hurricane Katrina everything
about the social, economic, and racial injustice of American society floated to the
surface. Nothing could be hidden from news cameras on the scene; no sanitized
'spin' could be given to the unfolding catastrophe" (51). But as these images of
deep-seated injustices indeed "floated to the surface," the media spun the story
by riffing on deeply engrained racialized, gendered, and classed stereotypes, which
have been historically used to legitimate and naturalize inequalities.

The victims of September 11 quickly became labeled as "heroes" even though they unknowingly stepped into the path of disaster, just as the hundreds of thousands did in the Gulf Coast region; however, the word "hero" was rarely heard in reference to that situation. Because the victims of September 11 were categorized as national heroes whose loss of life represented a painful loss to the nation, they required a type of mourning that manifested itself in the flood of contributions to the Digital Archive. By framing the victims of September 11 as American heroes, then, viewers were called upon to directly identify with the victims because they were fundamentally American, and so all of America suffered with them. Because the media chose to classify the victims of Hurricane Katrina as "refugees"—a highly racialized and classed category—such a categorization did not elicit a similar call for mourning. In an insightful article, Adeline Masquelier (2006) explains "refugees" as part of a "racialized discourse that, through its emphasis on responsibility and accountability, surreptitiously excluded poor New Orleans residents from its public, thereby helping to 'naturaliz[e] social inequality'" (737). Through their classification as "refugees," those affected by Hurricane Katrina became the antithesis of citizens, thereby distancing them from the American body politic. Thus, Hurricane Katrina was classified as a disaster merely because it occurred on U.S. soil, but in this case, the victims were refugees and consequently perceived as un-American, thereby merely requiring distant sympathy for them, rather than mourning with them.

CONCLUSION

While the significance of the media's representational force may not be an entirely new insight, the implications of this framing are profound not only for the real lives of those who suffered but also for the way our present becomes the past for the future. In other words, "the archive itself is not simply a reflection or an image of an event but also shapes the event, the phenomena of its origins" (Blouin and Rosenberg 2006, 2). Therefore, the content and structure of the two archives effectively create enduring cultural memories of the respective event. There is little doubt that these two digital archives will be seen as marking an important change in the way archives are constructed: they demonstrate the Internet's power to collect ephemera material concerning a nation's thoughts and feelings to an extent never before imagined. Moreover, because this archival material is stored on the World Wide Web, it is also readily available for viewing by a worldwide audience. Without critically analyzing the disparity in the contributions by indirect witnesses between these first two instances of digital archiving and its consequences for questions of national identity, one may gloss over or even forget the profoundly racialized, gendered, and classed society that the two events underscore amid the increasingly celebrated multicultural rhetoric. Thus, analyzing the production and content of these two archives alongside one another demonstrates that those issues of power do not subside as archives are made more inclusive through the use of the Internet.

NOTES

1. I borrow this phrase from Ann Laura Stoler's "Colonial Archives and the Arts of Governance" (2002). While Stoler creates this method of analysis for studying colonial archives, I believe it is just as important for the study of Internet archives.

2. These projects include the "Blackout History Project" (1998) and "Exploring and Collecting History Online" (2001).

3. Interview with the two staff members of the Digital Archive, March 4, 2009. The official titles of these two staff members are the Executive Director, American Social History Project/Center for Media and Learning, The Graduate Center, and Co-Principal Investigator for September 11 Digital Archive and Assistant Professor of History, John Jay College, City University of New York; and Managing Director, September 11 Digital Archive. I purposefully chose not to use their full names in this chapter. These two officials are hereafter referred to as CUNY staff members.

4. Unpublished interview data, February 19, 2009. The official title of this staff member is the Managing Director of the Center for History and New Media at George Mason University, hereafter referred to as CHNM managing director.

5. Unpublished interview data, February 18, 2009. The official title of this staff member is the Hurricane Digital Memory Bank Project Manager at the Center for History and New Media, hereafter referred to as the HDMB project manager.

6. Unpublished interview data, CUNY Staff members, March 4, 2009.

7. The effect of this type of racialization and sexualization of terrorists, which works to distance them from ideals of citizenship, is given significant attention in Rivard 2012.

REFERENCES

Abrash, Barbara. 2005. "Digital Democracy, Digital History: 9–11 and After." *Radical History Review* 93:96–100.

Aptheker, Bettina. 2005. "Katrina and Social Justice." In *Hurricane Katrina: Response and Responsibilities*, edited by John Brown, 48–56. Santa Cruz, CA: New Pacific Press.

Blouin Jr., Francis X., and William G. Rosenberg, eds. 2006. *Archives, Documentation, and Institutions of Social Memory: Essays from the Sawyer Seminar*. Ann Arbor: University of Michigan Press.

Brennan, Sheila A., and T. Mills Kelly. n.d. "Why Collecting History Online is Web 1.5." *Essays on History and New Media*. http://chnm.gmu.edu/essays-on-history-new-media/essays/?essayid=47. Accessed October 30, 2010.

Cohen, Daniel J., and Roy Rosenzweig. 2005. "Collecting History Online: Case Study: September 11, 2001." In *Digital History: A Guide to Gathering, Preserving, and Presenting the Past on the Web*. Philadelphia: University of Pennsylvania Press. http://chnm.gmu.edu/digitalhistory/collecting. Accessed November 15, 2009.

Cook, Terry. 2006. "Remembering the Future: Appraisal of Records and the Role of Archives in Constructing Social Memory." In *Archives, Documentation, and Institutions of Social Memory: Essays from the Sawyer Seminar*, edited by Francis X. Blouin Jr. and William G. Rosenberg, 169–81. Ann Arbor: University of Michigan Press.

Craven, Louise, ed. 2008. *What Are Archives? Cultural and Theoretical Perspectives: A Reader*. Burlington, VT: Ashgate Publishing Co.

Cox, Richard J. 2003. *Flowers After the Funeral: Reflections on the Post-9/11 Digital Age*. Lanham, MD: Scarecrow Press.

Derrida, Jacques. 1995. "Archive Fever: A Freudian Impression." Translated by Eric Prenowitz. *Diacritics* 25, no. 2: 9–63.

Foucault, Michel. 1976. *The Archaeology of Knowledge*. Translated by A. M. Sheridan Smith. New York: Harper and Row.

Gómez-Barris, M. 2009. *Where Memory Dwells: Culture and State Violence in Chile*. Berkeley: University of California Press.

Haskins, Ekaterina. 2007. "Between Archive and Participation: Public Memory in a Digital Age." *Rhetoric Society Quarterly* 37:401–22.

Hurricane Digital Memory Bank. 2005. "About Hurricane Digital Memory Bank." http://hurricanearchive.org/about/. Accessed November 1, 2009.

Lowenthal, David. 2006. "Archives, Heritage, and History." In *Archives, Documentation, and Institutions of Social Memory: Essays from the Sawyer Seminar*, edited by Francis X. Blouin Jr. and William G. Rosenberg, 193–206. Ann Arbor: University of Michigan Press.

Masquelier, Adeline. 2006. "Why Katrina's Victims Aren't *Refugees*: Musings on a 'Dirty' Word." *American Anthropologist* 108, no. 4: 735–43.

PRNewswire. "Sloan Foundation Grants $700,000 to Preserve Electronic History of September 11, 2001." March 8, 2002.

Rivard, Courtney. 2012. "Archiving Disaster: A Comparative Study of September 11, 2001, and Hurricane Katrina." PhD diss., University of California, Santa Cruz.

September 11 Digital Archive. n.d. "About the September 11 Digital Archive." http://911digitalarchive.org/about/index.php. Accessed October 1, 2009.

Stoler, Ann Laura. 2002. "Colonial Archives and the Arts of Governance." *Archival Science* 2, nos. 1–2: 87–109.

Sturken, M. 1997. *Tangled Memories: The Vietnam War, the AIDS Epidemic, and the Politics of Remembering*. Berkeley: University of California Press.

Life Bytes

Six-Word Memoir and the Exigencies of Auto/tweetographies

LAURIE McNEILL

In 2006 Larry Smith, a writer and magazine editor, realized his dream to start a publication "celebrating the explosion of personal media and the personal stories that celebrate the brilliance in the ordinary" (Smith 2006b). That magazine is *Smith*, an online "blog-a-zine" about "you and your neighbor and about people you haven't met yet . . . all with stories that frame our increasingly complicated world" (Smith 2006a). That focus reflects the Anglo-North American public's apparently voracious appetite for auto/biographical narrative[1]: "We just can't get enough of one another's lives," Smith explains, observing the different and daily practices of self-representation taking place in print and, more variously, over telecommunication networks (2006a). Given the key role played by new technologies in promoting these narratives and the lack of interest from print publishers, Smith turned to the Internet to launch his magazine, and quickly *Smith* became a major site for the production and consumption of online life writing, featuring myriad auto/biographical story "projects," including comics, videos, and written vignettes. In particular, *Smith* magazine is the home of Six-Word Memoir, which the site describes as a "populist, participatory, inspirational, and addictive" activity with a busy community of users who have contributed "hundreds of thousands" of mini-memoirs since the site launched in November 2006 (*Smith* magazine 2012b).[2] This project builds on the possibly apocryphal Hemingway challenge to write an entire narrative in six words (the example attributed to him: "For sale: baby shoes, never worn."). Launched as a contest in collaboration with Twitter, *Smith* sent subscribers one six-word memoir a day, and the site—and the practice—took off (*Smith* magazine 2012b). The site has spawned a YouTube series, four best-selling books, a board game, and, ubiquitously, a line of T-shirts. The six-word activity has become a popular pedagogical tool (the site features one "classroom" a month) and has been adopted by churches, youth groups, and "six-word slams." One member reports that, at her grandmother's funeral, mourners submitted six-word memorials to celebrate her life (Qui 2011). While *Smith* invited some celebrity contributions to its books, the majority of memoirs are produced, as Smith imagined, by "ordinary" individuals who upload their stories on the website.

Smith magazine's Six-Word Memoir—part contest, part collective auto/biographical act, part group therapy—highlights the key role played by online technologies in the ongoing popularity of memoir. Providing users with the invitation to see their lives as the material for what it calls a "good story" (Smith 2006a) and also with the means with which to make it public, *Smith* traded on the sense of untapped potential, facilitated by technological change, to build a community of auto/biographers, all equally engaged by each other's "good stories." But it was not only Larry Smith who observed technology's role in initiating a "golden age" of personal narrative (Smith 2006a): since 1991, when the World Wide Web made it possible to connect Internet content, millions of people have taken up digital technologies to tell their stories, in public, to potentially millions of readers, whether they are on blogs, Facebook, YouTube, or Ancestry.com. Six-Word Memoir is therefore one of thousands of websites in Anglo-North American culture, and particularly the United States, that responds to and builds social demand for what Sidonie Smith and Julia Watson call "everyday autobiography" (Smith and Watson 1996, 3). The popularity of online auto/biography, in its myriad forms, suggests that the Internet is serving and creating a shared sense that these interactive representations are how we make meaning of our lives. As one instance of this culture, Six-Word Memoir illustrates the unique ways that cyberspace is shaping (and is shaped by) the genres of life narrative, including memoir.

Six-Word Memoir is an instance of the identity technologies the Internet enables. These technologies include the hardware and software that users engage to produce and consume lives online, and this chapter considers the influential role these devices play in changing online auto/biography. But identity technologies also include the cultural and institutional apparatuses that can give shape to a desire to make and share stories, and the ways that users imagine making them. Such "technologies of self" (Foucault 1988) show online auto/biographers reinscribing very traditional social functions that the different forms of "autobiography" have served for centuries, including self-monitoring, therapy, and meaning-making. On the Internet, however, such functions are a necessarily collective act on a scale that is simply impossible offline. These shifting parameters of community and audience create and complicate generic expectations for auto/biographical acts.

THE AUTO/BIOGRAPHICAL CONVERGENCE:
CULTURE, GENRE, TECHNOLOGY

Millions of individuals make use of online technology in a collective act of "getting a life" (Smith and Watson 1996). In order to account for this explosion of personal narrative we need to consider the convergence of technological changes with genre and exigence—a sense of obligation, or, in Janet Giltrow's words, "the feeling that a certain sort of writing *should* be done, *now*" (Giltrow 2011, 54)—that began in the late 1990s in Western countries, particularly the United States, and carries over to the present. Online, the advances in software that launched Web 2.0 made the Internet accessible for everyday users, not just for computer specialists who knew HTML (Blood 2002). These developments have brought about what could be termed a democratization of publishing, since, in theory, "anyone" could make a story publicly accessible without negotiating the traditional publishing hierarchy. Simultaneously, offline, the rise of "therapeutic culture" (Furedi 2004) in Anglo-North American countries continued to groom social appetites for and consumer expectations of public confession. The genres of personal narrative apparently suited such exigencies perfectly, igniting a "memoir boom" (Gilmore 2001; Yagoda 2009; Couser 2012). This iteration of the boom mirrored the spirit of the online democratization of publishing,[3] in its particular focus on "true" stories by "ordinary" and often dysfunctional individuals (Gilmore 2001, 17) who came to fame, or at least public awareness, through their personal stories. In the United States, Couser argues, such "nobody memoirs" tend to feature a narrator from a "hitherto oppressed group," and are "more likely to be a tale of woe or suffering, rather than of a normal or happy life" (Couser 2012, 147). Furedi reads this interest in wounded selves as a product of the "therapeutic ethos" (Furedi 2004, 51) that is predicated on the public disclosure of traditionally private problems, as well as the pathologizing of such issues into mental illnesses (34–42, 68–72). The popularity from the 1990s on in "confessional autobiographies" by "nobodies" as well as celebrities (41) is a product of therapeutic culture. Just as the changing technologies of the Internet opened up publishing to a wider user base, changing cultural norms democratized "memoir" and "celebrity."

Carolyn Miller and Dawn Shepherd, in their analysis of the *kairos* that helps account for the rise of blogging in the 1990s, similarly situate the genre within North American discourses of celebrity, confession, and "public" and "private" that were undergoing significant shifts, propelled by reality television, celebrity scandals, and increased Internet usage in a culture shaped by an increasing "social psychology of self-disclosure" (Miller and Shepherd 2004). By the time that the more interactive online designs often described as Web 2.0 appeared at the end of the millennium, then, technology and culture had coalesced to prime public appetites for personal stories from celebrities and "ordinary" individuals alike. The 1999 launch of Blogger led to an explosion in blogging (Blood 2002), with hundreds of thousands of individuals launching their own blogs. Social network-ing sites appeared first in 1997 on SixDegrees, then Friendster, in 2002 (boyd and Ellison 2007), before being eclipsed by giants MySpace (2003) and Facebook (2004). In 2013, 1.1 billion people worldwide have active Facebook accounts, 79 percent of users come from outside North America, and 655 million mem-bers check in daily (Facebook 2013). North America has one of the highest Internet penetration rates, with 78.6 percent of its population using the Inter-net (Internet World Stats 2012). Lives on the web have unquestionably become part of everyday existence for a significant number of people. Through their cre-ation and sharing, these auto/biographical acts participate in an individual and collective enterprise of meaning-making, which reflects particular cultural un-derstandings of what it means to "get a life" and "have a life" in the digital era.

Both online and off, appetites for personal narratives remain piqued. Survey-ing the print and digital marketplace in the first decade of the new millennium, Ben Yagoda sees the memoir boom still in full force. "Autobiographically speak-ing," he notes, "there has never been a time like it. Memoir has become the cen-tral form of the culture: not only the way stories are told, but the way arguments are put forth, products and properties marketed, acts justified, reputations con-structed or salvaged" (Yagoda 2009, 28). Yagoda's description highlights the diverse functions that contemporary memoir has absorbed in a secular confes-sion culture in which "public displays of emotion" are not only acceptable but the dominant mode (Furedi 2004, 49). The digital shift that has made oppor-tunities for such public confession "infinite" (Moskowitz 2001, 246) has also extended the domain of memoir and the other forms of life narrative loosely grouped under the auto/biography umbrella by making them much more widely accessible: once Blogger and its competitors cleared the way for "push-button publishing for the people," as the company's original slogan declared (Blood 2004), private individuals could take to cyberspace to tell their own stories all the time. The memoir boom in print culture thus prepared the way for the online life-writing boom in its different forms, including Six-Word Memoir.

These technological, cultural, and generic shifts produced a new exigence, that sense of obligation or need to act in the face of "a thing which is other than it should be" (Bitzer 1968, 7) in this particular time and place. This urgency or obligation is part of the situation to which genre responds and is therefore both socially and generically created—the genre responds to and creates the social motivation. Miller explains that "exigence is a form of social knowledge—a mutual construing of objects, events, interests, and purposes that not only links them but also makes them what they are: an objectified social need" (Miller 1984, 157). Exigence "provides the rhetor with a socially recognizable way to make one's intentions known. It provides an occasion, and thus a form, for making public our private versions of things" (158). As Bitzer argues, the rhetorical situations that exigencies address require particular kinds of actions; responses must be "fitting," in that they "meet the requirements established by the situation" (Bitzer 1968, 9–10). Bawarshi suggests that "as individuals' rhetorical responses to recurring situations become typified as genres, the genres in turn help structure the way these individuals conceptualize and experience these situations, predicting their notions of what constitutes appropriate and possible responses and actions" (Bawarshi 2000, 340). How the situation will be perceived and responded to, and through which genres, will be shaped by culture, which "influences how situation is constructed" and "defines what situations and genres are possible or likely" (Devitt 2004, 25). For the Internet and the situations it engendered, the genres of life narrative had become that fitting response, given the mass communication and information exchange taking place online, informed by the culture of confession at the "intersection of the public and private" (Miller and Shepherd 2004). Miller and Shepherd claim that this "culture of self-disclosure . . . creat[es] individuals increasingly comfortable with being put on display," and increasingly desirous of consuming the displays of others, actions they are readily able to perform online (2004, n.p.). Writers who took up this kind of response did so in ways that upheld offline social norms and exigencies, including what Furedi calls the "therapeutic imperative" (Furedi 2004, 103), which dictates the appropriateness—even the requirement—of personal revelations. But not only would other people (potentially) care about one's ordinary life, one should also care about others'. In other words, because "anyone" can craft and share life stories online, "everyone" *should*, so part of the exigence included the engaged consumption as well as production of personal narratives.

In the early days of Web 2.0, that exigence might have been filled by blogs, and by bloggers linking to each other via rings or rolls. But in 2012 such practice became secondary to faster and larger and more corporatized narrative connections. For contemporary online memoirists, this continuous compunction to produce (and consume) life narratives arises out of the rhetorical situation of the Internet in its latest evolution, the age of the social network and the microblog.

Twitter and Facebook, as sites that unfold in "real time," demand a high level of participation, encouraging users to keep up a constant web presence, posting from home and on their mobile devices. Consistent novelty is essential to such sites' ongoing success: members want new material all the time; too much stasis and they will go elsewhere. The "networked self" of these kinds of digital auto/biographies, a responsive, regularly updated, and serial subject (McNeill 2012), has therefore been conditioned by these site practices to expect to produce and consume life narratives continuously and collectively as the "appropriate" responses to this situation. These auto/biographers labor under the condition of reciprocity: they will write, someone else will read, and add their own contributions (by commenting, retweeting, forwarding, or tagging, for example), to which the original writer will respond in the same manner; "feedback and reciprocity" are essential to the site experience (Oulasvirta et al. 2010, 238).[4] Indeed, users are positioned by these social networking sites to represent their lives as constituted by moments that have value and meaning and should be shared in ways that will generate response. To keep the site and the networked community it supports going, people have to keep posting, as do all sorts of people, not just celebrities or public figures who traditionally would expect a reception for sharing their stories with the world.

Online auto/biographers, then, must always be at the ready, continually updating their own narratives-in-progress and engaging with those of other members. As such, Six-Word Memoir and other sites that celebrate what Smith (2006b) calls "the brilliance in the ordinary" design a form of auto/biographical representation that demands the ongoing recitation of the everyday, the banal, and the relatable. Given this exigence, particular forms of memoir have developed that are fitting responses to the needs of the digital life narrator. I call these forms "auto/tweetographies" (McNeill 2011), short installments of life narrative, which share moments, experiences, and lives in miniature, and which will be updated or replaced regularly—daily or even more often—with new material.[5] Reflecting the status update or tweet, the two dominant models for these forms, these auto/tweetographies are brief and typically focus on the immediate moment, the content best suited to the microblogging or social networking situation. Antti Oulasvirta et al., in their analysis of microblogs *Jaiku* and *Twitter*, note that the "rapid disclosure of current activities and experiences" is essential to microblogging practices (and what distinguishes them from blogging), and this expectation "creates a pressure to continue sending status updates even at very mundane moments, as the sender's presence is constantly being created and re-created through these messages" (Oulasvirta et al. 2010, 238). This exigence to update drives content, pushing members to posts featuring "self-disclosure" of a particular kind: "most of the jaikus refer to the experiences and contexts of the poster *at the moment of writing*," with 83 percent of posts describing "the present moment" (243). The most dominant topics include "'working,' 'home,' 'work,' 'lunch,' and 'sleeping'" (248). Such posts, they argue, allow users to maintain a consistent site presence and thereby keep themselves and others engaged in the network (248).

So it seems that microbloggers, like academics, must publish or perish, and one's own life provides ample, if quotidian, material. In the early days of blogging, digital life writers faced similar pressures and responded similarly enough to produce the phenomenon pilloried as the "cheese sandwich" entry (Lankshear and Knobel 2003, 16), a sort of placeholder post that had little real content. On microblogs and social networking sites, such posts have become commonplace.[6] However, given that members are competing for the attention of their followers or "friends" on the network, they must master the art of the personal anecdote, find and burnish the gem in that cheese sandwich, so to speak. As Oulasvirta et al. put it, "it is in the interest of the teller to ensure that recipients find what is tellable or storyable in the object" (Oulasvirta et al. 2010, 239). The ascendancy—or at least acceptance as the norm—of such content reflects the diversification of practices in online life writing. Blogging remains popular, and is the place for longer entries (and not the banal), while microblogs and social networking sites call for these rapid-fire but often quite trivial life installments. Indeed, Oulasvirta et al. read this content as essential to the microblogging experience, which, they insist, "centers on *making the ordinary visible to others*" (238), and in so doing makes those ordinary moments significant. "By forcing oneself to think about what is *reportable* in an everyday experience," they argue, "the poster may be constructing the social meaning of those events" (248). Six-Word Memoir's editors echo this analysis, telling readers, "one way to make sense of a life is by breaking it down into short, meaningful bits" (Qui 2011). Importantly, however, posters do not need to construe such meanings alone, but in a networked environment, one in which members, and the site itself, help establish and reinforce norms and interpretations. On microblogs, members' comments and responses show how a network has "received and understood" a particular post. In so doing, "they *retrospectively legitimate* topics that as standalone objects might seem too mundane" (Oulasvirta et al. 2010, 243). Thus through publishing and reading these moments of life, users engage in a communal act of auto/biographical reflection and affirmation. They imbue these newer genres with the exigence of their antecedent genre, the blog: Miller and

Shepherd argue that blog writers and readers acted on "some widely shared, recurrent need for cultivation and validation of the self" in producing these texts (Miller and Shepherd 2004).

Clearly, Six-Word Memoir and related sites similarly answer an exigence many netizens feel to make lives—theirs and others'—meaningful through a collective act of (short) storytelling that generates discussion and response, as Anna Poletti has also observed about PostSecret (Poletti 2011, 26). Six-Word Memoir is therefore part of the process of "getting" one's life: making it understandable by reproducing it for publication, a process not hitherto available for the public at large. Only online is it possible or practical for these bits—or, rather, bytes—to be salvaged and then published and on such a broad scale. Before individuals could share lives over the Internet, such moments would not have had the potential validation of other readers or viewers, even though they may have experienced the exigence to share such material. Sites such as Six-Word Memoir set up such life ephemera and fragments as valuable and meaningful, the foundation for communities and the material that guides the telling of lives in the online memoir boom.

Auto/tweetographies, through their accessibility (available to anyone with an account on social networks or microblogs), brevity, and informality, along with the communal pressure to keep producing and consuming them, therefore embed auto/biographical acts in cultural consciousness. The modes of auto/biography become part of millions of people's daily routines: they now experience the social motive—the exigence—to log on and represent themselves and others. Surely this habit must shape offline lives, with users on the alert for "the reportable," thinking of how to shape experiences into status updates or tweets or even those six-word memoirs, designing utterances to suit the different audiences they address and fulfill the expectations of the communities in which they participate through their digital texts. Online technologies, then, have certainly influenced life writing practices, and the identities and communities they support. This insatiable interest in memory and meaning-making in multiple digital forms has also certainly influenced the development of Web 2.0: there are now more and newer platforms, programs, applications, and online sites, which construct and respond to the shared exigence to show and tell and read and respond to online lives. For instance, software and hardware designers have had to take into account—as well as create—users' "social need" (Miller 1984, 157) to stay connected to their communities, and thus sites such as Facebook, Twitter, Post-Secret, and Six-Word Memoir have "mobile" applications built into their designs. Digitization of memoir shows the mutual construction of identity technologies, with users shaping and being shaped by the web and by the genres of auto/biography.

Every day at *Smith* magazine's website, individuals compose hundreds of "micro-memoirs" (Yagoda 2009, 21), responding to the invitation, "One life. Six words. What's yours?" (*Six-Word Memoir* 2012). Ranging from the personal and confessional, poignant reflections on lives and moments, to witty wordplay and banal updates, these six-word memoirs reflect an active and committed membership deeply engaged by their own and others' lives and narratives. It is an apparently intimate space, where Larry Smith posts his own six words and occasionally comments on others' memoirs, at the same time that it is by now an established cultural institution drawing thousands of visitors. Six-Word Memoir constructs itself as a community site predicated upon the sharing of ordinary life stories, as Smith articulates, and it promotes its collaborations with social and non-profit organizations as ways of extending the good work the project does. The site's design and activities, however, indicate particular norms in place that guide memoirists in what they choose to narrate and how they should engage with other writers. In so doing, this auto/tweetography participates in a larger culture of digital self-help and normalizing that continue offline traditions of autobiography as a form of self-surveillance and social grooming. But as a commercial rather than personal or amateur site, it also serves other, less altruistic interests, and these ties must factor into how lives and stories are produced there.

On the site, users sign up and then submit their stories in one of several categories, or in video form on the Six-Word YouTube channel. Of the hundreds of daily submissions some will be picked by *Smith* staff as "featured memoirs," one of which becomes the "memoir of the day," and then a few are highlighted in the site's blog as "memoirs of the week." Still others will gain prominence as "most favorited" and "most commented," showing members' preferences and indicating the value the site places on sparking dialogue through submissions: the magazine pitches the *Six-Word* act as "a powerful tool to inspire conversation around a big idea, and a simple way for individuals to break the ice" (*Smith* magazine 2012b). More pragmatic concerns may also drive the site's encouragement of dialogue, since the more interaction members see, the more often they will visit the site and make their own contributions, growing the network and the content that it uses in other ways: the magazine also selects from this vast pool for its print publications. Memoirists are acutely aware of the potential for publication, half-jokingly debating in comments pages about whether submissions are "a six for the book" (e.g., DynamicDbytheC 2012). The contest element and possible book publication guarantee volume for the site, as users submit repeatedly in the hopes of being acknowledged by the community, at the very least through comments on their individual posts and ideally by the site's editors. This coaxing further fuels appetites for memoir—and in ways that print forms simply cannot—with a regular pool of contributors who supply new content and therefore keep readers coming back.

These rankings also introduce an element of competition and hierarchizing, which shape production of memoir in particular ways and demonstrate the more directive practices of publishers in the contemporary memoir boom, particularly for "nobody" memoirists (Couser 2012, 145). They certainly establish the value of the enterprise, giving it a particular cultural legitimacy that arises through selection even if, as with many major literary prizes, the selection criteria are unarticulated. They define what stories and, by extension, which lives are valuable, something the memoir categories also elicit since they reflect the kinds of topics they want memoirists to address. Although Six-Word has no specific directives for content beyond its word limit, the site's design and contest framework ensure that particular kinds of self-revelation take place that reflect popular understandings of memoir, particularly those that associate self-reflection with self-help, informed by therapeutic culture. While most of the site's submissions are posted to the default or main category "Life," users can also select from a range of other topics. "Moms," "Dads," and "Teens" find their own categories, while other subjects include "Jewish," "Resolutions," "America," and "Green Life." Although these fields must evolve to reflect users' submissions or requests ("Dads," for example, was added in June 2011), as well as the site's dominant national and cultural demographics,[7] they also establish frames through which memoirists imagine their lives/narratives. Sidonie Smith and Julia Watson (2010) describe the key role played by "coachers, coaxers, and coercers" of life narrative, those bodies issuing invitations or demands for individuals or groups to represent themselves "in the context of social institutions" (64–65). Reflecting and reproducing the values of such social institutions, these bodies emerge in particular storytelling situations and help "establish expectations about the kinds of stories that will be told and will be intelligible for others," what stories will be "appropriate" for each "site of narration" (69). *Smith* magazine positions itself as benign coach, encouraging members to think of their own lives as interesting subjects to share. "Everyone has a story," it announces encouragingly (*Smith* magazine 2012b). But its suggested categories serve as prompts to coax certain content in these memoirs, content that reflects *Smith*'s "USAmerican" (Bowering 1997) identity, one that values particular ways of living (as parents, for instance, and in environmentally conscious ways).

Taking their cues from these implicit and explicit markers of appropriateness and community identity, memoirists shape their own life writings to conform to Six-Word standards. Common threads deal with site comportment, with members raising questions about practices (e.g., "Who picks these featured memoirs, anyway?" [HoraceNelson 2011]) and clarifying "rules" (e.g., "Requests official ruling on hyphenation question" [midwestsensibily 2011]). Others remind the community of norms, particularly when a "crisis" is perceived. For instance, in response to certain memoirists flooding the site's page with multiple submissions, L2L3 writes, "New Sixer category births itself: Spamoirs," an entry that inspired forty-seven comments before the writer deleted the post when responses became too heated (L2L3 2012). In these instances, metagenre—reflexive commentary on form—helps community members groom new members and police violations, as Janet Giltrow has observed (Giltrow 2002, 187), and as such shows community identity in production: What values and sensibilities do members hold in common? How do they understand what they are doing, and how can they get others to understand (and conform to) those ways too? Notably, such discussions reflect concerns about behavior much more so than form. Six-Worders take a decidedly broad definition of "memoir," capturing overheard snippets of conversations (e.g., Steelpony shares "I never got to wear a Tiarra" [*sic*], a life narrative he "overheard in line at the supermarket") and observations about news and trends (e.g., algebragirl's commentary, "Can't believe the Kindle's not touchscreen") as well as inscribing their own lives. Such diversity suggests how auto/tweet practices rely on very loose interpretations of recognized literary forms to organize communities around the sharing of lives. The classification as "memoir," a literary genre currently enjoying critical and popular acclaim, may also lend prestige to these everyday narratives. As Six-Worder thesagittarian12 writes, "Future dictionary entry: 'memoir'—means 'anything.'" Perhaps memoir's apparent expansiveness helps account for the project's success: if theoretically "anything" counts (as long as it follows six-word norms), "anyone" can contribute. After all, "Everyone is a SMITH!" the site declares (*Smith* magazine 2012b). But these community reflections on and debates about genre, in concert with the site's design, help remind new and existing members that in fact institutional and cultural expectations undergird these auto/biographical acts and the identities they inscribe. Everyone may not, in fact, be "a SMITH."

We see instances of such expectations and grooming in the occasions that inspire "memoir booms" within the site itself. National or cultural holidays, events, and news stories generate streams of memoirs, with hundreds of writers chiming in their six-words to reflect on 9/11, thank veterans for their service on Memorial Day, respond to the death of Osama bin Laden, or celebrate the Fourth of July national holiday. These occasions, overwritten with national narratives of the United States, connect with cultural and social institutions to make Six-Worders align two exigencies: (1) the need to mark a national or cultural holiday or event, and (2) the need to inscribe themselves into that moment or event through personal narrative, often in ways that reflect dominant cultural norms. The personal and collective impulses collapse in an auto/tweetography, unfolding in real time, able to respond in the instant, and to keep responding with one's own contributions and comments on others'.

Such group responses illustrate the collective auto/biography these sites produce and coach, a composite narrative of individual acts that together create and reinforce meaning for these (assumed) shared experiences. Six-Word Memoir enables its writers to understand their "subject roles" and responses in these situations. Genres, Bawarshi (2000) notes, "carry with them social motives—socially sanctioned ways of 'appropriately' recognizing and behaving within certain situations—that we as social actors internalize as intentions and then enact rhetorically as social practices" (341). The Six-Worders' 2011 take on American Thanksgiving gives one example of such social action through genre. Featured submissions construct a story of the holiday as a harrowing experience, one marked by dysfunction (one's own, and, often, one's family's) and, by extension, narcotics. Loon narrates, "Ate wild turkey, drank Wild Turkey," while Believe suggests, "New holiday spice: Xanax in peppermill!" SKL (2011) notes there is "More than one turkey at table," and Jujeeball reels off his or her "Thanksgiving list: buy turkey, refill [V]alium." For its community, Six-Word Memoir is the "appropriate" response to the situation of fraught domestic rituals. These representations reproduce therapeutic culture's framing of the family and other institutions of private life as "toxic" sources of individual dysfunction (Furedi 2004, 70–75), and constitute a mutually affirming narrative of unhappy holidays and families for many site members. Though these responses are not the only Thanksgiving memoirs (others send out straightforward messages of gratitude and goodwill), they do offer a dominant model for Six-Worders as living imperfect lives but managing to rise above through (black) humor and, of course, six-word memoirs.

Participating in such public sharing in an online community, Miller and Shepherd argue, addresses motives of "social validation . . . through communicating with others and confirmation that personal beliefs fit with social norms." In these revelations, "self expression serves the intrinsic self-disclosure functions of both self clarification and self validation, enhancing self awareness and confirming already-held beliefs" (Miller and Shepherd 2004, n.p.). The lives at *Six-Word*, as this holiday installment suggests, very often mirror contemporary American understandings of the self as "vulnerable," "help-seeking," and unable to "cope with the trials of life" (Furedi 2004, 107), and of memoir as the way to articulate that self and its experiences. In contrast to the relentless positivity embedded in Facebook's auto/biographical coaxing, Six-Word Memoir, and related auto/tweetography/"humor" sites FML and My Life is Average, champion the ordinary, the "everyperson," as a universal and very "human" subject, and position the site itself to address the confessional and therapeutic needs of this "wounded" subject. Notably, most regular Six-Worders are serial memoirists, posting regularly, if not daily or even several times a day. (New members in particular produce torrents of six-words, though typically these trail off after the first rush, leaving only a few members guilty of "spamoirs.") These repeat performances suggest users experience a felt obligation to articulate foibles (their own, but sometimes others') in public, on a regular basis to a group of supporting and responsive readers as a form of self-validation. Such an exigence is produced in therapeutic culture that constitutes the goals of therapy as not "enlightenment" but survival (Furedi 2004, 104) and the afflicted as perpetually "in recovery" (e.g., Moskowitz 2001, 246–53). The auto/biographical here reinforces a cultural model of subjectivity, which is at once at home with its imperfections (as shared and reinforced by community members) and seeking ways to address those perceived flaws in a forum simultaneously constructed as both public and intimate, a close-knit community of sympathetic wordsmiths. Notably, one of Six-Word's memoir categories is "Resolutions," the perfect way for users to make public pledges of the ways they will change their lives for the better. These life installments that together "capture" a life, and here, lives, for closer examination (and thus revision) signal the generic and cultural influences on auto/tweetographies of the diary, a form popular in the self-help trade because of its accessibility and dailyness and thus ability to chart failure and progress (Bunkers and Huff 1996; Gannet 1992).[8]

While some of these daily memoirs may very well make it into "the book," the vast majority go unnoticed and unremarked. A few receive one or two comments, and even fewer move up the ranks to "most commented" and "most favorited." The payoffs for this unanswered majority thus must be personal, providing a creative outlet, sense of communal engagement, and, as some users put it, "free therapy." The memoirist Amapola writes, "Reading back own memoirs. Considering therapy," to which marymc replies, "This is therapy. Free therapy." Several other users chime in to support this idea, leading Amapola to conclude, "Yes, you're right! i think my next memoir will be: Thank you SMITH. Feeling better now. :-)." Such attitudes further reflect the site's construction of member subjectivities as "broken" and in need of repair, a repair enacted through participation in the Six-Word Memoir community. They also outline Six-Word's broader social mandates, its aligning of memoir with social actions beyond the strictly auto/biographical. As the editors imagine, by participating in Six-Word Memoir, members take the first step to engaging in broader dialogues about "big ideas" (*Smith* magazine 2012b) and challenging topics, such as illness, faith, or sexuality. Because *Smith* enables—and coaches—such steps, it seems to feel a particular responsibility to support members in what might be difficult situations; its affiliations with various social organizations indicate its sense of this potential for outreach and intervention that the auto/biographical act facilitates. These organizations include To Write Love on Her Arms, "a non-profit movement dedicated to . . . people struggling with depression, addiction, self-injury, and suicide," providing therapeutic and financial support (TWLOHA 2012). The site has created its own "TWLOHA" category for memoir submissions and links to the video Six-Word memoir of the actor James Earl Jones: "Help is real, hope is real," he counsels (TWLOHA 2012). Similarly, Six-Word's new "Dads" section partners with The Good Men Project, a "magazine as social movement," which aims to "foster a cultural conversation about manhood while supporting organizations that help at-risk boys" (The Good Men Project 2012).

Six-Word's community partnerships mirror those of other auto/tweetography sites, most particularly PostSecret, and thus suggest that auto/tweetographies embed exigencies of confession and therapy in microblogging genres. PostSecret, an art project-turned cultural confessional (Warren 2005), invites the public to submit anonymous confessions on the backs of postcards. It launched in 2004, and its almost immediate success surely helped establish the expectation that sites featuring the ordinary (and sometimes extraordinary) stories of private citizens have the potential to do much more than publish stories: the act of telling a story in public, even anonymously, may be transformative, empowering individuals (either producers or consumers) to create change on an individual or social level. As a result, sites' members may be seeking assistance at the same time that they are assigning meaning to their lives; perhaps the very act of such reflection creates crisis (indeed, this might be the foundation of the self-help industry). Given the particularly fraught situation created by PostSecret, with users required to confess secrets that are both "true" and "new" (Poletti 2011, 33), and therefore perhaps unprocessed, Warren has been careful to connect his community to resources. The site supports the suicide-prevention hotline Hopeline (Macauley et al. 2008, 97; Poletti 2011, 35), and contributes to the International Suicide Prevention wiki, linked on the site's main page.

PostSecret, Six-Word, and other auto/tweetography sites such as Makes Me Think ("an online community where people share daily life stories that provoke deep thought and inspire positive change") thus participate in a shared cultural understanding of situation that links auto/biographical reflection and therapeutic insights and actions. They also share the positive ethos of social networking giant Facebook, whose "mission is to give people the power to share and make the world more open and connected" (Facebook 2013). Each site builds on an apparently widely held exigence, produced by therapeutic culture, that people are not coping, that "the world" needs improving, and that such problems can be addressed through the regular online exchange of personal anecdotes and supportive commentary. That exchange, by extension, reproduces that exigence, in a process of mutual constitution Anthony Giddens termed "duality of structure." As Anis Bawarshi explains, "Human actors, in their social practices, reproduce the very social situations that make their actions necessary, possible, and recognizable, so that their actions maintain and enact the very situations that call for these very actions" (Bawarshi 2000, 353). The more we disclose in our online auto/biographies, the more we *need* to keep disclosing, as we continuously articulate our imperfections and failures.

Of course, Facebook's auto/biographical turn as advocate for making "the world" a better place persists without apparent irony at the same time the company turns the auto/biographical contributions of its members into millions of dollars in revenue, mainly through targeted advertisements based on the data site participants blithely supply (Kirkpatrick 2010, 235–86). It therefore reminds us not only of the lucrative nature of the self-help industry but also of the close proximity, in Web 2.0, of the personal and commercial, with socially produced websites, particularly social networks, capitalizing on the unpaid labor of the "prosumer" (Cohen 2008, 8). In many online auto/biographical forms, this commodification of lives and "online social relations" (9) goes hand in hand with more socially conscious motivations of these sites. The same activities that help members purportedly "heal" themselves and their community drive the bottom line for the more established auto/tweetography sites.

In this vein, Six-Word's affiliations extend beyond the social to the corporate, and reflect the new uses to which auto/biographical acts can be put in a Web

2.0 world. Auto/tweetographers at Six-Word Memoir and similar sites produce the content that all these sites use, in some way or another, for profit without financially compensating members for that work. Members' apparently blithe willingness to produce lives that become products that others sell or otherwise profit from suggests something about Internet culture that revises thinking about the agency and autonomy of auto/biographical subjects. For Six-Word memoirists, the opportunity to make their texts and lives public seems to trump concerns about ownership, copyright, or profit-sharing. Perhaps this response is part of the allure of the celebrity, or cyberlebrity, that online personal publishing delivers. For instance, in summer 2010, on the eve of the first Six-Word Memoir book publication, the site teamed up with Honest Tea beverage company (a "socially conscious" company, Larry Smith [2010] explains), with the company putting "100+ of the most thoughtful, inspiring, insightful, and funny Six-Word Memoirs" under the bottle caps; participants would be "considered for a bottle cap as well as a book." Similarly, another *Smith* story project, "Pregnancy" (2009), asks readers to submit their "amazing, unusual, or simply memorable pregnancy story" in ten words or less. This project pairs *Smith* with "Rick's Picks," a pickle company, in a contest in which winners ("six future moms and one dad") will be eligible for prizes including copies of the Six-Word Memoir book *Not Quite What I Was Planning* as well as jars of pickles (the "Rick's Picks Pregnancy Pack"). The grand prize winners will have their stories featured on the labels of Rick's new pickle product, "Slices of Life, 'the Pickle of Pregnancy'" ("What's Your Pregnancy Story?").

Putting aside the latter contest's recycling of stereotypes about pregnancy and the norms of experience it therefore reproduces for its readers, Six-Word's series of contests, publications, and other marketing maneuvers are remarkable in their ability to capitalize on members' appetites for—or at least benign acceptance of—using their lives/stories to provide free publicity for the magazine and other companies. These contest winners receive no payment for their memoirs nor do those memoirists published in the books (although they receive one free copy of the text). While users retain copyright to their work, they sign over to *Smith* a "Creative Commons Attribution" license, allowing the magazine to "use the submitted work for promotional, commercial, and non-commercial purposes, such as advertisements, books, and other products" (*Smith* magazine 2012a). While certainly the move is not new—companies have traded on consumers' free participation in promotional events for decades, and Facebook, as Cohen has discussed, has built its business model on such crowdsourcing (Cohen 2008, 8–10)—what is different is the scale of the enterprise, one made possible only by the Internet. Six-Word's campaigns demonstrate the social production of materials that Web 2.0 thrives on (Bruns 2008, 3–5), but they keep the traditional industrial model of profit in place: only *Smith* stands to gain financially from these ventures.

Auto/biography in these schemes is therefore an *interested* genre, turning the reflective and transformative ideals captured by the site's "self-help" and consciousness-raising elements to more pragmatic ends that serve corporate interests. On Six-Word Memoir—and PostSecret and Facebook, among other sites—the personal is (potentially) commercial, though not for the individual but for the institution that coaxes the individual. The rewards for the "produsers" end with the apparent realization of the ideals and the exigencies of both auto/biography and the Internet: the sharing of one's experiences in ways that reveal the self to the self and to others, the fostering of a potentially global but intimate community, and the support and exchanges inspired by participation in such a community. In a blog entry celebrating *Smith*'s sixth anniversary, Larry Smith quotes a comment by member MrsPremise that he takes as representative of the members' sentiments: "'I love this community, the books are the bonus'" (Smith 2012). Genre and technology pair with the ethos of both late capitalism and Web 2.0 to inspire the mass production of memoir that Six-Words coaxes and, literally, on which it capitalizes.

OUR MEMES, OUR SELVES

The pervasiveness and popularity of auto/tweetographies such as Six-Word Memoir, in addition to blogs, home pages, and other places where individuals inscribe themselves, illustrate how auto/biographical acts have become an inherent element of Internet culture and practices. The global economy for trading our stories remains robust, supporting individuals' participation in self-affirming communities and the corporate balances of the institutions that establish and profit from those communities. As a result, those institutions will keep finding ways to coach the free and regular uploading of selves and stories in ways that keep members connected to the site and each other, and to make sure that Larry Smith is right that "we just can't get enough of one another's lives." Those ways may not always be successful, even for well-established sites: in December 2011, for instance, Frank Warren had to discontinue the PostSecret iPhone app only three months after its launch when it was overwhelmed by inappropriate and even illegal content, including "pornographic, gruesome and threatening material" (Hernandez 2012). Going mobile invited a rogue contingent into the PostSecret community, one that disrupted its values of safety and mutual solace, and violated legal, moral, and generic norms upheld by its members. Perhaps the consolatory exigencies of auto/tweetographies mean these sites must remain small enough to practice "group therapy," with members engaging in community surveillance to insure that generic and social comportment is upheld. Despite the universalizing and welcoming rhetoric of such sites—PostSecret's comforting commiseration that "Everybody has secrets" ("PostSecret App Trailer" 2011) and *Smith's* reminder that "Everyone has a story"—their laissez-faire approaches do not extend to embrace libertarianism. Indeed, the normalizing impulses of Six-Word Memoir suggest quite the opposite, in the site's reaffirmations of comfortably mainstream, though left-leaning, Anglo-American ideals and constructions of subjectivities through the conforming frames of therapeutic culture (Wright 2008; Furedi 2004).

The cultural, technological, and generic apparatuses that gave rise to such sites therefore reflect a confluence of identity technologies, which shape how individuals live and report lives online. The serial production of lives and narratives in a responsive community of life writers that characterizes auto/tweetographies demonstrates a refocusing of the auto/biographical scope: memoir in this context and for these users is a synechdochic rather than definitive take on a whole life or even experience, and acquires significance through its mass production, the repeated, collective act of telling oneself into being in the company of others similarly engaged in such acts. The interactive, immediate, and serial quality of such online auto/biographical acts, and their fittingness for the rhetorical situations of digital and therapeutic culture particularly in North America, make a long run likely for "memoir boom 2.0."

NOTES

Anna Poletti and Julie Rak's thoughtful and probing editorial responses to this essay greatly refined my thinking about several of its claims. I am grateful for their supportive criticism.

1. In using the term "Anglo-North American," I refer to the English-language audience for the production and consumption of life narrative informed by the "memoir boom" and therapeutic culture. This public is certainly dominated by the United States but not limited to it, with participants from other countries, including the United Kingdom, Canada, and Australia. Throughout this chapter, "American" addresses the United States in particular, and not the continental Americas.

2. As of March 16, 2012, the site claimed that it contained 292,747 "recent memoirs," though it is not clear what the temporal boundaries of "recent" are.

3. Yagoda (2009) and Couser (2012), among others, point out that the late 1990s boom is just the latest in a series of epochs of high public demand for personal narrative, including those by "ordinary" individuals. Each of these booms will be inflected by the larger cultural needs and norms that the genres of life writing adapt to serve.

4. Bryant and Marmo's (2012) examination of interaction rules in Facebook "friendships" underscores the value placed on communicative exchange. In their study of college students' SNS practices, "I should expect a response from this person if I post on
his/her profile" was one of the five most important rules (12).

5. My nod to Twitter in this neologism focuses on the genres of microblogging, with
the "tweet" as the most popular (and thus recognizable) of them. Space here does not
permit me to take on a comprehensive analysis of uses and cultural practices of Twitter; for such discussions, see, for example, the work of danah boyd, Scott Golder, and
Gilad Lotan (2010), Courtney Honeycutt and Susan Herring (2009), and Ruth Page (2012).

6. Ironically, there are now blogs dedicated to the cheese sandwich. See, for example, *The Grilled Cheese Blog* (www.grilledcheeseblog.net) and *Grilled Cheese Social*
(www.grilledcheesesocial.com).

7. Data from web analytics site Alexa.com (2012) indicates that the site's visitors are
primarily females with some college education, and 64 percent of them come from the
United States.

8. I thank Sidonie Smith for suggesting this connection between Six-word Memoir
and the diary. I would like to call attention to the role of gender in cultural expectations
of both the diary and therapeutic culture, particularly given its largely female demographic (see n. 5). Katie Wright (2008), surveying feminist scholarship on confession
culture, summarizes that women in particular have been negatively affected by therapeutic culture and the ways it has "controlled and disempowered" them (326), though
she also offers a more recuperative reading of therapeutic culture (328–36).

REFERENCES

Alexa.com. 2012. "Statistics Summary for Smithmag.net." http://www.alexa.com/siteinfo/
    smithmag.net. Accessed May 14, 2012.
Bawarshi, Anis. 2000. "The Genre Function." *College English* 62, no.2: 335–60.
Bitzer, Lloyd. 1968. "The Rhetorical Situation." *Philosophy and Rhetoric* 1:1–14.
Blood, Rebecca. 2002. "Introduction." In *We've Got Blog: How Weblogs Are Changing
    Our Culture*, edited by J. Rodzvilla, ix–xiii. Cambridge, MA: Perseus.
———. 2004. "Hammer, Nail: How Blogging Software Reshaped the Online Commu-
    nity." *Rebecca's Pocket*. http://www.rebeccablood.net/essays/blog_software.html. Accessed
    January 29, 2009.
Bowering, George. 1997. *Bowering's B.C.: A Swashbuckling History*. Toronto: Penguin.
boyd, danah m., and Nicole Ellison. B. 2007. "Social Network Sites: Definition, History,
    and Scholarship." *Journal of Computer-Mediated Communication* 13, no. 1, article 11.
    http://jcmc.indiana.edu/vol13/issue1/boyd.ellison.html. Accessed August 2, 2011.
boyd, danah, Scott Golder, and Gilad Lotan. 2010. "Tweet Tweet Retweet: Conversa-
    tional Aspects of Retweeting on Twitter." In *Proceedings of the Forty-Third Hawaii
    International Conference on System Sciences, Kauai, Hawaii, January 5–8, 2010*. Los
    Alamitos, CA: IEEE Press. http://doi.ieeecomputersociety.org/10.1109/HICSS.2010
    .412.
Bruns, Axel. 2008. *Blogs, Wikipedia, Second Life, and Beyond: From Production to Pro-
    dusage*. New York: Peter Lang.
Bryant, Erin M., and Jennifer Marmo. 2012. "The Rules of Facebook Friendship: A Two-
    Stage Examination of Interaction Rule in Close, Casual, and Acquaintance Friendships."

Journal of Social and Personal Relationships. Prepublished April 25, 2012, DOI: 10.1177/ 0265407512443616. Accessed May 14, 2012.

Bunkers Suzanne L., and Cynthia Huff, eds. 1996. *Inscribing the Daily: Critical Essays on Women's Diaries*. Amherst: University of Massachusetts Press.

Cohen, Nicole. 2008. "The Valorization of Surveillance: Towards a Political Economy of Facebook." *Democratic Communique* 22, no. 1: 5–22.

Couser, G. Thomas. 2012. *Memoir: An Introduction*. New York: Oxford University Press.

Devitt, Amy. 2004. *Writing Genres*. Carbondale: Southern Illinois University Press.

Facebook. 2013. "Key Facts." http://newsroom.fb.com/Key-Facts. Accessed June 10, 2013.

Foucault, Michel. 1988. "Technologies of Self." In *Technologies of the Self: A Seminar with Michel Foucault*, edited by L. H. Martin et al., 16–49. London: Tavistock.

Furedi, Frank. 2004. *Therapy Culture: Cultivating Vulnerability in an Uncertain Age*. New York: Routledge.

Gannett, Cinthia. 1992. *Gender and the Journal: Diaries and Academic Discourse*. Albany: State University of New York Press.

Gilmore, Leigh. 2001. *The Limits of Autobiography: Trauma and Testimony*. Ithaca, NY: Cornell University Press.

Giltrow, Janet. 2002. "Meta-Genre." In *The Rhetoric and Ideology of Genre: Strategies for Stability and Change*, edited by Richard Coe, Lorelei Lingard, and Tatiana Teslenko, 187–205. Cresskill, NJ: Hampton.

———. 2011. "'Curious Gentlemen': The Hudson's Bay Company and the Royal Society, Business and Science in the Eighteenth Century." In *Writing in Knowledge Societies*, edited by D. Starke-Meyerring, A. Paré, N. Artemeva, M. Horne, and L. Yousoubova. Fort Collins, CO: The WAC Clearinghouse and Parlor Press.

The Good Men Project. 2012. "About Us." http://goodmenproject.com/about/. Accessed March 18, 2012.

Hernandez, Brian Anthony. 2012. "PostSecret App Discontinued Because of 'Malicious' Posts." *Mashable Tech*. http://mashable.com/2012/01/02/postsecret-app-discontinued -because-of-malicious-posts/. Accessed May 12, 2012.

Honeycutt, C., and Herring, Susan C. 2009. "Beyond Microblogging: Conversation and Collaboration via Twitter." In *Proceedings of the Forty-Second Hawaii International Conference on System Sciences, Waikoloa, Hawaii, January 5–8, 2009*. Los Alamitos, CA: IEEE Press. http://doi.ieeecomputersociety.org/10.1109/HICSS.2009.602.

Internet World Stats. 2012. "Usage and Population Statistics." http://www.internetworld stats.com/stats2.htm. Accessed May 30, 2012.

Kirkpatrick, David. 2010. *The Facebook Effect*. New York: Simon and Schuster.

Lankshear, Colin, and Michele Knobel. 2003. *New Literacies: Changing Knowledge and Classroom Learning*. Buckingham, UK: Open University Press.

Macauley, Maggie, Kendra Magnusson, Christopher Schiffman, Jennifer Hamm, and Arlen Kasdorf. "From Souvenir to Social Movement: PostSecret, Art, and Politics." *Young Scholars in Writing* 6:91–99. http://sfu.academia.edu/MaggieMacAulay/Papers/ 624118/From_Souvenir_to_Social_Movement_PostSecret_Art_and_Politics. Accessed December 12, 2012.

McNeill, Laurie. 2011. "Auto/tweetography: Producing and Consuming Identity on Social Networking Sites." Paper presented at the Modern Languages Association Conference, Los Angeles, CA, January 4–7.

———. 2012. "There is No 'I' in Network: Facebook and Posthuman Autobiography."
  Biography 35, no. 1: 101–18.
Miller, Carolyn. 1984. "Genre as Social Action." *Quarterly Journal of Speech* 70:151–67.
Miller, Carolyn, and Dawn Shepherd. 2004. "Blogging as Social Action." In *Into the
  Blogosphere: Rhetoric, Community, and Culture of Weblogs*, edited by L. J. Gurak,
  S. Antonijevic, L. Johnson, C. Ratliff, and J. Reyman. http://blog.lib.umn.edu/blogo
  sphere/blogging_as_social_action_a_genre_analysis_of_the_weblog.html. Accessed
  September 23, 2012.
Moskowitz, Eve. 2001. *In Therapy We Trust: America's Self-Obsession with Self-Fulfillment.*
  Baltimore: Johns Hopkins University Press.
Oulasvirta, Antti, Esko Lehtonen, Esko Kurvinen, and Mika Raento. 2010. "Making the
  Ordinary Visible in Microblogs." *Pers Ubiquit Comput* 14:237–49.
Page, Ruth. 2012. *Stories and Social Media: Identities and Interaction.* New York: Routledge.
Poletti, Anna. 2011. "Intimate Economies: PostSecret and the Affect of Confession."
  Biography 34, no.1: 25–36.
"PostSecret App Trailer—Everybody Has Secrets." 2011. *YouTube.* August 24. http://
  www.youtube.com/watch?v=jJF4-x4Xz3U. Accessed July 9, 2012.
Qui, Lisa. 2011. "Loved Wine in a Coffee Cup: Six Words for Grandma." http://www
  .smithmag.net/sixwordbook/2011/02/28/loved-wine-in-a-coffee-cup-six-words-
  for-grandma/. Accessed March 2, 2011.
Six-Word Memoir. 2012. *Smith Magazine.* www.sixwordmemoir.com. Accessed March
  23, 2012.
Smith, Larry. 2006a. "Editor's Letter." http://www.smithmag.net/about/letter/. Accessed
  February 23, 2012.
———. 2006b. "Our Birth Story." http://www.smithmag.net/2006/01/06/youre-never-
  eat-launch-in-this-town-again. Accessed March 2, 2011.
———. 2010. "Hey, What's Under That Bottle Cap? Six Words + Honest Tea." http://
  www.smithmag.net/sixwordbook/2010/06/03/hey-whats-under-that-bottle-cap-six-
  words-honest-tea/. Accessed March 20, 2012.
———. 2012. "Happy National Smith Day. And Now We Are 6." http://www.smith-
  mag.net/obsessions/2012/01/06/happy-national-smith-day-and-now-we-are-
  6/#more-1335. Accessed March 18, 2012.
Smith, Sidonie, and Julia Watson, eds. 1996. *Getting a Life: Everyday Uses of Autobiography.* Minneapolis: University of Minnesota Press.
———. 2010. *Reading Autobiography: A Guide for Interpreting Life Narratives.* Minneapolis: University of Minnesota Press.
Smith magazine. 2012a. "About and Writers' FAQ." http://www.smithmag.net/about/.
  Accessed March 2, 2012.
———. "The Six-Word Memoir Project." 2012b. http://www.smithmag.net/sixword
  book/about/. Accessed March 2, 2012.
TWLOHA. 2012. http://twloha.com/vision. Accessed March 2, 2012.
Wright, Katie. 2008. "Theorizing Therapeutic Culture: Past Influences, Future Direc-
  tions." *Journal of Sociology* 44, no. 4: 321–36.
Yagoda, Ben. 2009. *Memoir: A History.* New York: Riverhead Books.

Mediated Communities

Negotiating Identities/Queering Desires

Coming Out Online and the Remediation
of the Coming-Out Story

MARY L. GRAY

INTRODUCTION

I first started noticing that I was attracted to other girls when I was about 12 or 13. Before then, I can't even say that I knew gay people existed. But even when I was young I watched girls on TV and was amazed by them. I was over at my friend's house one night joking that I only watched *Baywatch* (my favorite show at the time) for the girls. After I said this, I realized it was true. It wasn't until about a year later, when I got on the Internet and found other people like me that I actually said to myself that I was bisexual. I've always been attracted to both sexes, but I found my true identity on the Internet. (Amy, age 15)

Amy, a white teenager living in the central region of Kentucky, cited the discovery of an Internet forum for lesbian, gay, bi, trans, queer (LGBTQ), and questioning young people as a defining moment in understanding her own bisexual identity.[1] Similar to many of her rural peers, Amy found that online representations of LGBTQ lives seemed more pivotal to this shift in her identity than fictionalized LGBT narratives, such as *Baywatch*'s campy queer subtexts or *Queer as Folk* and *Will and Grace*'s out-and-proud gay and lesbian characters. Fictional representations of LGBTQ people in popular media have long been theorized as a potential remedy to LGBTQ cultural marginalization and a cause for LGBTQ people to celebrate (Gross 2001; Gamson 1998; Doty 2000). Media visibility seemed a natural step in the progression for full rights and equal citizenship. The sociologist and feminist scholar Suzanna Walters convincingly argues that LGBTQ visibility in the media means that we are more widely seen but not necessarily better known (Walters 2001). While more images of LGBTQ people certainly stream into Americans' lives through television, films, and the Internet, the increase in visibility has not fully translated into pro-gay stances at the voting booth or in the halls of Congress. Accordingly, youth, many of whom are fleshing out the boundaries and meanings of their identity, are no more likely to know themselves through these fictional images, particularly given how rarely they depict rural places, than a straight person looking to fictionalized characters to make sense of LGBTQ people's lives. That is not to say that images of LGBTQ characters in popular media didn't inform (and fuel) the queering of Amy's desires. But the narratives of authenticity, of queer realness, that she found online by reading coming-out stories—from teens both in her state and living worlds away, following news bulletins posted to the National Gay and Lesbian Task Force and PlanetOut websites, and outlets for buying rainbow flags, jewelry, pride rings, and stickers—provided the grammar for a bisexual identity she eventually claimed as her own.

Engaging these online representations as a genre infuses them with what I refer to as queer realness. I draw on Judith Halberstam's prescient definition of realness which s/he asserts is "not exactly performance, not exactly an imitation; it is the way that people, minorities, excluded from the domain of the real, appropriate the real and its effects . . . the term realness offsets any implications of inauthenticity . . . realness actually describes less of an act of will and more of a desire to flaunt the unpredictability of social gendering" (Halberstam 2005, 51). Rural youth appropriate queerness as a possibility that is disparaged not only in representations of the rural but also in mass media depictions of LGBTQ people.

In referring to these representations of realness as a distinct genre I refer to the media scholar Jason Mittell's call to examine media texts as "sites of discursive practice" (Mittell 2001, 9). Instead of focusing on the aesthetic codes or features of the new media texts that might generically hold together, I apply Mittell's practice of analyzing sets of themes and patterns that surface across media texts, the audience members' experiences of those texts, and industry practices that consistently produce and recycle these themes and patterns (19).[2]

In rural contexts, Internet-based texts found on commercial websites, other young people's homepages, and regional e-mail–based discussion lists operate as a genre that queers realness. These texts lend materials to the labor of parsing out and responding to the expectations of LGBTQ visibility. Rural LGBTQ-identifying youth come to see themselves in terms made familiar through the narrative repetitions of self-discovery and coming out found in this genre. These digitally produced texts circulate the politics of LGBTQ identity and center on visibility as a hegemonic grammar for the articulation of identity. How much rural youth absorb and rework these identity categories turns on each young person's material conditions, cultural context, and history. As young people reckon with these genres, their negotiations highlight the recalcitrance of social categories, like race and class. Their narratives, in turn, necessarily trouble uncritical monolithic references to "the Internet" as the animating origin of transformation.

Many youth shared the belief that their identities expressed inherent desires that they were born with but that remained buried under the baggage of community norms and expectations of "having a family and settling down" in traditional heterosexual fashion. Their narratives of having been "born this way" echoed popular cultural understandings of sexualities and genders as expressions of one's core being (Lancaster 2003). Yet, arguably, Amy's identity didn't coalesce through isolated introspection and self-discovery. She described the year or so she spent online making sense of her fascination with *Baywatch* as a busy one "reading everything I could about gay people" and "hanging out in chat rooms talking with other kids about how they first knew they were gay and whether they thought I was gay or what words even made sense." Her processing of self-exploration, making sense of what "words even made sense," is indeed highly social. Amy's sense of what it means to be bisexual is, in practice, collectively organized through her interactions with what Bruno Latour (1996) calls "social actors"—from watching television shows and talking with friends, to surfing the Internet. From this perspective, rural youth sexualities and genders are best understood not as an unfolding state of biological fact confirmed in a moment of visually and textually mediated recognition but as residues of complicated dialogues—recirculations of coming-out narratives most notably—that increasingly involve digitally mediated renderings of LGBTQ identities complete with particular ways to dress, look, and speak. Urban and suburban youth might come across commercially or subversively produced LGBTQ images posted along public transit routes, pinned to community boards at local coffee houses, or embodied in the presence of gay/straight alliances and other LGBTQ-advocacy organizations. Rural youth, however, are unlikely to run across these images in their public spaces. As a result, they are more reliant on venturing out of town and exploring media to find the words and practices culturally saturated with queer realness.

A blend of fictional television characters and conversations with friends served as critical materials for Amy's queer-identity work. As her insights suggest, though, she found confirmation and a sense of "authentic" identity online. In this sense authenticity does not reside in Amy. It is a "manufactured" moment when "a place or event . . . conform[s] to an idealized representation of reality . . . a set of expectations regarding how such a thing out to look, sound, and feel"

(Grazian 2003, 10). Amy does not discover or possess her queer realness as much as she, like all of us, pursues a credible and sincere performance of that idealized representation in hopes that it will "come off as natural and effortless" (10–11). She notes that the absence of locally visible LGBTQ communities made it harder for her to precisely name—let alone act on—her attraction to both sexes. In the end, Amy's bisexual identity coalesced from watching *Baywatch*, being teased by friends, and reading the Internet-based musings of other young people.

Young people like Amy spoke about representations they found online as both resonances of their own experiences as well as evidence that others like them existed beyond their small communities. Drawing on a nineteen-month ethnographic study of digital media use among rural LGBTQ, queer, and questioning youth in the United States, this chapter explores how rural young people weave media-generated source materials into their identity work, particularly as they master the politics of visibility's master narrative event: that of "coming out."[3] Online representations, from noncommercial, youth-spun websites to subscription-based personal ads on for-profit media properties like PlanetOut and Gay.com, provide rural young people with materials for crafting what it means to come out as LGBTQ or questioning in rural contexts. While Martin Meeker (2006) described the formation of LGBTQ communities in the urban San Francisco Bay Area, no studies have focused specifically on youth in the rural United States, and their negotiations of a queer sense of self and the expectations of visibility that have become a feature of modern LGBTQ experience and popular culture. Case studies of rural sexualities and genders offer fresh vantage points to consider the links between larger structural issues, such as statewide social-service funding, regional race and class relations, media representations, and day-to-day processes of individual presentations and negotiations of identity.

QUEERING THE EFFECTS OF MEDIA VISIBILITY

If visibility is imagined to be the road to acceptance for LGBTQ-identifying people, much of that recognition circulates through representations in the media. Films, television characters, press accounts of social movements, AIDS reporting, plays, books, and the Internet are where most stories of queer desires transpire. These representations translate queer desires into LGBTQ-specific identities and give them a proper locale, but this is usually an urban area. Media, then, is the primary site of production for social knowledge of LGBTQ identities. This is where most people, including those who will come to identify as LGBTQ, first see or get to know LGBTQ people via social grammar, appearance, and sites of LGBTQ-ness.

Arguably, media's social force seems heightened (sometimes hyped?) in rural places not because of a complete absence of LGBTQ-identifying or queer-desiring individuals with whom rural youth might identify but because of the way rurality itself is depicted as antithetical to LGBTQ identities. Mass media consistently narrate rural LGBTQ identities as out of place, necessarily estranged from "authentic" (urban) queerness. These images teach rural youth to look anywhere but homeward for LGBTQ identities. Should we presume rural queer and questioning youth treat new media technologies as the latest vehicles of escape? Is it possible that for the rural youth who stay put, new media serve not primarily as "opportunities for the formation of new communities . . . spanning vast distances" but as opportunities to create and consolidate networks much closer to home that are otherwise absent from mass media representations? (Gross 2007, xi).

One of the difficulties in researching the role media play in the cultivation of a rural queer sensibility is that it is all too easy to fall back on the presumed properties of the technologies themselves to the exclusion of the social contexts that give technologies meaning.[4] Historically, technological innovations in the modern era simultaneously raise society's hopes and stoke its fears (Drotner 1992; Nye 1990; Marvin 1988; Sammond 2005). But no technology comes prepackaged with a set of "good" or "bad" traits (Turner 2006; Carey 1989). Unfortunately, until the novelty of a "new technology" tapers off or is displaced by something newer, researchers and cultural critics of media effects alike cycle through fixations on the good, the bad, and the ugly that comes hidden inside the box—whether it is a radio, a television, or the Internet. This has produced a lineage of media scholarship tightly focused on communication technologies as things that produce effects rather than cultural elements of the complexity of human interactions and our relationships with/to innovation itself. These debates over media's strong or weak effects rage on, regardless of the media in question.

Nonetheless, the tenor of these intellectual deliberations reaches a fever pitch when questions turn to media's potential influence on children. Young people have always been the screens onto which society projects its greatest fears (Waller 1990; Seiter 1993; Levine 2002; Jenkins 1998). More recently, with the advent of everything from MySpace to Gameboys, new technologies are presented in popular culture as sources of distraction, violence, or allure, which threaten the sanctity and safety of children. Janice Levine argues that rather than accept the statistical reality that children are more vulnerable to sexual harm at the hands of immediate family members, society projects its fears onto strangers, seeing media as one of several tools used to lure unsuspecting children. A case in point is the "pedophile panic" that spurred the drafting of the 1996 Communications Decency Act (Levine 2002, 20–44). This panic led to institutionalizing parental surveillance through codes for films and music, as well as v-chips and Internet-filtering software. These preventative measures presume and perpetuate the notion that media have direct and very negative effects upon children. Prevention logic suggests one can curtail certain behaviors by regulating access to these media or the content of media itself. The reality is, of course, far more complicated.

BREAKING THE MEDIA EFFECTS LOGIC

Media studies tend to approach the question of representations of social influence of media as a matter of impact. We think the medium itself carries certain properties and, therefore, inherent powers. New media promise to bring about change—slipping it in around mass culture. We attach cultural weight to it as we look to blogs to address our mistrust of mainstream journalism or turn to distance learning to address the increasing costs of higher education. But new media are part of mass culture—the stories they circulate remediate the stories already out there. While new media studies can perpetuate what the sociologist Claude Fischer diagnosed as media studies' penchant for "impact analysis," looking at rural young people's use of media offers us a different story (Fischer 1992, 8). For example, we might be tempted to imagine that new media technologies allow rural gay kids to escape their rural communities and find refuge, and recognition, online. But framing the question like this leads us down a dead-end road of inquiry, leaving many unable to explore how rural queer and questioning youth engage and transform media as they respond to expectations of visibility and the structures of familiarity that organize their offline experiences. Focusing on new media as spaces that produce online worlds fails to respond to the call of critical cyberculture scholars to examine how "[o]nline contexts permeate and influence online situations, and online situations and experiences always feed back into offline experience" (Baym 2006, 86). Media scholars like Nancy Baym call on us to "recognize that the internet is woven into the fabric of the rest of life" (86).

What we learn from reception and audience studies in media studies, particularly work done from a youth-centered approach by theorists like Ellen Seiter (1999; 2005) and Sonia Livingstone (2002; 2008), is that youth engage media in far more complicated ways than we assume. Seiter, for example, pioneered scholarship in children's use of the media, which worked to understand not only how children make meaning in their lives through their use of media but also how parental anxieties over children's media use spoke more broadly to societal tensions over what constituted "proper parenting," particularly that of the mother's role as moral guide. But much of the work on reception studies focuses tightly on the conditions for viewing, centered on the moment of reception itself. We wonder if it is possible to break out of this narrow focus to see the more complicated relationships between media and their meaning rather than effects in our everyday lives. Seiter and Livingstone respond to and challenge work that assumes media are deleterious to kids based on presumptions about the particular effects of the medium. They apply an ethnographic and qualitative approach to complicate what "effects" might look like in the lives of young people by studying their everyday uses of media. They treat young people as active agents and also as a culturally constructed demographic.

Another way for researchers to engage more complicated relationships between media and their meaning-making is through ethnographic approaches, which contextualize media engagements as part of a broader social terrain of experience. Performances of identities require tools: What tools are out there for rural youth to pick up if they seek to express a sense of self that doesn't square up with the heteronormative expectations around them? What allows for an iteration of a sexual or gender identity constructed in popular culture as antithetical to their rural communities? What kind of visibility can be performed here and through what means? What are the limits of these iterations? What do we need to politically tweak to make queer sexualities and genders more habitable to rural youth? Answers to these questions might be specific enunciations of identity or creating a politic, which does not see visibility as the primary goal, allowing an affinity and political kinship to take center stage.[5] Media engagements are one of many important discursive practices we integrate into our everyday lives. Media analysis cannot confine itself to an effects or an impact-measuring project if it hopes to contribute to understanding media as part, rather than the center, of sociality. A rich examination of new media takes stock of how central it is, how it comes to be seen as meaningful, and when it seems less relevant. As Nancy Baym argues, "Online spaces are constructed and the activities that people do online are intimately interwoven with the construction of the offline world and the activities and structures in which we participate, whether we are using the Internet or not" (Baym 2006, 86). The questions then become: What role do media engagements play in people's lives? When do they turn to media and when is it expendable background noise? When do media make a difference and what are the conditions that make these differences register as important or negligible? If we are to understand the relationship between media and young people's sense of their sexualities and genders, we need an approach that moves away from isolating media as conduits or contagions. Framing new media thus limits our ability to understand complicated individual and collective engagements with media.

To address this need for a more relational method to understanding media, I suggest concentrating on studies of media in situ. Archaeologists use this phrase to describe an artifact at the point of its unearthing or sighting, one that is still embedded in a deposit suggesting its age and cultural context. The concept of in situ embodies more than description of the artifact and its location, in this case, beyond the moment of reception. Although similar to media ethnographies of audience reception, my approach radically decenters media as the focus of study. Instead of examining audiences' reactions to specific programs or websites, I map the relationship between rural young people's experiences of a cluster of media engagements and a milieu, which is constitutive of its meaning. An in situ approach to media takes as the object of study the processes and understandings of new media among people within the context of their use. This approach requires tracing the circulations and layers of socioeconomic status, race relations, and location in the lives of those I met who make their media engagements meaningful to them. This approach focuses on how media engagements fit into a larger mosaic of collective identity work and does not assume a singular message or effect is (or can be) conveyed or transmitted.

THEORIZING YOUTH: APPLYING CRITICAL YOUTH STUDIES TO QUEER YOUTH IDENTITY WORK IN A DIGITAL AGE

Researchers typically assume that rural youth lack the resources, capacity, and support to actively foster difference in the seeming homogeneity of their small towns (Faulkner and Lindsey 2004; Flint 2004; Snively 2004). Rather than presume an absence of critical materials for identity formation, I draw on a sociological tradition that theorizes identity as a deeply social, contextual, and collective achievement instead of a psychological expression of an internal process of integration. Far from being the reflection of an inner drive, youth identities are cultural assemblages that work with the materials on hand.[6] I rely heavily on the scholarship that falls under the rubric of New Childhood Studies and critical youth studies (Adler and Adler 1998; Corsaro 2005; Fine and Sandstrom 1988; James, Jenks, and Prout 1998; Lesko 2001; Qvortrup 1994).

New Childhood Studies take adult researchers (and perhaps many of today's parents) to task for uncritically applying a developmental paradigm that frames young people's identity practices as playful experimentation rather than seeing these practices as ways of being in the world (Qvortrup 1994). Children and adolescents' articulations of identity are interpreted strictly as rites of passage on the way to adulthood. Under this rubric, young people's experiences of identity are simultaneously understood as the blossoming of an individual's unique character and, paradoxically, the timely appearance of universal characteristics particular to a phase of the human life course. New Childhood Studies challenges researchers to work against ahistorical, apolitical accounts, and universalizing developmental models of children and adolescents. In addition, New Childhood Studies offer a critical analysis of the "socially constructed nature of childhood and adolescence" replete with the cultural baggage of adult-centered views of the world (Best 2007, 11).[7]

Building on the work of New Childhood Studies, critical youth studies uses the insights and tools of cultural studies and critical studies in race, sexuality, and gender to engage children and adolescents as active agents and independent social actors rather than passive "subjects-in-the making" (Best 2007, 11). This approach attempts to foreground how power dynamics, including the researcher's relationship to youth participants, produce the cultural knowledge that shapes our understandings of young people. Working from this premise, critical youth scholars seek to acknowledge adults, children, and adolescents as cultural participants working in and through a dense network of power relations. This is particularly the case when it comes to the culturally charged discussion of youth sexuality. As Susan Driver argues, in reflecting on her own pioneering research examining queer youth's exploration of sexual desire through digital video, youth research must respond to and work against the heteronormative "conventional codes of academic knowledge" that "render ambiguous, indirect, and unstable ways of signifying [queer sexual] desire invisible" (Driver 2007, 308).

Studying rural queer and questioning youth identity formations builds on New Childhood Studies and critical youth studies in two important ways. First, unlike the independence and self-determination that define the queer youth political culture of national LGBTQ youth advocacy programs or queer-specific, urban-based resources and social services, rural young people's engagements with LGBTQ politics are marked by their interdependence with familiar queer adult advocates and non-LGBTQ allies. Since the 1990s and the visibility of "gay youth" as a cultural category, city-based queer youth activists envisioned their work as autonomous from that of adult queer activists (even though it was contingent on capital trickling down from adults). Rural queer and questioning youth have neither the peers nor the local tax base to imagine such independent political power. This echoes the broader disenfranchisement that challenges all rural-based political organizing efforts. As a result, studying rural queer youth identities requires critical scholars of youth culture to complicate youth-centered research models to account for adults' active participation in the construction of rural queer youth identity and community.

Second, I investigate rural queer youth identities as performative, socially mediated moments of being and becoming, or as Lisa Duggan puts it, identity construction as a "process in which contrasting 'stories' of the self and others—stories of difference—are told, appropriated, and retold as stories of location in the social world of structured inequalities" (1993, 793). I work against privileging youth experience in ways that could inadvertently essentialize queerness as a stable state of being that some youth possess.[8] Instead, I legitimize rural young people's claims to queer identities as, by definition, always more than "just a phase" or "experimentation" while questioning the presumption that identities ever start with or settle down to rest in the hands of individuals. My use of the metaphor of collective labor in a discussion of youth identity—talking about identity as work shared among many rather than the play of any one individual—is meant to recognize that the assembly and articulation of one's sense of self like any other social action is "work [that] always occurs in contexts" (Strauss 1993, 95–97). Queer identity work is the collective labor of crafting, articulating, and pushing the boundaries of identities. I frame youth sexualities and genders as labor carried out among and through people, places, media texts, and a host of other circuitous routes. Treating identity as work highlights the dynamic strategies youth and their allies must employ as they contend with the politics of visibility across these various work sites. It also acknowledges how political economies of gay and lesbian life intersect with consumption practices to produce genres of realness available for queer identity work. These materials are often commercial products themselves, hardly original or removed from the processes of commoditization. However, as queer scholars such as José Esteban Muñoz and Alex Doty have argued, audiences often rework hegemonic media representations through polysemic practices of queering and disidentification (Muñoz 1999; Doty 1993). I argue that rural youth do the collective labor of identity work differently than do their urban counterparts—not because rural queer youth have it inherently harder but because they confront different heteronormative/homophobic burdens and different identifications with the commercially mediated identities available to them. As a result, they bear the weight of a politics of visibility that was built for city living.

Imagined Terrain of Online Queerness

If there are any consistencies to the online sites rural youth such as Amy turned to, it would be that Mogenic, a nonprofit website produced in Australia by and for youth, was one of the more commonly cited destinations beyond Gay.com and Planetout.com. Mogenic's collections of coming-out stories, found on its message boards, were particularly popular. Other sites mentioned were Oasis Magazine Online, the Advocates for Youth website, the Advocates for Youth LGBTQ youth project, and the website for the Parents and Friends of Lesbians and Gays (PFLAG). This is by no means a comprehensive listing of the sites of queer realness that rural youth plumbed. Youth were just as likely to mention cruising the gay and lesbian sections of Yahoo as any LGBTQ-specific site. The meaning and use rural young people found in these sites are not easily discernible from the content of the sites themselves. The realities of new media access in rural U.S. communities further complicate any efforts to sum up the resources available to rural youth.

Paul DiMaggio and Eszter Hargittai (2001) make a compelling case that as diffusion of new media accelerates analyses of the digital divide, previously defined in binary terms of technology's presence or absence, we must consider "the dimensions of inequality" that delineate new media use (8).[9] DiMaggio and Hargittai's findings suggest that as information and communication technologies make their way to all corners of the globe through Internet cafés, schools, and government offices, researchers must pay even greater attention to conditions that reproduce social inequality through gradations in access as equipment, personal and confidential use, skills, and social support among new media users (8). For example, rural youth involved in this study had universal access to the Internet through computers available at their schools. Their state governments had invested heavily in school-based access through federal grants. But these grants also included some of the most sophisticated web-monitoring and filtering software available. Rural youth could not use their school's resources to examine the discourses circulating online about non-heteronormative gender or sexual identities because resources that discussed sexuality were summarily blocked. Even when young people reported being able to circumvent the filtering software, they did so at great risk because their passcodes for accessing school computers logged their browsing, e-mail, and chat exchanges.

Poverty and unemployment levels also dictated who might have access to a personal computer at home. Most of the working poor to lower middle-class youth shared computers with family members. Even in cases where they had

autonomous home access, youth frequently had only the most rudimentary ability to read more than text-based sites as most of the regions involved in my
research offer only dial-up service. A 2000 national study of access to broadband technologies indicated that only 5 percent of towns with populations below
10,000 had point-of-presence Internet service providers or other infrastructures
critical to providing high-speed services (Malecki 2003, 204). Cable and digital
subscriber line (DSL) services are still largely unavailable in rural Appalachia
(ConnectKentucky 2005; Malecki 2003, 201–14); ConnectKentucky 2007. This
speaks to the importance of considering not just the availability of new media to
rural queer and questioning youth but also the limits of that access for a range
of reasons.

Regardless of issues of access, youth must continually search for queer representations of realness as the Internet is always changing, constantly displacing
reliable locations for the kinds of reflections of realness they seek. Even though
at times difficult to track down, realness found in online narratives as compared
to fictional accounts in film and television indexes the limits of mass culture's
ability to bring visibility to LGBTQ-identifying people in rural communities.
They find comfort and familiarity in the narratives of realness circulating online. More so than fictional characters situated in urban scenes where a critical
mass of LGBTQ visibility is taken for granted, these stories resonate with the
complex negotiation of visibility and maintaining family ties that consume rural
young people's everyday lives. These digitally circulated representations of
LGBTQ identity categories interpellate rural queer youth by laying down a basic
narrative for the articulation of identity. At the same time, the amount rural
youth absorb or rework these categories has everything to do with each young
person's capacity to enact and publicly assert these categories. This approach to
studies of media's effects calls for a deeply situated understanding of media engagements beyond the reception of particular media texts.

Queer Realness

A media in situ approach applied to this fieldwork shows us rural queer youth
prioritizing particular genres of media engagement. Rural youth used the Internet, particularly engagements with youth-spun websites and personal ads on
commercial media properties like Gay.com, to confirm the existence of queerness beyond their locales and strategize about how to bring that queerness home
to roost. These genres as "discursive practices" are clearly experienced as sources
of information and, to some extent, unmediated truth about and for LGBTQ-
identifying people (Friedman 2006; Mittell 2001; Hanks 1987; Bauman 1986).

However, genres of queer realness are not defined by the aesthetic codes they might share as digital texts.[10] Internet-based personals, search-engine results, coming-out stories, and chat rooms as genres of queer realness provide moments of storytelling that transform the ways rural youth think and talk about their identities. As Richard Bauman notes, "When one looks to the social practices by which social life is accomplished, one finds—with surprising frequency—people telling stories to each other, as a means of giving cognitive and emotional coherence to experience, constructing and negotiating social identity" (Bauman 1986, 113). Rural youth are in the thick of these negotiations.

Darrin, a gay-identifying seventeen-year-old from an agricultural town of 6,100 people, sees websites, like the commercial portal PlanetOut.com, as "a place to feel at least somewhat at home." He adds, "But then I have to figure out how to make that home here too, you know? Chat rooms give me a place to go when I don't feel I can connect to others where I am." Amanda, a fourteen-year-old from Kentennessee, describes her experiences online as "pretty much the only place I can Google stuff or say my true feelings and not have everyone know about it." Darrin and Amanda's mention of commercial LGBTQ portals and search engines suggest that these genres offer a boundary public—a sense of place and the tools to find more resources—for their identity work.[11] For example, Sarah, age seventeen, from a town of 12,000 along the Ohio River separating Indiana and Kentucky, notes:

> When I'm on these sites, I like to read others' stories and experiences. I use web sites and search engines, like Google, most because they give the most info. I like personal stories, people's coming-out stories. How their family reacted. Going online and reading things from Betty DeGeneres [mother of lesbian comedian Ellen DeGeneres] on PlanetOut, where she does a little column. Trying to be as much of a sponge as I can when it comes to other people and their situations and how they handled themselves in those situations . . . using their experiences as possibilities for my own.

PlanetOut and its popular business partner Gay.com draw millions of visitors monthly.[12] PlanetOut, like other commercial sites that cater to community-specific niche markets, prominently promotes community areas and rotates spotlighted personal profiles along with designated message boards and chat rooms targeting youth, women, men, and a range of sexual and gender identities (Campbell 2005; Gamson 2003; Alexander 2002) LGBTQ-specific news and entertainment refresh each time one brings up the site's main page. Sarah's perusing and information sifting is familiar to all of us; she prioritized searching for coming-out stories and how-to's that could help her talk to family members about her queer identity. Sarah, like most of the youth I met, didn't want to escape from rural Kentucky. In part her desire to stay put was because of her close ties with family, but she, like several others I interviewed, also had no funds to leave her hometown and no educational training or particularly marketable job skills. Instead, she wanted to refashion her local circumstances with the help of what she discovered online. As I discuss elsewhere, "'family' represents a social safety net that is otherwise absent from the public infrastructure of impoverished rural communities" (Gray 2009, 139). Because this ethnographic study focused on youth who had not run away or been kicked out of their homes, I learned about the conditions for queering identity and publics in rural communities from young people who either did not want to leave their small towns or could not muster the means to do so.[13] Most were also minors and, therefore, had limited resources and legal rights to independence.[14]

Most of these young people were financially dependent on their parents. More broadly, despite their queer identity work, their communities embraced them because of their ties to local families. As such, families were primary sources of emotional and material support as well as social recognition and (sometimes begrudged) acceptance. Narratives that conveyed how to handle family anger, disappointment, and potential rejection were particularly important to these young people. Youth, like Sarah, were heavily invested in finding the commensurability between the tangible social worlds of their families and the referential connections to online LGBTQ communities. Tamotsu Shibutani called "audiences that are not obviously on the scene," like the ones Sarah encountered through her websurfing, "reference groups" (Shibutani 1961, 129). Shibutani argued that we orient and adjust our behaviors according to the reference group we envision. This process is complicated if one is at once learning about and seeking out markers of these reference groups. Rural youth needed to make their identities fit within the framework of "family."

The emphasis Shibutani puts on references to presumed but not presently queer is poetically illustrated among young people who use new media for what they refer to as "research." Joseph, for one, describes his early efforts to understand his attraction to boys this way: "when I was 11 or 12 years old, I started getting crushes on people, and I started going to search engines [on the Internet] and doing research about it . . . I just started doing research, and I found out what everything meant and that I was gay."

Justin, another fifteen-year-old questioning youth from a small Kentucky town of 4,500 on the Kentucky-Ohio border, describes his research this way:

When I first got the internet, my main goal was . . . I was about 13, I guess . . . of course, pornography 'cause I heard boys at school talking about it. When I first started, I would go lookin' for main places and they would have lesbians and gays in separate categories. Finally, I realized they [lesbians and gays] had their own [websites]. I had to search. It really was work. It was really, really hard to get onto these websites 'cause some of them had a block, and you'd have to hunt around for the ones that were free. Sometimes, you'd wait for a picture to download for five minutes! I was risking getting caught so I wanted to find something I really wanted to see!

The Internet presented both opportunities and challenges to Justin's research agenda. It required him to weigh his desires against the risk of exposure. He balanced the covertness and patience needed to find queer realness—primarily on personal listings on gay- and lesbian-specific websites—with his need to view something he could not see in his daily life. Josh also talks about the Internet as a means to explore his new community:

I was so uneducated about the gay life. I knew almost nothing. I mean like, gay terminology. People on the internet would use something and I'd be like, "What is that?" I didn't know. I didn't have a computer at home. I mean, I knew about a few things from other friends but most of them were, like things, you know, like how to act in a bar. Well, this is a dry county and we don't have any bars. And I don't think there's much in the Western Kentucky area where I'm from for gay people.

Josh doesn't attribute his ignorance of gay life to his rural surroundings. Indeed, Josh is no more "ignorant" than any young person steeped in the heteronormative world that shapes our lives. He recognizes that local places and people can provide some of the references he craves, but he also knows his lack of Internet access limits his ability to connect with them. Josh continues:

Online you're able to meet a lot more people than you are off-line. You may get five people at a Tri-State meeting [regional LGBTQ advocacy agency] one day and they may know two other people, so there's like 15 there. Online, I can talk to maybe 20 GLBT people in an hour! Since I live in a small town, where I know very few gay people, it gives me a sense that the gay community is small but when you get on the internet you realize the gay community is everywhere and it's huge!

Rural youth use genres of queer realness to symbolize and actualize their connections to a larger network of gays, lesbians, bisexuals, and transpeople. They
also use these media engagements with genres of queer realness to bring their
performances home, anchor them locally, and transform them into experiences
of self/senses of identity that can and do happen to youth "just like them."

Some young people seamlessly integrate genres of queer realness into their
construction of identity, but this is not always the case. To incorporate genres
of queer realness into an imagined sense of self, youth must traverse a dense
terrain of other social realities. They must weigh how doable or desirable such
realness is. As Shibutani notes, "each person performs for some kind of audience; in the drama of life, as in the theater, conduct is oriented toward certain
people whose judgment is deemed important" (1961, 129). Our inevitable align-
ments with multiple audiences lead us, as Shibutani puts it, to "violate the norms
of one reference group no matter what [we] do" (1961, 141). Disrupting (or queering) the norm stands out in rural communities where the audience is oriented
toward presumptions of familiarity.

THE CASE OF BRANDON:
NEGOTIATING QUEER REALNESS AND RURAL RACISM

Brandon and I e-mailed several times about his desire to share his story of
growing up as an African American in rural Central Kentucky. Brandon is self-
effacing, yet confident, a first-year student at a small college a few hours from
his hometown. He contacted me after reading an online announcement about
my research project, which had been forwarded to him by a friend involved with
their campus LGBTQ student group. We met in an activities room tucked in the
north wing of the campus student union. As Brandon waved effusively to people,
everyone—from custodians to students to administrators—returned his greet-
ing with a smile and a buoyant "Hey there, B." After graduating from a Catholic
high school in a town of 5,000, he had become a respected leader on campus
and was particularly known for his work as the president of the campus's Black
Student Caucus.

Brandon and I talked for nearly an hour about the organizing he did around
race issues at his high school. He laughed loudly but his voice belied exaspera-
tion as he recalled those early leadership experiences. "Any black student at my
high school knew that they were representing black with a capital 'B.' . . . We
were coming from two or three counties from around the region but when we
got to school, we became an instant community. . . . I used to joke with my best
friend, Lana, that we were the NAACP, BET, and NBA all rolled into one!"

Few people knew of Brandon's same-sex yearnings other than a young man on campus he had dated briefly and a smattering of friends he knew through online chat rooms and instant messaging. He had come out as bisexual to his friends in the Black Student Caucus only two weeks earlier. "I set them up really. I suggested we play a game of 'twenty questions' with the goal of sharing something with each other we'd never told anyone else. I've never been in a relationship with a girl here on campus and it didn't take my friends long to ask the obvious, 'Are you gay?'" Brandon said he felt more "whole" since what he dubbed "the big reveal":

> It, well, I was just feeling so split. The pressure to tell someone just seemed there all the time. It really became an issue for me beginning of this semester when the LGBTQ [student] group needed some help doing an HIV awareness project and approached the [Black Student] Caucus but the other members were like, "I don't want to work with the gay group!" . . . and I felt like such a fake pretending like I had nothing in common with these people [in the LGBTQ student group]. . . . I didn't feel like I could ignore the political struggles of a group I basically belonged to—even if no one knew—what kind of civil rights leader would I be?

I asked Brandon how his student activism and political organizing affected his sexual feelings and identity. He said:

> I've thought about this a lot lately. I've known for some time that I was attracted to both males and females . . . since probably sophomore year in high school . . . [*long pause*] . . . but, I guess . . . well, I felt like I had to choose between being black, I had to be either an African American student leader or labeled the "gay guy" and I saw what happened to kids labeled "gay." . . . I don't think I could have handled being rejected by other black kids. Being black was more important to me.

Brandon wondered aloud whether the pressure he felt to appear heterosexual would have been tempered if he'd attended a more racially diverse high school. His high school was in one of the few, nonurban areas of Kentucky with a sizable, visible, and well-established African American middle class. The rural communities surrounding Brandon's are typical of the racial makeup of rural Kentucky that are 90 to 96 percent white. In a very small town (population fewer than 3,000), this can mean literally one family of color keeps a town from registering as exclusively white. Similar to neighboring West Virginia, Kentucky has no adjacent townships of all or mostly black communities. Communities of color, predominantly African American but increasingly Latino families, exist in relatively segregated neighborhoods in the metropoles of Louisville, Lexington, and Bowling Green. There are a few towns associated with military bases and factories with sizable African American populations, but to respect Brandon's request for confidentiality, I do not specify the town or region in which he grew up. However, he does live in one of several communities where race relations have long been addressed by a powerful though small community of African Americans in coalition with white civil rights and labor organizers (Fosl 2002; Buck 2001).

Brandon felt his friends—black and white alike—accepted him because of his middle-class upbringing, which "put them all in the same kinds of clothes, neighborhoods, and high school classes." He felt he quickly rose to assume a leadership position as class president in his high school because of the ease with which he moved between his white and black friends. His high school had a history of welcoming discussions about race and social justice, so Brandon had room to advance projects like extensive Black History Month celebrations and forums on racially motivated hate crimes happening elsewhere in the state and across the border in Indiana. But when it came to opening up about his attraction to boys, he kept his feelings confined to a small circle of exclusively online friends:

> High school was a continuous battle between self-recognition or self-destruction. . . . It was a constant thing. . . . I realized that graduating from college, making achievements, all of that might not matter if people found out I was attracted to guys. So that was the sad part—why try to do good things if it wouldn't "count" 'cause I liked males? I think that was the reaction that most people in my life—family and friends—would have had. I wasn't courageous enough at that point to, like some of the people that I knew, to just go against the grain and come out. I think it was an ostracizing reaction for me to have, but it helped me survive this far.

Brandon sees his sexual desires as threatening to his closeness to family and friends, and his affirmation at school. Brandon does not possess the unequivocal self-acceptance and "sense of integrity and entitlement" that Steven Seidman defines as the "post-closeted gay sensibility" of today's gay youth identity (Seidman 2002, 75). Brandon's relationship to a bisexual identity is more complicated, however. Seidman does not suggest all gay people are "beyond the closet," but does claim that in this unprecedented age of gay visibility most gay Americans "live outside the social framework of the closet" (Seidman 2002, 9).

But as the anthropologist Martin Manalansan (2003) argues in his ethnography of gay Filipino men's negotiation of sexual identity and diasporic life, gay identity in the United States is "founded on a kind of individuation that is separate from familial and kin bonds and obligations" and "predicated on the use of verbal language as the medium in which selfhood can be expressed" that do not have parallels or translate seamlessly in the social organization of Filipino life in the diaspora (23). Brandon's struggle is as much with these generic expectations of distance between gay identity and family as with heterosexism. Brandon needs to reconcile the demands of distancing, which Manalansan describes as fundamental to U.S. gay identity with his need to maintain family ties and recognition as a local African American leader. Seidman suggests that the identity negotiations Brandon confronts are exceptions to the rule attributable to the challenges individuals face when they must synthesize sexual identities and racial or other core identities (Seidman 2002, 43). Even though Seidman's focus is on a wide group of individuals, many still raise the question of why are those who privilege gay visibility valorized as "beyond the closet," and youth of color, rural young people, and other individuals with core identities vying for recognition seen as in denial? Seidman's liberationist approach configures the closet as the residue of a past "social system of heterosexual domination" that can be conquered through choosing recognition and coming out (217–18, n.10). For rural youth, particularly rural youth of color like Brandon, the politics of LGBTQ visibility do not provide greater access to unequivocal pleasures of acceptance and identification, and put at risk the necessities of familiarity.

Brandon expressed ambivalence about coming out to his friends and family but did find solace and a way to negotiate the expectations of visibility through what he called his "gay outlet":

> The summer before my junior year, I got work as a station assistant at our local public radio station. I spent evenings stocking and entering things into a database in the basement of the station. The computer I worked on had internet access, no filters like the computers at school, which I wouldn't have touched with a 10-foot pole! So one night, I don't even know what I typed in; I just found chat rooms with guys looking to hook up with other guys. But I also found websites about political stuff. . . . There was a whole world of people talking about being bisexual . . . well, not as many people talking about that but at least I could see places that were for people like me. . . . This was my gay outlet. . . . I could read personals, stories about people my age telling their parents about their feelings. . . . I could even find rooms for chatting with people living near my hometown!

For Brandon, reading online personals and coming-out stories was a way to experience what coming out to his parents might feel like at a time when his ability to talk about his bisexuality seemed incompatible with his identity as a young, progressive African American student leader in rural Kentucky. Ironically, his online explorations reinforced the racial reality of his daily life:

> You know, no matter how many times I went into the Kentucky chat rooms on
> Gay.com or looked at personals on places like PlanetOut, I never once saw another
> black kid my age living in my area. . . . I didn't find anything for black kids any-
> where! Maybe that says more about my computer skills? [*laughs*] I don't know if
> that means I'm the only one—I doubt it . . . all of the personals I read either said
> they were white guys looking for white guys or race didn't matter . . . but it mat-
> ters a lot to me!

Youth, like Brandon, use new media to temporarily patch the incongruence or alienation between their sexual desires and other social worlds. They must reckon this mending with the resources locally available to continue their identity work. Brandon's "gay outlets" attended to parts of his experiences of identity. These engagements with genres of queer realness also reminded him that while "gay outlets" could offer the promise of connection with others "like him," these others would necessarily reproduce the segregation and racism of his surroundings.

The Case of John W.:
Negotiating Gay Identity and Queer Desire

John W. generously made room for us to sit down by clearing away stacks of sheet music and leftover coffee cups from his weathered, plaid couch. He offered a quick apology for the apartment's disarray. "Sorry, the dudes I live with are kind of pigs." We met shortly after he answered my call for participants, which circulated through his college diversity coalition's e-mail list. John W.'s tattoos and facial piercings together with the safety pins holding his jeans together fit the moniker of "progressive punk rocker" he proudly claimed. He had recently declared himself "gay," but he wasn't sure if that identity resonated deeply with him.

A nineteen-year-old white, middle-class college student, John W. grew up in a factory town of 10,000 and prided himself on being one of the "edgy kids." He continues to commute on weekends from the college he attends to his hometown. Of his high school, he says, "There really weren't too many different kinds of kids. There were the jocks, which I tried to be. There were the smart kids and a few African American kids." John W. grew up in a strict Catholic household where sexual desires were not discussed. He recalls memories from as early as five years old when he realized that tying himself to his backyard swing set and hanging from its bars sexually excited him. "I really didn't know what bondage was at that point. Sometimes I even say that maybe my sexual attraction is more towards bondage than male or female." He found friends early on with whom he could share and act out some of these desires: "I don't know if the other cliques got into a little bit more of the alternative lifestyle of having sex or doing sexual things than my group of friends. I would probably think that my group of people was more apt to doing things a little bit different because we were different in the first place." In describing his forays into sexual play, John W. continued:

> I had this friend; I think he's straight. But he would come over, and we would get drunk. We just started tying each other up. I was between 15 and 16. One time we were at his house and we were looking at a *Playboy* and then there was like a couple pictures in the back of some guys lifting weights, and he was like, "Do you like that?" "Yeah." He asked me if he could do me up the butt, so I was like, "Okay, sure." As soon as he came and pulled out, he was like, "What have I done? I can't do this again." I haven't talked to him in a while. We didn't leave on bad terms. That's just when I started wondering if maybe I was gay.

John W. singles out his move to a midsized college town and subsequent access to the Internet as the means through which he acquired what he described as the language for his innate desires:

> In high school, I didn't really have too much access to the Internet because it was newer at the time and slower and, of course, all the school computers had software trackers and filters on them. We didn't have a computer at home either. When I came to college, my sophomore year, I got a computer, so I had instant access to the Internet. Before I had a computer I didn't have any sense of what I'd find online. I just typed in so many things on the computer and just learned about what to type in, what to find. I think with Gay.com I probably just typed in www.gay.com, like randomly, and found that this was the access to all the perverts like me. That's when I started learning about bondage and the terms, what BDSM was and S&M, and I just, I can't remember how I started looking for groups.

Websites were critical to John W.'s process of naming his desires, but they also played an important part in his search for local belonging in communities of practice organized around his new identity:

Three or four years ago you'd have a hard time finding something to do with leather or bondage or whatever around here, but now about every weekend there's a party. So the Internet has allowed all that to come forth. . . . Before I met my boyfriend [at the campus LGBTQ group], I was actively involved with a BDSM bondage group that met in South Central Kentucky area. I would travel and play around with male and females—mostly safe sex. I was actively involved with that group.

For John W., claiming a gay identity was a means toward a more salient identity: "I have to emphasize that my sexual interests are a big part of who I am, and my attraction for men . . . I don't know. I'm not all that sure that I feel gay like the other guys I meet who are gay. Like my current boyfriend, he's really gay, wants to settle down with one other guy and isn't into bondage at all." When asked how he was different from other gay men his age, John W. responded that from reading websites and negotiating his current relationship, he had the sense that being gay came packaged with a set of expectations, such as monogamy and normality, "like working at a regular job and settling down."

As John W. saw it, "bondage just comes with a desire to play with other people. I'm not just out to have sex. I'm fulfilling this internal need." Identifying as "gay" made it easier for him to find other men with whom to have the intimacy and sexual connection he desired, even if a gay identity did not squarely fit his sense of self and his range of desires:

Gay.com really isn't that great for me because a lot of people aren't into bondage. But I go to the "Kentucky" chat room because you know that you're probably going to find somebody near you. A lot of people will travel two or three hours to meet somebody. You can't just like hit on a guy on campus 'cause you don't know. I can find people on campus that I would have maybe one-night stands, but I really didn't have fun because there was no bondage. If I didn't have access to computers, I don't know what I would do.

The websites and online communities John W. finds don't confirm an identity for him. Rather, he picks up definitions to pragmatically serve his sexual desires. This process of sorting through the available terms led to his identity as a young gay man. But his gay identity is an approximation; he has ambivalence with the category "gay," but he finds utility in it. Digital representations of what it means to be "gay" have been undeniably vital to John W.'s sexuality. But they also underscore the frustration of what philosopher Kenneth Burke long ago noted: "to define or determine a thing is to mark its boundaries" (Burke 1969, 24).

CONCLUSION

Until recently, Brandon felt his bisexuality was incommensurate with his racial identity; John W. questions whether his identification with bondage fits with his understanding of "gay." Presuming that rural youth in the United States are isolated from LGBTQ identity formation, and from the processes that can queer one's normative sense of self, ignores how identities settle on our skin. The politics of LGBTQ visibility compel Brandon and John W. to put sexual identity ahead of their familial, racial, and queer desires. Nonetheless, Brandon and John W. teach us that we need to change our perception of the closet as an open or shut door. Closets are, in part, shaped by the "compulsory heterosexuality" that structures our everyday interactions (Rich 1980). Culturally, we all work under the assumption that individuals are heterosexual (and "male" or "female") until "proven" otherwise. Rural communities' material dependencies on structures of familiarity and the value placed on conformity as a sign of solidarity intensify the visibility of compulsory heterosexuality's hegemonic sexual and gender norms. Brandon's experience of what is commonly referred to as "the closet" challenges Seidman's assertions of, or hopes for, an America beyond the closet as long as we hitch a generic and universalizing logic of visibility to queer difference.

Like most teens, Brandon and John W. grew up with gay visibility readily available in the media. They knew what "gay" meant, but it was an identity category otherwise conspicuously unfamiliar to and popularly depicted as out of place in their rural surroundings. Both Brandon and John W. searched for identities that would lend authenticity to their own desires but that they could also experience locally. But identities, as the rhetorician and AIDS activist Cindy Patton has argued, "suture those who take them up to specific moral duties" (Patton 1993, 147). The ascribed moral duties of visibility and normative sexual mores that Brandon and John W. associated with the genre of "gay" realness they found online conflicted with the moral duties that already deeply engrossed them locally. The genre of "gay" available to them as a commodity through online coming-out narratives and personal ads provided partial relief to their search for realness. However, the packaging of gay identity's "auxiliary characteristics," those hegemonic behaviors and affective dispositions represented as integral to the status role of "gay," read as incommensurate with other pieces of their sense of self (Brekhus 2003). Their rural locales did not present them with options to tune out this dissonance. This is not a case of the Internet opening netherworlds of desire and identification unavailable in the everyday lives of rural queer youth. Instead, Brandon and John W.'s engagements with genres of queer realness demonstrate the dialectical production of modern LGBTQ identities that, by definition, draw on narratives driven by a politics of visibility.

Narratives of isolation reflect the ascendancy and dominance of a self-discovery/disclosure paradigm, which structures not only LGBTQ lives but also modern notions of how identities work (Seidman 2002; Giddens 1992, 200). What we call "the closet" springs from the idea that identities are waiting to be discovered and unfold from the inside out. Authenticity hinges on erasing the traces of others from our work to become who we "really" are. To leave the traces of social interaction visible is to compromise our claims to authenticity and self-determination (Giddens 1992, 185). Genres that queer realness simultaneously expand and consolidate the possibilities of identity—by prompting youth to rework the unmarked categories of heterosexual, male, and female—embrace their burgeoning non-normative desires. They then rearticulate LGBTQ identities as "real," "natural," "unmediated," and "authentic." In this sense, identity, even the most intimate, personal senses of self, can be explored as deeply social and highly mediated. With this in mind, how might we shift away from framing rural young people's sexualities and genders as, simply, unfolding states of being stunted by what we presume they lack? How might we, instead, come to see identities (theirs and ours) as a cultural process akin to what the philosopher Gilles Deleuze characterizes as the folding in from the outside?

The transformative power of self-identification to organize politics, culture, and intimacy depends on countless others. Social identities as agents of change are not isolatable to individual bodies or locations. Highly dynamic dialogues between local, material conditions and modern, commercial renderings of LGBTQ identities produce particular ways to dress, speak, and look for rural youth. For the youth with whom I worked, representations of the real—online coming-out stories and electronic personal ads in particular—were crucial. These genres of queer realness expand their sense of place, home, and belonging within queer social worlds.

Beyond a moment of visibility provided by mainstream television and film, genres of queer realness circulate compelling images of peers on a similar quest for verity and viability. This validation is particularly pressing in rural areas where community members rely on being known and knowable—familiar—to people around them. Internet-based genres of queer realness offer rural youth possibilities for both recognition and acknowledgement of seeking that recognition in places one is presumed to already be familiar. This genre of realness has the power to authenticate queerness through the textual and visual rhetoric of LGBTQ visibility that is (seemingly) real and tangible somewhere, even if it is not easily found in a small town. But how is the increased visibility of queer realness through media discourses taken up in people's lives? What are the practical applications of these media texts and discourses? What do these youth do with the expectations of visibility that are so central to the identity politics of the LGBTQ social movement? Instead of trying to gauge how media effects impact individuals, we should look at everyday uses and practices of media engagement.

NOTES

1. The inclusion of "queer" and "questioning" in the name of the forum Amy found online was not an anomaly. Several of the most commonly cited youth-specific websites and discussion forums referenced queer and questioning if not in their titles then in their FAQs. Arguably these terms, typically left undefined, operated as umbrella terms or placeholders for a spectrum of sexual and gender identities and practices that these sites and their offline counterparts meant to include. While queer and questioning challenge heteronormative structures of teenage life in multiple ways, they can also operate as stabilizing identity categories. I use the word "queer" throughout this chapter to signal my own desire to consider how a moniker that denaturalizes norms associated with sexual and gender identities might also paradoxically operate as an identity category. Drawing on scholar Shane Phelan, I maintain that the usefulness of the term "queer" may be that it names "an unstable identity process" (Phelan 1997, 60) less intentionally claimed by individuals than unpredictably carried out through their interactions.

2. Mittell does not specifically have ethnographic studies of media in mind, but his culturally situated notion of genre resonates with work in anthropology that examines how audiences and listeners interact with generic conventions. See William Hanks (1987); Richard Bauman (1986); and more recently Sarah Friedman (2006) for exemplars of this approach to genres as discursive practices.

3. Fieldwork for this project took place between September 2001 and April 2003, and in several short follow-up trips in the summers of 2004 and 2005. Thirty-four young people, ages fourteen to twenty-four, provided most of the interview materials; a broader group of youth allowed me access to participate and observe their everyday lives. I anchored my research in several small towns and rural communities, most with populations between 900 and 15,000 in what is referred to by the U.S. Census and Appalachian Regional Commission as the Central Appalachian Region.

4. As the media scholar Steve Jones recently argued, the fact that the Internet "comes to us at a screen's remove should not remove from our consideration the realities (socially, politically, economically, or otherwise constructed) within which those who use it live and within which the hardware and software, markets and marketing operate" (Jones 2006, xv).

5. Lisa Duggan (1992) suggests just such an approach. Duggan (22) cites Donna Haraway's (1985) reference to the feminist Chela Sandoval's use of the notion of "oppositional consciousness" to construct identities, which resisted naturalization but sought, instead, a foundation of coalitional politics built through common cause.

6. For a representative sample of studies that approach identity as a sociological construction see Strauss (1959); Giddens (1991); G. H. Mead and Morris (1934); and Goffman (1959); specific studies of youth identity include early studies by M. Mead (1932)

and Whyte (1943). For studies specifically dealing with the career of homosexuals, see Humphreys (1970) and Ponse (1978). See also the more recent work of Brekhus (2003), and his concept of suburban gay male identities as transmutable categories that can serve as actions, objects, or characteristics depending on the social situation. I hope this project builds a serviceable bridge between interactionist/constructionist perspectives on identity and poststructuralist perspectives on subjectivity. For the latter, the self is much less coherent and more of a "consequence" of discourse and power. Arguably, an interactionist approach and conceptualization of identity makes a bit more room for agency and resistance. On this point, see Flax (1990, 192–221).

7. For a recent and thorough review of this literature and its implications for youth research, see Best (2007, 1–38).

8. Many readers will recognize that this approach to identity is indebted to the work of Judith Butler and her use of Esther Newton's notion of performance as iterative acts that produce the chimera of a stable identity (Butler 1990). See also Barbara Smith's (1981) work on the social construction of personal narrative.

9. See also DiMaggio, Hargittai, Neuman, and Robinson (2001, 307–36).

10. I draw from the work of scholars on drag and the importance of "realness" in performing gender as a category such as Butler (1990; 1993); Halberstam (1998); and the earlier work of Newton (1972). Unlike hyperbolic performances of gender popularly associated with drag, "realness" seeks to embody rather than parody gender norms.

11. There is an ongoing, vibrant discussion of the critical role of information and communication technologies (ICTs) in the construction of spaces. For example, Morley and Robins (1995) offer a theoretical analysis of how ICTs—particularly globally circulated mass media consumption—disrupt the traditional boundaries of the nation-state. These authors argue that ICTs afford a different kind of geography and assert corresponding global/local dialectics. The anthropologist Debra Spitulnik (2002) takes a more linguistic approach to the ways in which communicative practices and their everyday discursive engagements with media technologies, such as portable radios in Zambia, produce spaces of cultural mobility. Zizi Papacharissi (2002, 9–27) more recently argued that the virtual spaces of new media offer potential for a revival of the public sphere. See Curry (1996) for a more provocative discussion of the distinction between "space" and "place" that bears heavily on the question of whether new media can be considered locations of any sort.

12. PlanetOut and Gay.com merged in 2001. For a discussion of their business model, see Campbell (2005, 663–83).

13. Unfortunately, there are no studies that could provide a more in-depth discussion of the numbers of youth who leave or stay in rural communities in relation to the resources available to them to negotiate a queer sense of identity. The census data suggests a slow and steady "brain drain" from the parts of Appalachia where I did the bulk of my fieldwork, but these data do not easily track the ebb and flow of specific young people in and out of the area or attempt to determine why some youth stay or leave, and the social, political, and economic factors that feed into these decisions.

14. Studies from the late 1980s to the present (Housing Assistance Council 2002; Hoover and Carter 1991; Fitchen 1992; and Cloke, Johnson, and May 2007) have consistently shown that U.S. rural communities have few, if any, shelters, outreach programs, or minimal services. Homelessness is often invisible because individuals with

insecure housing use car campers, parks, and private homes as temporary shelters, and there are no centralized support services where these individuals could be counted.

REFERENCES

Housing Assistance Council. 2002. *Taking Stock: Rural People, Poverty, and Housing at the Turn of the 21st Century*. Washington, DC: Housing Assistant Council.

Adler, Patricia A., and Peter Adler. 1998. *Peer Power: Preadolescent Culture and Identity*. New Brunswick, NJ: Rutgers University Press.

Alexander, Jonathan. 2002. "Homo-pages and Queer Sites: Studying the Construction and Representation of Queer Identities on the World Wide Web." *International Journal of Sexuality and Gender Studies* 7, nos. 2–3: 85–106.

Bauman, Richard. 1986. *Story, Performance, and Event: Contextual Studies of Oral Narrative*. Cambridge: Cambridge University Press.

Baym, Nancy. K. 2006. "Finding the Quality in Qualitative Research." In *Critical Cyberculture Studies*, edited by David Silver and Adrienne Massanari, 79–87. New York: New York University Press.

Best, Amy L. 2007. *Representing Youth: Methodological Issues in Critical Youth Studies*. New York: New York University Press.

Brekhus, Wayne. 2003. *Peacocks, Chameleons, Centaurs: Gay Suburbia and the Grammar of Social Identity*. Chicago: University of Chicago Press.

Buck, Pem Davidson. 2001. *Worked to the Bone: Race, Class, Power, and Privilege in Kentucky*. New York: Monthly Review Press.

Burke, Kenneth. 1969. *A Grammar of Motives*. Berkeley: University of California Press.

Butler, Judith. 1990. *Gender Trouble: Feminism and the Subversion of Identity*. New York: Routledge.

———. 1993. *Bodies That Matter: On the Discursive Limits of "Sex."* New York: Routledge.

Campbell, John Edward. 2005. "Outing PlanetOut: Surveillance, Gay Marketing and Internet Affinity Portals." *New Media and Society* 7, no. 5: 663–83.

Carey, James W. 1989. "Technology and Ideology: The Case of the Telegraph." In *Communication as Culture: Essays on Media and Society*, edited by James W. Carey, 201–31. Boston: Unwin Hyman.

Cassell, Justine, and Henry Jenkins. 1998. *From Barbie to Mortal Kombat: Gender and Computer Games*. Cambridge, MA: MIT Press.

Cloke, Paul John, Sarah Johnson, and Jon May. 2007. "The Periphery of Care: Emergency Services for Homeless People in Rural Areas." *Journal of Rural Studies* 23:387–401.

ConnectKentucky. 2005. *Internet and Broadband Use in Kentucky: Statewide Results from the 2005 County Level Technology Assessment Study*. http://www.connectkentucky.org/NR/rdonlyres/DCD506F1-D29-DC4-A421-02C91C8751C9/0/61_TECHNOLOGY_STATISTICS.pdf.

———. 2007. *2007 Kentucky Technology Trends: Results of the 2007 ConnectKentucky Residential Survey*. http://www.connectkentucky.org/_documents/2007KentuckyTechnologyTrends_residential_6-11-08.pdf.

Corsaro, William. 2005. *The Sociology of Childhood*. 2nd ed. Thousand Oaks, CA: Pine Forge Press.

Curry, Michael R. 1996. *The Work in the World: Geographical Practice and the Written Word*. Minneapolis: University of Minnesota Press.

DiMaggio, Paul, and Eszter Hargittai. 2001. *From the "Digital Divide" to "Digital Inequality": Studying Internet Use as Penetration Increases*. Working Paper 19. Princeton, NJ: Center for Arts and Cultural Policy Studies, Woodrow Wilson School, Princeton University.

DiMaggio, Paul, Eszter Hargittai, W. Russell Neuman, and John P. Robinson. 2001. "Social Implications of the Internet." *Annual Review of Sociology* 27:307–36.

Doty, Alexander. 1993. *Making Things Perfectly Queer: Interpreting Mass Culture*. Minneapolis: University of Minnesota Press.

———. 2000. *Flaming Classics: Queering the Film Canon*. New York: Routledge.

Driver, Susan. 2007. "Beyond 'Straight' Interpretations: Researching Queer Youth Digital Video." In *Representing Youth: Methodological Issues in Critical Youth Studies*, edited by Amy L. Best, 304–24. New York: New York University Press.

Drotner, Kirsten. 1992. "Modernity and Media Panics." In *Media Cultures: Reappraising Transnational Media*, edited by Michael Skovmand and Kim C. Schrøder, 42–62. London: Routledge.

Duggan, Lisa. 1992. "Making It Perfectly Queer." *Socialist Review* 22, no. 1: 11–31.

———. 1993. "The Trials of Alice Mitchell: Sensationalism, Sexology, and the Lesbian Subject in Turn-of-the-Century America." *Signs* 18, no. 4: 791–814.

Faulkner, Audrey Olsen, and Ann Lindsey. 2004. "Grassroots Meet Homophobia: A Rocky Mountain Success Story." *Journal of Gay and Lesbian Social Services* 16, nos. 3–4: 113–28.

Fine, Gary Alan, and Kent L. Sandstrom. 1988. *Knowing Children: Participant Observation with Minors*. Newbury Park, CA: SAGE Publications.

Fischer, Claude. 1992. *America Calling: A Social History of the Telephone to 1940*. Berkeley: University of California Press.

Fitchen, Janet. 1992. "On the Edge of Homelessness: Rural Poverty and Housing Insecurity." *Rural Sociology* 57:173–93.

Flax, Jane. 1990. *Thinking Fragments: Psychoanalysis, Feminism, and Postmodernism in the Contemporary West*. Berkeley: University of California Press.

Flint, Colin. 2004. *Spaces of Hate: Geographies of Discrimination and Intolerance in the U.S.A.* New York: Routledge.

Fosl, Catherine. 2002. *Subversive Southerner: Anne Braden and the Struggle for Racial Justice in the Cold War South*. New York: Palgrave Macmillan.

Friedman, Sara L. 2006. "Watching Twin Bracelets in China: The Role of Spectatorship and Identification in an Ethnographic Analysis of Film Reception." *Cultural Anthropology* 21, no. 4: 603–32.

Gamson, Joshua. 1998. *Freaks Talk Back: Tabloid Talk Shows and Sexual Nonconformity*. Chicago: University of Chicago Press.

———. 2003. "Gay Media, Inc.: Media Structures, the New Gay Conglomerates, and Collective Sexual Identities." In *Cyberactivism: Online Activism in Theory and Practice*, edited by Martha McCaughey and Michael D. Ayers, 255–78. New York: Routledge.

Giddens, Anthony. 1991. *Modernity and Self-Identity: Self and Society in the Late Modern Age*. Stanford, CA: Stanford University Press.

———. 1992. *The Transformation of Intimacy: Sexuality, Love, and Eroticism in Modern Societies*. Stanford, CA: Stanford University Press.

Goffman, Erving. 1959. *The Presentation of Self in Everyday Life*. Garden City, NY: Doubleday.

Gray, Mary L. 2009. *Out in the Country: Youth, Media, and Queer Visibility in Rural America*. New York: New York University Press.

Grazian, David. 2003. *Blue Chicago: The Search for Authenticity in Urban Blues Clubs*. Chicago: University of Chicago Press.

Gross, Larry P. 2001. *Up from Invisibility: Lesbians, Gay Men, and the Media in America*. New York: Columbia University Press.

———. 2007. "Foreword." In *Queer Online: Media, Technology, and Sexuality*, edited by Kate O'Riordan and David J. Phillips, vii–x. New York: Peter Lang.

Halberstam, Judith. 1998. *Female Masculinity*. Durham, NC: Duke University Press.

———. 2005. *In a Queer Time and Place: Transgender Bodies, Subcultural Lives*. New York: New York University Press.

Hanks, William. 1987. "Discourse Genres in a Theory of Practice." *American Ethnologist* 14, no. 4: 668–92.

Haraway, Donna. 1985. "A Manifesto for Cyborgs: Science, Technology, and Socialist Feminism in the 1980s." *Socialist Review* 15, no. 2: 65–108.

Hoover, G. A., and M. V. Carter. 1991. "The Invisible Homeless: Non-urban Homeless in Appalachian East Tennessee." *Rural Sociologist* 11, no. 4: 3–12.

Humphreys, Laud. 1975. *Tearoom Trade: Impersonal Sex in Public Places*. Chicago: Aldine Pub. Co.

James, Allison, Chris Jenks, and Alan Prout. 1998. *Theorizing Childhood*. New York: Teachers College Press.

Jenkins, Henry. 1998. *The Children's Culture Reader*. New York: New York University Press.

Jones, Steve. 2006. "Dreams of Fields: Possible Trajectories of Internet Studies." In *Critical Cyberculture Studies*, edited by David Silver, Adrienne Massanari, and Steve Jones, ix–xvii. New York: New York University Press.

Lancaster, Roger N. 2003. *The Trouble with Nature: Sex in Science and Popular Culture*. Berkeley: University of California Press.

Latour, Bruno. 1996. "On Interobjectivity." *Mind, Culture, and Activity* 3, no. 4: 228–45.

Lesko, Nancy. 2001. *Act Your Age! A Cultural Construction of Adolescence*. New York: Routledge Falmer.

Levine, Judith. 2002. *Harmful to Minors: The Perils of Protecting Children from Sex*. Minneapolis: University of Minnesota Press.

Livingstone, Sonia M. 2002. *Young People and New Media: Childhood and the Changing Media Environment*. Thousand Oaks, CA: SAGE.

———. 2008. "Taking Risky Opportunities in Youthful Content Creation: Teenagers' Use of Social Networking Sites for Intimacy, Privacy, and Self-expression." *New Media and Society* 10, no. 3: 392–411.

Malecki, Edward J. 2003. "Digital Development in Rural Areas: Potentials and Pitfalls." *Journal of Rural Studies* 19:201–14.

Manalansan, Martin F. 2003. *Global Divas: Filipino Gay Men in the Diaspora*. Durham, NC: Duke University Press.

Marvin, Carolyn. 1988. *When Old Technologies Were New: Thinking about Electric Communication in the Late Nineteenth Century*. New York: Oxford University Press.

Mead, G. H., and Charles W. Morris. 1934. *Mind, Self and Society from the Standpoint of a Social Behaviorist*. Chicago: University of Chicago Press.

Mead, Margaret. 1932. *Coming of Age in Samoa: A Psychological Study of Primitive Youth for Western Civilization*. New York: Blue Ribbon Books.

Meeker, Martin. 2006. *Contacts Desired: Gay and Lesbian Communications and Community, 1940s–1970s*. Chicago: University of Chicago Press.

Mittell, Jason. 2001. "A Cultural Approach to Television Genre Theory." *Cinema Journal* 40, no. 3: 3–24.

Morley, David, and Kevin Robins.1995. *Spaces of Identity: Global Media, Electronic Landscapes, and Cultural Boundaries*. New York: Routledge.

Muñoz José Esteban, 1999. *Disidentifications: Queers of Color and the Performance of Politics*. Minneapolis: University of Minnesota Press.

Newton, Esther. 1972. *Mother Camp: Female Impersonators in America*. Englewood Cliffs, NJ: Prentice-Hall.

Nye, David E. 1990. *Electrifying America: Social Meanings of a New Technology, 1880–1940*. Cambridge, MA: MIT Press.

Papacharissi, Zizi. 2002. "The Virtual Sphere: The Internet as Public Sphere." *New Media and Society* 4, no. 1: 9–27.

Patton, Cindy. 1993. "Tremble, Hetero Swine!" In *Fear of a Queer Planet*, edited by Michael Warner, 143–77. Minneapolis: University of Minnesota Press.

Phelan, Shane. 1997. "The Shape of Queer: Assimilation and Articulation." *Women and Politics* 18, no. 2: 60.

Ponse, Barbara. 1978. *Identities in the Lesbian World: The Social Construction of Self*. Contributions in Sociology 28. Westport, CT: Greenwood Press.

Qvortrup, Jens. 1994. *Childhood Matters: Social Theory, Practice and Politics*. Brookfield, VT: Avebury.

Rich, Adrienne. 1980. "Compulsory Heterosexuality and Lesbian Existence." *Signs: Journal of Women in Culture and Society* 5:631–60.

Sammond, Nicholas. 2005. *Babes in Tomorrowland: Walt Disney and the Making of the American Child, 1930–1960*. Durham, NC: Duke University Press.

Seidman, Steven. 2002. *Beyond the Closet: The Transformation of Gay and Lesbian Life*. New York: Routledge.

Seiter, Ellen. 1993. *Sold Separately: Children and Parents in Consumer Culture*. New Brunswick, NJ: Rutgers University Press.

———. 1999. *Television and New Media Audiences*. Oxford: Clarendon Press.

———. 2005. *The Internet Playground: Children's Access, Entertainment, and Mis-education*. New York: Peter Lang.

Shibutani, Tamotsu. 1961. *Society and Personality: An Interactionist Approach to Social Psychology*. Englewood Cliffs, NJ: Prentice-Hall.

Smith, Barbara Herrnstein. 1981. "Narrative Versions, Narrative Theories." In *On Narrative*, edited by W. J. T. Mitchell, 209–32. Chicago: University of Chicago Press.

Snively, Carol A. 2004. "Building Community-Based Alliances Between GLBTQQA Youth and Adults in Rural Settings." *Journal of Gay and Lesbian Social Services* 16, nos. 3–4: 99–112.

Spitulnik, Debra. 2002. "Mobile Machines and Fluid Audiences: Rethinking Reception through Zambian Radio Culture." In *Media Worlds: Anthropology on New Terrain*, edited by Faye D. Ginsburg, Lila Abu-Lughod, and Brian Larkin, 337–54. Berkeley: University of California Press.

Strauss, Anselm L. 1959. *Mirrors and Masks: The Search for Identity*. Glencoe, IL: Free Press.

———. 1993. *Continual Permutations of Action*. New York: Aldine de Gruyter.

Turner, Fred. 2006. *From Counterculture to Cyberculture: Stewart Brand, the Whole Earth Network, and the Rise of Digital Utopianism*. Chicago: University of Chicago Press.

Waller, Gregory A. 1990. "Situating Motion Pictures in the Pre-nickeloden Period: Lexington, Kentucky, 1897–1906." *Velvet Light Trap* 29:12–28.

Walters, Suzanna Danuta. 2001. *All the Rage: The Story of Gay Visibility in America*. Chicago: University of Chicago Press.

Whyte, William Foote. 1943. *Street Corner Society: The Social Structure of an Italian Slum*. Chicago: University of Chicago Press.

"Treat Us Right!"

Digital Publics, Emerging Biosocialities, and the Female Complaint

OLIVIA BANNER

We want our health to become a number.
—WALTER DE BROUWER, Quantified Self website, February 16, 2011

We live in an era filled with claims that the latest information technologies herald a new age in understanding how the body works. From personal genome testing to biotracking devices, from 3-D MRIs to bioscopies, our biotechnologies promise to make visible the invisible and to ferret out core truths encoded at the cellular level. At the center of these promises operates a fundamental faith that data and statistics exist in an unmediated relationship to truth. Although our daily bombardment by statistics may prove jarring, creating an endless anxiety about negotiating risk (Woodward 2008), we are increasingly offered means by which data and statistics—and the means to produce them—are made comfortable and familiar to us. This is no longer a discourse available only to the chosen few of a techie elite. We are all potentially nothing more, but also nothing less, than our data.

This article investigates such familiarizing practices of making the subject informatic—that is, where subjecthood and identity are conferred through participation in a discourse of data—with a particular focus on how female members of patient-networking websites enlist these practices. These sites are points of biomediation, where a digital representation of an illness is accepted as corresponding to the truth of the body, and where the social construction of an illness is contoured as well as challenged by people with the illness. This biomediation is linked to the current fetishization of data evident in new practices such as lifelogging, where people track minute fluctuations to their physical and mental states with the goal of improving their health, and it forms the basic ground of operations for patient-driven medicine. Building on the popularity of face-to-face patient support groups as well as early online support groups (Usenet newsgroups, for example, and LiveJournal), and fueled by the increased use of the Internet for all things relating to health (Fox 2011), patient-networking websites have helped to foster the belief that the Internet, through its ability to assemble and harness large quantities of data from volunteer donors of information, might offer a set of new techniques for biomedical breakthroughs. These sites ask participants to engage in self-tracking practices, in which they record fluctuations to their symptoms through daily updates that turn variable affective states (e.g., moods, fatigue levels, pain levels) into the "raw data" of statistics. Through self-tracking and the transformation of affect into data, such sites advance a process of informatic subjecthood, where the participant actively engages her interpellation (Althusser 1970) by informatics discourse and then views herself as a potential ongoing source of data, which becomes a gift to the health commons.

For Paul Rabinow (1996), biosociality, or group affiliation and self-definition formed around shared physical or biochemical markers, constitutes a primary—if not the most significant—mode for the organization of identities today. As instances where biosocialities form, these patient-networking websites present an arena in which a Foucauldian "anatomopolitics" is intrinsically linked to biosociality—that is, where the individual learns to discipline and regulate her body through the terms delimited by her biosocial community (Foucault [1978] 1990, 139). Fostering the idea that the individual user can learn from members of her biosocial community, such cyberbiosocialities join the individual practices associated with anatomopolitics to a biopolitics of the biosocial community. Discourses of individual self-empowerment—the attendance to one's own corporeal existence—apparent throughout patient-networking sites mesh with entreaties to empower the biosocial community at the same time (Rose 2006).

This kind of informatic subjecthood takes place on PatientsLikeMe.com (hereafter PLM), a site that is significant for a number of reasons. It is the largest site of its kind, with more than one hundred thousand users (as of 2011). Many of the illnesses and syndromes that it currently includes are notoriously contentious diagnoses, ones that scholars have problematized as historically and culturally shifting and under constant negotiation (Martin 2009; Orr 2006). The definitions of these diagnoses that circulate in popular discourse are often multiple and variable, and thus people so diagnosed are aware of the instability of their own diagnoses, as well as the politics that drive recognition of and research into their conditions. This is true of the two illnesses I discuss here: fibromyalgia and chronic fatigue syndrome (hereafter FM/CFIDS),[1] illnesses affecting primarily women and whose online communities therefore produce specifically female digital publics, where women sometimes reflect on the social conditions that determine how medicine constructs their illness; this gives new media scholars the opportunity to reflect on what opportunities these sites afford women to actively challenge biomedicine. I argue that once users engage in the informatic practices available on PLM, where the site represents the body and its symptoms through the language of biomedicine, the patient's ability to understand her illness as situated within a larger sociohistorical context is attenuated. This practice of self-quantification amplifies a dynamic whereby together patients generally accept the terms offered by biomedicine through which to understand their illnesses. The informatic subjecthood constructed on PLM contributes to the construction of the illness itself.

Social Construction, Biomediation, and the Female Complaint

In her account of FM/CFIDS, Susan Greenhalgh describes this phenomenon within the rubric of social construction, here applied to the idea of illness itself. For Greenhalgh, "Constructivist perspectives on illness have . . . show[n] that illness is not so much a real phenomenon—although it has biological bases and produces genuine discomfort—as it is a phenomenon that is *made real* by the operations of medical science. It is 'socially constructed,' or brought into being, by the specific practices, technologies, and styles of reasoning by which it is studied and represented by researchers and diagnosed and treated by clinicians" (Greenhalgh 2001, 24). Because Greenhalgh supports this conclusion with an autoethnographic study, her example leaves out the manner in which a *group* of people who share the diagnosis circulate meanings and practices among themselves. By analyzing such a community, this chapter shifts the emphasis in social construction from "the operations of medical science" as the primary site through which an illness is made real to an understanding of how an illness is made real by new processes of subjectification, through the biosociality afforded by the Internet.

This sort of subjectification is a process of *biomediation*. I use this term in conversation with Eugene Thacker. For Thacker, biomedia are those sites where biotechnology meets biota in ways that expand on what the biological has been able to do, allowing for biological substances to be used in novel ways. Such expansions depend on the technical understanding of life as digital and informatic (Thacker 2004). Although he constrains the term "biomedia" specifically to media used in laboratories (e.g., gel electrophoresis, petri dishes, recombinant

DNA), I extend it to arenas where biological states are mediated through digital and informatic modes of representation. PLM is such an arena, where bioinformatic tools allow for the subject to recontextualize herself not only as an embodied subjectivity more generally but also as a body upon which medical technologies like genetic therapies or pharmaceuticals can work.

Because biomedia take as their fundamental ground a digital mode of operation in which the body can be coded so that media and technologies can re- and decode it, self-tracking projects, where users track changes to their physical and mental states through software programs and therefore turn physical experience into data, constitute a prime example of the biomediated body. Those who self-track engage the practice in the hopes that it will one day join with other techniques based on data and informatics in which the body and its processes can be maximized, manipulated, and managed. Through practices of turning the self into data, embodiment itself begins to be contoured through statistical data. These notions of bodies as digital and/or informatic become, through lived experience, engrained on and within bodies. We can investigate the phenomena of these patient websites as spaces in which an illness is understood as integral to the self and identity and is transformed into informatic language in a digital context, which then contributes to a fetishization of the self-as-data, now made available for biomedical research.

In an illness that mainly affects women, such informatic subjecthood changes the stakes for what Lauren Berlant (2008) has deemed the "female complaint"— the registering of "complaints" specific to women through affective intimate publics. In the case of FM/CFIDS and PLM, site administrators are aware that medical professionals often ignore or dismiss women diagnosed with these conditions. The site therefore includes features designed to create a new media intimate public sphere like those Berlant describes. The site is a space where strangers who share a history, in this case their diagnoses and the long travels they took to get those diagnoses, come together to share their stories, where "the consumers of [it] *already* share a worldview and emotional knowledge that they have derived from a broadly common historical experience" (viii). In Berlant's descriptions of them, intimate public spheres accrue particularly strong affective attachments through the consumption of commodities designed to make women *feel* a commonality. In PLM, this affective attachment is achieved through participation in what PLM conveys as a "complaint" lodged at the institution of biomedicine itself, which constitutes members' common sphere of affective investment. As in Berlant's assessment of the intimate public sphere generally, in these biosocialities the possible political import of female complaints becomes subsumed by the fact that the intimate public sphere never truly goes public and/or becomes a democratic form of collective action. These new media forums of biosociality divest their illnesses of the historical and social context that have produced them, leaving their users at the whim of the site itself to formulate the shape their complaint will take.

SELF-TRACKING AND PATIENT-DRIVEN MEDICINE

Logging data and tracking daily experience in medical contexts and for purposes of self-monitoring is by no means new—patients have long been asked to monitor and chart their symptoms (Martin 2007). Yet its deployment within electronic forums is transforming the nature of how individuals view themselves, how they perceive their bodies, and how they conceive of the collectivities to which they feel they belong, all of these mediated by the all-powerful statistic.

Walter de Brouwer's proclamation in this chapter's epigraph demonstrates the fascination with and desire for statistics and data that circulates among the gurus of our contemporary information economy. De Brouwer's statement appears on the Quantified Self website, a community blog of reports by information-industry workers who are engaging in a fledgling practice called lifelogging. Lifelogging practitioners track and record the minutiae of their biodata, from food eaten to blood pressure measurements, and they sometimes use video and audio technologies to record their daily experiences. The purpose of lifelogging, in the words of the futurist Kevin Kelly, is personal growth through analysis: "Deep comparative analysis of your activities could assist your productivity, creativity, and consumptivity" (Kelly 2007). Lifelogging functions as a technology for self-optimization within a capitalist economy, allowing a person maximum efficiency for the most effective insertion into the capitalist practices of producing and consuming and, in the practices of informatics-based capitalist economies, of creating software or online content. It also expands the terrain for the current fetishization of data.

But these information workers do more than simply grant to data the mystical powers often given fetish objects; they also participate in the wider biocapital processes by which somatic data is reified into a commodity. As many have noted, the information-economy industries and their workers participate in an ongoing process by which digital technologies are exalted as liberatory forces through the "empowerment" they provide; and as digital technologies increasingly allow for data about the body to be collected, these discourses promote the data itself as the mode for empowerment (e.g., Liu 2004). Walter de Brouwer's claim that "we want our health to be a number" is typical of lifeloggers (de

Brouwer 2011). Once reduced to data, "health" becomes not only a site for intervention, modification, and optimization but also becomes a commodity, which
can be valued and exchanged within the biocapitalized market. It should not
come as a surprise that the founder of PLM, Jamie Heywood, is himself deeply
enmeshed in the information industry: he was a Silicon Valley software engineer who prospered during the dotcom boom. His company uses Web 2.0—the
participatory web—under the aegis of driving a new wave of medical innovation, which the site, like others of its kind, refers to as "patient-driven medicine." This type of medicine is being fueled by the technological transformations
of the cyber realm: because online forums allow companies immediate access
to patients, a range of issues that have bedeviled the pharmaceutical industry
can be overcome. These include the low percentage of successful recruitment
and retention of patients for clinical trials, the time lag between clinical trials
and reporting of results, regulations concerning privacy and sharing data, and,
perhaps most significantly, the enormous cost of clinical trials (Allison 2009).
Web 2.0 and patient-networking websites overcome these problems because they
allow easy recruitment of trial populations, immediate reporting of results, a
significant reduction in costs for pharmaceutical drug delivery, and an easy
means of working around current privacy and consent concerns, since patients
volunteer to participate. Patient-driven medicine and its Web 2.0 existence are,
therefore, a boon to pharmaceutical companies. The phrase "patient-driven medicine," though, connotes that such sites are part of a grassroots effort, as though
patients themselves can determine the course of research. Yet in its use of the
word "patient," the phrase suggests the extent to which someone who experiences an illness must, when encountering these sites, also feel and understand
herself within the context of the contemporary neoliberal medical industry. In
other words, to engage in patient-driven medicine, and to log in as a "patient like
me," the participant sees herself as a biomedicalized subject, fully interpellated
by the practices, discourses, economics, and socialities of modern medicine.

   That understanding hinges on being not only able to represent identity as data
but also understanding that representing oneself through data contributes to
the company's broader aims. "Our goal," says PatientsLikeMe's "About" page, "is
to enable people to share information that can improve the lives of patients diagnosed with life-changing diseases. To make this happen, we've created a platform
for collecting and sharing real world, outcome-based patient data . . . and are
establishing data-sharing partnerships with doctors, pharmaceutical and medical device companies, research organizations, and non-profits."[2] Users are made
aware that when they voluntarily provide information about their symptoms and

treatments, PLM then sells it to corporate clients, some of which research causes of diseases but many of which are pharmaceutical companies interested in testing or developing new treatments. Like other Internet community sites, the patient communities at PLM also function as support groups; in this they are no different from various LiveJournal groups or from other health-related sites such as Inspire or MyInvisibleDisabilities. However, PLM significantly differs in two aspects: first, in its role as a corporate entity that sells data; second, in its interface, where users are asked to report on their symptoms and are offered minutely detailed analyses of variations of symptoms over time.[3]

PATIENTSLIKEME AND FM/CFIDS

The largest biosocial community on PLM is the FM/CFIDS community, with approximately 35,000 users (as of June 2013).[4] Estimates of prevalence for both illnesses vary: most recently, the incidence of CFIDS in the general U.S. population was estimated at 2.45 percent (Reeves et al. 2007); for fibromyalgia the incidence has been estimated at 2 percent (Wolfe et al. 1995). Figures on incidence vary according to which symptom criteria are employed, and misdiagnosis is also common. Both illnesses are characterized by, among multiple other symptoms, widespread musculoskeletal pain and fatigue. They are of particular interest to my study of female biosocialities for a number of reasons. First, they are poorly understood, and their definitions undergo constant redefinition. Second, due to new findings of the possibilities of a viral cause for CFIDS, there has been an increase in CDC funding as well as press reporting on it, and thus the possibility of greater public awareness for it.[5] As syndromes, only their symptoms can be treated (rather than their causes, in the case of diseases). In contemporary fashion doctors generally prescribe a range of pharmaceuticals, from antidepressants to opioids, in a "throw the spaghetti and see what sticks" fashion. To date, the FDA has approved three drugs for the treatment of FM, all of them repurposings of antidepressant or antiseizure compounds. The numbers of people with these illnesses and potential prescriptions mean that pharmaceutical companies are extremely interested in them. With increased attention and a wider range of possibilities for causation, PLM continually revamps its website to attend to these new formations.

Third, with these particular illnesses the diagnoses are given predominantly to women, at a ratio of nine women to every man. Following in a long line of female maladies that have been ascribed psychosomatic etiologies, FM and CFIDS have for years not been recognized as "real" illnesses. Doctors often dismiss those with symptoms as depressives or as hypochondriacal. Both FM and

CFIDS have been bedeviled by the politics of research into women's health issues, which is often underfunded. Patient-networking sites with FM/CFIDS communities are therefore instructive in what they reveal about how women use them to register specifically female complaints against biomedicine.

In order to address the main symptoms of these illnesses—musculoskeletal pain and debilitating fatigue—PLM uses a "Pain and Fatigue Rating Scale" (PFRS) as its main feature for tracking symptom fluctuations. When a user logs in, the homepage first entreats her to update her symptoms, which it calls "InstantMe." Once the user updates this, she is taken to her homepage, where the dominant visual is her PFRS chart, which differs significantly from traditional methods of representing the body's pain, such as the McGill Pain Questionnaire. On that questionnaire, one adjective may correspond to pain caused by, for example, arthritis, and another to pain caused by nerve damage, and it also includes a visual representation of the human form.

Unlike the McGill Pain Questionnaire, which maps pain onto an image of the body, the PFRS is presented as a graph. The "language" of pain is therefore no longer situated on the body: embodied experience is made fully statistical and digital. Because the graph is customizable according to duration of time, the ability to so manipulate symptoms increases their existence as pure data, as numbers to which calculations can be performed and then rearranged. Pain becomes quantifiable. In addition, the PFRS, unlike the McGill Questionnaire, does not exist within the context of the embodied clinical interaction. In an almost paradoxical dynamic, pain is disembodied and abstracted through this procedure, thus losing its affective nature and its chance to communicate something other than what the graph represents as numerical and abstract. Since this scale is envisioned as a potential way for physician and patient to communicate electronically in order to monitor a patient's condition, it also encourages the loss of the face-to-face encounter.

The emphasis on the patient as generator of data is evident in the site's rating system, where users are awarded stars according to how often and how thoroughly they update their profiles. At its most basic level, this rating system constructs the sense that there are "good" site participants and those who are "less good," in this way emphasizing the importance of daily updates. These "reward" stars, which promote increased use of the site and direct other users to view those profiles with greater star awards, indicate only how much a user has contributed to defining herself through her data. In the site's words, "Profile stars indicate how much health information you are sharing. The more you share, the more you can understand about your own experience with your condition and the more you are helping others to learn."[6]

PLM's personal profile pages ("About Me") are the site's one area where users have the freedom to represent themselves as they wish: they can upload a photo and provide a biographical sketch. Here, biographical profiles generally address a user's status within the household as mother, daughter, and/or wife in terms of caretaking roles; job status, particularly how FM/CFIDS has affected the user's role in the workforce; and often a summary statement about the user's attitude toward the disease, toward biomedicine, or toward their spiritual inclination. One user includes the following biographical note:

> I was diagnosed with fibromyalgia about 4 months ago. I have been having mus-
> cle and joint pain since I had cervical fusion on my neck in April of 2007. I am a
> grandmother raising 4 grandkids. They are helpful most of the time with doing
> chores and things I can no longer do. My husband is a truck driver so he is gone
> alot [sic]. I was a registered nurse before I began having problems. I miss nursing
> but I just can't do it any more. On days it is cold or raining things really act up. I
> can tell better than the weather man when a storm is coming. I am looking for
> others to share ideas with.

Often users supply details about their medical history. Another member writes:

> I used to be very outgoing and full of energy. Slowly and without any red flags
> something changed. I just started hurting. I thought at first I had muscle soreness
> from exercising or overworking in the garden etc. but it kept happening and from
> very little exertion. I had what I described to my doctor something that felt like
> carpel tunnel pain everywhere . . . or at least near my elbows, wrists, knees, neck,
> shoulders and my hips. . . . The hips are the worst for me. The pain gets so severe
> I can not walk well or sit down without help . . . and no one can even touch the
> skin of my legs without causing me pain. That is a hard thing with 3 kids needing
> their Mom. I did my own research and figured out what was going on and went to
> the doctor with some things printed out and she and I went through the steps of
> testing me for every disease possible and doing the pressure points test 14 for me.
> I began realizing some of my triggers and also taking Cymbalta which seemed to
> help quite a bit and [X]anax for anxiety. I learned to rest more and not take on
> HUGE assignments and responsibilities and to say no sometimes. Which is hard
> for me because I like to do things for people. I feel for everyone with this condi-
> tion . . . it sucks.

A third member outlines her reasons for using the site:

> I'm a 41 y/o wife and mom of 2 children ages 10 and 12. I've been married for 15yrs. I live in beautiful Colorado. I look forward to meeting others who are living their life with similar conditions and learning from them and their experiences. I believe that patient experiences are helpful to others in finding treatments that could work to get our life back to as close to what it was prior to becoming ill. I look forward to connecting with others through this site.

When users visit others' profile pages, then, they gain from these condensed profiles a sense of familial relations and work life, as well as the particular form the individual user's illness takes. Users express their worries that they've disappointed their families, or otherwise failed to live up to domestic obligations. Also evident is the desire to support other people with the illness. From this informal sampling of members' profiles, it is safe to conclude that a majority of users in the FM/CFIDS community articulate their reason for joining the site as a need for support and for finding out how other people with FM/CFIDS manage their illnesses. While the site promotes an ethos that tracking and measuring biodata also contributes to a biomedical commons, this is not the primary reason why members use it—or at least, it is not one that they make explicit in their self-representations. Rather, they use the site in order to escape their failures in the domestic sphere and to find a safe space in which to openly talk about private, sometimes embarrassing, physical difficulties.

The forums register livelier and deeper traces of affect and emotion than what appears in the foreshortened and immobile icons/biographical profile. In the forums, patients complain about doctors, about how fibromyalgia impacts their individual lives, about difficulties in their working lives, and about each other when they engage in flame wars. Yet because these forums are places for communications between members and not intended for the eyes of medical professionals, there is no communication of frustration with the medical profession to those working within it. Such frustrations instead are channeled back into the forums. This type of female complaint (Berlant 2008) exists within a circumscribed self-referential circuit, a community of complaint that addresses only itself.

For Berlant, the female complaint expresses itself through a conventionality that "keeps people attached to disaffirming scenarios of necessity and optimism in their personal and political lives" (2008, 2). This produces a social life in which sentiment is rendered important, where a slant toward the "intelligence of affect, emotion, and good intention produces an orientation toward agency that is focused on ongoing adaptation, adjustment, improvisation, and developing wiles for surviving . . . the world as it presents itself" (2). Similarly, the site encourages just such an orientation, where, by airing their grievances, members then can share ideas about how to adapt and survive—how to make do. The focus on sentiment over a more clearly articulated debate crystallizes in the forms of visual representation that often appear in forums. Possibly due to privacy concerns, many users do not post photos of themselves as profile icons. Rather, they often use icons that participate in an aesthetic language of conventionality, sentimentality, and cuteness, which reflect the impotency of this space of complaint. Representative icons include a jovial baby duck, a unicorn, and an image of Tinker Bell. The cuteness of these images draws on an ongoing language of women's sentimentalized and infantilized culture. They also register, as Sianne Ngai (2010) has argued of the cute aesthetic more generally, how physically small and vulnerable their creators feel, or, indeed, the "smallness" of their illness, which is denigrated by a biomedical complex that dismisses it and by a culture that has ignored it. In one forum titled "say it in pictures—photos only! no text allowed," the "cute" pictures such as those just described were followed by images that veered away from the cute and sentimental and dipped into a bleaker realm. Here, the animals, if cute, were no longer prancing happily about, but rather twisted in pain, and some animals were fantastic or grotesque; another image was Frida Kahlo's famous self-portrait where her spine is a fractured column and punctured with nails; and other images recalled a Tim Burton–esque aesthetic of creepiness and Gothic horror. As entries in a forum conversation, which evolved over time, each picture implicitly commented on the ones before it, and the later images contain an implicit critique of the cuteness in the earlier photos. Whether the images are dark and edgy, ironic and humorous, or mundane and conventional, they mark out their users' frustrations with how to represent how they feel. When a member creates a forum organized around photos, she addresses pain's intransigence for linguistic representation. Through their desire to find an alternate form of expressing embodied and affective experience, these forums critique the PFRS scale as an inadequate method for representing the embodied experience of illness.

The ways in which users of these forums communicate their feelings to each other contrasts markedly from how a much-discussed public service announcement about fibromyalgia represented the illness to the public (National Fibromyalgia Association 2007). First appearing on broadcast and cable channels in 2006, the PSA was produced by the National Fibromyalgia Association and the pharmaceutical giant Pfizer, which manufactures a blockbuster drug, Lyrica, that the FDA had recently approved for the treatment of fibromyalgia. In the commercial/PSA, the opening black screen announces in white letters that the people who appear are not actors; each person, the majority of whom are women, then attests, in overlapping vignettes in which their words blend into each other, to their muscle and joint pain, their fatigue, their difficulties sleeping. The tone of the PSA is overall one of sadness: its testifiers sometimes tear up, cry, and bear pained expressions. The music accompanying the advertisement is meant to make viewers feel this sadness, until the final moments when a voiceover encourages viewers to visit a website for more information, and the music then becomes uplifting. Viewers are asked not just to empathize so that illness can be acknowledged but also to see this illness within the sphere of a female sentimentalized complaint. Such knowledge, as the final screen directing the viewer to the Pfizer website indicates, is always circumscribed by the operations of capitalist biomedicine.

A similar mode of empathic identification operates throughout PLM: although members support each other and develop a community in its forum spaces, the purpose of the community is to contribute to the development of biomedical treatments. The site itself is populated with reminders that it functions as an antidote to the dehumanization patients face when visiting doctors in today's managed-care settings, where appointments are crammed into fifteen-minute sessions, where a patient is often shuffled back and forth between specialists who don't coordinate care, and so forth. Within the FM/CFIDS community, site administrators are constantly developing new ways to address users' complaints about the ways they are treated by doctors and the medical industry (often gathered under the slogan "Treat Us Right!"). The site therefore attempts to address the "ugly feelings" (Ngai 2007) inspired by the biomedical encounter—feelings such as frustration, anxiety, and anger, all of which have been expressed by its users. It does so by incorporating a discourse of hope, which it proffers as intrinsically tied up with its statistical project that will "fix" modern medicine. This investment in hope is apparent in the site's research page, which for a few years linked to genetic sites and thus participated in the hope-filled discourse that underpins contemporary genetics.[7]

As entries into the emerging digital public sphere, these sites must be understood in terms of their engagement with publics and counterpublics offline. According to Michael Warner (2005), counterpublics, unlike publics, do not depend for their existence on the circulation of texts; rather, they often occupy liminal and temporary spaces, those of performance, for example. In the cyber realm, counterpublics form through the performative space afforded by cyberactivity, and in this, the users of PLM come together to form a counterpublic, which comments on, diverges from, and often critiques dominant biomedical discourses about their illnesses. Like other counterpublics, they would seem potential generators of counterdiscourses that could foment political critique. Yet the site itself channels all critique into its project where self-definition through data might contribute to the amelioration of the counterpublic's complaint through advancing modern bioinformatics.

PLM and other patient-networking sites must be located within their broader cyber ecology—that is, the multitudinous and varied areas from which users gather information about, respond to, and engage with their illnesses. If we move beyond PLM to other support sites and individual blogs, we can ask how much they achieve what Susan Greenhalgh has called for: the telling of stories that might contest "the medical construction of one's identity, the transformation of the person one always thought one was into 'patient with diagnosis'" (Greenhalgh 2001, 324). One example of this practice can be found in the blog *Fibro World: Adventures of Fibro Dot.*[8] This blog presents an interdependent relationship between caregiver and fibromyalgic—a mother and her sick daughter, whose name is anonymized to "Dot." This blog demonstrates a different approach to understanding how this illness creates affective relations and involves care work. Like those cute images so often used on PLM, *Fibro Dot's* images participate in a sentimentalized conventionality. The use of a hippo cartoon and somewhat juvenile fonts suggest an innocence and youthfulness, a "cuteness," which might sabotage its potential for sociopolitical critique. *Fibro Dot's* posts are primarily written by the mother, who describes family events, difficulties with running errands, preparing meals, and notes her daughter's progressions and regressions. One entry describes the mother's fears about how her daughter will survive once the mother has died, detailing their particular bond as caregiver and care receiver in light of a somewhat absentee father/husband figure, and the certainty that the healthcare system will not provide the kind of personalized and consistent care that the mother provides. Dot's mother worries, "I am starting to creak in funny places, and it would be remiss of me not to start planning for the distant future now." She considers the following candidates for her replacement as primary caregiver:

> *Dot's Father*: unfortunately believes that Dot is physically fine and that her mind
> is subconsciously causing her pain. He opposes any help I give her because, according to his reasoning, I am perpetuating her helplessness and preventing her from

moving, vacuuming, and healing. When I am not home to care for Dot, I can't count on him, so he is obviously not in the running as a possible replacement caregiver, or caregiver supervisor.

Dot's Siblings: are busy with their own lives and are not in the position to provide the actual care she needs on a daily basis, but they could probably hire a caregiver and oversee Dot's care. I suspect I will have to broach the subject with them at some point to see if they are amenable.

Our Health Care System: is not even a consideration. However, we are looking at Canada and The Netherlands where there is comprehensive health care the likes of which will never be seen in the U.S. Scandinavia is not eligible because fibro people do not do well without sunlight and warmth. At first, a Dutch husband seemed like a joke but circumstances have convinced Dot that it wouldn't hurt to learn a few Dutch phrases like "going Dutch" or "I love your tulips," etc.

By contextualizing the experience of illness, the blog moves away from illness as only symptoms and toward illness as mediated by social context. Dot's mother critiques the paucity of support from other family members, implicitly critiquing the view that FM is "all in the head," and she explicitly addresses the sociopolitical context that does not provide support for its citizens who are ill.

The desire to see the illness as more than just something that affects an individual, but rather as played out within a complicated web of relationships, is reflected in one of the blog's goals, described on its "About Us" page as "to hear the stories of other caregivers." In attempting to establish a community of interdependent relationships, this blog emphasizes the formation of a public sphere, which might address the context in which illness is lived. Here, a language for addressing fibromyalgia—even representing it—is established and implied. Such a language takes the form of conversations, of multiple voices contributing to constructing a portrait, which would address the absence of a public conversation about how the illness affects its caretakers as well, and thus, implicitly, the lack of attention from insurance companies, the medical profession, and, in a larger sense, the entire umbrella of a government that does not attend to those most vulnerable among its population and leaves them, and their families, without a safety net. Across these sites, the intimate digital public is offered as an alternative to the fractured and sometimes damaging intimacy of the nuclear family.

Another such digital public exists among people with FM/CFIDS who use YouTube as a space of testimonial. People with FM/CFIDS post short videos that they've produced for a small group of potential viewers, including the YouTube user's family and friends. In these cases, testimonial serves the means of education (see e.g., Miss2 2008). Other videos often serve to substantiate the reality of fibromyalgia itself, indicated most clearly in the title of one YouTube video, "Fibromyalgia Is Real" (PainFoundation 2008). David Serlin (2010) writes that "YouTube and its counterparts provide an opening for those who wish to engage public health discussions beyond the clinic or the classroom toward some uncharted horizon" (xiii).[9] In the case of FM/CFIDS videos, YouTube allows users to occupy and address the very arena of public discussions about their health that they feel current biomedicine ignores. Although instructional and/or educational, these videos also contain an implicit empathetic address in their attempt to provoke the viewer into feeling *for* those who are ill and for their plight.

For Berlant (2008) the outcome of the female complaint as it deploys modes of empathetic identification has been to recuperate any political critique by a focus on the personal and the domestic. In offering a counterpublic that is not dominated by the language of personal data, instances such as *Fibro World*'s page and YouTube videos arguably provide one of the few spaces where critique (political or not) may be registered. For without a language of politics, and one that relentlessly centers the gendered nature of this illness, these lives may continue to be lived online in a manner that repeats the way they are lived in private— that is, attended to by pharmaceuticals, unexamined within a sociopolitical framework. In patient websites, by sharing individual "narratives," or at least by sharing individual experience of diseases, for the greater good of a disease community, these stories fail at any political interventions. They instead increase the life lived through its diagnosis and increase the process through which only that which is quantifiable is of relevance to understanding illness.

CONCLUSION

In the case of medicalization discourses online, it is time to revisit earlier claims that the cyber realm opens up identities to postmodern ideals of fragmentation, multivocality, and performative play (Poster 1990, 1995; Turkle 1995). Not only patient-networking sites but also the sort of networked lifelogging community encouraged by Quantified Self operate through underlying assumptions about cyber- and bioinformatic technologies and truth: first, that identity will be reportedly truthfully; and second, that they themselves contribute to efforts to find the "truth" about health and well-being. One might understand this as opposite the performative aspects of MySpace or Facebook. When it comes to health management, the move to make bioinformatics part of the construction of a privately defined yet publicly enunciated self attenuates the performative aspect of the modern digital subject.

Where PLM does seem to support certain claims made around postmodern identities is in the fact of the site's instability. In an attempt to move away from the essentialism inherent to identity politics, which must define a set of people through reference to a fixed attribute, Lennard Davis (2002, 9–32) has made the claim that disability instantiates a dismodernist identity position, since it is in all ways an unstable and unfixed category: a category to which all people will eventually belong; a category that people enter and exit; and a category that defies a stable definition. PLM reflects this instability. When it first debuted in 2004, the site addressed only a few conditions, among them ALS and multiple sclerosis. Soon after, it expanded to include more than ten conditions, which it divided into "rare" and "common" (among the latter were anxiety/depression, diabetes, and bipolar). In winter 2011, the site shut itself down except to existing members in order to broaden its categories once again; it announced that it would, in the future, attempt to have an online community for *every* illness and condition. In addition, it no longer would constrain users' participation by requiring them to maintain separate profiles for discrete conditions; now a user could be a member of multiple communities and could visit the forums of any community. The user with FM/CFIDS attempting to access her forums, for example, would see not only FM/CFIDS forums but also those of related communities (with a high incidence of co-morbidity) as well as the entire PLM population. One illness community therefore became not only its own biosociality but rather entered an entire field of biosocialities. With this change, the site magnified its presence as the keeper of data and the accumulation of data as a disruptive force. By contributing to an individual disease community, the user was now contributing not only to the good of that particular biomedical community but also to the overarching goals of patient-driven medicine.

Users of PLM are enrolled in a cyberbiosociality that mediates their illnesses in such a way to draw them further into biomedical discourses. As much as "patient-driven medicine" claims to represent a challenge to modern biomedicine, in its cyber form it seems another in a long line of practices through which the individual is made subject to modern biopower's discourse of statistics, and especially to its twenty-first-century fetishization of data and information. Still, if we listen closely we can hear the tremors of discontent with this form of subjectification, even if they are no more than images cut and pasted from other cyber venues, and even if they form just another node on the circuit by which the female complaint circulates only among its own members.

NOTES

1. Some notes on terminology: FM/CFIDS have historically been categorized as syndromes, since they have no identifiable cause but are rather a cluster of symptoms. There is contention within the medical community about whether FM/CFIDS should be classified as disease or syndrome; therefore, in this chapter I use the more general term "illness," which includes within it the subjective quality of how the individual perceives herself. These are separate diagnoses, but their symptoms often overlap, and, in keeping with the practice of PLM itself that collapses the two into one disease category, I delineate them as one terminological entity, "FM/CFIDS." When referring to a particular illness, I use its separate term. In 2013 the PLM site again updated its terminology to reflect that patient advocacy groups were calling on the medical establishment to refer to CFIDS by its more scientific-sounding name, myalgic encephalitis, and changed the community's title to "FM/CFIDS/ME." However, as this article was written about the 2011 site, I use the earlier term.

2. See http://www.patientslikeme.com/about, accessed March 2010.

3. This is not the only site of its kind, however. CureTogether creates reports (about treatment effectiveness) after users self-report their data. With a link to upload one's personal genetic testing data, the site clearly intends to enter the field of patient-driven medicine. Unlike PLM, CureTogether has no support-group forums. But like PLM it participates in a fetishization of data, evident in its homepage slogan: "CureTogether gives you access to 10.3 million data points shared by 25,000 members across 586 conditions." It is unclear whether this slogan is addressed to users or to corporate clients interested in "data points." It also demonstrates the conflating of the two: understanding the self as data points, and understanding that self as potentially circulating commercially.

4. PLM has undergone multiple updates since its initial debut. The particular version analyzed here was last accessed in April 2011. It should be noted that the site has undergone a major revision since then; however, most of the features I discuss in this article appear as well in the revised site.

5. The best chronicle of the history of CFIDS (Johnson 1996) revisits these arguments and explains how the very name "chronic fatigue syndrome" has served to belittle the condition, which in Britain retains the more scientific and less connotation-heavy "myalgic encephalitis," (see Johnson 2009).

6. See http://www.patientslikeme.com/help/faq/My%20Profile.

7. PLM has partnered with 23andMe, which indicates that at some point it has entertained the possibility of integrating genetic test data and thereby incorporating one of the major arenas of today's informatics of the body/self.

8. The *Fibro World* blog was available at http://www.fibroworld.com/, which is no longer active. Blog quotations are taken from copies in my files.

9. Serlin's comment is made in the context of scholarship on public health crises. Although FM and CFIDS have not historically been constructed through public health-crisis discourses, this is no longer the case, due to recent studies linking CFIDS to a virus. Among the countries treating CFIDS as a potential public health crisis and therefore banning those with it from donating blood are Australia, Britain, and Canada.

REFERENCES

Allison, Malorye. 2009. "Can Web 2.0 Reboot Clinical Trials?" *Nature Biotechnology* 27:895–902.

Althusser, Louis. 1970. "Ideology and Ideological State Apparatuses." In *Lenin and Philosophy and Other Essays*. New York: Monthly Review Press.

Berlant, Lauren. 2008. *The Female Complaint: The Unfinished Business of Sentimentality in American Culture*. Durham, NC: Duke University Press.

Davis, Lennard. 2002. *Bending over Backwards: Essays on Disability and the Body*. New York: New York University Press.

de Brouwer, Walter. 2011. "Health Internet of Things." http://quantifiedself.com/2011/02/hit-%E2%80%93-health-internet-of-things/. Accessed August 30, 2011.

Foucault, Michel. (1978) 1990. *The History of Sexuality*. Vol. 1. Translated by Robert Hurley. New York: Vintage Books.

Fox, Susannah. 2011. "Peer-to-Peer Healthcare." Last modified February 28, 2011. http://www.pewinternet.org/Reports/2011/P2PHealthcare.aspx.

Greenhalgh, Susan. 2001. *Under the Medical Gaze: Facts and Fictions of Chronic Pain*. Berkeley: University of California Press.

Johnson, Hillary. 1996. *Osler's Web: Inside the Labyrinth of the Chronic Fatigue Syndrome Epidemic*. New York: Crown.

———. 2009. "A Case of Chronic Denial." *New York Times*, October 20.

Kelly, Kevin. 2007. "Lifelogging, An Inevitability." Last modified February 21, 2007. http://www.kk.org/thetechnium/archives/2007/02/lifelogging_an.php.

Liu, Alan. 2004. *The Laws of Cool: Knowledge Work and the Culture of Information*. Chicago: University of Chicago Press.

Martin, Emily. 2009. *Bipolar Expeditions: Mania and Depression in American Culture*. Princeton, NJ: Princeton University Press.

Miss2. 2008. "I have Fibromyalgia." Last modified October 6, 2008. http://www.youtube.com/watch?v=3rY1X2SYLog&feature=related.

National Fibromyalgia Association. 2007. "Facing Fibromyalgia, Finding Hope." http://www.youtube.com/watch?v=SMCECMsW1RE. Accessed March 28, 2011.

Ngai, Sianne. 2007. *Ugly Feelings*. Cambridge, MA: Harvard University Press.

———. 2010. "Our Aesthetic Categories." *PMLA* 125, no. 4 (October): 948–58.

Orr, Jackie. 2006. *Panic Diaries: A Genealogy of Panic Disorder*. Durham, NC: Duke University Press.

PainFoundation. 2008. "Fibromyalgia Is Real." Last modified September 8, 2008. http://www.youtube.com/watch?v=3nIfvomIxic.

Poster, Mark. 1990. *The Mode of Information: Post-structuralism and Social Context*. Chicago: University of Chicago Press.

———. 1995. *The Second Media Age*. Cambridge: Polity Press.

Reeves, William, James F Jones, Elizabeth Maloney, Christine Heim, David C. Hoaglin, Roumiana S. Boneva, Marjorie Morrissey, and Rebecca Devlin. 2007. "Prevalence of Chronic Fatigue Syndrome in Metropolitan, Urban, and Rural Georgia." *Population Health Metrics* 5, no. 5. doi:10.1186/1478-7954-5-5. Accessed August 1, 2012.

Rose, Nikolas. 2006. *The Politics of Life Itself: Biomedicine, Subjectivity, and Power in the Twenty-First Century*. Princeton, NJ: Princeton University Press.

Rabinow, Paul. 1996. "Artificiality and Enlightenment: From Sociobiology to Biosociality." In *Essays on the Anthropology of Reason*, 91–111. Princeton, NJ: Princeton University Press.

Scarry, Elaine. 1987. *The Body in Pain: The Making and Unmaking of the World*. Oxford: Oxford University Press.

Serlin, David, ed. 2010. *Imagining Illness: Public Health and Visual Culture*. Minneapolis: University of Minnesota Press.

Thacker, Eugene. 2004. *Biomedia*. Minneapolis: University of Minnesota Press.

Turkle, Sherry. 1995. *Life on the Screen: Identity in the Age of the Internet*. New York: Simon and Schuster.

Warner, Michael. 2005. *Publics and Counterpublics*. New York: Zone Books.

Wolfe, Ross, J. Anderson, I. J. Russell, and L. Hebert. 1995. "The Prevalence and Characteristics of Fibromyalgia in the General Population." *Arthritis Rheumatology* 38:19–28.

Woodward, Kathleen. 2008. *Statistical Panic: Cultural Politics and Poetics of the Emotions*. Durham, NC: Duke University Press.

Cyber-Self

In Search of a Lost Identity?

ALESSANDRA MICALIZZI

TALKING ABOUT ONESELF ONLINE: FRAGMENTED IDENTITIES

This chapter presents a review of the empirical findings resulting from a study about virtual communities dedicated to perinatal death mourning and carried out in 2009. The objective of the research was to determine whether the Internet could develop a new area for socialization and discussion of a loss, with reference to mourning, that is not yet fully recognized socially. In consideration of the delicacy of the theme and the difficulty of meeting the women who had these experiences, I divided the fieldwork into two phases. During the first phase, I used the ethnographic method and participated as a researcher in three online communities for six months.[1] I was able to create bonds with some of the women and started the second phase of the research, in which twenty-five e-mail interviews were sent out on the theme of loss and on the meaning of participating in a virtual community.

In recent developments across a range of disciplines, the idea of a monolithic identity, stable and predestined, has been replaced by a perspective that sees identity as a "process," a complex and constant ongoing work that regards the individual, his relations, and the contexts he moves in. As Di Fraia argues, "rather than an original and unchangeable piece of data, or an immutable property an individual *has*, identity is conceived of as something that one *does*, like a task one continues to perform throughout one's life" (Di Fraia 2007, 37). One preeminent approach in this reappraisal of identity is the narrative approach that views identity as constructed through cognitive and communicative processes based on stories. The capacity for narrative is a skill unique to the human species and dates back to the acquisition of language (McAdams 1993; MacIntyre 1988).

According to this approach, narration is part of the process of construction of identity both individually and socially. At the level of the individual, there is the purely organizational aspect; an individual understands her own identity through the process of narrative: "a process through which facts, events or situations relevant to the self are understood through their position within the narrative theme" (Smorti 1997, 48). The structuring of the self, therefore, has a narrative form, as McAdams (1993) suggests when discussing the narrative process of constructing personal myths; these are coherent and structured narratives of the self. From this point of view, identity can be defined as "a temporally defined narrative fiction whose principal task is to supply, subjectively and objectively, a consistent recognition tool adapted to the type of social organization to which one belongs" (Pecchinenda 2008, 21). Identity organized through narrative provides a subjective sense of self-continuity because it symbolically integrates the events of an individual's personal experience into the story a person tells about his or her life (Douglas 1982). In this sense, "each human being knows, without even wanting to, that he is a *narratable self* immersed in the spontaneous self-narration of his memory" (Cavarero 1997, 48). At the social level, the definition of identity presented by Bruner (2003) is pertinent, as it stresses that the subject's story of himself is not found exclusively "within a person but also outside him, in those contextual 'blocks,' the pieces of the world that narration brings inside the subject" (Smorti 1997, 31). The final result is what Bruner defines as the *distributed self* that transcends the individual's identity and is disseminated in the stories that others construct, consciously or otherwise, about that person (Bruner 2003). "From this perspective, identity and narratability are two sides of the same coin, different discourses referring to the same reality" (Di Fraia 2007, 43). In other words, each individual's identity is not only the result of an interior process but is also the result of an ongoing interaction between the most significant relationships in which one is involved, relationships that contribute to the creation of an interwoven fabric of ontological stories. Ontological narratives, as Somers (1992) defines them, are about the self; they allow the individual to express the personal identity to others. Writing (or talking) about oneself is a narrative process that involves others, in a dialogue that takes shape in the narration itself. The role of the other is fundamental because he is a witness to our being in and of the world: "[B]asically, we need others to understand who we are and, for this reason, we *are speaking to ourselves* when we constantly tell our story to others" (Di Fraia 2007, 46).

These ontological narratives are also exchanged by personal media, and above all on the Internet. For this reason and from this perspective, it is interesting to examine the relationship between narrative and the Internet. According to Walker's (2001) definition, the Internet is basically a narrative technology, a specific relational context where fragmented stories are shared. It is important to specify that online stories have special characteristics that put them halfway between traditional writing and oral communication. This is reflected in the critical use of the terms "secondary orality" (Ong 2002), spoken-written language (Mininni 2004), or post-orality (Lamberti 2007) to describe online exchanges. These labels underscore the hybrid nature of the Internet as a site of storytelling: on one hand, the immediacy and the spontaneity typical of face-to-face conversations; on the other, the interposition of writing and a technological interface. This aspect has implications for both the issue of identity and the study of the narratives produced and exchanged online. From the narrative point of view, using the Internet for storytelling typically results in fragmentation, producing short excerpts, reduced and often abbreviated to minimize writing time.

From the standpoint of identity, talking about oneself online produces narrative in the context of the liberating power of spontaneity and of the reflective depth of considered writing. At the same time, the interposition of an interface helps to create an intimate, protected space, ideal for self-disclosure (Pennebaker 1997). With regard to identity, the technical characteristics of the Internet and the mediation of writing help the user to regulate her online presence (Waterworth, Waterworth, Mantovani, and Riva 2010; Riva 2010), to spread it out, distribute it, and adapt it to his most *attended* relational contexts (Helmond 2010; Turkle 1995).[2]

In this sense, the Internet can be considered an identity technology, one of the available "digitalized extroversions of psychological processes, through which every human being constantly produces and reproduces his identity" (Di Fraia 2007, 36). Further, the participatory nature of the World Wide Web and the Internet can be a psycho-relational device (De Kerckhove 2001) through which it is possible to enter into relationships with others. In other words, it is an interactive technology where writing about oneself becomes a form of participation shared with others, where the story is openly shared, in many spaces and in many fragmented narratives. The result is that the chronological dimension of the narrative—the positioning of the story in time and the chronology of events within the narrative—is expanded to include a spatial dimension, no longer a single, defined space but a multitude of spaces and relational contexts.

Perinatal Death Mourning: Linguistic and Cultural Resistances

The issues outlined earlier—individual identity as ontologically determined by narrative, the negotiation of identity narratives with others in the definition of the individual and social self, and the Internet as a narrative technology—are critical to understanding the analysis that follows. I discuss perinatal death mourning, which refers to the loss of a child during pregnancy or before completing the second month of life (Ravaldi 2006). From a narrative point of view, perinatal death is a very painful turning point; besides completely reorganizing one's life story, it also puts some aspects of individual and social identity into question. When I began my research, I wondered if the Internet, as a narrative technology, could make the process of reorganizing one's identity easier by providing areas in which to share painful experiences. In what follows, I address the question that opened this brief chapter: Can the Internet provide a place where one can recover a lost identity, which in the case of perinatal death mourning refers to the woman's lost identity as a mother?

Before discussing the data, I contextualize the topic of social identity more specifically in reference to mourning. First, I want to clarify that certain discursive and cultural conditions exist that prevent perinatal death mourning being recognized as an experience of real loss in Italian culture. In particular, cultural traditions tend to underrate the strength of the psycho-affective bond formed between mother and child during pregnancy. This aspect is emphasized in common linguistic usage: the expression "parents-to-be" is used to identify a couple expecting a child, as if to say that the expectations and practices associated with the role become effective only when the child is born.[3] The same can be said for the expression used to refer to an unborn child as "a baby on the way."[4] In this case as well, there is a cultural propensity to not acknowledge the existence of a child until after birth—its official arrival. Within this discursive context, it is common to refer to the period of pregnancy as "the waiting." It is difficult, then, for individual women to alter such a linguistically—and therefore culturally—entrenched view, which maintains that the loss of a child during pregnancy is not a real loss but only a missed "appointment" (Ravaldi 2009).

Referring in general to the loss of a daughter or a son, Fornataro points out that "when the partner dies, who remains is called widow; when a parent dies, the child is orphan. When a son dies, there isn't a word that can express what that man and that woman (parents) are. It misses the word, it misses the name to say that" (Fornataro 2012).

Because maternity is often an event shared with significant others, whether relatives or friends, when perinatal death occurs, though, the reactions of others are very important for the mother who suffers it. In most cases, because it is generally considered not to be a true loss, the "failed parents," and specifically the mother, are urged to bring about another pregnancy. This naturally has a severe psychological effect on the mother, whose grief goes unacknowledged (Ravaldi 2006).

In examining these experiences from a narrative standpoint, both situations lead to disavowal of one's identity. In the first case, the loss of the child is denied; therefore, the painful experience of the mother is not recognized in narratives produced by others or able to be narrated coherently to others by the woman affected. In the second situation, the mother denies her identity as a mother and tries to repeat an experience that did not end well. During the life of a woman who was preparing herself to become a mother, the loss of an unborn child is a turning point, a crucial moment of sudden redefinition of her story. Such a sudden change at the experiential level must affect the story one tells.

In the case of mourning—or any traumatic event—the emotional turmoil of the first phase of the loss often leads to silence (Pennebaker 1997). And it is a silence that conceals the overwhelming need to talk about oneself and one's child, and the deep need to forget on the part of the social surroundings.

The fear of forgetting becomes even stronger in the case of perinatal death mourning, where there are often no concrete objects—images, odors, objects used by the lost child—to which memory can be attached (Ravaldi 2006). The fear that one's child will not be recognized socially complicates the process of coping with the loss. The case of perinatal death mourning, therefore, is important for thinking about identity, social and individual, because two critical aspects come into play: first, the need to feel recognized socially as a person who has suffered an affective loss; second, the drama of having to renounce a social role that had been developing as part of one's identity.

The Internet and Lost Identities: A Case Study

Before discussing the theme of digital identity as proposed and developed within these communities by the participants, I need to identify a few elements that could help define the situation in Italy, both on and off the web. In Italy, perinatal death mourning receives no support from the national health care system and, similarly, there are only a small number of virtual spaces dedicated to sharing this experience.[5] Nevertheless, in the past few years, there have been numerous initiatives designed to raise awareness and form groups, which were principally spontaneous and local associations. For example, it was within one of the groups in the study that chatting was first used to meet and discuss in groups. The participants tried to create a setting for mutual self-help groups.

Second, perinatal death mourning is often thought to be a purely female experience, since the mother is seen as the only person involved. This cultural

legacy is reflected also in the virtual communities, which were exclusively composed of women during my period of study. There have been changes also in
this area. On association sites dedicated to perinatal death mourning, reference
is now being made to initiatives, both virtual and real, that involve fathers and
in some cases also grandparents and other relatives. In any case, it is typically
the mother who recounts the loss of a child. As Cavarero reminds us, "old witches
or wise wet-nurses, grandmothers or storks, fairies or sibyls, are seen throughout literature to testify to the source of female narration. . . . Women tell stories
and there has always been a woman at the source of the power of enchantment
in every story" (Cavarero 1997, 158).

Regarding the organization of the sites examined, in the three communities
it is possible to read the messages and the various comments without having to
log in, but the reader must log in to leave a message or comment on the forum.
Usually, access to a community stems from an initial personal contact via e-mail
with the moderator, followed by a period of participation "in the wings," without presenting oneself to the group. Only after becoming familiar with the other
users' messages can the new participants introduce themselves, and from that
moment they can participate fully in the community. The cycle is as follows:
acclimation, introduction, participation, taking on responsibility, and exiting
from the group.

The first period coincides with a time of exploration of the new digital environment (*acclimation*), a step that usually comes right after the loss of a child.
When I asked Alice's mom to tell me the story of her "presence" in the group, she
said: "Initially, I didn't sign up, I spent hours reading what others had written,
but I was not able to 'come out'! Maybe because to do so meant telling myself 'It's
all true, and it really happened and you can't go back. I am also a special mommy
and Alice will not come back to me.' Alice died December 2 and I signed up on
January 9, if I remember correctly. It was time to face everything, but, most of
all, to be hugged by other magnificent mommies." The possibility of participating, as stated earlier, is conditioned by the creation of an account. This moment
has interesting implications for identity. As shown by the nicknames they chose,
most women who enter the community develop their identity around their
denied motherhood. Almost all of them use the first name of the child they lost,
followed by mommy (as in "Alice's mom"). In addition, the images they choose
to sign their messages refer to maternity or to a neonatal image.

The *introduction* phase, which sanctions the sharing of one's own story with
the rest of the group, begins the moment a mother recounts the details of her
loss and the painful and traumatic moments that followed. One of the most

common times is when the mother comes home from the hospital, to a house where everything reminds her of the pregnancy. As a narrative, therefore, the presentation phase is sharply focused on the loss with specific references to motherhood without a child. The response by other users is a warm welcome to the group, whose members define themselves as "special mommies." This process is important to establishing social identity: it encourages recognition of motherhood, albeit prefaced by the modifier "special." This feeling of being understood and accepted is the main motivation behind joining an online group. It should be emphasized that in Italian there is no word for a parent who has lost a child, which again underscores society's difficulty in recognizing this condition, with even greater resistance in the case of perinatal death mourning.

An interviewee explained to me the role of the forum by these words: "[L]ittle by little I recovered my serenity, thanks also to them [the other mothers in the forum], sharing highs and lows, expressing our outrage at all those idiotic comments made by the people we ran into every day!" *Participation* starts with daily visits to the forum that take the form of writing about oneself and reading the responses and messages written by other "special mommies." It is also possible to tell the group about taboo feelings: the sense of uneasiness experienced in contact with one's loved ones, the desire to give up, the anger about superficial comments made by others.

Both reading other entries and the responses from group members are extremely helpful to the newcomer in developing a strong sense of belonging and normalizing their own experiences, returning them to the realm of ordinary, everyday life. When I elicited a metaphor to describe the participation to the group, Claudia Ravaldi answered: "Being part of the forum is like having another family in the sense that you belong to a group where personal bonds are strengthened by sharing difficult experiences and they grow with reciprocal exchange and help!" (Claudia Ravaldi, Lapo's mommy, meeting facilitator). Significantly, one respondent described the community as a "mirror," a place to see oneself reflected in the stories of others. In the words of another group member, these moments of identification and recognition make it easier to develop selective affinities and establish special relationships that involve a small number of users. Often, these bonds are based on very similar shared experiences, making recognition even stronger. Through regular narrative exchanges, the special mommies contribute to creating a sense of virtual togetherness (Bakardjieva 2003).

At this point in the participation phase the loss itself, at first narrowly defined, expands into a narrative that focuses more on remembrance, and the experiences shared with the child during pregnancy. But it is also a time when one reflects on one's own identity, often in a process that involves distancing oneself from "others," represented by everyone in the social context who chooses to remain silent, to not remember, to be unreceptive to memories of an "almost-born" child. The boundaries of the group strengthen in this constant confrontation with the indifference of a social context unwilling to integrate painful experiences. Sofia's mommy is a senior participant and she describes her new role in the community: "I felt the unstoppable need to tell my story as a way to know my child—that no one can ever know directly if not through me—something I would have liked to do very much even outside the Internet, but people never want to talk about it and that hurts us *mommies* a lot. It means that for them, these children never existed, but this doesn't happen in the forum. We talk about our babies freely." The *taking responsibility* phase is the moment in which the acknowledgement of being special mothers helps the participants to rebuild bonds, including those outside the Internet, and become stronger when confronted with the stories of newcomers, whom they try to protect and support. Women who feel they have made some progress in dealing with their loss provide support for newcomers. In terms of narration, messages intended for others predominate, with content less focused on the self and personal experiences, and much encouragement for those going through rough times, sometimes through explicit references to their own stories and experiences.

The last phase, *exiting from the group*, coincides with the acceptance of one's experiences, the relegation of the emotional loss to an area of the memory. It is the moment when one wishes to distance oneself from pain and return to the life-world (Husserl 1972).

Through the in-depth interviews, I achieved a better understanding of the motivations that led women to participate in a virtual group and of the differences between "real life" and online experience. The unanimous opinion of the members confirms a number of key theories of identity and narrative. Substantially, in the community, it is possible to recognize one's lost identity as a mother and one's painful and inconsolable emotional state, due to the loss of your child through producing, sharing, and listening to others' narratives of loss. Reading others' stories and comparing them with one's own experience through interaction in the forum is fundamental to feeling fully understood: an experience completely unknown outside the online community. The sense of discomfort depends on the fact that both loved ones and health care staff are often unprepared to face this type of situation: in fact, mothers who have lost an unborn child are usually admitted to the maternity ward, in beds alongside new mothers.

The principal reason that women enter the forum and continue to partici- pate is the respect for their own denied identity. The women I interviewed stress that in the community you feel understood, accepted for what you are (a mother), and are thus able to open up and tell your stories without being judged by oth- ers who have not experienced the same situation and almost always underrate it. To this relationship is added all the values connected to the technology of the Internet, as explained by Marida, a meeting facilitator, who underlines the role of the online group in managing inexpressible emotions: "the online group is an area that welcomes illegitimate pain and suffering. Here we feel understood more easily by those we share with, who have also suffered a loss: it is possible to share a grievous emotional burden and therefore feel partly relieved. I can express my fears, my anxieties at any moment, so I feel less alone. It's an emer- gency room that is always open and can be reached immediately."

"Being a Mommy Again": How the Internet Works

This brief chapter provides a picture of virtual contexts as an environment for social sharing in which it is not only possible to develop a new identity but also to rediscover fragments of one's self that may have been lost or questioned on the social level. Perinatal death mourning is an example of a situation in which there is a discrepancy between the social self—defined by how others see you— and the individual's perception of the self (Pecchinenda 2008).

The Internet provides an "alternative space" for narrative that, in the case of perinatal death mourning, performs an important function. First, the commu- nal boundaries have precise limits, defined by some procedural and technolog- ical markers. These limits don't deal with filters to the platform set by the login but rather the meaning of the identity behind the choice of a particular account name. Users access the community with a nickname that expresses the identity denied them—as mothers. In this way, introducing themselves through traits unrecognized offline, these women are free to elaborate what they feel without compromises or social restrictions. To investigate the reasons that led the mom- mies to find an answer online, Luca's mommy answered, "I was not able to talk about it with anyone because I had been assaulted with a load of banality, a flood of clichés that made me feel worse instead of better, and so, after shutting myself off from the real world, I decided to look elsewhere for comfort or also for simple discussion." At the same time, writing about oneself on the Net is of fundamental importance to those elaborating a loss and trying to make sense of a traumatic experience. Written language, even if concise, instantaneous, and im- mediate, forces the users to take advantage of a more linear and rational process

of communication than spoken discourse. The Internet thus defines the boundaries of another area and, at the same time, acts as a buttress supporting the
details of an autobiographical story that is often full of painful emotions.

In terms of interactive technology, the web also gives members of this community the possibility of reflecting on their own entries and those of others. At
the base of participating in the community there is the mimetic identification
mechanism (Morin 2003) that allows members to cope with a traumatic experience, like losing a child, and to emerge from the sense of solitude and estrange-
ment that comes from the way one is perceived by others. Identification, in fact,
helps to reinterpret an experience as something ordinary; identification, then,
eliminates the sense of not belonging and "being different" that comes with the
experience. Paola's mommy describes to me how she felt after the loss of her baby,
underlining the unconscious search of isolation from the rest of the world:
"[M]ourning is such an all-encompassing event that it takes over all the aspects
of life, you completely change, it upsets all your habits and the way you look at
life . . . and only someone who has had the same experience can really understand. This is why one seeks distance from other people and needs to find someone who 'feels' the same thing. The forum is the shortest way."

With identity, the mechanisms of recognition and identification help mourners regain control over their lives and reach a "turning point." On one hand, the
definition of a different context shared with others who have experienced the
same thing helps them to not only be recognized but also recognize themselves—
as mourners. On the other hand, within the community area you have a chance
to discuss, to take possession of your identity as a mother, a woman who has
waited and lived with a child, and then to distance oneself and start to process
the loss. Therefore, the Internet is also a place for social recognition, a place
where it is possible "to be a mother again" and to satisfy this role through the
preservation of the memories of the lost child. With regard to the initial question that opened this chapter, the findings provide a positive answer. The interactive contexts followed the mourner in the double passage of identity: from
expectant mother to mourner; from mourner to special mommy.

The principal theories regarding the mourning process (Kaplan 1996) show
how the "work" of elaboration (Freud 1917) is done at the moment one is able
to interiorly shift the associations with the memory of the deceased. The process
ends when it is possible to disassociate the pain of the tremendous loss from
the images of who was lost, putting it in an interior space created specifically
for the memory of the moments shared with a loved one. The web and, above

all, the community contribute to making this passage possible, defining a space in the memory and letting the mourner recover her lost identity.

NOTES

1. See www.sullealidiunangelo.it; www.ciaolapo.it; and http://genitoridiunastella.it. All three communities began as private initiatives and were operated by parents who had lost children in the pre- or neonatal stage. The most active forum was the Ciao Lapo Association; besides being the most structured it is the most consolidated in Italy, and is directly managed by a psychiatrist. The base principle that guides this experience is reciprocity, or sharing, and reciprocal recognition of each other's stories.

2. About the idea of the electronic distributed self, note the position of Helmond (2010) that uses the expression "Identity 2.0" to give the sense of fragmentation and collaborative construction of personal and social identity.

3. The literal translation from Italian of "futuri genitori" is "future parents."

4. The literal translation from Italian of "bimbo in arrivo" is "baby on-arrival."

5. During the period the research was conducted, I found five virtual communities dedicated to perinatal death mourning in Italy.

REFERENCES

Bakardjieva, Maria. 2003. "Virtual Togetherness: An Everyday Life Perspective." *Media, Culture and Society* 25, no. 3: 291–313.

Cavarero, Adriana. 1997. *Tu che mi guardi tu che mi racconti*. Milan: Feltrinelli.

Bruner, Jerome. 2003. *Making Stories: Law, Literature, Life*. Cambridge, MA: Harvard University Press.

Douglas, Mary. 1982. *In the Active Voice*. London: Routledge & Kegan Paul.

De Kerckhove, Derrik. 2001. *Architettura dell'intelligenza*. Milan: Testo&Immagine.

Di Fraia, Guido. 2005. *Storie con-fuse: Pensiero narrativo, sociologia e media*. Milan: Franco Angeli.

———. 2007. *Blog-grafie: Identità narrative in Rete*. Milan: Guerini.

Fornataro, Maria Ida. 2012. "Quando muore un figlio." In AAVV, *Riflessioni e testimonianze sul lutto*. Last modified December 6, 2012. http://www.gruppoeventi.it/riflessioni -sul-lutto-mainmenu-33/7-aiuto/23-quando-muore-un-figlio.html.

Freud, Sigmund. 1915. "Mourning and Melancholia (1914–1916)." In *The Standard Edition of the Complete Psychological Works of Sigmund Freud*, edited by James Strachey, 14:237–59. New York: W. W. Norton.

———. 1917. "On the History of the Psycho-Analytic Movement." In *The Standard Edition of the Complete Psychological Works of Sigmund Freud*, edited by James Strachey, 14:7–97.

Helmond, Anne. 2010. "Identity 2.0: Constructing Identity with Cultural Software." Proceedings of the Miniconference Initiative, University of Amsterdam, January 20–22.

Husserl, Edmund. 1972. *Die Krisis der europäischen Wissenschaften und die transzendentale Phänomenologie*. Milan: Il Saggiatore.

Jedlowski, Paolo. 2005. *Un giorno dopo l'altro: La vita quotidiana tra esperienza e routine*. Bologna: Il Mulino.

———. 2000. *Storie comuni: La narrazione nella vita quotidiana*. Milan: Bruno Mondadori.

Kaplan, Louise J. 1996. *No Voice Is Ever Wholly Lost: An Exploration of the Everlasting Attachment between Parent and Child*. New York: Simon and Schuster.

Lamberti, E. 2007. "Oralità, scrittura, post-oralità e funzioni della memoria." In *Memoria e saperi: Percorsi transdisciplinari*, edited by Elena Agazzi and Vita Fortunati, 299–314. Rome: Meltemi.

MacIntyre, Alasdair. 2007. *After Virtue: A Study in Moral Theory*. 3rd ed. Notre Dame, IN: University of Notre Dame Press.

Mininni, Giuseppe. 2004. *Psicologia e Media*. Rome: Laterza.

McAdams, Dan P. 1993. *The Stories We Live By: Personal Myths and the Making of the Self*. New York: Guilford Press.

Morin, Edgar. 2003. *La méthode*. Vol. 5, *L'humanité de l'humanité l'identité humaine*. Paris: Soeil.

Ong, William James. 2002. *Orality and Literacy: The Technologizing of the Word*. New York: Routledge.

Pecchinenda, Gianfranco. 2008. *Homunculus: Sociologia dell'identità e autonarrazione*. Naples: Liguori.

Pennebaker, James W. 1997. "Writing about Emotional Experience as a Therapeutic Process." *Psychological Science* 80:162–66.

Ravaldi, Claudia. 2006. "L'elaborazione del lutto nella morte perinatale: Passare attraverso l'assenza." Last modified April 13, 2006. http://www.ciaolapo.it/lutto/elaborazione-del-lutto-nella-morte-perinatale.html.

———. 2009. *Piccoli Principi: Perdere un figlio in gravidanza o dopo il parto*. Florence: Boopen.

Riva, Giuseppe. 2009. "Is Presence a Technology Issue? Some Insights from Cognitive Sciences." *Virtual Reality* 13, no. 3: 159–69.

———. 2010. "Using Virtual Immersion Therapeutically." In *Use of Technology in Mental Health: Applications, Ethics and Practice*, edited by Kate Anthony, DeeAnna Merz Nagel, and Stephen Goss, 114–23. Springfield, IL: Charles C. Thomas Publishers.

Smorti, Andrea, ed. 1997. *Il Sé come testo: Costruzione delle storie e sviluppo della persona*. Firenze: Giunti.

Somers, Margaret R. 1992. "Narrativity, Narrative Identity and Social Action: Rethinking English Working-Class Formation." *Social Science History* 16, no. 4: 591–630.

Turkle, Sherry. 1995. *Life on the Screen: Identity in the Age of the Net*. New York: Simon and Schuster.

Waterworth, John A., Eva L. Waterworth, Fabrizia Mantovani, and Guiseppe Riva. 2010. "On Feeling (the) Present: An Evolutionary Account of the Sense of Presence in Physical and Electronically-Mediated Environments." *Journal of Consciousness Studies* 17, nos. 1–2: 167–78.

Walker, Jill. 2001. "Distributed Narrative: Telling the Stories across Network." Paper presented at the AoIR Conference, Brighton, September 21. http://jilltxt.net/txt/Walker-AoIR-3500words.pdf. Accessed August 8, 2012.

Homeless Nation

Producing Legal Subjectivities through New Media

SUZANNE BOUCLIN

Homeless Nation (HN) is a Montreal-based nonprofit organization dedicated to "democratizing technology" throughout Quebec and elsewhere in Canada (Homeless Nation 2002, 1). Its primary vehicle for doing so is a website that has been designed "for and by the street community" (1).[1] In step with new user-friendly media (file-sharing, portable cinematographic equipment, camera-ready phones, and new exposition venues such as YouTube), HN has, since 2003, provided access to interactive communication technologies (e-mail, blogging) and training in new media technologies (digital cameras, sound equipment, and editing software) to its members.[2] The organization boasts more than six thousand users and one hundred guests (or "members"). To become a member, one has to create a user account with a password and valid e-mail address. Members can then log into the site and change or update their "profiles" by adding audio-video content, posting images, contributing to a weblog, and, more recently, report a missing person. Like other social media, there is also a "wall" function whereby members can post comments on their profile page, which all other members can view and to which they can respond. Street-involved people who use the HN social media write poetry (Hatrackman 2011), post information about rallies (Richard 2010), and suggest appropriate shelter (Richard 2010) or other survival strategies such as how to cash a check without identification (Tupper 2006) and how to pass a driver's test (JohnGraham 2011). Contributors provide "life updates" (Nick 2010) and also express political views such as critiquing cuts to social programs (Colinford 2010; Sue 2007).

The overarching goal of HN is to facilitate the street community's ability to "tell their stories and have their voices heard" through written, audio, and video testimonials (Homeless Nation 2002, 3). In developing HN's mandate, the film-maker Daniel Cross was inspired by the photographic images archived by the

Farm Security Administration, especially the images of migrant workers during the dustbowl era that were meant to "capture" the lived reality of rural poverty in America (3). Cross believed that HN could be a space that provides "a class of people underrepresented in mainstream media" the "opportunity to create unique and poignant works of art" (4).[3]

Homeless Nation's sizable aims include constituting a forum for the "virtual and actual" street community to develop a "national collective voice" and to "create dialogue between Canada's homeless and mainstream society" (Homeless Nation 2002, 6). Importantly, their normative aim is to "change" and even "save people's lives":

> Homeless people are transient; they can disappear off the streets without a trace. A fact made all too painfully clear with the . . . murders of Vancouver's "pig farmer" case. Imagine if there had been a simple bulletin board site for street people in Vancouver to dialogue and leave messages on; this atrocity could have been acted upon years earlier. (Homeless Nation 2002, 4)

Anecdotal evidence suggests that Homeless Nation has had a direct impact on a number of street-involved individuals; at least three people have drawn explicit connections between using the skills they learned through Homeless Nation and finding stable work and/or stable housing (Bouclin 2011).

Some of the discourse deployed in the above quote by Homeless Nation is problematic. For instance, in discussing the trial of serial killer Robert Picton, there is no gender or race analysis of the fact that the "people" he murdered were primarily Aboriginal women, many from Vancouver's Downtown East side, some who were street-level prostitutes. There is no mention that Aboriginal women continue to navigate systemic racism daily, and the grossly unaccountable criminal justice system is in part responsible for the violence they endure. Moreover, there are contradictions and dangerous assumptions that inform the view that one can ever "give voice" to another. Nevertheless, I argue here that Homeless Nation's richness lies less in its capacity for broad-scale social transformation but more in the more mundane and tacit ways it reflects, generates, and embodies what I call *street law*.

Street law refers to the governance of and by people who are street-involved— individuals among the assemblage of people, who unlike people who are *not* street-involved, are homeless or precariously housed, and engage in non-recognized, devalued, or prohibited income generation and survival tactics on and through the street. Street law can be officially enacted law (often in written form), which is used to regulate interactions and relationships on the street. In this sense, street law may be "vagrancy type" legislation (dictating when and where people can panhandle), camping bylaws (banning the erection of temporary shelter), and municipal guidelines around health and safety standards (controlling the spread of infections and diseases among shelter users and staff).[4] Street law can also be conceptualized in less positivist and instrumentalist ways. Consequently, it does not have to be limited to externally imposed, formally enacted, written rules. Street law is the network of implicit and indirect rules to which we turn when determining appropriate ways of being and interacting on the street. Street law, it follows, is most meaningful when it is imagined, framed, and communicated by the people most concerned with the effects of its governance.

Homeless Nation generates more intuitive or implicit street law by helping constitute at least three kinds of subjectivities. First, street-involved people are archivists documenting the street law that already exists as it is framed and communicated by the people most concerned with it. Second, street-involved people are artists, generating alternative visions of street law, which disrupt more official and, often externally imposed, understandings of law. Third, street-involved people are mediators, which constitute norms by furthering conditions of interactions among multiple street users.

In these endeavors, HN fosters conditions of agency for street-involved people. Rather than simply assuming that they must respond to official state-based legal normativity, HN members project what Robert Cover calls "an imagined future upon reality" (Cover 1985, 1604). By collecting footage, creating performance pieces, and furthering conditions of dialogue among a range of legal subjects, HN members constitute and express street law at once *as it is* and how it *should be*. In addition to facilitating such practices among its members, the site takes on, in itself, a jurisgenerative capacity by also performing the functions of archivist, artist, and mediator. Homeless Nation helps develop relationships based on proximity instead of those that are organized around confrontation, indifference, or fear. Consequently, Homeless Nation is implicated in the processes through which street-involved people and their interlocutors can constitute new, and potentially more empowering, legal subjectivities built around understanding, specificity, and care.

HOMELESS NATION AS ARCHIVE

Homeless Nation was initially imagined by its founder as a "street archive" of people, an "Internet documentary project" and "web-based digital memory of and from the street" (Homeless Nation 2002, 4). It was intended to take the form of an experimental documentary comprised of footage taken by street-involved people and HN volunteers (1). The "heart" of the archive would be the "immense collection of homeless voices and stories" and the "thousands of personal web pages . . . created, archived and updated" by HN members (6). The HN site would store audio-video files on the Internet in the hope of "documenting the voices of homeless Canadians," and to make sure that these stories will "not be lost" (Homeless Nation 2009, 1). The expectation was to share these narratives with the broadest audience possible (6).[5]

By claiming to provide a collective memory, HN runs the risk of presenting a homogenized vision or a representation of the "homeless Canadian," reduced in diversity of recollections (Bastide 1970). More than simply preserving stories, HN collects, redefines, and transmits localized histories of the street community. Through filmed interviews with various interlocutors and by organizing data in interactive ways, HN members constitute new information about the specific situation of individual street-involved people. Like any archive, HN can be "revolutionary and traditional" at once, as Derrida (1995, 5) reminds us. HN's practices raise questions about the limits of representation and of interpretation; they also invite engagement with the ways these concepts intersect with notions of identity, memory, evidence, and authenticity.[6]

The street archive is a necessarily partial framing device, which conceals, highlights, cleans up, demeans, defends, challenges, includes, and excludes other accounts of the same event. Like the formal legal processes that define and contain street-involved people *as* homeless, the street archive is not an unambiguous collection of facts about homelessness or street life. The video archive of "homeless voices" that are available on the website is limited to people who access the site, have learned to upload audio-video files or other testimonials, and have deemed this venue the appropriate means to express their views. Unlike the formal definitional, classifying, and containment processes from which street-involved people have been excluded, the street archive is described and imagined primarily by street-involved people and their allies. Although the street-community members have rarely been active participants in decision-making processes or pieces of legislation that directly impact their lives, the street archive can operate as a corrective that showcases individual lives rather than caricatures embodied in legislation, such as the "aggressive panhandler" constituted through "safe streets" acts.

Namely, the HN archive has recently been used to store alternative understandings of street law, which in turn have, to a limited extent, been incorporated into the official legal order. Images collected by HN members in Victoria,

British Columbia, were submitted as evidence to substantiate the claim by anti-poverty activists that the city's bylaws against camping in public violated home-less people's right to life, liberty, and security of the person (Richard 2009).[7] Homeless Nation's legal relevance is less that it provides a record of existing street law. Rather, HN problematizes other archival-based claims to truth about the rules that govern interactions on the street by drawing attention to their incompleteness. Homeless Nation contributors authenticate and legitimate par-ticular versions of street involvement by archiving audio-visual data. This indi-rect indictment of formalized legal structures may well rescue street-involved peoples' everyday realities from the ways of thinking that individualize and blame them for sometimes atrocious, often challenging, living conditions. It also invites perception of the complexities and contradictions inherent to their life situations in ways that suggest how they are also agents of social change.

The HN archive puts into sharp relief how the containment of memory in written formal law is porous and incomplete; in so doing, it also articulates a different expression of street law, which includes the memories of those indi-viduals coping most with its exigencies.

Homeless Nation does not, however, explicitly aim to integrate the street com-munity into formal legal mechanisms through its archival practices. In fact, while some members support such initiatives, others adamantly oppose navi-gating the formal legal system in any way.[8] Consequently, it functions more as a medium for artistic expression and a venue for generating dialogue.

Homeless Nation's Visions of Street Law

Homeless Nation was also designed to bring non-street-involved people into "homeless spaces." Outreach workers would capture sounds and images and up-load them to the HN website, providing "accurate video" and "panoramas" of street life to the "general public" (Homeless Nation 2003, 6). The mobile cam-era, in the hands of HN constituents, would convey "a feeling of life on the street" in ways that "artistically . . . immerse the average Canadian into the sites and sounds of the homeless experience" (Homeless Nation 2002, 6). "Mainstream society" could, as a result, access HN's website and be "placed in an environ-ment familiar to a homeless person" (Homeless Nation 2003, 3) when watching such footage. According to Daniel Cross, non-street-involved people would, through HN, be confronted with "the drone of rush-hour traffic under the Gar-diner Expressway . . . the wail of sirens at Pigeon Park . . . scores of discarded needles at Place Pasteur . . . [and] the din of hundreds of men eating soup at the Salvation Army" (3). Anyone who accesses the HN site—presumably "the public and [members of formal] institutions"—would "explore the spaces lived in by homeless people, to feel the texture of what it is to live on the street" (Homeless Nation 2002, 14). HN's normative aim is to elicit a particular response from the site's targeted audience: "a virtual feeling of what homelessness is all about" (15).

There are contradictions in such discourse. Conceived as a means through which broader society can witness street life, HN seems to reproduce and reinforce a version of "poverty tourism," the problematic subject-object assumptions in which it is embedded, and how these play out in ethnographic endeavors to cinematically engage with globalized socioeconomic inequality.[9] The language used by Cross does little to differentiate HN's footage from the increasingly large body of documentaries about street-involved people that rely on voyeuristic methodologies, many of which have done a disservice to the street community by reinforcing romanticized and tired stereotypes about life on the streets.[10]

To be fair, HN's own normative commitment is to create films made *with* the street community through collaborative practices, with the use of auto-cinematography, within disciplinary paradigms that favor filmmakers' immersion in their subject's social networks and daily lives, through methods that encourage members' "control [over the] distribution of their own voice and image" (Homeless Nation 2003, 26).

These commitments do, at times, translate into practices that will help produce meaningful images. The HN facilitators—people "on the ground" working directly with, or themselves members of, the street community—deploy a discourse than is subtly different than that circulated within HN's policy materials. There is a shared understanding that street-involved people are wary (and with reason) of the media and researchers, and the objectification that occurs in both these media. As Chris, an HN member and contributor, explains, in response to a news report in which he is cited through filmed interview footage: "When you do a media interview, you can talk on camera for an hour, two hours, five hours, but when they show this on TV . . . just a few words, a sentence, that's all you're ever going to get. They're not going to be able to run an hour of videotape straight, showing them following me around and asking me every single question that they ask me. . . . That's why we have Homeless Nation" (Tupper 2006, 1).

Moreover, there is a shared belief that the goal is not to capture images of the street community for external purposes but rather, as Ash, an HN member and coordinator, explains, to engage in a collaborative creative process: "As soon as I mention we're a participatory media project, people get their backs up right away. 'Media,' it's like this scary word. 'You're going to take a photo of me, or you're going to film me doing something.' A lot of people have had bad experiences with being misrepresented." He explains that rather than "just taking a photo of someone . . . without talking to them about where that photo's going to be used," HN members approach other street-involved people in the spirit of artistic collaboration: "Hey, we're part of this project. This is what we're doing. Do you want to be involved . . . ?"[11] In so doing, the perspectives that HN afford work against the voyeuristic and anthropological gaze encouraged—unwittingly perhaps—by its founder. HN also complements while being qualitatively different from more hierarchical perspectives relied upon by antipoverty activists who are "returning the gaze" onto formal legal actors.[12] According to one of HN's staff members, staff ultimately take on a "facilitative" role rather than a strictly archival or activist one: "We use video and online technologies to give the homeless a voice. We empower and act as a vehicle, but do not decide on content/issues. Many people from the street community might want to blog about human rights violations, but they may also just want to blog about their shitty day or the new dog they got."[13]

Consider the video montage "This Is the Best Place on Earth" (Vancouver Outreach Team 2009). Through voice-over the clip satirically and playfully criticizes the British Columbia government for displacing waves of homeless people during the Olympics while deploying actual footage of already poor living conditions in Vancouver (Homeless Nation 2009). By way of mobile cameras in the hands of HN members, viewers are brought into the city spaces that street-involved people navigate, but rather than "experiencing poverty," shot structures and editing choices position the viewer to experience the way HN members regulate space rather than simply representing it. In the clip mentioned earlier, interlocutors are invited into certain places (we see dumpsters and hear people talking on a stairwell); we are also excluded from others that are nonetheless explicitly and implicitly signified (we see the graffiti on one of Vancouver's iconic shelters; we also see the decaying structure of a flop house to which we are not granted access). It is HN's members who ultimately decide whether interlocutors are welcome. In so doing, they produce new urban spaces and new modes of interaction among them for multiple street-users. In these moments, when street-involved people present themselves as subjects in their cinematic mapping of the city, they hold themselves up as authoritative participants in and interpreters of the world they represent. By providing a view that is materially from the ground, HN operates as a kind of tracking shot of life on the street via a network of moving cameras operated by HN's members.[14] Through the camera eye that "moves among" its subjects, people who are not street-involved are invited to draw on a multitude of information to get a sense of how street-involved people form relationships on and with relation to the street, and how those relationships develop and shift over time. In so doing, HN provides new visions of street law.

HOMELESS NATION AS MEDIATOR

Homeless Nation has more recently de-emphasized its archival (documenting the voices from the street) and expository (showing the street) pursuits, and has taken on a life of its own as mediator. HN proposes to capitalize on the "interactivity potential" of new media to generate dialogue among street-involved people and between the street community, support groups, and the broader public (Homeless Nation 2003, 7). Homeless Nation aims to do so on two levels: first by "unifying the voice of the homeless," and second by inviting "the rest of Canada [to] talk directly with homeless people on discussion boards" and "hear unique first person stories from the street" in ways that will ultimately "breakdown" any "stereotypes" to which they adhere (Homeless Nation 2003, 6).

Homeless Nation endeavors to realize this ambition by taking on the role of host, medium, and mediator as a material, virtual, and symbolic site of interaction. In generating these conditions of interaction, HN also constitutes the street law through which multiple constituents represent and evaluate shared rules for acceptable interactions on the street.

Homeless Nation is a *host*, a materially created "hospitable environment of involvement and inclusion" (Homeless Nation 2003, 11) and a means through which street-involved people could "access a national community" and thereby gain a "sense of belonging" (26). According to one understanding of the hospitable relation, the host is constituted by defining and treating the guest as someone who is different than herself (Derrida and Dufourmantelle 2000). Similarly, the guest in HN's hospitable relation is the street-involved person's other.[15] This is true despite the fact that HN members are precariously housed and are themselves "guests" of their community partners (often community cafes and shelters) that lend them a physical space with computers and other furnishings. There is little doubt that it is the street community who ultimately determines who will have access to these facilities. Nonetheless, each community venue where HN finds a material base is intended as "a central point for artists, activists, and homeless people to interact physically (brainstorm, training, and the like) in assisting each other to develop unique ways to interact" (Homeless Nation 2003, 10).

On another level, HN is a virtual space that is moderated by volunteers and staff. The site provides a venue for articulating immediate concerns (such as the missing persons' forum mentioned earlier), and long-term commitments to generate conditions of empowerment through information on housing rights and guidelines for health and safety on the street. As noted in relation to the clip "Best Place on Earth," HN is often used as a medium through which people can enact judgment of policies, practices, and individual actors who further entrenched social inequities by uploading videos commentaries and visual evidence of negative interactions.

Finally, HN is a symbolic space through which the tensions that exist between individual street-involved people and their immediate "others" may be relieved. This is true whether interlocutors are other street-involved people, family members, service providers, police, or more distant "others," such as policy makers or judges.

Homeless Nation performs this symbolic mediation by providing both a physical space to ground contributors and a virtual space through which they can enact judgment. Homeless Nation functions as mediator, constituting a symbolic site that fosters dialogue and negotiation among diverse members of the street community in ways in which, ideally, all interacting parties take responsibility for their level of commitment to one another and have exchanges, which will challenge the boundaries between those who are street-involved and their real/imagined others.

In deploying discourse such as "merging art and technology," "bridging the gap between the rich and the poor," and "bringing together Canada's homeless and mainstream society" (Homeless Nation 2009, 1), HN attempts to embody Robert Cover's symbolic conception of law, namely, as a conduit between normative "worlds that are" and those "that might be" (Cover 1992, 176). HN members articulate alternative relationships through a social site that offers new configurations for interactions that are not present in face-to-face interactions. As danah boyd suggests (boyd 2007, 120), these new relationships are organized around persistence (speech acts leave a trace), searchability (community is constituted through the search and discovery of "like minds"), replicabilty (through cut-and-paste functions, the original becomes indistinguishable from the "copy"), and invisible interlocutors (it is impossible to know who will fall upon particular utterances made in networked spaces). Homeless Nation embraces social media as a means of complicating and fundamentally altering how street-involved people engage as citizens and how they interact with one another and with the broader public.

Constituting Legal Subjectivities
through New Media

To Daniel Cross, the Internet "holds limitless potential and promise," and "communication" through new media "solves problems in a democracy" (Homeless Nation 2003, 12). According to this view, HN is a vehicle through which street-involved people can become full and engaged agents and citizens. As with some of HN's other well-intentioned discourse, here too we witness what Darin Barney has astutely cautioned against in his critical analysis of social media. Through our engagement with new and emerging media technologies, information, communication, and participation have become surrogates for motivation, judgment, and democratic action (Barney 2008). As a result, rather than furthering conditions of agency and democratic participation for street-involved people, HN may well simply be "settling for publicity" rather than promoting conditions of substantive equality (89). Nevertheless, HN's value lies less in its ability (1) to effect broad structural changes through members' small-scale endeavors to persuade actual, imagined, or ideal audiences of the legitimacy of their interpretations and claims through blogging and uploading audio-video files; (2) to foster a general ethos of dialogue and respect; and (3) to create a material and virtual space for multiple voices, regardless of the status of the person making the utterance (whether from the "street" or not). It is in this way that HN may actually achieve its normative aims. That is, its contributors are in the unique position to produce footage that can make audiences "want to kick and yell," and "do something" about the injustices that the street community negotiates daily.[16]

In its ideal state, then, HN embodies a kind of translocal and transtemporal community (De Sousa Santos 2002)—in this case the street/non-street dyad—by generating conditions of reciprocity or interchange and of common purposes. Through the sites (the individuals, the physical space, the virtual, and the metaphoric space) and sights of Homeless Nation (from the street, of the street, of the public, for the public, through creativity rather than confrontation), the distinction between users and their intended audience is reconfigured as a street community and one that is constantly shifting as people move in and out of their roles as content-providers/knowledge producers and content-receivers/ knowledge consumers.

It is through the interaction of these multiple interpretative communities that HN members constitute a legal community. Through the HN medium, interlocutors are invited to take the perspective and consequently evaluate the normative commitments of street-involved people, who advance their personal laws, through the narratives they circulate and the images they construct.[17] This is not to say that there is a "street *sub-culture*,"[18] yet, if we take culture as a set of practices interwoven with *all* social practices, then clearly there is a street *community*. That is, each member of HN has his or her normative commitments, like any other person's, which are constituted by and graspable through reference to shared values and norms, including, perhaps, those of a discrete social group (Nedelsky 1989, 7). More than returning the gaze on formal legal actors or responding to other normative structures, HN members assert their jurisdiction to govern interactions on the street, to speak as a community with shared normative expectations, endowed with the authority to use, reject, and recraft official law's language, its form and content, in order to adjudicate when conflicts arise and, thereby, to express new relationships.

POSTSCRIPT

Since I began writing this piece, and despite receiving numerous awards from the World Summit, the Canadian New Media Association, and the Society for New Communications Research, the Homeless Nation pilot project has been denied any sustained core funding from the government. As a result, the Montreal, Vancouver, and Victoria HN outreach programs have been forced to shut down. Despite this financial loss, organizers cobbled together some money through independent fundraising to hire a national moderator to continue to track user trends and to ensure that content was posted by contributors. Members continued to post blog entries and videos until about 2010, when that money also ran out. The last HN blog posting I have been able to retrieve was from PaulFBurnside, a Vitoria-based "street poet" who used HN as a primary vehicle for sharing his work.

Since then, web activity has consistently decreased and by 2012 user-generated activity seemed to stop entirely. Currently, Homeless Nation has been taken over by posts and e-mails generated through spambots, programs that harvest e-mail addresses to send unsolicited messages. While the temporary shutdown of HN operations has been a serious blow to the street community, there is some hope. In Victoria, for instance, HN contributors have used their skills to record and post videos and commentary through a similar endeavor titled "Street Stories." The project was developed out of the University of Victoria and local nonprofit organizations.[19] Moreover, I am recruiting volunteer moderators and working with community members and students in Ottawa to develop a train-the-trainer manual and workshop series. Our goal is to facilitate conditions in which HN is less reliant on government funding and instead places street-involved contributors at the helm to revive HN as a space for articulating, critiquing and reassessing street-involved peoples' multiple and shifting online and legal subjectivities.

NOTES

1. See generally http://www.homelessnation.org/en.

2. According to HN volunteers, most street-involved people they interviewed had some post-secondary education, knew how to use a computer, and had access to the Internet. The survey's analyst concluded that "to assume that they do not possess the ability to interact with a technology the rest of us take for granted is an insult to the intelligence of homeless people" (National Homeless Survey n.d., 4). It is worth noting that their findings do not attend to differences in access to new media and formal education based on age, gender, and race differences among street-involved people.

3. In relation to his other documentary projects, Cross writes that "personally and artistically" he was "tired of cutting out all the stories/characters that [did not] fit into the narrative arch." His belief was that the street archive would become a "new way of presenting the voices of [his] subjects directly to the audience" (Homeless Nation 2002, 4).

4. See for instance: *Safe Streets Act*, RSO 1999, c. 8 (prohibiting "aggressive" panhandling); *Victoria (City) v. Adams*, 2008 BCSC 1209, [2008] BCJ No 1708 (an attempt by the municipality to ban the erection of temporary housing); and Ministry of Health and Long Term Care, *Interim Guidance for the Prevention and Control of Tuberculosis in Homeless Shelters and Drop-In Centres* (policy recommendations for the policy recommendations of the city of Toronto).

5. Interestingly, unlike *Copwatch*, which also uses new media to further conditions of justice, the HN archive is not limited to documenting oppressive police practices. *Copwatch* is an informal network of self-governing volunteer collectives. It first emerged in the United States based on the model implemented by the Black Panther Party. Members of the BPP would foot patrol and keep a watch over police officers in predominantly African American neighborhoods. They would intervene if individual officers became intimidating or abusive. The broad aims of *Copwatch* are to foster police accountability, to document and prevent police brutality, and to safeguard the rights of citizens. While goals of different collectives vary, most collectives engage in community legal education and videotape interactions between police and the public. They also tend to be an important presence in leftist protests and demonstrations, collecting witness statements and archiving violent and nonviolent interactions (Berkeley *Copwatch*, n.d.).

6. The archive has been theorized and historicized broadly across disciplines. See, for instance, Osborne (1999 [the archive as it relates to the history and historiography of science]); Spivak (1985 [the archive as furthering of colonial knowledge]); Foucault (1972 [the archive as site of a discursive formation and system of enunciation]); Agamben (2009 [the archive as any media with the functionalities to capture, determine, shape gestures, behaviors, or discourses]); Deleuze (1988 [referring to Foucault as the "new archivist"]). For a recent collection of essays on the question of the archive, see Robertson (2010).

7. *Victoria (City) v. Adams*, 2008 BCSC 1209, [2008] BCJ No. 1708; and *Victoria (City) v. Adams*, 2008 BCSC 1363, 299 DLR (4th) 193.

8. For instance, at the request of a Homeless Nation moderator, I developed a project through which members of the street community could forward legal questions

anonymously through my profile page. A group of pro bono law students under my supervision would then attempt to provide timely and useful information to be posted as general guidelines for all HN members. While the project was embraced with considerable enthusiasm, one HN member responded to our post with: "Never."

9. Consider the discussion around the movie *Slumdog Millionaire* and criticisms that it amounts to "poverty porn" (exploitation of the lives and experiences of the global poor for entertainment or other gratification by Western consumers). See generally Sengupta (2010).

10. Compare the Fredericton-based filmmaker Doug Sutherland's documentary, which follows Brian Jones—a forty-year-old bank executive who has made the decision to live "on the street" for one week. For a sample of some of the (albeit mixed) responses the film has received, see http://www.cbc.ca/canada/new-brunswick/story/2010/01/29/nb-bank-manager-streets-600.html.

11. Interview with Ash, cited in Tupper 2006.

12. Compare *Copwatch*'s countersurveillance tactics through which individuals return the gaze and "watch the watchers." In so doing they resist formal law's authority to define who is a legal subject and who is a legal agent.

13. E-mail from Chris Aung-Twin, former Homeless Nation coordinator, June 15, 2010.

14. Homeless Nation contributors constitute legal subjectivities much like the "tracking shot" in cinema facilitates conditions of agency within viewers and the film's subjects (Bouclin 2011, 149–65). The tracking shot is a species of long takes, which permits a greater depth of field. As an unbroken sequence, the tracking shot works to preserve spatial and temporal unity, even as it invites multiple interpretive possibilities through relations of proximity among and between bodies, objects, and spaces. The tracking shot constructs relations in a continuous way, by tracking and archiving interactions over time, instead of imposing meaning through juxtaposition or confrontation. André Bazin argues that shots in long takes function this way "when the essence of the event is dependent on the simultaneous presence of two or more factors in the action" (Bazin 1967, 127).

15. To be hospitable, the host must first have to authority to host (through ownership and identity). He or she must also have a measure of power over the guest: the hospitable relation is destroyed the moment the person being hosted takes over the house by force (Derrida and Dufourmantelle 2000, 150–51).

16. For a rich discussion on the utopian aspirations that documentary film will contribute to leftist political struggles, see Gaines (1999).

17. In her critical engagement with the liberal understanding of "autonomy," Jennifer Nedelsky argues that it is not a quality that "one can simply posit about human beings" but rather, being autonomous requires the ability to "develop and sustain the capacity for finding our *own law*" and therefore the relationships and personal practices that may "foster that capacity" (Nedelsky 1989, 7).

18. The anthropologist Oscar Lewis (1959) coined the controversial concept "subculture of poverty" in reference to autonomous subgroups that socialize members into behaviors and attitudes that perpetuate their own poverty. The concept "*subculture*"— and what distinguishes that understanding of people as members of a discrete population or social group from concepts like "community," from "public," from "society"—is highly contested. Some interlocutors note that the use of the prefix "*sub*" in this conceptualization of group affiliation connotes a secondary status (subaltern, subordinate)

within the broader social life, whose members ascribe themselves or are given by others a deviant identity, often linked to other markers of identity including race, class, gender, sexual orientation, and so on. Others point to the ways in which belonging within a subculture opens the possibility to contest and renegotiate subordinate status and to constitute new modes of status. Still others perceive the subcultural as neither inherently progressive nor resistant but more likely as part of the shattered and shattering quality of life. For an introduction to the contested terrain of subcultures, see Hebdige (1979) (comparing "innovative" subculturalists to "imitative" mainstream consumers). On the uneasy relationship between subcultural theories and feminisms, see McRobbie (1980). For other analyses that complicate the binary oppositions in earlier discussions of the subcultural, see Gelder and Thornton (1997).

19. See http://pswm.uvic.ca/pswm-program-programa-pswm/street-stories-research -project/.

REFERENCES

Agamben, Giorgio. 2009. "What Is an Apparatus?" In *What Is an Apparatus? And Other Essays*, 14. Stanford, CA: Stanford University Press.

Bastide, Roger. 1970. "Mémoire collective et sociologie du bricolage." *L'Année sociologique* 21:65–108.

Barney, Darin. 2008. "Politics and Emerging Media: The Revenge of Publicity." *Global Media Journal* 1, no. 1: 89–106.

Bazin, André. 1967. *What Is Cinema?* Vol. 1. Berkley: University of California Press.

Berkeley *Copwatch*. 2011. "Refuse to be Abused." http://www.berkeleyCopwatch.org/. Accessed August 12, 2011.

Bouclin, Suzanne. 2011. "Street Law's Sites, Sights and Media." PhD diss., McGill University.

boyd, danah. 2007. "Why Youth (Heart) Social Network Sites: The Role of Networked Publics in Teenage Social Life." In *Youth, Identity, and Digital Media*, edited by David Buckingham, 119–42. Cambridge, MA: MIT Press.

CBC News Canada. 2010. "N.B. Banker Spends Week Living on Streets." Last updated January 29, 2010. http://www.cbc.ca/canada/new-brunswick/story/2010/01/29/nb-bank -manager-streets-600.html.

Cohen, Stanley. 1972. *Folk Devils and Moral Panics*. London: MacGibbon and Kee.

Colinford. 2010. "Woodwards Protest." Last modified December 1, 2010. http://home lessnation.org/node/18288.

Cover, Robert. 1992. "Nomos and Narrative." In *Narrative, Violence, and the Law: The Essays of Robert Cover*, edited by Martha Minow, Michael Ryan, and Austin Sarat, 95–172. Ann Arbor: University of Michigan Press.

———. 1985. "Violence and the Word." *Yale Law Journal* 95:1601–29.

Deleuze, Gilles. 1988. *Foucault*. Minneapolis: University of Minnesota Press.

Derrida, Jacques. 1995. *Archive Fever: A Freudian Impression*. Chicago: University of Chicago Press.

Derrida, Jacques, and Anne Dufourmantelle. 2000. *Of Hospitality*. Translated by Rachel Bowlby. Stanford, CA: Stanford University Press.

De Sousa Santos, Boaventura. 2002. *Towards a New Legal Common Sense*. London: Butterworths.

Foucault, Michel. 1972. *The Archaeology of Knowledge*. Translated by A. M. Sheridan Smith. New York: Pantheon Books.

Gaines, Jane. 1999. "Political Mimesis." In *Collective Visible Evidence*, edited by Jane Gaines and Michael Renov, 84–102. Minneapolis: University of Minnesota Press.

Gelder, Ken, and Sarah Thornton. 1997. *The Subcultures Reader*. New York: Routledge.

Hatrackman. 2011. "God." Last modified November 8. http://www.homelessnation.org/en/node/21488.

Hebdige, Dick. 1979. *Subculture: The Meaning of Style*. London: Methuen.

Highmore, Ben. 2002. *Everyday Life and Cultural Theory: An Introduction*. London: Routledge.

Homeless Nation. 2002. *Homeless Street Archive*. Montreal.

———. 2002. *National Homeless Survey*. In author's files.

———. 2003. *Street Archive: Cyberpitch Funding Proposal*. Montreal.

———. 2009. "About Homeless Nation." Last modified January 1. http://www.homelessnation.org/en/node/16973.

———. 2010. "Missing." Last modified September 9, 2010. http://www.homelessnation.org/en/missing.

JohnGraham. 2011. "Tips to Pass Motorbike Test." Last modified August 19. http://homelessnation.org/en/node/21546, archived at http://artilib.org/20098161-tips-to-pass-motorbike-test.html.

Lewis, Oscar. 1959. *Five Families: Mexican Case Studies in the Culture of Poverty*. New York: Basic Books.

McRobbie, Angela. 1980. "Settling Accounts with Subcultures: A Feminist Critique." *Screen Education* 34:37–49.

Ministry of Health and Long Term Care. 2011. "Interim Guidance for the Prevention and Control of Tuberculosis in Homeless Shelters and Drop-In Centres." http://www.toronto.ca/health/tb_prevention/pdf/guidance_homeless.pdf. Accessed August 12, 2011.

Nedelsky, Jennifer. 1989. "Reconceiving Autonomy: Sources, Thoughts, and Possibilities." *Yale Journal of Law and Feminism* 1:7–36.

Nick. 2010. "Update." Last modified December 20. http://www.homelessnation.org/en/node/19601.

Osborne, Thomas. 1999. "The Ordinariness of the Archive." *History of the Human Sciences* 12, no. 2: 51–64.

Richard. 2009. "Homeless Nation Video Helps Win Court Case." Last Modified December 9. http://www.homelessnation.org/en/node/17939.

Richard. 2010. "Shelter 2010–2011." Last modified November 1. http://homelessnation.org/node/19454.

Robertson, Craig. 2010. "Historicizing the Archive." *Communication Review* 13:1–4.

Safe Streets Act. RSO 1999, c. 8.

Sengupta, Mitu. 2010. "A Million Dollar Exit from the Anarchic Slum-world: *Slumdog Millionaire*'s Hollow Idioms of Social Justice." *Third World Quarterly* 31, no. 4: 599–616.

Spivak, Gayatri. 1985. "The Rani of Sirmur: An Essay in Reading the Archives." *History and Theory* 24, no. 3: 247–71.

Sue. 2007. "Abusive Relationship vs. Abusive Gov't." Last Modified June 28. http://www.homelessnation.org/node/5548.

Tupper, Peter. 2006. "Curbside Internet for the Homeless." *Tyee*. Last modified November 22. http://thetyee.ca/Life/2006/11/22/HomelessNation/.

Vancouver Outreach Team. 2009. "This Is the Best Place on Earth." Last modified November 12. http://www.homelessnation.org/node/12548.

Victoria (City) v. Adams, 2008 BCSC 1209, [2008] BCJ No 1708.

Victoria (City) v. Adams, 2008 BCSC 1363, 299 DLR (4th) 193.

Williams, Raymond. 1974. *Television, Technology, and the Cultural Form*. New York: Schocken Books.

REFLECTIONS

Autobiography and New Communication Tools

PHILIPPE LEJEUNE,
translated by KATHERINE DURNIN

The topic of this chapter is "How new communication tools have changed auto-biography"—a vast and tricky subject. I do not to attempt to prophesy but rather to analyze the terms of the question. I use the word "autobiography" in its broad meaning here as the written expression of a life by an individual. There are at least three different types of autobiography that must be distinguished:

- The *retrospective story of a life*, or a significant part of that life, told in writing for the purpose of communication or transmission. This is a rare and difficult act that requires an effort at composition and entails risks even if it is private; the purpose is to transmit a memory, a worldview, an experience, and values. Rare indeed, but one aimed at visibility.
- The *personal diary*, which may be used to construct memories, to sooth painful emotions, or to stand back from one's life and examine it as it moves along. This is, in contrast, a very common activity that has no rules and usually ends up in the wastebasket.
- The *correspondence*, which is addressed to someone at a distance, is a reciprocal act aimed at maintaining a relationship and has no formal limitations.

These various forms or behaviors, which I have just defined as though each had an unchanging essence, are by no means eternal. They have not always existed, and they will not always exist; they have undergone myriad changes over time under the impact of various factors—some of which, in fact, have involved changes in "communication tools."

One must take a very long view to see that it is not only autobiography (the written expression of the self) that changes with social structures and communication tools but also the way in which we manage and think about our identity.

There is no set "I" that remains identical throughout the history of humankind and simply expresses itself differently depending on the tools at hand. In this case, it is the tool that shapes the craftsman.

If you look at the history of the diary, which is nearly as long as the history of humankind (in the form of account books, administrative archives, chronicles, and the like), you will see that the shift from collective journal to personal diary was possible only in civilizations that had paper (for example, eleventh-century Japan and Europe beginning in the late Middle Ages), a necessary but not a sufficient condition, since other civilizations may have had paper but did not make the same use of it (this is true of China, which invented paper, and the Arab world, which transmitted it to Europe).

How was it possible that the Greco-Latin world was able to develop a certain "care of the self," in Michel Foucault's expression and, at the same time, develop a capacity for the daily recording of administrative and management information without ever thinking of applying that capacity to the care of the self? As far as we know, there is no personal diary dating from antiquity. Was it for lack of paper? Because reading was still done aloud? After all, silent reading did not become widespread until the Middle Ages.

I will refrain from asking other equally complicated, obscure, and controversial questions. In my opinion, though, autobiography, regardless of its ancient roots, is a modern genre. Despite the prestigious but little-imitated example of Saint Augustine, autobiography only really developed during the Renaissance, in a bourgeois merchant civilization that had recently just discovered printing. And rhetorically, would Montaigne have written his *Essays* if printing had not existed?

None of these things explain everything, but the diary only came into its own with paper, and autobiography with printing. As long as people wrote on wax tablets, as long as texts had to be copied out by hand in order to be disseminated, as long as people read aloud, the self did not have a chance.

I have used these distant examples in order to avoid the blind spots of the present. But think for a moment about the distinctions I have just drawn between autobiography, diary, and letters. Are they not breaking down before our very eyes? It seems clear that the Internet and blogs are reshuffling the cards, erasing some distinctions that we thought were set in stone when in fact they were the projections of short-lived communication tools. The blog, for example, eliminates the distinction between diary and correspondence, and also between public and private. On the other hand, it heightens the difference between the instantaneous and the long-term—or in Régis Debray's (2000) terms, between communication and transmission.

This brings me to another tricky point: analyzing the second part of my title, "new communication tools." I find it worrying and somewhat mind-boggling to realize that what is still *new* to me—computers (which I have been using since 1991), e-mail, personal websites—may already be *old* to those of you who take photographs with your cell phones, navigate with a GPS, and read Montaigne on an iPad.

Which brings me to the crux of the matter: new communication tools are not only changing autobiography—the expression of a life—but are also attacking life itself. In using the verb "attack," I am touching on another sensitive point: the problem of value. We can speak of these changes with joy or with regret. Very few of us adopt a neutral stance. Is this a good thing or a bad thing? People used to have a soul; now they have Google. People used to have a guardian angel; now they have a GPS. We used to have time, but now we have none. It used to be that the postman came once a day and delivered a letter or two. Now, on the two monitors hooked up to my computer, I can write my deep thoughts in one file while also keeping an eye on the new messages that land effortlessly in my inbox, standing out in boldface. In the past, phone calls had to wait their turn. I used to take my time as I pondered my reply, and my correspondent had to take into account the time it took for the mail to arrive. Now I reply quickly, because if I fail to respond within twenty-four hours people think I have died. I have sung this song in a minor, negative key, and I shall leave it up to you to answer by singing an uplifting hymn to speed.

Thus, the new communication tools have two features: fusion and speed.

Fusion: At first, in the 1980s and 1990s, it might have seemed that, after a century of innovations focused on sound and pictures (the telephone, film, radio, and television), information technology and the Internet marked a return to writing. This was not entirely false, but it quickly became apparent that writing, which came to the fore initially, had been rehabilitated only to be melded with the other media (sound and pictures) in a new language that incorporated all three.

Speed: Searching for and creating information have become almost instantaneous, and distance no longer matters. The new communication tools are so powerful that (in the negative version) they are overwhelming our human capacities and so will reduce us to anxiety or idiocy, or (in the positive version) they are forging a new type of human. It is no longer a matter of the (altered) expression of a life that remains the same but of a profound change in life itself wrought through its relationship with time. Today, everything moves so quickly that our identity can no longer rely on the permanence of the world around us.

The devalued past collapses and the future disappears, because tomorrow is already today. We are losing our long-term connections, our rootedness in the past, and the ability to project ourselves into the future, all of which allowed us to construct a narrative identity. We are skating along swiftly in a present that annihilates the past and denies the future.

So here we are at the heart of the problem. This analysis of the breakdown of autobiographical identity in a world that is moving too fast is seen repeatedly in texts about the "postmodern" world. In a book recently published in French by the Italian philosopher Fabio Merlini (2011), *L'Époque de la performance insignifiante: Réflexions sur la vie désorientée*, he predicts outright the breakdown of autobiographical memory (85ff.). But my examples come from a German sociologist, Hartmut Rosa (2010a), on the conclusions he reached in his book *Accélération: Une critique sociale du temps* (2010b). The two main points are the reversal of intergenerational transmission and the breakdown of narrative identity:

TRANSMISSION

In premodern society, before big industry, the present bound together at least three generations, because the grandfather's world was scarcely different from the grandson's, and grandfathers could still transmit their know-how and values to grandsons. During the high modern period in the first half of the twentieth century, the present shrank to a single generation: a grandfather knew that his grandchildren's present would be different from his own. He no longer had much to teach them; the younger generations became carriers of innovation, and their task was to create a new world—as they did in 1968, for example. But in our belated modernity today, the world changes many times in a single generation. A father no longer has much to teach his children about family life, which is constantly reorganizing itself, or about the jobs of the future or new technologies. You hear eighteen-year-olds talk about "before" when referring to how things were when they were ten. A young specialist will show an expert only slightly older than him what is "up to date." The present is becoming foreshortened and more fleeting and our sense of reality and identity is being shaped by the same forces.

IDENTITY

Before now, modernity and the idea of progress promised us that ultimately people would be freed from political oppression and material want, and would be able to live self-determined and freely chosen lives. This idea is based on the assumption that we all have something like a "life project," our own dream of what might be called the "good life." That is why people in modern societies developed true narrative identities, which allowed them to tell the story of their experiences like a story of conquests, albeit with some stumbling blocks strewn along the way, but one that led toward the "good life" of their dreams.

But now it is becoming impossible to develop even the outlines of a life project. The economic, professional, social, geographical, and competitive landscape has become too fast-changing for anyone to predict plausibly what our world, our lives, most of our careers, and we ourselves will be like in just a few years. Identity is no longer based on assertions such as "I'm a baker, I'm a socialist, I'm married to Christine, and I live in Paris." Now we say, "I'm a baker for the time being, I voted for the socialists but I won't next time, I've been married for five years to Christine, who wants a divorce, and although I've lived in Paris for eight years, I'm moving to Lyon this year for my work."

We might ask ourselves whether these warnings are overblown and whether narrative identity, the very purpose of which is to harmonize the past and the present, might not have another trick up its sleeve. But we might also ask ourselves, in all honesty, whether there is not a great deal of truth to them—a truth that will only become clear in the next generation, once those now living active lives reach the age of retirement and memories.

I have to admit that I do not know the answer, probably because I cannot bring myself to announce, on behalf of a forlorn modernity, that autobiography is dead. I can only indicate some points of reference derived from my own necessarily limited experience and look at each of the three "genres" of autobiographical expression that I distinguished at the outset, but in a different order.

The Diary

In 1988 and 1998 I conducted two surveys asking for individual accounts from people who kept personal diaries. The purpose of the second survey, ten years after the first, was to gauge the changes that had been brought about with the advent of the personal computer, to which I myself had been converted in 1991. In 1998 more than half of the responses came from other "converts"—neither surprising nor significant given that that was the aim of the survey. We analyzed the advantages and disadvantages, and the changes in the environment and methods of a practice, which remained completely private. But what about diaries on the Internet? We no longer had to conduct a survey: all we had to do was go and look. From October 1999 to May 2000, and for the entire month of October 2000, I was glued to my screen looking at *all* cyberdiarists writing in

French. "All" was not many. There were sixty-eight of them in October 1999 and double that number a year later. I started out with a negative view of them and within two weeks I was completely won over. It was a passionate conversion experience, and the start of many friendships. I soon realized that this was something *different*: I called it "network intimacy." Technology had made it possible to reconfigure relationships, giving rise to a new type of friendship between strangers—people who recognized and gravitated toward one another because of their diaries. Naturally, this intimate sociability is quite different from the self-expression of a solitary diary, which is often less studied and more sincere. A great deal of self-control is exerted; constant care is taken to achieve a positive and appealing self-presentation; the diarists must write regularly so as not to lose their audience, and they engage in direct or indirect dialogue with other diaries; in addition, there is a tendency to form groups and communities.

Another characteristic feature of online diaries is the new way in which they process time spatially, through *retrochronology*. The past of the text is not behind it but in front of it, or rather under it, floating to the surface only to be pushed down in turn by the next entry. This is the order of curricula vitae, which start in the present and go back through time, presenting things not in the glorious order of accomplishment but in the disappointing order of dissolution: the applicant ends up in the cradle. In cyberdiaries, you enter the past going backwards and with jumps: it takes some painful gymnastics to read the texts in the order in which they were written. Time no longer flows—it floats and then sinks. The present comes before the past and surfaces toward nothing.

The online diary thus offers a new social construction of identity and a new construction of time.

My book (Lejeune 2000) described an avant-garde practice almost in real time. Today, eleven years later, it has become an archaeological study, bearing witness to a world that has disappeared. Cyberdiarists were rare in 2000 because you had to be able to set up your own website and only a small percentage of the French population had an Internet connection. Then, suddenly, Internet connections became widespread, blog platforms began to appear in 2003, and Facebook started up in 2004. Today there are millions of blogs, although they are so fleeting and ephemeral and cover such a wide range of topics, often far from intimate, that it is difficult to say what we are counting. A new type of sociability has sprung up. People have a blog, a website, or a Facebook page; they "tweet" the way people used to leave a calling card: it is the minimal and almost obligatory way of existing socially. In the past, it took an exceptional stroke of luck to appear in the public media; today anyone can do it, except that with the whole world in the media now, no one takes any notice. Still, everyone can take a shot at it. In any case, it was impossible to predict in 2000 what the Internet would look like in 2011, and it will no doubt be amusing to reread this text in 2022 or 2033.

But has everything really changed? Do new technologies wipe out the old ones? Are there still some miserable Luddites who continue to keep their diaries just for themselves, by hand, in notebooks? The answer is yes, and their numbers have not declined in France. We know this from the results of the latest survey by the Ministry of Culture on "the cultural practices of the French," a survey that is conducted every ten years and that, since 1988, has included a question on the practice of keeping a personal diary. Here is how Olivier Donnat (2008) analyzed the responses that year:

> It is interesting to note that the success of blogs and personal websites has not consigned the personal diary to the dust heap, since this form of writing is still virtually as widespread as it was in 1997 and the profile of its practitioners has barely changed: overall, twice as many women as men keep personal diaries (10% compared to 5%), particularly as adolescents and students (one-quarter of young female students keep diaries compared to 9% of their male counterparts).
>
> In addition, the writing methods seem to have changed relatively little, with most people still using paper, regardless of age: 74% of people who keep a diary use a notebook or sheets of paper, 18% use a computer and 8% use both. However, personal diaries seem to be an exception in this regard, as the use of computers has become much more prevalent for other forms of personal writing. . . .
>
> The writers who have continued using paper are mainly older and less educated women. This can likely be partly explained by the fact that some do not own a computer, but the fact that two-thirds of them have access to the Internet shows that most instances reflect a real preference for paper, at least for certain types of writing.

So the landscape is changing, but less than one might think. The APA (Association pour l'Autobiographie), which some friends and I founded in 1992 to collect and preserve all the unpublished autobiographical writings that people wanted to entrust us with, is receiving just as many personal diaries as ever, in the form of either manuscripts or typescripts.

The real question is what will happen to diaries on the Internet that are no longer set down on paper. Does using an immediate form of communication mean that any possibility of intergenerational communication has been lost? I have a two-part answer to that question.

In my survey (Lejeune 2009), I came across an unusual pioneer, a young student who went by the name of "Mongolo" (I never found out his real name). While keeping an online diary, he also theorized subtly and profoundly about this new practice. He had also created two collective websites, one titled "Souvent" ("Often") that encouraged regular diary writing (to be a member you had to write in your diary at least two or three times a week), and the other to prolong the life of abandoned diaries, allowing them to remain on the Internet in the "Orphanage for Personal Diaries." "Orphanage" obviously sounded better than "retirement home" or "cemetery," because orphans have a future. But do they really? When Mongolo himself stopped keeping his diary, instead of putting it in his own orphanage he shut down the orphanage at the same time! Seeing this, I proposed that he deposit both his diary and his orphanage with the APA. He did this, but only in the form of CDs, without attaching a hard copy as I had suggested—something that we did not do either. These CDs are thus the only remaining public trace of the pioneer online diaries from 1999 to 2000.

The situation has changed since then. In France, in 2006, the copyright law extended copyright to the Internet, and the Bibliothèque Nationale de France (BNF) and Institut National de l'Audiovisuel (INA) were entrusted with recording a snapshot of the entire French-language Internet twice a year. This large-scale "capture" is carried out by robots unbeknownst to anyone. Many people are naïve enough to think that when they close down their blog or website, they are erasing everything. Not so. The memory of it remains *forever*. I was able to check this with my "Autopacte" website, which is preserved in its entirety every six months. Anything I have removed in the meantime will be stored *forever*.

In addition to this massive data capture, the BNF is working on building some collections of texts that are archived more intelligently. It has asked the APA to assist it in compiling an anthology of personal diaries and web pages. One of our members, Bernard Massip, together with a small group of cyberdiarists, is helping to make the selection. This anthology of about a thousand websites exists only in electronic form, of course, and has no equivalent on paper.

CORRESPONDENCE

Correspondence is undergoing an even more radical transformation than the diary because, in this case, handwritten letters and e-mail are used for the same purpose, whereas the diary is aimed at two different ends—public or private. Unfortunately, the survey on French cultural practices does not include a question about correspondence. It did have one related question in 2008, but that was only about e-mail. Still, we all know from personal experience that e-mail has largely replaced handwritten correspondence and telephone calls. I receive far fewer letters, and the telephone rings less often. While the letter and the telephone still occupy a special place, it is shrinking with each passing day. Letters are (reasonably) resistant because people still like paper, ink, envelopes, stamps, the handwriting of a loved one, shoeboxes to keep old letters in, and waiting for the mailman, and because truly personal expression still seems to require writing by hand. But their role is gradually shrinking, and people are gradually getting used to entrusting increasingly intimate messages to e-mail, despite its unfortunate tendency for indiscretion. The telephone is still holding its own: people have a taste for the human voice, for the immediacy of dialogue, and especially for the telephone's ability to take on new functions that make it yet another portable computer.

E-mail takes us into a world of fast-paced exchanges (with less time for reflection and maturation), writing quickly (people make a lot of errors and reread less, which is paradoxical since, unlike with paper, correction is easy and leaves no trace), the disappearance of signs of the individual (gone are personal handwriting or a signature), the possibility of multiple addressees (with the "cc" function), a powerful ability to copy and forward messages, the ability to save a copy of everything and find anything (but remember that nothing is ever lost or forgotten), but also the possibility that someday everything might be lost.

Autobiography

Properly and strictly speaking, autobiography was supposed to be the subject of this reflection, but here I am running short of time—I must speed things up, and will only be able to touch on it. I will make two observations about its good health, to reassure those of you who were afraid it might disappear.

My first observation is that it has withstood the arrival of the Internet. Granted, in technical terms, there is nothing stopping someone from publishing a relatively long autobiography by posting it on the Internet. But who would actually read it? So far, the only things people read on the Internet are short texts or series of fragments: a diary entry, a letter, yes, but not a two-hundred-page narrative. For long texts, when it is real reading and not just skimming, people still turn to paper. When they receive a two-hundred-page attachment, they print it out to read it. Will things change with e-readers and tablets? Perhaps. But for the time being, when it comes to publishing, for example, if an author publishes his autobiography on his publisher's website, as Martin Winckler (2002, 2004) did, he does so in the fragmented form of a series, one chapter at a time; he would never post the whole thing at once. So the full-fledged autobiographical narrative remains primarily on paper. We must imagine electronic autobiography moving in a completely different direction. Not as a coherent text, modeled on the book, but a creation that uses the very form of the new media by taking advantage of their creative potential: hypertextuality (the construction of a whole out of fragments tied together by networks of links and escaping from the linear form of the book) and remediation (the combined use of text, pictures, and sound). For the past thirty years we have seen the development of the autobiographical graphic novel (ever since Spiegelman's *Maus*) and autobiographical film (the masterpiece being, in my opinion, Alain Cavalier's *Le Filmeur*). By the same logic, one can imagine new forms appearing on the Internet, forms that will probably be closer to self-portrait than autobiography—nonlinear forms that will make greater use of the possibility, which the book lacks, of evolving over time the way a blog does. I am probably describing something that already exists but that I am not yet aware of because I have not navigated the Internet enough.

My second observation is that autobiography on paper is booming. You have only to look at the number of texts deposited with the APA in recent years or at the publishing market to see that the classical forms of autobiographical texts are doing fine and, at least for the time being, are withstanding the dizzying acceleration of lived time that I mentioned earlier. The APA is receiving just as many narratives covering a single life, or the major events of a life, or even family histories (people having developed a passion for genealogy, spurred on by the uploading of public archives on the Internet and the development of websites such as Geneanet), and just as many narratives telling the story of a personal crisis or ordeal. In the past ten years, we have even seen an amazing transformation in the physical presentation of the typescripts we receive: the binding, the formatting, the ever greater number of illustrations—everything is getting better. These handcrafted products are becoming just as attractive as books, and sometimes surpassing them, particularly when it comes to the number, quality, and presentation of photographs. Independent and assisted self-publishing is on the rise. At the very moment when we are entering what François Bon (2011) calls the "post-book" period, the book form seems, paradoxically, to be making an extraordinary comeback because economically and technically it is now accessible to every enthusiast. It is no longer for professionals alone, nor is it destined for the market; rather, it is facilitating a new form of family sociability. People make thirty copies and send two of them to the APA, which it will deem "unpublished." Since the APA was established in 1992, the boundary between published and unpublished texts has become blurrier, and our assessment criteria more flexible.

And are we seeing a withering away of autobiographical production in the book publishing world? Not at all. Documentary autobiographies (which relate to social problems or contemporary history) continue to sell just as well as ever. And there has been a real upsurge in "literary" autobiographies. I will end by mentioning a work that Véronique Montémont (2011) submitted for her PhD dissertation titled "Petite cartographie des écrits égotropes, 1975–2010" ("Minor mapping of egotropic writings, 1975–2010"). Why does she coin this new term "egotropic"? To broaden her field of observation, to exclude nothing, and at the same time to get a better grasp of historical changes, particularly in the borderline experimental areas sometimes (but not always) referred to as "autofiction." Her corpus, which includes some 120 published texts and which she has analyzed with the latest methods (using the "Frantext" database), shows that unlike the model texts of the genre, contemporary texts eagerly embrace hybridization and fragmentation. Autobiography uses the resources put at its disposal by all other literary forms and no longer clings to the classical unifying narrative. These new forms often express troubled and problematic identities, but is that not the raison d'être of autobiography? And by favoring hybridization and fragmentation, these literary works, published in book form, are using the very methods that we see in the virtual world. Could it be that our "accelerated" world has found the forms demanded by our new "narrative identities," be they paper or electronic?

REFERENCES

Couleau, Christèle, and Pascale Hellégouarc'h, eds. 2012. *Les Blogs, écritures d'un nouveau genre?* Itinéraires 2. Paris: L'Harmattan.

Bon, François. 2011. *Après le livre.* Paris: Seuil.

Debray, Régis. 2000. *Introduction à la médiologie.* Paris: P.U.F.

Donnat, Olivier. 2007. "Internet et moi." *La Faute à Rousseau* 45 (June): 25–27.

———. 2009. *Les pratiques culturelles des Français à l'ère numérique: Enquête 2008.* Paris: La Découverte/Ministère de la Culture et de la Communication.

Lejeune, Philippe. 2000. *"Cher écran . . .": Journal personnel, ordinateur, Internet.* Paris: Seuil.

———. 2009. *On Diary.* Edited by Jeremy D. Popkin and Julie Rak, translated by Katherine Durnin. Honolulu: University of Hawai'i Press.

Merlini, Fabio. 2011. *L'Époque de la performance insignifiante: Réflexions sur la vie désorientée.* Translated from Italian by Sabine Plaud. Paris: Éd. du Cerf.

Montémont, Véronique. 2011. "Les mots pour se dire: Petite cartographie des écrits égotropes (1975–2010)." Unpublished *habilitation* (postdoctoral) thesis, Université Lille III.

Moulard, Cécile. 2004. *Mail connexion: La conversation planétaire*. Vauvert: Au Diable Vauvert, 2004.

Rosa, Hartmut. 2010. *Accélération: Une critique sociale du temps*. Translated from German by Didier Renault. Paris: La Découverte.

———. 2010. "Au secours! Tout va trop vite." Interview by Frédéric Joignot. *Le Monde Magazine*, August 28, 11–17.

Simonet-Tenant, Françoise. 2007. "'Écris-moi': Enquête sur la lettre aujourd'hui." *Cahiers de l'APA* 37 (October): 72.

Winckler, Martin. 2002. *Légendes*. Paris: P.O.L.

———. 2004. *Plumes d'Ange*. Paris: P.O.L.

The Blog as Experimental Setting

An Interview with Lauren Berlant

ANNA POLETTI *and* JULIE RAK

THE PROCESS

JULIE: How did you come to your blog writing process? What made you decide that you were going to prepare your posts in advance?

LAUREN: My process has developed over time into a thing that is relatively reliable, although I don't post regularly. In 2004 I published a piece called *Unfeeling Kerry* where I describe why I didn't really like blog writing at that time, which, among many academics, involved adapting theory to polemics, to the opinion form. I wasn't really interested in shooting off quick responses to immediate stimuli. I wasn't interested in being, as it were, an affect register keyed to prescriptive conclusions about what appeared for a moment to be significant events. So, instead, it seemed to me that if *Supervalent Thought* could be cast as a research blog, my task would be to try to figure out the contours of a problem in relation to a project. In a short piece you can only begin to approach a problem and see what shifts because of your mode of approach. I tended to articulate those problems in terms of phrases and keywords: for example, there is a series on "the encounter" and one on "the combover" as a form of subjectivity and social experience. There is also a series on the problem of thinking about life at its edges—the suicide materials, the *Do You Intend to Die?* sequence. All of this slight movement has been very important to developing the final chapter of my next book, where the question is what it means not to want to attach to the world, which I take profoundly to be an experience of biopolitics.

I decided that because it was a research blog it ought to be my project to be developing things. It was also an opportunity to think about the way I write, since I am a bad writer. My process is a lot like making pie crust. I try carefully and slowly to push a problem into a new contour by making a new context for it—I feel like I'm very slow compared to other people. So I don't know about a "decision" I made, but this turned out to be my process.

So one thing about the process is that because it was a research blog, I felt like it was important for the entries to develop thought. The other thing is that, as I'm trying to learn how to write so I couldn't just be, you know, just casting things off quickly. So there's a lot of ongoing revision. I think that the writing in *Cruel Optimism* (2011) was transformed by writing the blog because I have a more available style now than I had in previous work.

JULIE: What was it about the form of blogging that made you think it was a good medium for this kind of writing?

LAUREN: Well, again, I wasn't thinking of it as a good medium for where I was at the time. It's a developmental medium; it's an experimental medium for me.

COMMUNICATION: WRITING TO HUMANS

LAUREN: My interest in the blog was to try to think about writing as communication . . . rather than the way I think about it when I'm writing normally, which focuses on my fidelity to the idea and the question. When I'm writing out of fidelity to the idea and the question, my writing tends to involve longer sustained abstractions, and when I'm writing to humans . . . I'm much more likely to be closer to a storytelling modality.

ANNA: How did you know that people would be reading your blogs, was it a speculation on the form?

LAUREN: Yes: I think the medium and genre of the blog presumes such a rhetorical orientation for the writer, a hybridized public, personal voice: but I didn't make any conscious empirical predictions about the destiny of the blog, or really have fantasies about it. Because one doesn't know what will happen. I didn't really care or consider outcomes. My blog actually gets quite a few hits. But I don't know how much *reading* there is. But then there's hardly any reading anywhere anyway . . .

JULIE: Is it important to you to just know that you get readers or do you . . . are the comments significant in terms of what you're doing?

LAUREN: Well, you know, I was very inspired—although I hadn't read it at the beginning—by Latour's *Reassembling the Social* (2005). His argument is that we ought to have four notebooks with different kinds of data in them and to think about how the data speak to each other. I wasn't really thinking about writing to people at the time, but about reorganizing how I mediate thought. I was just thinking, "I want to be a better writer. I'm not a good writer because my work is too closed off and people find it very hard to attend to it."

And although people are willing to do the work for some writers, and it's not like they're *not* willing to do the work for me, I think I get a lot more criticism for the difficulty of my work than I want to. And I don't *really* understand why it's difficult—that's the other thing. I mean, since it's not difficult for me. It's rhythmical and spiraling, working figurally as much as argumentatively. But one thing that I know is that after people have heard me give a talk, my work is much easier for them to read. So there is something about the grain of my spoken voice that I need to learn how to translate into my writing. Because of that I am working on my writing; additionally, no one has really trained me to write critical theory, and I wasn't happy about many normative practices of writing about it or with it. I had been trained to write and at a certain point people just said, "This is what she does." And, you know, mazel tov to her, and good luck. And so . . . and then I just felt I needed to take writing on as a project. Plus, the kind of work I want to write isn't going to sound like continental philosophy. Since no one was training me, I was self-training. For these reasons the blog is not centrally motivated by how [people] read my work "as theory," what Derrida or Žižek would say about it, and so on.

I'm happy when people write comments, though. I try to respond to those comments, especially since most people are actually kind of cowardly in fact and so they will often write me e-mails and not put comments on the bottom because they don't want to seem like fans. So I actually have quite a big response audience to the blog that doesn't get manifested on it. And I'm grateful for that. I'm grateful for anyone who takes the time to read anything because who has time to read anything? I'm grateful for being taken seriously. But the project of learning how to write in a way that would make it possible for my thought to be found, and for me not to exact too much patience from people, was central to my own thought about what the blog could train me to do. So when I say it's a research blog I mean also that it's a training blog, and I'm really very serious about that.

THE BLOG AS TRANSFORMATIONAL ENVIRONMENT

ANNA: So that leads to my question, which draws on your formulation of the transformational environment, following Bollas, in *The Female Complaint* (2008), where you write: "Christopher Bollas describes the optimism a new object of attachment organizes as a 'transformational environment.' Extending Winnicott's notion of the transformational environment, Bollas argues that when someone recognizes a new attachment she seeks to desire herself in the desire she elicits from another. This version of herself is not someone who already exists but one that the transformational environment provided by the new object will help to bring into being" (239). Would you describe your use of the blog as creating a transformational environment for your writing?

LAUREN: That's what it is, yes. My love of Bollas has a lot to do with his translation of object into scene. And thinking about the way a classroom, for example, is an environment that enables people to unlearn things and learn things, and also to be in the space of abeyance and not knowing how to have the next thought. That part of teaching is a really important part of writing for me also. Even prior to reading Bollas I talk about this orientation toward writing in the introduction to *The Queen of America Goes to Washington City* (1997), where I say that, as a writer, I perform an operation on the object in, as it were, real time, in the real time of writing and reading. Otherwise I could just say, "The fetus is X," but what I want to show is how the fetus got to be that way; I also want to show what it would look like to have a different kind of sentence in which the fetus could operate. And this is because my very strong view is that if you don't change the form of knowledge along with changing knowledge, you're not actually changing knowledge. What you're doing is you're putting new topics in old clothes. And I've had big debates about this with scholars I quite respect who feel very strongly that it's our job to be useful in a way that makes people feel more powerful and entitled when they've finished rather than less, and that therefore I ought to have an obligation to produce rational, critical, normative argument in my work such that when you finished reading it you would have "a takeaway point" that you could use in other arguments, rather than learning how to comprehend differently or feel more awkward in relation to your object in such a way that makes an entirely different environment around it. I'm really interested in making a different environment around the object because I'm interested in worlding.

So I don't mean to make a claim that my work is radical because there are people—Katie Stewart or Jackie Orr or people like that—whose critical writing is much fiercer in its refusal of metadiscourse and refusal of utility. And I want to be useful, actually. I enjoy explaining and I really like clarity. But what I try to do is to slow down the process of the transformation of the object in relation to the critical work and to allow the object to be a genuinely live resource for me.

What's interesting about the difference between an actual transformational environment and writing is that an actual transformational environment comes out of the child's need, the child induces a relation to be open to its own becoming-different within the anchoring. But, when writing is the transformational environment, the author is having to create it and induce people to get attached to it: so there's a whole question of how you get people attached to the situation in which they will also become different. And, I think, when you teach gender and sexuality studies you're making a similar kind of quite intense demand on people, asking them to take something through which they have constituted the truth of themselves and to become different in real time in relation to that thing. That is an extremely difficult project, and that's why writing this way is harder. Maybe I'll get better at it, and one of the questions that always puzzles me—and one thing I'm trying to experiment with in the blog—has to do with how much one's writing is taken over by the event of the writing. So usually when I write about literature or art I work very closely with the exemplum in order for it to make the environment in which the problem I'm working on is changing. In the blog I'm trying to have a lighter touch in relation to my encounters so that the encounter isn't dominating the scene of writing, but enables the loosening or floating of the concept. But it is a platform for launching a thought through the human voice that is still very present in the analysis.

JULIE: You have an entry from December 2007 where you talk about lightness in relation to Facebook: "I said to her that one point of Facebook is to inhabit the social as a play of play; of having a light impact, of being ordinary, of being acknowledged, echoing, noodling," all these things. If this is Facebook (and we thought this was a fascinating way to talk about Facebook) then would you say that blogs have a heavy impact or a heavy intimacy or make strong connections as opposed to weak connections?

LAUREN: Well, I don't want to generalize about blogs because there are so many different kinds. In general I feel that people are melodramatists. So in general I feel that the blog form has an amplifying function with respect to intention and voice. Trolls are meaner, humor is edgier, satire is edgier. Melodrama is more melodramatic. Trauma is more traumatized. So . . . in that regard, I think, my blog is unusual in that it is exploring a variety of different affective atmospheres for relationality both performatively and referentially. It talks about comedy an awful lot. And tries to think about what it would be like to have a more gestural relation to the social . . . a lighter touch in relation to the social. It talks a lot about awkwardness and other forms of the comic, and tries to think a lot about what it would mean to imagine a world in which there was a lot more give and elasticity than is the case in the world of melodrama that, I think, saturates almost all writing by almost everybody, you know. So Facebook is different, and I think Facebook is a place where there's mostly melodrama. People's status updates sometimes are merely, "I had a donut," but often they become, "I had a donut that provides intense delight or drama or impact that's profound." I see it myself, like, I'll write something about a mood I'm in but by the time everybody comments on that it, it becomes a huge event I had, you know? Even if it was an incident that passed and wasn't profound—hardly anything is! But the medium eventilizes the evanescent, so often, because of the technicalities of comment-building. At the same time, in a different frequency that accompanies all the checking in, Facebook does allow other forms of ordinariness that are just sweet and episodic, which is incredibly important in relation to being in the ordinary of other people's lives with whom you're not living in the same space. That's a particular function of Facebook and Twitter and the other forms of social media that are about the right now and the instant. I love poking, you know, because I think it's just a way of saying, "I'm with you," "I thought about you today." And it doesn't have to have a message. It doesn't have to be expressive or philosophical. It just has to take the form of being-with. And I've been thinking a lot about this in my work; about the difference between citizenship, membership, belonging, and being-with, and wanting to see if it's possible to get more and more and more formal as a way of trying to think differently about vicissitudes of attachment in social space.

ANNA: When you were talking about it earlier in relation to teaching, it seems to me that what the blog offers you is a kind of co-presence that the book or the academic journal, the traditional modes of publishing, don't allow you to have. In those forms, you publish and then you take up a position of distance: "I'm leaving the room, there you go. I'll leave everyone in the room with my thinking and wait to hear from you about what you think." Whereas the blog's actually allowing you to stay in the room but create a transformational environment, creating an environment that allows you to stay in it while other people engage in it.

LAUREN: Right. It's always a surprise. Although I don't write it for the people to come in, so it's not like I'm sitting there waiting, you know, like one of those feminists in the dark with no light bulb. I'm not sitting there waiting for a hit or response, although it's also interesting when the blog gets taken up. . . . It's interesting because to me the phrase "What people are doing online" is not a description of identity. And so one of the things you're trying to do is to say maybe that's a good way of describing what "online relationality" is. It's a practice-based and experimental, experiential model that is different from something like expressive projection, which is, I think, how people mostly think about the writer's "voice." *Supervalent Thought* is a training ground; I wasn't doing it so that I could have a voice. It was so I could have writing.

ANNA: I would suggest that this idea of a training ground is actually more common than we think it is. The veneer of confident, assertive performance, of the polemic that gets associated with the blog, even when people examine more tentative blogging projects, overlooks the fact that many people are using the blog as a means of creating scenes for themselves to encounter others in.

LAUREN: Well, there are a lot of blogs where people actually are training each other, such as pro-ana [pro-anorexia] blogs or knitting blogs. Even political blogs where people are trying to hash out positions are pedagogical but I think *training* is slightly different. I mean, I think there are pedagogical blogs aimed at forging *forms of life*, but it is less common for the blogger to try to build a skill for transformed *modes of thought*, this is less common. But certainly it's an experimental form in the nineteenth-century sense, and some people are making it up as they go along, that's a really important part of it. And mostly they're making it up collectively.

GENRE AND IDENTITY: WHAT COUNTS AS AUTOBIOGRAPHY?

LAUREN: Should we talk about blogs as part of the expansion of life writing genres? In your hats as traditional life writing scholars you would have thought that a blog with an "I" voice would be generating a kind of autobiographical continuity throughout the blog.

JULIE: Yes, even without its participation, in a sense.

LAUREN: Exactly. And my blog has an explicit polemic against this, right?

JULIE: Yes.

LAUREN: It says, "I'm not interested in aspiring to autobiography; I'm interested in biography as a launching pad for other kinds of thought and conceptualization." But there is autobiography in the blog. One of the pieces, in the *Do You Intend to Die?* sequence, is about my cousin . . . there are a few relatives who pop up in the blog. There is autobiography there, but it's there because it helps clarify something. It's there because in the blog I'm using everything I know: that's what I meant earlier by noting the centrality of the genre of "the encounter" to the blog. One of the things blog writing has clarified for me as an intellectual is that I bring everything I know to the table when I'm engaging a problem, whether it's thinking, teaching, or ordinary conversation. And I bring everything I know to the blog. I bring stuff that happened in my history, I bring stuff that happened in my current life, an encounter I had in airports—I don't have any time in my life, and so the airport is one of the places where I feel free to write whatever I want to because I'm waiting. You might have noticed that the productivity of waiting is one of the kind of key tropes of the blog, you know, like getting up in the morning or Christmas vacation or these aleatory moments when I don't have to be productive in an ordinary way or when I'm so tired of one kind of thought that my mind like explodes into another kind of thought. I often point out my pleasure in brainstorming while going running and what it means to be filled with thought and to try to get back to record it. So it's interesting to ask, if I'm not doing traditional life writing and yet autobiography is in there, what does it mean that autobiography is being put in contact with many other kinds of conceptualization in order to change the contours of knowledge? And that seems like the kind of question about which you would want us to talk. Were you the most gratified when you saw autobiographical writing in the thing [the blog]?

ANNA: I am very interested in thinking about the autobiographical as a means of thinking. You've said it very well yourself, that you encounter the autobiographical content as a means of thinking. I'm attracted to autobiography in a non-narrative context because I'm very interested in texts that people create that demonstrate their thinking or their fantasies or their processing, generally.

LAUREN: Right, in that sense it's autobiography in your larger sense of what autobiography is: a record of the scenic-ness of processing.

The Scene

LAUREN: Well, for me the blog is more like *The Arcades Project* (1999) or some other kind of scenic imminent writing. The existence of that gives me permission to think that the blog is intellectual work. But on the other hand, other things that are like *The Arcades Project* I don't like as well. I worry about this, but then I'm not publishing this as a book so I don't have to make a claim on anybody when I'm doing this. The freeing part is that I'm not making a claim that this is knowledge that anyone should encounter. But if they do and they learn things from it I'll be thrilled . . .

JULIE: One of the things that I really love about *The Arcades Project* is that Benjamin was interested in the question of whether you change knowledge when you change the frame for it.

LAUREN: But *The Arcades Project* is very hard to read too.

JULIE: It can be. But I did not read the entries in order, and I read one a day for a while. If I read a blog that way it would be better, because I could just drop in to it. And then I can drop away from that. This kind of reading is really interesting to me because it signals what the autobiographical is when it is not dependent on orderly narrative. That's the stuff that I get really excited about.

LAUREN: I'm really surprised by that, that is that . . . you see *The Arcades Project* as autobiography.

JULIE: I [*thinks a bit*] yes, I do. I think it's because people make a terrible mistake when they think that the theory is only in File N. That's not what Benjamin is trying to do. He's trying to make a way of organizing what he's seeing and to me that is the life trace for him. The other project that I like that's like that is Raymond Williams's *Keywords* (1985) because it's non-narrative organizing of knowledge. It's a deep drill through all kinds of words and concepts.

LAUREN: I'm very surprised at your conjecture of those things.

JULIE: Really?

LAUREN: Yes, I am. I mean on some level, somebody could say they're the opposite, that Raymond Williams is saying, "Here's a keyword and here is the story of that word. The word is itself a kind of magnet for a narrative that will tell you how it got to be that way right now." And Benjamin is refusing meta-explanation. So at one level I can see what you're describing but on another level, they seem quite different.

JULIE: But I like the fact that they have a database approach to thinking about how to organize it. And that is what I like about online writing.

LAUREN: Right. And that's what I feel like I don't do, to taxonomize into topics. But when I'm in a particular research phase or a particular teaching phase I will often pursue a problem in a series that brings incommensurate knowledges and idioms into contact. Then the blog becomes a scene for walking around a problem. So my blog work is much more subjectified in a sense that it's much more infused with vicissitudes in my perspective on things than either of those two more formalist texts. But that's because Benjamin's decision was to not explain how he got there. You know, he just got there. Whereas I want to . . . I want to tell you how I got there. I was sitting in the airport and this thing happened and these other people were there. So it's just interesting to consider if what we have in common here is a body of work that understands the ordinary as episodic, that understands that you can't have a continuous narrative of knowledge but rather a kind of clustering of situations. This is also Foucault's model of genealogy. And, and then there's something about the relation of the personal to the impersonal, even in Williams, he's thinking

about it all the time. I mean *Keywords* is one of the great texts about subjectification, subjectivity. In other work, Williams is very explicitly personal. I'm
really trying very hard not to reproduce the thing that we were always de-
constructing. You know, the hierarchy of the objective to the subjective and
the privileging of argument over narrative. I was inspired by Lyotard, in
"One of the Things at Stake in Women's Struggles," saying, "We know the rev-
olution will have been achieved when there is no longer a difference between
the sentence, 'the soup is on' and the sentence, 'it is true the soup is on.'" And
I'm there, you know, I really think it doesn't matter in my work, whether
you're in one of those sentences or the other; that there's some other kind of
thing that is being performed in the work that isn't about confirming norms
of legitimation. The focus is on how to move a problem that I'm trying to
engage. That's what I hope anyway.

The Scene as a Suspension Bridge

JULIE: We are really taken by your discussion of scene in the entry "Crossover/
Combover: a Performance Piece." Here's some of what you wrote: "Like all
genres, the scene is a suspension bridge, defined not by events but by wob-
bly atmospheres in proximity to a disturbance. So if a scene appears as a shift
within the ongoing, the happening becomes event in its apprehension. What
we've grasped without understanding it, not in facts or narrative that come
to stand as facts. The story about X and in the psychoanalytic sense of the
primal scene, the subject becomes conscious of their non-sovereignty in an
encounter with a threatening situation and gets stuck in the affect of the atmosphere." Why are we interested? First of all, we're interested in how you understand the scene as a genre.

LAUREN: I have a lot to say about that. In *Cruel Optimism* I was working out
the problem of the genre of the scene in relation to the cinema of precarity
and the question of what the genres of a time are in crisis or a transition where
you understand yourself to be in a scene but you don't know what its genre
is yet. You don't know if the scene is going toward tragedy or comedy or
some kind of mixedness or is just a nothing episode that has no impact. You
don't have a sense of its arc. You just have a sense of its intensity and the emerging shape of its intensity. So in psychoanalysis, what is a scene? A scene exists
where there is a perturbation in an atmosphere that overwhelms, that reveals
and unravels structure, but it also induces a kind of stuckness in relation to
the revelation of the event. That is, it produces a kind of slowness or a paralysis or incapacity.

And so, you know, in the famous "A Child Is Being Beaten" (1919) Freud imagines that the subject overhears something in another room and imagines that he is occupying all of the positions in that scene. Or take "the primal scene." In the primal scene you come in, you come into a room and you are overwhelmed by a thing you see such that your seeing of it is accompanied by an over-presence of affect that makes it impossible to narrate it away and to narrate yourself away from it. The scene is an enigma, and raises the question of how you move it and move in relation to it.

JULIE: Is it that sense of cathection where there is no disengagement, there can be no reflection?

LAUREN: Well, cathexis is a really important part of reading in the sense that you are attached to a thing and that attachment becomes the condition of your endurance. Although there are a lot of minor cathexes, like being cathected to chocolate, that do not anchor subjects. But the major cathexes are different. At a conference last week, the anthropologist Katie Stewart asked us to write from a scene, and I thought, "Well, I'll write from the scene of writing." In the scene of writing, what we discover is that people float genres in which it was possible to take up a lot of different kinds of position. That's what a scene is. And that's what it means for the scene to be a suspension bridge.

All genres are the opportunity to walk around a variety of outcomes and happenings in relation to a particular kind of scene.

JULIE: It's much better than thinking about genre as law.

LAUREN: Yes. Genre as law is a ridiculous conceptualization because obviously it's not law, although Derrida's version in "The Law of Genre" locates law where it hits its limit, folds in on itself, and unravels. Genre is barely even a contract, even though I have occasionally metaphorized it as a contract in the sense that there's a normative expectation in contact with a genre that you will inhabit content in a certain kind of way or that you will encounter a certain kind of logic. But of course since there is also the expectation that you will encounter certain kinds of obstacles to that logic and that content, it becomes a much more complicated thing: it's a horizon of expectation but it's not a law. When people are excited, they're excited for the same reasons they get disappointed, which is there was a kind of surprise they either enjoyed or didn't enjoy in relation to it.

JULIE: As in, "I read this Oprah book and I expected to hate it but I did not."

LAUREN: That's right, exactly. And in that case its genre is really identical with its brand as opposed to its genre . . . its actual literary genre. So one of the things that became interesting with Oprah books was that there were lots of different kinds of them she actually liked but by being branded as Oprah books you expected a certain intensity of sentimentality in relation to truth. And it could be fiction and it could be nonfiction. It could be present, it could be prior, it doesn't really matter. But you thought you were going to have an intense emotional event and that there would be revelation in relation to it. And that's the me-genre of the Oprah brand, which is really, really interesting in relation to other histories of literary genre.

So when I am thinking about a scene, you know, I'm just very interested in the becoming-event of something. A scene is a disturbance that can become event. And that can take on a narrative shape, and that can start to have resonances with other events in that genre. But you often don't know what the event of the scene will be until you spend some time with it, so . . .

ANNA: So in that sense, do you think the blog, for you, is a space where the scene's actually easier to make apparent than in other forms? Thinking of it as one of your many choices of spaces in which to write.

LAUREN: I don't know. I think in my more extensive narrative critical work, part of my job is to work scenically as a way of describing the phases of development of a problem. There isn't ever a thing I've ever written that isn't in sections. So one thing is . . . I've thought about this because of you guys, because of your interest in my blog I have thought about this, that I always section my work and that my sections and the length of my blog entries are pretty similar. But the satisfaction of a blog entry as genre is that I'm making this scene for a problem and that scene isn't identical to the encounter that might be generating it.

ANNA: In that sense, writing for the blog allows you to maintain fidelity to the scene, whereas in other kinds of writing—as you said earlier—you feel obligated to maintain a fidelity to the problem.

LAUREN: Exactly.

JULIE: That disjuncture between writing a scene for a problem, and its nonidentity with the encounter, gets at the heart of what we want to think about with respect to online identity in this collection. We think that many of things we have seen about online identity do not make this kind of distinction, and we're really interested in thinking about it.

LAUREN: I'm just curious about the word "identity" there because I wouldn't have thought we were talking about identity just now.

JULIE: No.

LAUREN: So it's interesting.

JULIE: Our larger project is to try to do that. But we know that we don't want to think about identity apart from identification, and we don't necessary want to think about it as concomitant with the idea of the subject.

ANNA: For me "identity" is actually a problem in how we approach thinking about what people are doing online, because it has been a dominant frame for understanding what they are doing and *how* they are doing it. There is a tendency to think of most of these things through the framework of identity. But, what if we thought about it as autobiography? As creating a scene? A suspension bridge? It seems to me that we need to expand the range of concepts and be more precise in our use of the term "identity" to better grasp what is happening online.

DOING IT IN PUBLIC: RESISTING DEAD GENRES

LAUREN: And I don't know exactly why I decided to do it in public either. I think it was mainly because most of the genres that we write in as professional interpreters are dead genres; that is, people don't enjoy reading what we write, they don't look forward to reading it, they read (when they do) out of duty to their own professionalism. If that. And they do not induce optimism about world-building through critical interpretive work. I'm trying to create different kinds of platforms and voicings and modes of expression for that. I don't want my students to be writing work they wouldn't read if they hadn't a professional obligation. I don't want my colleagues who are participating in very strong world-building and attention-cultivating projects to work in forms that are a violation of their own rich minds. And I think most people are doing that. And I wish they wouldn't. And so I myself don't want to. And I've been lucky compared to many because I was so de-skilled and disassociated from the world when I was young that I wrote books and articles that looked innovative when really they were just the thing I could do at the time. But I think now there's actually a kind of ethical and political compulsion to get people to write work they can stand behind as writing.

And I want to create situations of solidarity with that project. And so that's why I ventured the project of changing my own critical writing in public, because I thought it probably is good . . . it probably matters—although I didn't know if it would matter to anybody—to think that criticism could look different and that criticism could look engaged and fierce and meditative and magnetize so many different kinds of knowledge that we have in relation to enigmas that we're finding very, very hard to clarify. That was the hope that I had when I started doing it, anyway, and it still matters a lot to me, to place politically and conceptually transformative projects of change and solidarity formation in relation to how we organize knowledge.

JULIE: To follow and maybe end, is the emphasis on encounter in your blog connected to that kind of ethics?

LAUREN: Yes.

JULIE: Would you like to speak about that?

LAUREN: I've written a lot about being a colleague, you know, something that we do all the time and that most people are pretty bad at, including me on occasion, but I care about it a lot as a genre. One thing about teaching and being a colleague is that you can learn from any encounter with anything. That's at the heart of *Cruel Optimism*, that you can be attached to anything and it can create the possibility of a world for you. And that any, any kind of encounter could produce a new potential for relationality. And, if I'm trying to change knowledge and its objects, and trying to think about the aesthetic in terms of affective development, it has to be in such a way that criticism and world-building don't look like antithetical processes or the irrelevant in relation to the relevant, but actually are continuous with each other. Then the encounters that organize so many of my posts are very important to me as genres that induce aesthetics. Because after all, aesthetics is the place where a certain kind of encounter with form is the scene where you're open to the possibility of becoming different. I'm actually kind of like that in general, in my ordinary life. Any encounter that I have is a thing that can light me up in a way that can make another kind of encounter possible. Leo Bersani said once in my presence that trauma is a moment when your brain lights up in a way that it hasn't done before. And I was like, "But that's what learning is." And that's what delight is too. It's not just trauma. That's why I work on nonsovereignty as the foundational dynamic of sociality because becoming undone isn't just the end of something, it's also the possibility of becoming different.

Contributors

OLIVIA BANNER is a lecturer in the Department of English at Rice University, where she teaches courses on medicine, media, and literature. She is also a member of Medical Futures Lab, based in Houston, Texas. Her book, *Biomediations: Identities after the Genome Projects*, is forthcoming.

LAUREN BERLANT is the George M. Pullman Distinguished Service Professor of English at the University of Chicago. Her national sentimentality trilogy— *The Anatomy of National Fantasy* (1991), *The Queen of America Goes to Washington City* (1997), and *The Female Complaint* (2008)—has now morphed into a quartet, with *Cruel Optimism* (2011) addressing precarious publics and the aesthetics of affective adjustment in the contemporary United States and Europe. Her work on affect, writing, and mediation has motivated a number of works, such as *Intimacy* (ed., 2000); *Compassion: The Culture and Politics of an Emotion* (ed., 2004); *Desire/Love* (2012), and, with Lee Edelman, the forthcoming *Sex, or the Unbearable* (2014). As coeditor of *Critical Inquiry*, she has also compiled *On the Case* (special issue of *Critical Inquiry* 2007). She blogs at *Supervalent Thought* and is also a founding member of the art/activist group Feel Tank Chicago.

SUZANNE BOUCLIN is an assistant professor of the Faculty of Law at the University of Ottawa. Her work and research crosses feminist studies, film and communications studies, and criminology. She teaches feminist jurisprudence, law and poverty, law and cinema, and alternative dispute resolution. She has published in the *Canadian Journal of Women in the Law*; *Public Law*; *Race, Gender and Class*; the *International Journal of the Humanities*; and in several collections of essays, including *The Arts and the Legal Academy: Beyond Text in Legal Education* (2013).

ROB COVER is an associate professor of communication and media studies at the University of Western Australia, where he teaches media theory and professional and creative media practices. He researches and writes on digital media theory, with an emphasis on the contemporary context and uses of interactive media and its implications for identity; population as a concept, including the ethics of population-size debates and composition through migration and debates over refugees; and sexuality and youth, including youth health communication and LGBT suicide. He has been published in journals such as *Continuum: Journal of Media and Cultural Studies, Convergence, New Media and Society, Journal of LGBT Youth, Body and Society*, and *Media International Australia*, among others. His recent book is *Queer Youth Suicide, Culture and Identity: Unliveable Lives?* (2012).

MARY L. GRAY is a senior researcher at Microsoft Research New England and an associate professor of communication and culture, with adjunct appointments in American studies, anthropology, and gender studies at Indiana University. Her work focuses on how people use digital and social media in everyday ways to shape their social identities and create spaces for themselves. Her most recent book, *Out in the Country: Youth, Media, and Queer Visibility in Rural America* (2009), examined how youth in rural parts of the United States fashioned "queer" senses of gender and sexual identity and the role that media—particularly Internet access—played in their lives and political work. Her current research includes work on the experiences of workers and requesters contributing to online labor platforms, and the importance of location and place in the context of mobile technologies.

MELISSA GREGG is Principal Engineer and Researcher in Residence for the Intel Science and Technology Center for Social Computing at the University of California–Irvine. She has a PhD in gender studies from the University of Sydney and specializes as a cultural theorist and ethnographer. Her publications include *Work's Intimacy* (2011), *The Affect Theory Reader* (coedited with Gregory J. Seigworth, 2010) *Cultural Studies' Affective Voices* (2006), and *Willunga Connects: A Baseline Study of Pre-NBN Willunga* (2011).

HELEN KENNEDY is senior lecturer in new media in the Institute of Communications Studies at the University of Leeds. She has published widely on new and digital media. Her recent research has focused on forms of new media work, covering topics such as web design, web standards, web accessibility, free labor, and, most recently, social media monitoring and intelligence work.

PHILIPPE LEJEUNE taught French literature at the University of Lyon (1966–72) and then at the University Paris-Nord (1972–2004). His research focuses on auto-biography (*L'Autobiographie en France*, 1971; *Le Pacte autobiographique*, 1975) and on the practice of keeping diaries (*"Cher cahier,"* 1990; *Le Moi des demoi-selles*, 1993; *"Cher écran . . .,"* 2000; *Un journal à soi: Histoire d'une pratique*, 2003). In 1992 he founded the Association for Autobiography (APA), which collects, reads, and archives all the unpublished autobiographical writing entrusted to it. The APA also publishes a review, *La Faute à Rousseau*. In 1995 Lejeune created a research team "Genesis and autobiography" (ITEM/CNRS) and published two books of "genetic criticism" (*Les Brouillons de soi*, 1998; *Autogenèses*, 2013). Two collections of his work have been published in English: *On Autobiography* (1989) and *On Diary* (2009). His website is www.autopacte.org.

LAURIE MCNEILL is an instructor in the Department of English and co-chair of the Coordinated Arts Program at the University of British Columbia. She specializes in genre and auto/biography studies, with a particular focus on digital forms of self-representation, including social networking sites and blogs, analyzing how the interface of genre, technology, and culture shapes the ways individuals make meaning of experience. Her work on these subjects has been published in *Biography* (2012), *Genres in the Internet* (2009), and *Language and New Media* (2009). She is also engaged in research on best practices in collaborative learning and teaching in multidisciplinary cohort programs.

ALESSANDRA MICALIZZI completed a PhD in communication and new technologies at the Istituto Universitario di Lingue Moderne (IULM) and had a four-year postdoctoral fellowship during which she studied online mourning. She continues to collaborate with the Department of Communication, Behaviors and Consumption at IULM and works as a consultant for private institutes of research such as Abis sas and Episteme. Emotions, identities, and the practices of sharing narratives online are her areas of interest. Her first book is *Like Another World: Practices of Socializing the Experience of Loss On and Off Line* (2012).

AIMÉE MORRISON is an associate professor of English at the University of Waterloo, where she teaches courses in new media theory and practice. She has recently published on personal mommy blogging as a life writing genre, on the political character of the Internet, and on the use of personal computers in romantic comedy. Her work on Facebook is part of a larger, ongoing project titled "Deciphering Digital Life Writing," supported by the Social Science and Humanities Research

Council of Canada. With Heather Zwicker and Erin Wunker, she cofounded the feminist academic blog *Hook & Eye*. Follow her on Twitter: @digiwonk.

LISA NAKAMURA is a professor in the Department of American Cultures and the Department of Screen Arts and Cultures at the University of Michigan–Ann Arbor. She is the author of four books on digital media and identity: *Race and Cyberspace* (2000); *Cybertypes: Race, Ethnicity, and Identity on the Internet* (2002); *Digitizing Race: Visual Cultures of the Internet* (2007), winner of the 2010 Association of Asian American Studies Book Award in Cultural Studies; and *Race After the Internet* (2011), coedited with Peter Chow-White. She is working on a manuscript titled "Workers Without Bodies: Race, Gender, and Social Media" and has presented work on digital labor in virtual world games, racism and homophobia in console games, and user-generated campaigns to critique and publicize uncivil behavior and image practices online.

ANNA POLETTI is a lecturer in literary studies at Monash University, where she is co-director of the Centre for the Book research unit. Her research interests are autobiography beyond the book, diy culture, and identity technologies. She is the author of *Intimate Ephemera: Reading Young Lives in Australia Zine Culture* (2008), and, with Gillian Whitlock, coedited a special issue of *Biography: An Interdisciplinary Quarterly* on autographics.

JULIE RAK is a professor in the Department of English and Film Studies at the University of Alberta, Canada. She is the author of *Boom! Manufacturing Memoir for Popular Markets* (2013) and *Negotiated Memory: Doukhobor Autobiographical Discourse* (2004). She edited *Auto/biography in Canada: Critical Directions* (2005), with Jeremy Popkin coedited Philippe Lejeune's *On Diary* (2009), and with Andrew Gow coedited *Mountain Masculinity: The Life and Writing of Nello (Tex) Vernon-Wood* (2008). She is completing a SSHRC-funded book titled *Social Climbing: Gender and Mountaineering Writing*.

COURTNEY RIVARD is a fixed-term faculty member in the Department of English and Comparative Literature at the University of North Carolina, Chapel Hill. She received her doctorate from the University of California–Santa Cruz in the Department of Politics with an emphasis in both feminist studies and Latin American and Latino studies. She has published "Critique Matters, Too: Review of *Museum Matters: In Praise of the Encyclopedic Museum* by James Cuno" (*E-misférica*, May 2012) and "Collecting Disaster: National Identity and the

Smithsonian's September 11th Collection" (*Australasian Journal of American Studies*, 2013). More broadly, Rivard researches the politics of archiving as it relates to the production of notions of race, gender, sexuality, national belonging, and cultural memory.

SIDONIE SMITH is the Mary Fair Croushore Professor of Humanities and the Director of the Humanities Institute at the University of Michigan. Julia Watson is a professor of comparative studies at Ohio State University. They have co-written *Reading Autobiography: A Guide for Interpreting Life Narratives* (2001; expanded edition, 2010), and coedited five collections: *De/Colonizing the Subject: The Politics of Gender in Women's Autobiography*; *Getting a Life: Everyday Uses of Autobiography*; *Women, Autobiography, Theory*; *Interfaces: Women, Autobiography, Image, Performance*; and *Before They Could Vote: American Women's Autobiographical Writing, 1819–1919*. Smith and Watson have also coauthored essays including "Witness or False Witness? Metrics of Authenticity, Collective 'I'-Formations, and the Ethic of Verification in First-Person Testimony," "The Trouble with Autobiography," "The Rumpled Bed of Autobiography: Extravagant Lives, Extravagant Questions," and others. Smith has published *Moving Lives: Women's Twentieth Century Travel Narratives* (2001); *Subjectivity, Identity, and the Body* (1993); *A Poetics of Women's Autobiography* (1987); and, with Kay Schaffer, *Human Rights and Narrated Lives* (2004), as well as several coedited collections and numerous essays, most recently on Mary Rowlandson's captivity narrative and posthumanism, and on aspects of human rights. Watson's recent essays are on Alison Bechdel's *Fun Home*, Bobby Baker's *Diary Drawings* and posthumanism, and authenticity and ethnicity in autoethnography.

Index

absence, 29–30, 100, 108, 170–71, 174, 177, 211
accumulation, 73, 106, 213
activism, 19, 70, 77, 82, 92, 107, 175, 183, 233
actor, 5, 43, 56, 71, 76, 80, 84, 169, 175, 209, 239
adolescence, 167–91. *See also* teenager; youth
adultery, 99–101, 104–11
advertising, 10, 47, 49–50, 85, 114, 159, 170, 178, 190
advocacy, 82, 169, 175, 181, 214n1
aesthetics, 78, 100, 168, 179
affordance: coaxing and, 112–19; definition of, 4–7, 10, 12, 97; in Facebook, 125–27
agency: and autobiography, 93n1, 159; and Facebook, 116, 175; and Homeless Nation, 241n14; and an interactionist approach, 191–92n6; Internet users and, 4, 7, 9, 49, 71, 92–93, 208; street people and, 231–38; subjectivity and, 39n1
album (online), 56, 85, 114, 119
algorithm, 72, 85, 113, 124, 127–28
anonymity: and authenticity, 77; offline and online, 56; online, 25–27, 29–31, 35–39; in PostSecret, 80–81
anthropology, 191n2, 192n11, 241–42n18

anxiety, 11, 57, 66–67, 99, 101, 107–8, 173, 225
archaeology, 174
archive: association with fixed identity, 34; digital, 10, 16; digital snapshot of French Internet as, 248; and Facebook, 66; Homeless Nation as, 229–33, 240n3, 240n6, 241n14; of life stories, 82–84; personal vs. database, 72–74; of the self, 91–92; of September 11 and Hurricane Digital Memory Bank, 132–43
artifact, 85, 113, 126, 134, 174
artist, 19–20, 83–85, 139, 231
arts, 53, 233
assemblage, 43, 71, 91, 113, 174, 230
attachment, 18, 31, 71, 105, 201
audience: and access to information, 141; actual and ideal, 238; and communal witnessing, 106; communicating to a wide, 232; community and, 145; direct communication with, 240n3; experiences of, 168; on MySpace, 51, 74–75; online, 6, 74–75; and paratext, 81–82; performance and, 191n2; performing for an, 180, 182; for photo albums, 119; as a public, 36; queering and, 176; reception studies of, 174; and social media interfaces, in digital life writing, role of, 126n7; studies of, 172; utterances and, 151

authenticity, 9, 28, 73, 75–77, 80, 100, 133, 168–69, 171, 190, 232–33
authorship, 91, 113, 125–26
autobiography: and the autobiographical pact, 17; definition of, 3–5, 21n1; of everyday life, 144–47; and media theory, 77; and narrative, 8–12; offline published versus online digital, 112–16, 149–52, 247–49; online profile as, 60; published, 70; as a scene, 19; and the self, 71–72. *See also* biography; memoir
autographic, 113, 127
automediality, 77–78
autonomy, 70–71, 159, 175, 178, 241n17
avatar, 19–20, 43–44, 48, 78–79, 83, 91

Baym, Nancy, 30, 38, 70, 172–73
Berlant, Lauren, 12, 17–19, 75, 107, 201, 207, 212
biography: as a digital form, 126; online collective, 159–61; as part of auto/biography, 3–8, 21n1; as part of a social media profile, 60, 65, 124. *See also* autobiography
biosociality, 198–202, 204, 213
bisexual, 51, 167–70, 182–84
blog, 77, 147–48, 162n6. *See also* weblog
bodies, 31, 45–48, 50, 56, 78–79, 153, 190, 201–2, 241n14. *See also* embodiment
boredom, 100, 104, 106
boundaries, 31, 71, 79–80, 84, 113, 127, 161, 168, 176, 192n11, 224–26
boyd, danah, 68, 128n3, 162n5
boys, 50, 180–81, 184
bricolage, 78, 91–92
broadband, 178
browser, 43, 118, 177
bulletin, 43, 168, 230
bytes, 144–45, 147, 149, 151, 153, 159, 161

camera, 42, 50, 76, 140, 229, 233
capitalism, 10–11, 66, 77, 108, 160, 202, 209
celebrity, 11, 51, 74, 76, 91, 114, 116, 145–47, 149, 159
cell phone, 13, 50, 82, 100, 103, 160, 249

childhood, 49–50, 81, 99, 119, 171–75, 224
cinema, 229, 241n9, 241n10
circulation, 10–11, 72–73, 83, 103, 169, 209
citizen, 4, 11, 17, 20, 43, 50, 73, 108, 141–42, 167, 211, 238, 240n5
civilization, 248
classification, 140–42, 154, 214n1, 232
clinic, 200–205, 212
coaxing (autobiographical), 112–17, 119, 125–27, 153, 160
coercion, 105, 114–16, 119, 126, 153
commerce, 169, 176
commodification, 73, 92, 116, 128n4
commodity, 11, 79, 176, 201–3
commons, 159, 199
communication: asynchronous, 27; avatars and, 43; between patients and doctors, 217; digital, 46, 66, 126; and intimacy, 101; mass, 148; mobile devices and, 107; nonlinguistics modes of, 82; online, 17–18, 30, 58, 238–39; oral, 219, 226; relevance of Judith Butler's work to, 56; technologies of, 48, 162n4, 177, 192n11, 229; tools of, 10–11; youth, 55
community: of auto/biographers, 145; avatars and, 79; biosociality and, 200; FM/CFIDS, 204–12; formation of, 52n2, 81; forums, 213, 221–27; genre and, 154; idea of, 14; identity and, 25; and LambdaMOO, 45; model for, 106; networked, 149–61; online, 12, 33–34, 84, 155, 204, 213; of practice, 124; practices of, 100; queer, 15, 177–84; self, relation and, 92; street, 238; of users, 82, 144; virtual, 80, 217; websites, 16; youth and, 169–73
computer: access, 138, 177, 181, 187, 240n2; digital records, 136; discarded, 49; and distance learning, 26–27; hardware and software, 5; identity, 58; and identity theft, 116–18; industry, 47; and phone-tracking, 99; specialists, 146; usage of, 106

confession, 20, 35, 70, 75, 80–81, 91, 100, 116, 146–48, 152, 162n8

consciousness, 4, 8–9, 17, 151, 160, 191n5

consumer, 4, 11, 71, 92, 99, 115, 117, 119, 126, 146, 159, 201, 238, 241–42n18

consumption, 36, 43, 66, 85, 112, 144, 148, 161, 176, 192n11, 201–2

convergence, 5, 7, 17, 146

Couldry, Nick, 5–7, 71–72, 77

counterpublic, 209–10, 212

Couser, G. Thomas, 146, 153, 161n3

culture: commercial, 118n4; and community, 16; contemporary, 3; digital, 46, 50; extra-marital relationship and, 109n4; Italian, 220; mass, 178; media, 104; and memory, 133; metropolitan, 102; online, 30, 145; popular, 48, 170–73; postfeminist, 108; print, 4, 8, 147; self-identification and, 190–91; of simulation, 28; street, 239; subculture, 241–42n18; technological, 116; therapeutic, 145–61; of usage, 113; women's, 17, 208; and work, 105; youth, 82, 175–76

curation, 73, 79, 92, 137–38

cyberculture, 25, 37, 48, 93, 172

cyberrace, 12, 42–43, 47, 49, 51–53

cyberspace, 29, 37, 44, 48, 50, 145, 147

cyborg, 47, 71

database, 64, 72–73, 84, 116, 126–28, 134

Deleuze, Gilles, 26, 31, 57, 64, 101, 190, 240n6

democracy, 10, 29, 44, 49, 51, 132, 137, 146, 202, 229, 238

demographic, 75, 100, 109n1, 153, 162n8, 173

Derrida, Jacques, 56, 91, 133, 232

diary, 5, 17, 20, 104, 119, 126, 134, 247–48

diaspora, 51, 85

digitization, 151

discourse: anti-immigration, 49; of autobiography, 3, 19; biomedical, 204, 209–10, 212–13; celebrity, 146; civil, 102; of confession, 20, 80; corporate, 79–80; of Homeless Nation, 230–40; identity and, 218; of identity, 31; and informatics, 198–202; media, 191n2; offline, 65; performativity and, 58–61; popular, 55–56; public, 122; racial, 45–48; racialized, 141; risk, 62; scholarly, 114; selfhood in, 59, 63, 66, 84, 192n6; of sexuality, 178; spoken, 226; Twitter, 14

disease, 203–4, 206, 212–14, 231

diversity, 3, 28, 43, 154, 232

documentary, 20, 137, 231–32, 240n6, 241n10

documentation, 6, 73, 137

domain, 76, 147, 168

Duggan, Lisa, 103, 176, 191n5

Eakin, Paul John, 8, 18

Ellison, Nicole B., 55, 66, 147

embodiment, 48, 64, 71, 73, 78–79, 83, 93n1, 201

ephemera, 62, 66, 136–37, 141, 151

essentialism, 26, 30, 42, 44, 51, 57–58, 63, 176, 213

ethnicity, 34, 36, 43, 47, 50, 59, 67, 78–79

ethnography, 28–29, 132–33, 170, 173–74, 180, 191n2, 217

exigence, 124, 144, 146–51, 160–61, 233

Facebook, 5, 10–12, 43, 62–67, 72, 83, 112–28, 145–49, 151, 156, 159–62

fame, 49–51, 146

families, 70, 139, 180, 184, 211

feminism, 40, 104, 107, 162n8, 167, 241–42n18

fibromyalgia, 199–212

fiction, 47, 56, 58, 65, 167–69, 178, 218

Foucault, Michel, 56–64, 107, 133, 145, 199, 240n6, 248

Freud, Sigmund, 226

gays, 177, 181–82

gender: alternative, 29–30, 177; analysis, studies, 263; difference, 100, 109n1, 109n2, 240n2; discrimination, 99, 140; Fordist ideas of, 106; genres of writing

gender (*continued*)
    and, 6; as an identity category, 47–48,
    51–52, 59, 65–67, 78–79, 82–83, 132,
    139, 162n8, 168–69, 173–77, 179,
    191n1, 241–42n18; and illness, 212;
    norms, 189; and online identity, 32–
    35, 46, 59; in an online profile, 60,
    114; performativity, 63, 192n10;
    stereotypes, 140; transgender identity
    and, 19; virtual, 44
genealogy, 70, 82, 85, 91
generation, 9, 48, 82, 92, 133, 230
genetics, 201, 209, 214n3
genre: of auto/biography, 152, 160,
    248, 251; blog, 150, 260; collegiality
    as, 272; of confession, 80; dead, 271;
    of digital life writing, 113; of the
    encounter, 265; and exigence, 17,
    146; of freshman "Facebook," 127;
    of home pages, 32; law of, 269; of
    life narrative, 145–48; of life writing,
    5–6, 161n3, 265; and liveness, 51;
    and media engagement, 178–79; of
    memoir, 154; of microblogging,
    157, 162n5; and queer realness, 1
    68–69, 176, 182, 186–90; as a scene,
    19–20, 268; as social action, 155;
    of speech and writing, 117–19; of
    work-based romance, 106; of
    writing, 18
geography, 11, 34, 55, 82, 119, 192n11
Gilmore, Leigh, 146
Giltrow, Janet, 146, 154
girls, 109n2, 167
governance, 64, 230–31
government, 64, 116, 136, 177, 211, 239
governmentality, 9, 73
GPS, 73, 99, 249
graphics, 43–44, 109n1, 139–40

Halberstam, Judith, 76, 168
Haraway, Donna, 28, 48, 191n5
Hayles, N. Kathryn, 71
heteronormativity, 84, 173, 175–77, 181,
    191n1
heterosexuality, 104, 169, 183, 190

homelessness, 95, 192–93n14, 229–33,
    238–41
homepage, 168, 205
homosexuality, 192n10
HTML, 146
humanism, 4, 71, 91
humanities, 94

identity: and anonymity, 35–37; in auto-
    biography studies, construction of,
    7–10, 30–34, 60, 71, 82–84, 101,
    191n6, 213, 217–18; biomedical,
    210–12; and the body, 42; categories,
    73, 78–79, 93n1; and community,
    25–31, 153, 174; and cultural mem-
    ory, 133–34, 137–41; as decentered,
    30–31; definition of, 39n1; digital, 11;
    encoded, 100; on Facebook, 12, 14;
    and informatics, 198–203; lost, 220;
    and narrative, 9, 219; offline, 57;
    online, 3–4, 13–14, 17, 20, 38–39, 77,
    167; and performativity, 56–62; print,
    4; racial, 42–51; resistant, 15–16;
    sexuality and, 167–90; shared, 5;
    social, 221–28; and social networking,
    55–59, 62–64; as a technology, 145,
    161, 219; virtual, 28–30; youth, 173–
    90. *See also* selfhood
ideology, 5, 44, 49, 71, 77, 82, 84, 92, 116,
    139
illness, 10, 18, 76, 146, 198–205, 209–14
inauthenticity, 76–77, 115–16, 168, 202,
    230, 233, 238
inequality, 26, 44, 49, 77, 140–41, 176–77
informatics, 198–202, 214n7
infrastructure, 127–28n2, 178, 180
institution, 107, 119, 145, 152, 154, 160,
    201
interactivity, 43–44, 49, 56, 58, 64, 71, 92,
    145, 147, 161, 226, 229, 232
interface, 4–5, 12, 31, 43, 57, 115, 117,
    119–20, 124–27, 204
Internet: access, 240n2, 254; accessibility,
    146; affordances, 5; anonymity, 32,
    35–36, 42, 56; archives, 132–38, 231;
    and autobiography, 93n4, 160; and

biosociality, 200; cafes, 177; and collective memory, 84; as a convergence of media technologies, 7, 81, 84; cultural studies approaches to, 25–31, 38; culture, 159–60; as a democracy, 238; diaries, 251; and ephemera, publishing, 144–48; filtering, 172; identity, 28–30, 37; and life writing, 112; and narrative, 225; new genres, 17–18; as a public space, 10, 145; and racism, 47, 78; research material on, 120; security, 99; service providers, 178; as a shared space, 151; storytelling, 219–20; subjects, 4; users, 12, 173; as a utopic space, 20, 44, 46, 83; as a venue for community, 204, 217–18, 224–26; as virtual, 46; and web 2.0, and user profiles, 73; as a youth space, 169–70, 178–90. *See also* web
interpellation, 63–64, 71, 178, 199, 203
intimacy: and adultery, 101–5; and confession, 80–84; and online surveillance, 100; and online users, 75, 106–9; sexual, 188, 190; threats to, 211
iPhone, 100, 160

justice, 184, 230, 240n5

Kipnis, Laura, 100–101, 104, 108–9

legality, 11, 100, 109n3
Lejeune, Philippe, 10–12, 17
lesbians, 177, 181–82
lifelogging, 198, 202–3, 212
life writing, 3–6, 21n1, 70, 78, 90, 112–19, 120–28, 144–61, 265–66. *See also* autobiographyliteracy, 48, 82, 100, 108
LiveJournal, 72, 199, 204

McRobbie, Angela, 104, 241–42n18
mediation: Homeless Nation as, 237; as identity-work, 20; and illness, 198; of the Internet and writing, 219; and the relationship of technology and subjectivity, 77; and self-representation, 6. *See also* remediation

meme, 112, 160
memoir, 5, 70, 112, 116, 119, 127, 144–54, 159–64. *See also* autobiography
memory, 9, 18, 85, 132–33, 136, 141, 224, 226, 233, 247
metadata, 93n8
method: of archival collection, 135–38; of auto/biography and new media studies, 113–14; in auto/biography studies, 7, 118; digital, 132–34; ethnographic, 217; ideas about in different fields, 3–4; relational, of representing physical pain, 205; for the study of online identity, 12–13, 126–27; and the subject of inquiry, of corporate marketing, 79
methodology, 6, 17, 38, 57, 114
microblogging, 148–51, 162n5
Mittell, Jason, 168, 178, 191n2
MUD (Multi-User Dungeon), 28–30, 36, 43
multimedia, 6, 27, 72, 79, 84, 92, 125
MySpace, 50–51, 55, 59, 62, 64–65, 72, 147, 171, 212

narrative: adultery, 104; and autobiography, 7–11, 18–20, 144, 256; as democratic, 232; digital life, 113; and identity, 16, 79, 217–17, 250; LGBTQ, 167–70, 189; life, 17, 21n1, 71, 84, 91–92, 119, 126–55; master, 15; online, 72, 90, 178, 219; and online storytelling, 219–21, 225; and paratexts, 85; personal, 89, 134, 145, 192n8; and scene, 266–67, 270; structure in memoirs, 119; studies, 78
neoliberalism, 11, 43–44, 65, 82, 91, 203
nonprofit, 152, 177, 229, 239
normativity, 4, 66, 83–84, 107, 112, 190, 230–31, 238–39

ontology, 51, 56, 108, 218

paratext, 82, 85, 93n6, 119
performativity, 8, 12, 55–59, 62–68, 75, 176, 210, 212–13

person, 7, 30, 58, 70, 82, 91
platform, 51, 106–7, 114, 126–27, 151, 203, 225
Poletti, Anna, 10, 75, 80, 113, 125–26, 127n1, 151, 158
populate, 25, 28, 126, 209
population, 126, 147, 178, 183–84, 191n3, 203–4, 211, 213
pornography, 51, 160, 181; of poverty, 241n9
portal, 37, 179
Poster, Mark, 150, 212
postfeminism, 104, 108
posthumanism, 6, 91
postmemory, 18, 84
postmodernism, 28, 30–31, 44, 61–62, 66, 91, 212–13, 250
PostSecret, 80, 151, 160–61
poststructuralism, 56–57, 63, 66, 75, 191–92n6
poverty, 51, 177, 233, 241–42n18
presence, 19, 105, 149–50, 169, 177–78, 213, 222, 240n5
privacy, 7, 11, 62, 67, 80–81, 100–101, 113–16, 120, 128n7, 203
productivity, 12, 37, 48, 64, 75, 107, 202
products, 10, 42, 47, 71, 147, 159, 176
profile: on a dating site, 72, 76; and digital selfhood, 65, 79; on Facebook, 67, 114–15, 124, 126–28, 127n1, 162n4; on Homeless Nation, 229; maintenance of, 61, 62–63, 91, 106; on medical sites, 205–8; mental, 93n4; on PlanetOut, 179; on a social network , 43, 51–52, 56–60; storage of, 73
prosthetic identity, 18, 78, 84, 91
psychoanalysis, 9, 18, 44
psychology, 3–5, 68, 117, 147
public, 77, 85, 146, 178, 180, 198, 200, 209, 213
publicity, 49, 99, 115, 139, 159, 238
public sphere, 75, 192n11, 201–2, 210–11
publisher, 49, 144, 153, 255–56
Publisher (status update interface on Facebook), 125

queer, 84, 167–71, 173–83, 190–91. *See also* sexuality

race, 42–44, 47–52, 78, 83–84, 140–42, 183–84. *See also* racism
racism, 12, 42, 47, 49, 78, 136, 182, 230. *See also* race
Rak, Julie, 4, 8, 128n9
reader, 40, 74, 93n4, 145, 150–51, 153, 159, 222
reality, 30, 38, 49–50, 71–72, 75–76, 124, 146, 169, 171–72, 212, 218, 230–31
realness, 76, 168–70, 176–79, 181–82, 190–92
reflexivity, 71, 85, 91
relationality, 70–71, 113, 174
remediation, 12, 20, 77, 167, 172. *See also* mediation
rhetoric, 20, 47, 74, 92, 104, 148, 161–63, 190, 248

safety, 52n1, 160–61, 171–72, 180, 207, 211, 231, 237
scene, 12, 17–20, 59, 138, 140, 178, 180
searching (online), 62, 73, 91, 175
secrecy, 11, 80, 100–101, 161
security, 11, 93n8, 99, 101, 108, 230, 233
selfhood, 4, 26, 29–30, 35–37, 55–59, 62, 64, 71, 75, 77, 81, 91–92, 146, 160
sentimentality, 207–10
serial, 63, 149, 161, 230
sexuality, 46, 62–63, 78, 82, 107, 157, 175, 188, 190, 263
sign, 44, 175
Smith, Sidonie, 8, 112, 145, 153
SMS, 7, 107, 109n4
social networking, 12–15, 55–67, 79, 103, 128n6, 132, 147–63
society, 42, 48, 59, 61, 101, 107, 116, 173, 175–76, 191n3, 200, 217, 221, 230, 241–42n18
sociology, 3, 10, 167, 172, 174, 191–92n6
soul, 63–64, 249
spam, 136, 154, 239
spying, 99–100, 109n1

statistics, 66, 100, 147, 171, 198–99, 201–5, 209, 213

status update, 13–14, 59, 61–62, 79–80, 90, 112–17, 119–25, 128n7, 149, 151

stereotype, 12, 59, 78, 140, 159

structuralism, 44, 101, 107, 170, 238

subculture, 241–42n18

subjectivity: autobiographical, 93n1, 156; blog as a form of, 259; construction of, 55–59, 62–63, 77–78; demands for, 12; as distinct from identity, 39n1; embodied, 198–201; as a fantasy, 48; female, 128n5; human, 26, 30; in *Keywords*, 268; liberal ideas of, 4; middle-class, 108; online, 44, 64–65; postmodern, 91–92; poststructural, 192n6; theories of, 31

subscriber, 85, 144, 178

suburbs, 109n3, 169, 191–92n6

subversion, 44, 82, 169

Supervalent Thought, 17–18, 259, 265

surveillance, 18, 56, 76, 81, 92–93, 99–101, 105, 108, 116, 152, 161, 172

symbol, 100, 118, 182, 218

symptom, 51, 67, 199–200, 202–5, 211

systems, 9, 29, 78, 116, 133, 230

tactics, 127, 230, 241n12

tech, 100, 120, 145

technology: of the archive, 133; and biology, 200–203; and blogs, 128n9; cultural, 67; and culture, 147; as democratizing, 229; digital, 47–48, 66, 82, 105–9, 146, 225, 240n1; as ethically neutral, 171–72; and Facebook, 116–17, 128n2, 128n6; gender and, 109n2; genre and, 160–61; GPS, 99; and identity, 12, 15, 20, 219; interactive, 226; love as, 101; love for, 92; and monitoring, 81; narrative and, 218; new media, 43, 177–78; and personal narrative, 145; science and, 114; and the self, 11; speed of, 11; video, 19; as a way to survive an event, 18

teenager, 153, 167–68, 191n3. *See also* adolescence; youth

telecommunication, 47, 49, 144

template, 72, 78, 80, 84–85, 92, 137

temporality, 18–19, 37, 66, 108, 161, 218, 241n14

terrorism, 88, 139–40, 142n7

testimonial, 82, 211–12, 229, 232

testimony, 73, 100, 209, 222

transgender, 19, 65, 82, 92. *See also* queer

transgression, 76, 79–80, 107

translation, 78, 82, 227n3, 227n4

transnational, 74, 77, 82, 85

transparency, 77, 101, 107, 114

trauma, 18, 84–85, 221–22, 225–26

truth, 6, 66, 75–77, 88, 107, 133, 138, 178, 198, 212–13, 233, 263, 270

Tufekci, Zeynep, 62, 67

Turkle, Sherry, 25–26, 28–31, 44, 58, 92, 212

Twitter, 55, 128n6, 144, 149, 151–52, 154, 159–63

unconscious, 12, 58, 62, 226

usage, 113, 117–18, 146

users: as archivists, 137, 139; avatars of, 79; in communities, 12, 144–47; complaints of, 209–10; creative, 122; as creators of online content, 89–91, 118; on dating sites, 76; and digital life narrative, 113–14; and Facebook, 14, 124–28; group dynamics of, 222–23, 225; hostile, 75; human, 117; identities of, 55; as individuals, 4, 199; and informatics, 199–208; and interaction with software, 120; of the Internet, 3, 5, 7, 47, 99–100, 107; as life-loggers, 15; need for engaged, 115; of new media, 177; and online copyright, 159; and online memoirs, 157; online participation and, 149–53; and racism on the Internet, 42–43; and self-presentation, 44, 50, 60, 71–82; of shelters, 231; social, 30; and social networking, 52n2, 58–59; status updates and, 123; street community of, 238–39; student, 121; subjectivity of, 57, 62–67; testimonials of, 212–14;

users (*continued*)
and trauma, 85; as an unsatisfactory term, 93n2; user-friendly media, 229; utopian views of, 49–50
utopia, 16, 43–44, 47, 49, 83, 241n16

victim, 76–78, 80, 139, 141
viewer, 141, 151, 209, 211–12, 241n14
violence, 51, 66, 79, 82, 171, 230
virtual, 29, 38, 91
visibility, 50–51, 167–68, 170, 172–73, 175–76, 178, 184, 190–91, 247
vision, 83, 100, 231–33

Watson, Julia, 8, 10, 13, 112–16, 119, 145–46, 153
web: application, 118; archival possibilities of, 73, 92; and auto/biographical genres, 151–52; browsers, 43; corporatization and, 81; decline in activity on, 239; ecosystem of, 127; and Facebook, 114; HTML forms on the, 121; and identity-work, 16; interactive quality of the, 226; as a memory site, 85, 231; mourning on the, 221; "1.0," 56; pages, 25, 28, 34, 59, 71, 232; presence, 149; programming, 125; programs, 134; self-curation and, 79; and social networking, 132; technologies of the, 75;

"2.0," 3–4, 49–52, 58, 70, 83, 128n2, 146–47, 151–61, 203; users, 44; World Wide, 33, 36, 141, 145, 219. *See also* Internet
webcam, 72, 76, 90
weblog, 72, 162n6, 229. *See also* blog
website: analysis of, 14; as an art project, 88–89; collective, 72, 256; creation of, 252–53; genealogical, 74; and Homeless Nation, 16, 229, 232–33; Jakob Nielsen, 128n5; Karelog, 109n1; LGBTQ, 168–91; news, 100; patient-networking, 199–209, 212; personal, 79, 89, 249; photosharing, 136; Quantified Self, 198; racial stereotyping on a, 50; as a research instrument, 83; Six-Word Memoir, 145; *Smith* magazine, 158; spousebusting, 103; versions, 34–35
Whitlock, Gillian, 7, 113, 127
workers, 48–49, 100, 202, 230, 233

Yagoda, Ben, 146–47, 152, 161n3
youth, 55, 82, 145, 168–84, 190–96, 210. *See also* adolescence; teenager
YouTube, 49, 52n6, 55, 71–72, 76, 79, 100, 136, 145, 152, 211–12, 229

Zuckerberg, Mark, 101, 115

Wisconsin Studies in Autobiography

WILLIAM L. ANDREWS
General Editor

Robert F. Sayre
The Examined Self: Benjamin Franklin, Henry Adams, Henry James

Daniel B. Shea
Spiritual Autobiography in Early America

Lois Mark Stalvey
The Education of a WASP

Margaret Sams
Forbidden Family: A Wartime Memoir of the Philippines, 1941–1945
Edited with an introduction by Lynn Z. Bloom

Charlotte Perkins Gilman
The Living of Charlotte Perkins Gilman: An Autobiography
Introduction by Ann J. Lane

Mark Twain
*Mark Twain's Own Autobiography:
The Chapters from the "North American Review"*
Edited by Michael J. Kiskis

Journeys in New Worlds: Early American Women's Narratives
Edited by William L. Andrews, Sargent Bush, Jr., Annette Kolodny,
Amy Schrager Lang, and Daniel B. Shea

American Autobiography: Retrospect and Prospect
Edited by Paul John Eakin

Caroline Seabury
The Diary of Caroline Seabury, 1854–1863
Edited with an introduction by Suzanne L. Bunkers

Cornelia Peake McDonald
*A Woman's Civil War: A Diary with Reminiscences of the War,
from March 1862*
Edited with an introduction by Minrose C. Gwin

Marian Anderson
My Lord, What a Morning
Introduction by Nellie Y. McKay

American Women's Autobiography: Fea(s)ts of Memory
Edited with an introduction by Margo Culley

Frank Marshall Davis
Livin' the Blues: Memoirs of a Black Journalist and Poet
Edited with an introduction by John Edgar Tidwell

Joanne Jacobson
Authority and Alliance in the Letters of Henry Adams

Kamau Brathwaite
The Zea Mexican Diary: 7 September 1926–7 September 1986

Genaro M. Padilla
My History, Not Yours: The Formation of Mexican American Autobiography

Frances Smith Foster
Witnessing Slavery: The Development of Ante-bellum Slave Narratives

Native American Autobiography: An Anthology
Edited by Arnold Krupat

American Lives: An Anthology of Autobiographical Writing
Edited by Robert F. Sayre

Carol Holly
*Intensely Family: The Inheritance of Family Shame and
the Autobiographies of Henry James*

People of the Book: Thirty
Scholars Reflect on Their Jewish Identity
Edited by Jeffrey Rubin-Dorsky and Shelley Fisher Fishkin

G. Thomas Couser
Recovering Bodies: Illness, Disability, and Life Writing

John Downton Hazlett
My Generation: Collective Autobiography and Identity Politics

William Herrick
Jumping the Line:
The Adventures and Misadventures of an American Radical

Women, Autobiography, Theory: A Reader
Edited by Sidonie Smith and Julia Watson

José Angel Gutiérrez
The Making of a Chicano Militant: Lessons from Cristal

Marie Hall Ets
Rosa: The Life of an Italian Immigrant

Carson McCullers
Illumination and Night Glare:
The Unfinished Autobiography of Carson McCullers
Edited with an introduction by Carlos L. Dews

Yi-Fu Tuan
Who Am I? An Autobiography of Emotion, Mind, and Spirit

Henry Bibb
The Life and Adventures of Henry Bibb: An American Slave
Introduction by Charles J. Heglar

Diaries of Girls and Women: A Midwestern American Sampler
Edited by Suzanne L. Bunkers

Jim Lane
The Autobiographical Documentary in America

Sandra Pouchet Paquet
Caribbean Autobiography:
Cultural Identity and Self-Representation

Mark O'Brien, with Gillian Kendall
How I Became a Human Being:
A Disabled Man's Quest for Independence

Elizabeth L. Banks
Campaigns of Curiosity:
Journalistic Adventures of an American Girl in Late Victorian London
Introduction by Mary Suzanne Schriber and Abbey L. Zink

Miriam Fuchs
The Text Is Myself: Women's Life Writing and Catastrophe

Jean M. Humez
Harriet Tubman: The Life and the Life Stories

Voices Made Flesh: Performing Women's Autobiography
Edited by Lynn C. Miller, Jacqueline Taylor, and M. Heather Carver

Loreta Janeta Velazquez
The Woman in Battle: The Civil War Narrative of Loreta Janeta Velazquez,
Cuban Woman and Confederate Soldier
Introduction by Jesse Alemán

Cathryn Halverson
Maverick Autobiographies:
Women Writers and the American West, 1900–1936

Jeffrey Brace
The Blind African Slave:
Or Memoirs of Boyrereau Brinch, Nicknamed Jeffrey Brace
as told to Benjamin F. Prentiss, Esq.
Edited with an introduction by Kari J. Winter

Colette Inez
The Secret of M. Dulong: A Memoir

Before They Could Vote:
American Women's Autobiographical Writing, 1819–1919
Edited by Sidonie Smith and Julia Watson

Bertram J. Cohler
Writing Desire: Sixty Years of Gay Autobiography

Philip Holden
Autobiography and Decolonization:
Modernity, Masculinity, and the Nation-State

Jing M. Wang
When "I" Was Born: Women's Autobiography in Modern China

Conjoined Twins in Black and White:
The Lives of Millie-Christine McKoy and Daisy and Violet Hilton
Edited by Linda Frost

Four Russian Serf Narratives
Translated, edited, and with an introduction by John MacKay

Mark Twain
Mark Twain's Own Autobiography:
The Chapters from the "North American Review," second edition
Edited by Michael J. Kiskis

Graphic Subjects:
Critical Essays on Autobiography and Graphic Novels
Edited by Michael A. Chaney

Omar Ibn Said
A Muslim American Slave:
The Life of Omar Ibn Said
Translated from the Arabic, edited, and with
an introduction by Ala Alryyes

Sister: An African American Life in Search of Justice
Sylvia Bell White and Jody LePage

Identity Technologies: Constructing the Self Online
Edited by Anna Poletti and Julie Rak